Responsible Research and Innovation

Responsible Research and Innovation provides a comprehensive and impartial overview of the European Commission's Responsible Research and Innovation (RRI) framework, including discussion of both the meaning and aims of the concept, and of its practical application.

As a governance framework for research and innovation, RRI involves four key perspectives: ethical, economic/business, legal and governance and political. The book is organised into chapters covering these different dimensions. The authors provide different viewpoints on these aspects, in order to offer guidance from experts in the field, while at the same time acknowledging the interpretative openness of the RRI frameworks.

Robert Gianni is a postdoctoral researcher at Sciences Po Paris and Ethics Expert at the European Commission. The current aim of his research is to critically scrutinise the different registers of the justification of technological innovation and their repercussions within society.

John Pearson is Ethics and Research Integrity Policy Officer at the Free University of Brussels. He has previously held positions at the KU Leuven and at the University of Namur. His research interests include Responsible Research and Innovation, deliberative democracy and republican political theory.

Bernard Reber is a philosopher, Research Director at the National Center for Scientific Research (CNRS) and member of the Political Research Center of Sciences Po, Paris. He has been a member and Deputy Director of the CNRS Research Center, Meaning, Ethics and Society, based at University Paris Descartes, Sorbonne, Paris.

Contributors:

Xavier PAVIE, PhD
Professor at ESSEC Business School
Research Associate IREPH – University Paris Nanterre

Dr. Ganesh Nathan
University of Applied Sciences and Arts Northwestern Switzerland (FHNW)
ESDES Business School, Lyon Catholic University (UCLY).
Business School Lausanne (BSL)

Routledge Studies in Innovation, Organizations and Technology

Dynamics of Knowledge-Intensive Entrepreneurship
Business Strategy and Public Policy
Edited by Franco Malerba, Yannis Caloghirou, Maureen McKelvey and Slavo Radosevic

Collaborative Innovation
Developing Health Support Ecosystems
Edited by Mitsuru Kodama

Innovation Drivers and Regional Innovation Strategies
Edited by Mario Davide Parrilli, Rune Dahl-Fitjar and Andrés Rodríguez-Pose

Information Theft Prevention
Theory and Practice
Romanus Izuchukwu Okeke and Mahmood Hussain Shah

The New Production of Users
Changing Innovation Collectives and Involvement Strategies
Edited by Sampsa Hyysalo, Torben Elgaard Jensen and Nelly Oudshoorn

Foundations of Information Systems
Research and Practice
Andrew Basden

Social Inclusion and Usability of ICT-Enabled Services
Edited by Jyoti Choudrie, Panayiota Tsatsou and Sherah Kurnia

Strategic Marketing for High Technology Products
An Integrated Approach
Thomas Fotiadis

Responsible Research and Innovation
From Concepts to Practices
Edited by Robert Gianni, John Pearson and Bernard Reber

For more information about the series, please visit www.routledge.com/Routledge-Studies-in-Innovation-Organizations-and-Technology/book-series/RIOT

Responsible Research and Innovation

From Concepts to Practices

Edited by Robert Gianni, John Pearson and Bernard Reber

LONDON AND NEW YORK

First published 2019
by Routledge
2 Park Square, Milton Park, Abingdon, Oxon OX14 4RN

and by Routledge
52 Vanderbilt Avenue, New York, NY 10017, USA

First issued in paperback 2020

Routledge is an imprint of the Taylor & Francis Group, an informa business

British Library Cataloguing-in-Publication Data
A catalogue record for this book is available from the British Library

Library of Congress Cataloging-in-Publication Data
A catalog record for this book has been requested

ISBN 13: 978-0-367-58821-2 (pbk)
ISBN 13: 978-1-138-20934-3 (hbk)

Typeset in Times New Roman
by Deanta Global Publishing Services, Chennai, India

Contents

Illustrations

Figure

Tables

Foreword[1]

From responsible innovation to responsible innovation systems

Richard Owen

About eight years ago I was invited to a meeting with a high-ranking civil servant at the UK Government's Department of Business, Innovation and Skills to brief him on a large international programme on the risks of nanosciences and nanotechnologies that I co-ordinated for the UK Research Councils. He ushered me into his London office, where I gave a presentation about the programme with details concerning the science and technological innovation being undertaken. He was very interested in this. At the end of the presentation, I had two additional slides. I was a little anxious about presenting these, but I took a gamble. 'Evidence-based regulation is always destined to play catch up with disruptive areas of emerging science and innovation like nanotechnologies', I said to him, 'don't you think we need to develop a governance framework that includes but goes beyond regulation, one which includes but goes beyond risk assessment. Something like a framework for "responsible innovation"?' I went on to briefly sketch what such a framework might involve. He stared at me blankly, as if I had been speaking a completely unknown language. After a short pause, he said: 'Well thank you for coming in'. Then he led me out of the office, picked up a printed page of paper containing my short biography and photograph and drew a thick red line right through my image with a fat red pen. Looking up he saw the expression on my face. 'Oh, don't take it personally', he said, 'it's just to remind me later that we've met and I'm done with you'.

Given that response, I could have been forgiven for concluding that the concept of responsible innovation would have a very limited future. Looking back over the eight years since that meeting, it now seems clear that that would have been quite an erroneous conclusion. A lot has happened since in the world of responsible innovation (RI). We have witnessed the rapid growth of a community of academic (and policy) scholars working on the topic and a proliferation in the number of publications on RI from those in academia and policy, including an academic journal dedicated to the subject. We have seen emerging conceptual frameworks that have helped frame and give meaning to a concept that seems to many to be (heuristically, intuitively) *right*, but needed substance and, to be honest, some intellectual underpinning and rigour. This is, in no small measure, due to a commitment by the European Commission to Responsible Research and Innovation (RRI) that was announced in 2011 and has continued since. Notable was the Science in Society work programme in the latter stages of FP7 which funded four projects (two research projects: GREAT and RES AGORA and two co-ordination and support actions: PROGRESS and RESPONSIBILITY). This book features important contributions from authors directly or indirectly involved in this first clutch of projects. As the EC's ambition for RRI grew further, significant funding emerged in the now rebranded 'Science with and for Society' programme in Horizon 2020, where RRI is now a cross-cutting issue. We have seen some jump on the bandwagon, and some make careers in it. We have seen an EU Declaration on RRI emerge from Rome in 2014, building on earlier declarations such as the Lund Declaration of 2009. We have seen a number of member states developing policies and programmes for RI or RRI, for example the UK, Holland and Norway. We have seen the EC's RRI discourse uncomfortably coalesce on a set of important but somewhat disparate policy 'keys' – gender, governance, ethics, stakeholder and public engagement, science education – that may in turn now change again to a 3 O's agenda of 'open science, open innovation and open to the world'. These remind us of RRI's status as not only an emerging academic field and social movement, but a policy and political artefact. We have seen ambitions for implementation, for *mainstreaming* RRI across the European Research Area, and beyond. And, as a sure sign that RI and RRI have arrived, we are seeing a growing body of critique from scholars. This includes contestation and even blunt, outright anger by some scientists and technologists who see responsible innovation as a post-modernist tool of social coercion, control and political correctness that scapegoats technology, innovation, science and the sanctity of human progress. One can imagine Michael Polanyi looking down at us from on high and smiling wryly.

RI, and particularly RRI, are discourses in the making and are interpretively flexible. It is important to recognise that what responsible innovation purports to be is yet to be settled. These are discourses that are in an active process of discursive translation that is yet to stabilise. In the earlier parts of the current decade, a number of definitions emerged, as well as a set of processual dimensions that do seem to be withstanding the test of time and on which there seems to be at least some agreement. In 2015, Fern Wickson and Ellen-Marie Forsberg neatly summarised these as a focus on research and innovation addressing significant societal needs and challenges (there are strong links to social innovation and 'Mode 2 science' in this respect); a process that actively engages and responds to broadly-configured knowledge from a range of stakeholders (i.e. knowledge co-production and inclusive deliberation); a concerted effort to anticipate and think through envisaged impacts and potential problems, identify alternatives and reflect on underlying values; and to ensure this combined anticipatory, reflective and deliberative knowledge is responded to in terms of the goals and trajectories of innovation and science aimed at this as a process of adaptive learning, integrated and embedded into and around research and innovation itself. To these I would add the importance of openness and transparency, and indeed, more generally, a commitment to opening up the purposes, motivations, intended (and unintended impacts) of techno-visionary science and innovation to reflection and deliberation, where consensus is not necessarily the goal. This, as Vincent Blok's chapter makes clear, is far from straightforward, particularly when we consider innovation in a competitive market economy where information asymmetry (even if this is tempered through selective opening up via 'open innovation') is key to increasing market share and corporate profit.

When we look at responsible innovation in such processual terms, these dimensions seem reassuringly familiar (at least to scholars of science and technology studies): indeed RI rests on important antecedents and foundations in this regard. From ELSA and anticipatory governance to technology assessment in its various forms and the sociology of expectations (which Armin Grunwald expands upon in his chapter), RI restates and refines these earlier iterations. Indeed, some have accused RI as being old wine in new bottles, addressing a set of wicked problems concerning science, technology and innovation governance that have haunted us for many decades, but just under a different name. I feel there is some truth in this, depending on how one frames RI, but it is also a little harsh. It is true to say that RI addresses some problems that have dogged society at least since the end of the Second World War and probably much further back, perhaps even as far back as the Enlightenment. Given the power of techno-visionary science and innovation to create futures that are inherently unpredictable, one of these is the thorny problem of unexpected and unpleasant surprises, and the dilemma (and illusion) of control. There has been much written on this subject elsewhere. Suffice here to say that techno-visionary science and innovation, in particular the disruptive type, are always associated with uncertainties, ignorance, ambiguities, (ethical) dilemmas and the potential for unexpected surprises. The unexpected has to be expected to happen, since these are socially constructed and politically, ethically, environmentally, culturally and socially entangled. Their context of use is key: they can be reconfigured, and reengineered for different purposes: this is the problem of many hands.

This presents us with a well-known dilemma of control in which we trade off potential benefits and opportunity losses against the potential for harm, lock-in and path dependency. Faced with such inevitable ignorance and uncertainty, we can try and understand the phenomenon of *emergence* and aim for socially robust science and innovation, in which we take different kinds of knowledge seriously in hand with the science and innovation process itself and in which we develop a systemic capacity for responsiveness to that broadly-configured knowledge. The dimensions of RI that have been articulated aim to provide a conceptual framework to support this, under which specific tools (for example foresight and vision assessment discussed by Grunwald) can be integrated and deployed.

But of course the problem of unexpected surprises is not the only – perhaps, I suggest, not even *the* most important – problem responsible innovation attempts to address. RI is also aimed squarely at purposes, motivations, values and intended impacts. It adds to the question 'How do we proceed under conditions of ignorance and uncertainty?', the question 'What kind of future do we want science and innovation to bring into the world?' In doing so, we are compelled to explore the goals and values that frame and underpin innovation, how these are arrived at and their normative anchor points: who defines the 'right impacts' of innovation (and how), considerations that the reader will find explored in more detail in the chapter by Simone Arnaldi and colleagues. We are in effect asking what kind of innovation do we not only want, but what innovation do *we need* in a society facing a future that is increasingly fragile, unsustainable, unequal and unjust. If innovation has the power to create futures, surely we need to harness that power to secure our future, or at least leave options open for future generations? RI is challenging the banality of innovation, to change its cognitive frame, to reframe it, challenging it to focus less on producing stuff for the market and concentrate on the priority job of securing a sustainable, just, equitable and flourishing future for our people and planet.

RI is often conflated in this sense with innovation aimed at 'Grand Societal Challenges'. But is it also hitched to a post-modernist, post-Capitalist world view? The answer is that your guess is as good as mine, for in truth there has been little exploration beyond the process into the politics of RI itself; to date, this political analysis has been quite under-developed in the RI literature. If RI aims for a different modality of science, innovation and society, a different politics, what exactly is that modality, what exactly is RI's political imaginary? Does RI, for example, privilege a Habermasian-inspired model of deliberative democracy over expert informed, representative democracy in which we allow others to make decisions concerning the agendas, goals and risks of innovation on our behalf? Such discussion on the politics of RI and the context and norms that frame innovation challenge us to collectively raise our heads beyond keys and O's and engage with *second-order reflexivity*, which the GREAT project usefully described as how 'society, and modern rationality in particular work, […] not only a reflection on our own actions […] but a reflection on how the presupposition, the governance principles and the values determine our way of acting'. The concept of second-order reflexivity is an important theme in this book, explored in detail in the chapter by Gianni and Goujon.

If RI differs at all from concepts that it evolves from, it is then that it asks us to reflect on what being responsible is in the face of the power of innovation to create different futures and the power of innovation to co-produce uncertainties and dilemmas with those futures in the making. In doing so, we need to understand what the word 'responsible' means. One of the strengths of this book is its desire to focus on the word responsibility. This is crucially important to anchor any conceptual framework for RI in a coherent framing and understanding of the polysemic and slippery term 'responsible'. After all, ultimately RI has to be about being responsible, acting responsibly, and – fundamentally – taking responsibility for the futures science and innovation seek to create through activities we do in the present, as far as this is possible. Without an understanding of how responsibility is framed, configured and enacted, there is no 'responsible' in RI. The chapters in this book unpack a word that is deeply ambiguous and often black-boxed. The reader will find chapters (by Pellé, Gianni, Pavie and Reber, for example) in which such future-oriented dimensions of responsibility as care and responsiveness become significant, dimensions of responsibility that are helpful for understanding the responsible in RI.

But of course, any discussion of responsibility cannot be done in a vacuum: there is a history and present to responsibility, just as there are historical foundations for RI. As Reber discusses in his chapter, these responsibilities are informally or formally codified through extant norms and rules (e.g. the norm of science to objectively search for the truth underpinned by codes of research integrity, or codes of research ethics relating to research on human subjects or animals): these norms and (soft or hard) rules define role responsibilities – who does what, who is responsible for what and who is accountable for what in the production of knowledge and futures. RI as an approach is one that advocates for inter- and transdisciplinarity, for knowledge co-production, for reflecting on values in disciplines where the principle of excluding values is the norm. This plays havoc with deeply engrained role responsibilities, as these are currently defined, and causes concern, and indeed resistance.

This is, in no small measure, because such norms are embedded in a larger system. They are tied to institutional logics, to organisational evaluation and career progression processes and reward and incentive regimes (e.g. in universities). It is second-order reflection and critique on this bigger picture, the *science and innovation system*, that I believe is the next frontier for RI, and for which this book lays important foundations. One of RI's lasting legacies should be to create an important entry point for a more prominent and critical STS lens into the concept and practice of innovation itself, even if the term responsible innovation is consigned to history; this, as someone reflecting on seven years working in a business school, is sorely needed. RI's focus on science and technology has been at the expense of the very innovation systems within which science and technology development (and the institutions in which these are conducted) are increasingly located, increasingly implicated, increasingly complicit. Over the last 50 years, we have moved from a post-Second World War linear model of innovation to one which my colleague John Bessant has described as 'knowledge spaghetti'. This emphasises an innovation systems approach, as national innovation systems, as regional innovation systems, as technological innovation systems. As Henry Etzkowitz maintains, concepts such as the triple helix, in which there is a deep intertwining of government, industry and universities, and in which the entrepreneurial university plays a central role, are *the* universal contemporary model of innovation. I am not sure this is completely true, as anyone studying grassroots technologies and innovation in the so called 'developing world' will, I hope, agree. However, there can be no denying the hegemony. As a recent leading scientific advisor to the UK government told my university on a recent visit: 'we have been very good in the past at converting money into excellent science. The challenge is now to turn excellent science into money'.

Notwithstanding the evolution of such concepts as social innovation and quadruple and even quintuple helix models (which in themselves perhaps start to inspire and draw on some of the thinking from STS), the point is that RI has to address the innovation system, and, I would argue, reframe it. In doing so, we need to consider the contours and features of current innovation systems and the knowledge economy. We need to consider how we reconfigure these: the actors and institutions involved, their elements and functions, the configuration of knowledge flows, the competencies required, the normative ends and the socio-political context in which these sit. Without addressing the innovation system we cannot take responsibility for the futures this system is currently producing, or configure this system to secure a better future for us all. What does a responsible innovation system look like, and what are its implications? This book provides the groundwork for us to begin answering this question.

Richard Owen, University of Bristol,
September 2017

Note

1 This foreword was inspired by a keynote speech I presented at the final (Go4) conference of the FP7 RRI projects (GREAT, PROGRESS, RES-AGORA and RESPONSIBILITY) in January 2016 at the European Commission, Brussels.

Introduction

RRI: A critical-constructive approach

Robert Gianni, Bernard Reber and John Pearson

The recent changes in the economic production process together with the acceleration in the development of communicational technologies, projecting their range on a global scale, have increased the requests for different types of regulation within the realm of science and technology. Besides, the process of 'democratization' in European societies, which has incurred a radical turn since the beginning of the seventies, has required the constant development of new forms of inclusiveness and dialogue between citizens, experts and policy-makers (Donzelot 1994; Sykes & Macnaghten 2013; Boltanski & Chiapello 2007; Reber, 2006, 2011). These historical processes, which have been running in parallel for a long time, have nowadays become closely related to one another. The new challenges connected to a more flexible and circular economy have become more and more dependent on the capacity of research to produce new, revolutionary and sustainable outcomes. However, the critical damage caused by an extractive technology-based economy together with increasingly demanding requests for the well-being of present and future generations are steering the production process towards different ways of achieving profitable results. It is not by chance, then, that the technical and strategic logics pertaining to science and the economic sphere have been integrated into what we now call research and innovation. If, by definition, research is done for the sake of knowledge, without necessarily complying with its exploitation, innovation is a recent epistemic and pragmatic category directly dealing with the possible marketization of its products (Godin 2015; Blok and Lemmens 2015; Bessant 2013).

Innovations are often processes or products deriving from the universe of scientific research, although we cannot delineate a necessary relation between the two. However, given the acceleration in their development as well as the unforeseeable increase in their effects, it appears unfeasible to regulate their scope or steer their paths according to traditional regulatory frameworks.

Already since the seventies, different regulatory frameworks have been put in place in order to prevent science from drifting in dangerous directions, by trying to assess the risks related to a specific process or products. Accordingly, certain initial forms of technology assessment and risk assessment have helped to understand the foreseeable impact of science and technology. But the ambitious possibility of assessing and thus preventing risks has recently, slowly but firmly, been giving way to the acknowledgement of the 'cunning of uncertainty' related to future scenarios (Nowotny 2015; Grinbaum & Groves 2013; Lee & Petts 2013; Grunwald 2016; Reber 2017a, 2017b). Instead of trying to prevent risks according to traditional top-down procedures, it is now time to turn towards more positive processes in order to make a co-construction of the future that we want and therefore decide what the right impacts are (Gianni 2015; Kuhlmann et al. 2016; Maesschalck 2017; Owen et al. 2013; Von Schomberg 2013).

It is in this general framework and following this tradition that we should unlock the reasons, scope and principles underlying this fairly new regulatory framework named Responsible Research and Innovation (RRI).

The objectives of RRI are often said to be intuitive because of the agreeable positive understanding of the word responsible. Its different definitions all rely on the fact that it should tend towards "socially acceptable, socially desirable ends" (Von Schomberg 2011; Owen et al. 2013; EC 2012), or at least "expand the range of options" (Van den Hoven 2013), and that the procedural requirements accompanying such objectives are just because they are receiving and operationalizing those strong societal claims calling for a democratization of science and a moralization of the economy (Muniesa & Lenglet 2013).

The originality of RRI with respect to other assessment paradigms is not always free of discussion (Fisher & Rip 2013), highlighting several similarities with respect to Technology Assessment, Participatory Technology Assessment, Constructive Technology Assessment Precautionary Principle(s) etc. However, despite their evident similarities, it is also possible to detect some differences. The most important one is most probably exemplified by the adoption of the word 'responsibility', which entails a wide range of meanings covering different layers of societal regulatory codifications (Gianni 2016; Vincent et al. 2011; Pellé & Reber 2015, 2016). In this way, responsible practices are not relegated to political processes anymore but are ascribed to all actors involved in the development process (Fisher & Rip 2013). Furthermore, besides its individual origins, which have too often reduced its scope to legal competences (Ricoeur 2000), responsibility has more recently assumed a proactive, positive and collective understanding which changes its overall sense in the scope of RRI (Jonas 1984; Grinbaum & Groves 2013; Stahl et al. 2013; Owen et al. 2013).

However, the fertility of such an ambitious and broad framework cannot escape from incurring a series of shortcomings, critiques and confusion. These are generated not only by its different interpretations but also – and mostly – by the difficulty of 'translating' its general sense into all the different, plural worlds cherishing our societies (Reber 2016, 2017a, 2017b).

It is in this sense that we thought of operating a distinction between different perspectives. This does not represent a division, but the possibility of adopting different views on the same topic so as to unveil more aspects. For this reason, more critical contributions have been included in this volume to highlight and promote the dialectics between institutional frameworks and contingent, contextual perspectives.

It is through this dialectic that new forms of freedom will be developed and preserved within a framework able to integrate them in a relation where individuals recognize each other and are meaningfully interacting, a relation no longer of intersection but of interconnectedness (Brudney 2014).

This book aims at recalling the underlying principles, the general objectives and the advantages of RRI, both at the normative and the functional level. There are at least two ways of operating an analysis of a regulatory framework like RRI. The first approach is to analyse what RRI is actually capable of according to its theoretical limits and practical obstacles. The attempts subsumable under this reference criterion adopt a critical perspective, and they generally unveil distances between theory and practice, confusions in the general understanding of the notion and mismatches between intended purposes and actuality.

A second approach is to propose what RRI should or could be by focusing on the construction of its tools. This constructive side can be nourished by the indication of formal tools or by addressing the criteria to 'evaluate' its objectives and results. These analyses tend to indicate good ways ahead rather than highlighting shortcomings, although the two sides are never completely detachable.

We believe that this book embraces an exhaustive spectrum of both methodologies by unpacking most of RRI's features and actual barriers, but also by offering a wide range of indications on how to engage in the construction of responsible societies.

We decided to build the **first part** of this volume on the ethical features of RRI for several reasons. First of all, because – according to an understanding of ethics, which defines it as the just regulation of contextual dynamics among different social sectors aimed at pursuing individual freedom – RRI is a potentially powerful ethical notion. Accordingly, Gianni has highlighted the implicit but fundamental connection between responsibility and freedom for a just development of RRI. Also, Grunwald has demonstrated that the challenge of a responsible approach to R&I cannot be decided at the scientific level. If innovation faces an apparent paradox in wanting to neutralize the uncertainty connected to its reason for being, responsibility, if reduced to its original epistemic domain, also cannot be more than an empty box. It is at the ethical level that the epistemic formulas can be nourished by contextualized perspectives towards a hermeneutic approach, forming "narratives about possible future developments involving visions, expectations, fears, concerns and hopes which can hardly be assessed with respect to their epistemological validity".

Following the same line but operating a fundamental connection to its political origins, Reber makes an interesting parallel between RRI; Ethics Reviews, which are already mandatory at the European Commission (EC); and research integrity. By highlighting the importance of a legal or legally sound framework, he also traces the distance between ethics within review processes and RRI, where it forms only one of the six keys of the EC. This is the first attempt to analytically discuss the different relationships between EC keys and to propose moral innovation according to different combinations of moral responsibility understandings. It is at the moral level, indeed, that we should look for fertile ground to address all the challenges arising from our pluralistic societies. On such ground, we can adopt responsibility, a rich conceptual 'constellation', as the just connector between individual and social dynamics.

The **second part** of this volume investigates the actual limits of RRI with a special focus on its political dimension. Here, the two complementary sides of the analysis on RRI are integrated. These critical contributions all focus on highlighting some actual difficulties of RRI, which can potentially endanger a harmonized, effective and legitimate implementation of this notion. In fact, all three contributors warn us against the danger which could lead to fruitful differences, internal to the discourse of RRI to ruptures, unbridgeable distances caused by a lack of concrete communication. If Klassen *et al.* rightly point at the dangerous deafness between academic research and policies, Pearson highlights the confusing differences intervening within research funding agencies at the national and supranational level in Europe. Guske and Jacob enlarge this argument by warning against blindness with respect to the concrete dynamics ongoing in actual research practices, and call for a deeper inclusiveness of a different range of actors.

If these gaps are most probably ascribable to processual mechanisms, other warnings are raised in the **third part** of this book. Here, the authors, by hinting at the potential dangers of an instrumentalization of the notion, define a series of requirements necessary to distinguish and protect RRI from pursuing top-down approaches in the establishment of 'acceptable' outcomes of R&I.

Arnaldi et al., while rightly emphasizing the flexibility embedded in the concept of responsibility, also connect RRI with its general but fundamental normative ground, present in the European Charter of Human Rights, so to define what could be seen as ethically acceptable. In this way, they propose a model of new governance able to combine fundamental rights with soft and hybrid regulatory instruments.

Gianni and Goujon define the formal processes needed to implement an ethical governance of RRI. If participatory processes are widely recognized as fruitful components of current governance approaches, the two authors point out that they are not sufficient to establish a necessary legitimacy of the process. In fact, if participation is not followed by a concrete integration of those contextual claims, then it remains an inefficient or poor rhetoric tool. Accordingly, in order to be able to overcome these invisible barriers, the authors suggest adopting a second-order reflexivity, one able to question, at different levels, the framework itself. In this way, and following a pluralistic perspective, RRI can fulfil its expectations of being a co-constructive framework.

Lenoir highlights the same risks by distinguishing RRI from neo-liberal strategies for keeping open contingencies. It is through this openness that RRI will be able to host future needs, claims and values into a framework that will not disregard any difference.

The **fourth part** of our contribution focuses on economical, business and management perspectives. The starting point is the clear analysis operated by Blok et al. – this analysis of transparency is one of the few warnings about the absolutization of procedures and/or values in the RRI discourse. By relying on the most important features in the field as a benchmark, the authors go through the differences between a substantive and a procedural approach to RRI, showing that in both cases we can still find processes fulfilling some conditions, but which cannot be considered responsible.

It is against such a procedural and anonymous understanding of RRI that we can put together the essays written by Sophie Pellé and Xavier Pavie.

Pellé has analysed Joan Tronto's fruitful indications in order to show the normative importance of a care ethics conjugated into feminine terms.

Xavier Pavie has continued his long-lasting approach of synthesizing the philosophical–existential presuppositions of a virtuous approach with the strategic mechanisms aimed at increasing value. By hinting at the common origin of the word 'value', Pavie has once again shown the closed interdependency and strategic efficiency of an ethical approach to RRI. And it is at the crossroads of the different developments of the value that we have to address the challenges of RRI. It is here that we need to find an understanding of responsibility that is able to keep normative references together with contingent applications. As clearly exemplified by Nathan, it is at the very core of the development of a circular process of R&I, at the design phase, that we should approach such an understanding of responsibility, or it will otherwise remain an inefficient contingent reaction to protests.

References

Bessant, J. (2013). Innovation in the Twenty-First Century. In: R. Owen, Bessant, J. and Heintz, M. (Eds.), *Responsible Innovation. Managing the Responsible Emergence of Science and Innovation in Society*, Hoboken (NJ): John Wiley & Sons, pp. 1–25.

Blok, V. and Lemmens, P. (2015). The Emerging Concept of Responsible Innovation. Three Reasons Why It Is Questionable and Calls for a Radical Transformation of the Concept of Innovation. In: B.-J. Koops, Oosterlaken, I., Romijn, H., Swierstra, T. and Van den Hoven, J. (Eds.), *Responsible Innovation 2: Concepts, Approaches,and Applications*. Dordrecht: Springer, pp. 19–35.

Boltanski, L. and Chiapello, E. (2007). *The New Spirit of Capitalism*. London: Verso.

Brudney, D. (2014). The Young Marx and the Middle-Aged Rawls. In: J. Mandle and Reidy, D. (Eds.), *A Companion to Rawls*. London: Wiley-Blackwell, pp. 450–471.

Donzelot, J. (1994). *L'invention Du Social. Essai Sur Le Déclin Des Passions Politiques*. Paris: Seuil.

European Commission. (2012). *Science with and for Society*. Available at: https://ec.europa.eu/programmes/horizon2020/en/h2020-section/science-and-society.

Fisher, E. and Rip, A. (2013). Responsible Innovation: Multi-Level Dynamics and Soft Intervention Practices. In: R. Owen, Bessant J. and Heintz M. (Eds.), *Responsible Innovation. Managing the Responsible Emergence of Science and Innovation in Society*. Hoboken (NJ): John Wiley & Sons, pp. 165–184.

Gianni, R. (2015). Framework for the Comparison of Theories of Responsible Innovation in Research. *GREAT Project*; http://www.great-project.eu/D5.1.

Gianni, R. (2016). *Freedom and Responsibility. The Ethical Realm of RRI*. London/New York: ISTE/Wiley.

Godin, B. (2015). *Innovation Contested – The Idea of Innovation Over the Centuries*. London: Routledge.

Grinbaum, A. and Groves, C. (2013). What is 'Responsible' about Responsible Innovation? Understanding the Ethical Issues. In: R. Owen, Bessant J. and Heintz M. (Eds.), *Responsible Innovation. Managing the Responsible Emergence of Science and Innovation in Society*. Hoboken (NJ): John Wiley & Sons, pp. 119–142.

Grunwald, A. (2016). *The Hermeneutic Side of Responsible Research and Innovation.* London/New York: ISTE/Wiley.

Jonas, H. (1984). *The Imperative of Responsibility: In Search of Ethics for the Technological Age.* Chicago: University of Chicago Press.

Kuhlmann, S., Edler, J., Ordóñez-Matamoros, G., Randles, S., Walhout, B., Gough, C. and Lindner, R. (2016). Responsibility Navigator. In: R. Lindner, Kuhlmann, S., Randles, S., Bedsted, B., Gorgoni, G., Griessler, E., Loconto, A. and Mejlgaard, N. (Eds.), *Navigating Towards Shared Responsibility in Research and Innovation. Approach, Process and Results of the Res-AGorA Project.* Karlsruhe, pp. 135–158; https://indd.adobe.com/view/eaeb695e-a212-4a34-aeba-b3d8a7a58acc.

Lee, R. J. and Petts, J. (2013). Adaptive Governance for Responsible Innovation. In: R. Owen, Bessant, J. and Heintz, M. (Eds.), *Responsible Innovation. Managing the Responsible Emergence of Science and Innovation in Society.* Hoboken (NJ): John Wiley & Sons, pp. 143–160.

Maesschalck, M. (2017). Reflexive Governance for Research and Innovative Knowledge. London/New York: ISTE/Wiley.

Muniesa, F. and Lenglet, M. (2013). Responsible Innovation in Finance: Directions and Implications. In: R. Owen, Bessant J. and Heintz M. (Eds.), *Responsible Innovation. Managing the Responsible Emergence of Science and Innovation in Society.* Hoboken (NJ): John Wiley & Sons, pp. 185–194.

Nowotny, H. (2015). *The Cunning of Uncertainty.* Oxford: Polity.

Owen, R., Bessant, J. and Heintz, M. (Eds.) (2013). *Responsible Innovation. Managing the Responsible Emergence of Science and Innovation in Society.* Hoboken (NJ): John Wiley & Sons.

Pellé S. and Reber, B. (2015). Responsible Innovation in the Light of Moral Responsibility. In: *Journal on Chain and Network Science, Special Issue: Responsible Innovation in the Private Sector*, 15(2), pp. 107–117. http://www.wicanem.wur.nl/Tracks%20-%20Responsible%20Innovation%20in%20Chains%20and%20Networks.htm; http://www.wageningenacademic.com/doi/abs/10.3920/JCNS2014.x017.

Pellé, S. and Reber, B. (2016). *From Ethical Review to Responsible Research and Innovation.* London/New York: ISTE/Wiley.

Reber, B. (2006). Technology Assessment as Policy Analysis: From Expert Advice to Participatory Approaches. In: F. Fischer, Miller G. and Sidney M. (Eds.), *Handbook of Public Policy Analysis. Theory, Politics and Methods*, New York, Public Administration and Public Policy Series. New York: Rutgers University/CRC Press, 125, pp. 493–512.

Reber, B. (2011). *La démocratie génétiquement modifiée. Sociologies éthiques de l'évaluation des technologies controversées*, collection *Bioéthique critique*, Québec, Presses de l'Université de Laval, 2011.

Reber, B. (2017a). *Precautionary Principle, Pluralism, Deliberation. Science and Ethics.* London/New York: ISTE/Wiley.

Reber, B. (2017b). RRI as Inheritor of Deliberative Democracy and the Precautionary Principle. In: *Journal of Responsible Innovation.* ISSN: 2329-9460 (print) 2329-9037; (online) Journal homepage: http://www.tandfonline.com/loi/tjri20.

Ricoeur, P. (2000). *The Just.* Chicago: Chicago University Press.

Stahl, B., Eden, G. and Jirotka, M. (2013). Responsible Research and Innovation in Information and Communication Technology: Identifying and Engaging with the Ethical Implications of ICTs. In: R. Owen, Bessant, J. and Heintz, M. (Eds.), *Responsible Innovation. Managing the Responsible Emergence of Science and Innovation in Society.* Hoboken (NJ): John Wiley & Sons, pp. 199–215.

Sykes, K. and Macnaghten, P. (2013). Responsible Innovation – Opening Up Dialogue and Debate. In: R. Owen, Bessant, J. and Heintz, M. (Eds.), *Responsible Innovation. Managing the Responsible Emergence of Science and Innovation in Society*. Hoboken (NJ): John Wiley & Sons, pp. 85–107.

Van Den Hoven, J. (2013). Value Sensitive Design and Responsible Innovation. In: R. Owen, Bessant J. and Heintz M. (Eds.), *Responsible Innovation. Managing the Responsible Emergence of Science and Innovation in Society*. Hoboken (NJ): John Wiley & Sons, pp. 75–83.

Vincent, N., van de Poel, I. and Van den Hoven J. (Eds.) (2011). *Moral Responsibility, Beyond Free Will & Determinism*. Dordrecht: Springer.

Von Schomberg, R. (2011). *Science, Politics, and Morality: Scientific Uncertainty and Decision Making*. Dordrecht: Springer.

Von Schomberg, R. (2013). A Vision of Responsible Research and Innovation. In: R. Owen, Bessant, J. and Heintz, M. (Eds.), *Responsible Innovation. Managing the Responsible Emergence of Science and Innovation in Society*. Hoboken (NJ): John Wiley & Sons, pp. 51–74.

Part I

Ethical features of Responsible Research and Innovation

1 The discourse of responsibility

A social perspective

Robert Gianni

Introduction

The notion of Responsible Research and Innovation (RRI), recently launched by several national funding agencies and adopted by the European Commission (EC) in 2011, has become increasingly important for the development of publicly funded research (Pearson Ch. 5). The EC is the major financier for research in Europe, and its guidelines play a crucial role with regard to the objectives and methodology that different stakeholders involved in research practices should and will pursue. However, the understanding of how a single general framework can and should work in different domains still represents one of the main challenges for scientists and policy-makers. The necessary level of abstraction of a regulatory policy must come to terms with its application and the specific measures that it requires.

It is not an easy task to disentangle the complexity of RRI because of the different perspectives it needs to embrace and the necessary flexibility it requires in order to be adapted to different contexts. Furthermore, such flexibility can undergo attempts at instrumentalization, generating an ambiguous and counter-productive scenario. However, a flexible pattern does not imply that RRI-related words are unconstrained or totally arbitrary. The meaning of the acronym RRI can and should be decided according to a political vision put in place through dedicated actions (van Oudheusden 2014; Gianni 2016).

At first sight, innovation, research and responsibility can be seen as belonging to at least two clashing conceptual paradigms. On the one hand, the dimension of research and innovation tends, although with clear differences, towards the construction of a more technological future according to strategic and technical rules (Schumpeter 1934; Bessant 2013).[1] On the other hand, the dimension of responsibility is strongly anchored to a normative ground, defining duties and barriers for actions (Vincent et al. 2011). This presumed heterogeneity then raises some doubts about the possible convergence of two paradigms following divergent methodologies. How can we facilitate the integration of these two methodologies without losing their aims and spirit? How can research and innovation be boosted if we burden them with too many rules and other normative features? At the same time, what kind of Research & Innovation (R&I) are we going to promote if projects are constructed while ignoring what society stands for and considers valuable?

The discrepancies in the interpretations of RRI and the difficulty in reaching a shared perspective (Owen et al. 2013) are the fruits of the ambiguity and cross-disciplinary nature of the words embedded in it. Thus, beside the useful analyses on the framework as such (Owen et al. 2013; Van den Hoven 2014; Grunwald 2011; Kuhlmann et al. 2016; Jacob et al. 2013; Spaapen et al. 2015), several authors have started to propose alternative perspectives, in order to clarify issues that are often simply due to a common crystallization of the concepts.

From my perspective, such a hermeneutical operation has been taking two main paths. The first one is formed by those contributions that highlight the normative bases of R&I in order to show some implicit features and the benefits of the adoption of a normative framework. These attempts have been brought about by some authors who have tried to redraw the galaxy of innovation in socio-ethical terms (Godin 2015; Blok and Lemmens 2015; Bessant 2013; Pavie 2014; Van Den Hoven 2013; 2014; Moldashl 2010). A second track has been one of proposing an analytic reading of responsibility that tries to distinguish all its different senses (Vincent 2011). These operations have the great merit of having clarified all the differences embedded in such a polysemic concept. However, I see few examples of how to integrate the different acceptions of responsibility in a way that could be fruitful for R&I (Pellé & Reber 2015; Pellizzoni 2004; Pavie 2014). Accordingly, this chapter attempts to propose a picture of responsibility that is stronger in tackling the problems arising from its terminological ambiguity without dismissing such fertile plurality.

We will achieve such an attempt by making explicit the underlying sense and scope of the concept of responsibility. By defining the relation between its different meanings, we will obtain an ethical understanding of responsibility. In the last part, I will suggest that the political and institutional nature of the discourse on responsibility should be the actual grounds for implementing RRI.

Responsibility: The construction of a polysemic concept

Subjective efforts and objective rules

Certain recurrent ethical and political terms are inclined towards inflation, which can increase their role but often also brings a loss of value. The concept of responsibility is surely one of the main victims, having undergone such a process in recent years (Ricoeur 2000). If, on the one hand, its flexibility represents a powerful aspect in order to cope with social pluralism, on the other hand this pluralism often appears in terms of idiosyncrasy, generating doubts about the possibility of a consensual understanding of responsibility and thus of its utility. Not only different social domains may interpret responsibility in different ways, but also, within the same domain, an understanding of responsible practices can be subject to differing interpretations. Societal actors are now called to be responsible in different occasions and with different meanings according to concrete situations and the related social dimension. Alain Ehrenberg, for instance, has highlighted how individuals are so exposed to quests for responsibility that they often perceive it as an unreachable model, generating psychological pathologies (1998).

Responsibility is growing not only in quantitative terms but, increasingly, also in terms of quality. Ibo van de Poel and Nicole Vincent have listed several meanings in the wake of Hart's famous example (2011). According to Pellé and Reber (2015), we can find even more understandings of responsibility than those listed by Hart. Being used with major frequency in different domains, these applications have also contributed to a semantic multiplication, which makes it hard for stakeholders to hold onto a common understanding of responsibility.

On the basis of the different usages of responsibility, we can identify two major conceptual paradigms, which are often seen as difficult to integrate.

The first one is probably the strongest, even in our daily comprehension, and applies a classical reading of a deontological character. It relies on the perspective that, in order to assess concrete effects and to prevent bad consequences, actions need to be imputed to an actor who is accountable for the outcomes. This understanding is mostly retrospective and defines the limits of what an agent should do. A particular closeness to the realms of law and deontological morality, highlighting what should or must not be done, has often contributed to shedding a negative light on the concept. Among this range of perspectives, we can include the different legal and moral models aimed at establishing the borders of individual duties.[2] Stemming from a strong European juridical tradition of scholars interpreting Kantian deontological doctrines, the aim of this conceptual framework is to define the *objective* cognitive conditions for identifying an actor with an action so as to guarantee a common ground for justice (Kelsen 2005; Hart 2008; Kant 1997; Vincent *et al.* 2011). Therefore, the main focus is on the distinction and the definition of terms like accountability, liability and blameworthiness.

A significant variation of this understanding of responsibility, which, in many respects, still belongs to an 'objective' framework, is that of trying to assess actions according only to consequences. Agents assume a responsible perspective when they make decisions according to the criterion of maximizing the positive outcomes of an action. Although we can list several different interpretations of what counts as a positive outcome, the common ground is the necessity to adopt objective, often quantifiable, criteria.[3] This stream has the great merit of defining limits and attributing specific actions to agents so to maintain a general understanding of duty. In this sense, it regulates existing relationships and aims at guaranteeing fundamental justice. It is mostly retrospective or, eventually, framed by a risk assessment methodology.

However, because of their strong relation to an objective framework, these attempts have to prescind from contextual or existential considerations. Similarly, they tend to focus on the rules within which an individual can move, and by doing so, they often overlook the rules themselves, the value-based clashes arising in societies, and most of all, they cannot provide stable indications about those interactions not yet regulated by a normative framework. The complex patterns in which R&I is embedded in their activities must surely rely on objective normative criteria, but they also require softer regulatory forms as well as policies aimed at constructing a common future.

A second conceptual paradigm in the exegesis of the concept of responsibility has been entering more and more into our daily comprehension, to the point that it has become a solid conceptual counterpart to the objective paradigm. According to this framework, it is not sufficient to regulate through objective criteria based on abstract norms and rules for two main reasons. The first is that negative effects are already present, proving a sort of incapacity of objective criteria to protect society from negative outcomes (Jonas 1984; Beck 1992). The second is that these kinds of frameworks are, in principle, neutral with respect to moral pluralism and unable to account for uncertainty, which is the core issue of R&I (Nowotny 2013; Reber Ch. 3; Gianni & Goujon Ch. 8). Consequently, abstract normative frameworks need to be overcome or at least integrated by subjective efforts. Thus, agents are exhorted to recognize their individual role in the determination of the future and in taking care of it. The consequences of individual actions are extended to the point that they become, in principle, infinite, increasing the sense of responsibility not only in quantitative but also in qualitative terms (Ricoeur 2000). This understanding is prospective; it looks at the future, and focuses on what can be done, generating a positive aura around itself (Pellé & Reber 2015). Within this conceptual framework, we can include all those attempts aimed at contrasting a technocratic drift through the shift towards a more emotional and more existential effort. We can group these contributions in their promotion of behaviours based on care and virtue. The importance of this paradigm is its focus on the need to extend responsible behaviour beyond the borders of deontological rules in order to cover all those private and unregulated spaces of human action. It also matches the orientation towards the future, typical of R&I, and holds great rhetorical power by promoting subjective and existential values (Jonas 1984; Beck 1992; MacIntyre 2007; Blok 2016; Pavie 2014; 2017).

The limit of these kinds of approaches is that they often underestimate the necessity for an intersubjective regulation, able to combine individual actions into an institutional effort (Gianni 2016). Individual actions, in order to be effective, require the equal efforts of other actors in a shared framework.

Furthermore, neo-liberal rhetoric has recently started to use this 'existentialist' discourse, pushing on individual efforts according to 'valuable' reasons as a motivating discourse for increasing productivity and dismissing social aspects. The instrumental ends behind some of these slogans are often difficult to distinguish from those plausible efforts aimed at improving our wellbeing (Boltanski and Chiapello 2007; Hartmann and Honneth 2006; Stehr 2008). This ambiguity has also contributed to shedding a grim light on the concept of responsibility and its scope (Eagleton-Pierce 2016; Arnaldi and Gorgoni 2016).

On the one hand, then, we find a more objective stream, worried about defining stable criteria for distinguishing responsible from irresponsible actions. These criteria can be legal rules, calculations or any kind of objective reference useful for establishing a clear link between an action and an actor. On the other hand, responsible behaviours are conceived as subjective expressions of individuals concerned about the(ir) environment and willing to make an additional effort.

The problem with a regulatory framework like RRI is that it needs to encourage an efficient process without losing legitimacy (Lenoir 2016). The question is then which conception of responsibility could be the most apt to obtain such a result, considering that both evidence some limits. As noticed by Jean Louis Genard, analytical theorization often distinguishes what is empirically conjoined (1999). Both registers, the subjective and the objective one, tend to restrict their analyses to a specific field of inquiry with a strict methodology, without addressing the overall relational framework of responsible practices where actors often cannot, or do not want to, ignore its different sides. If we consider these two perspectives, neither of them seems to completely fit in the framework of R&I. Encouraging researchers and innovators to act according to legal rules appears more a tautology than a groundbreaking framework. In addition, it is logically wrong and morally bad to enhance the functions of right so as to become the sole driver in constructing our future (von Schomberg 2011). Similarly, by limiting responsibility to a subjective goodwill, we run the risk of falling into a relativist scenario where each actor can decide if and how to care, rendering responsibility an empty word (Ricoeur 2000). Besides, as shown by Ricoeur, caring about our environment or our siblings cannot and should not prescind from a legal basis according to which someone must be accountable for negative consequences (Ricoeur 2000).

Despite all the different interpretations of responsibility, though, the basic reason for its adoption in the different realms is that it has always represented a fruitful and powerful regulatory tool. Already in 1884, J. E. Labbè defined responsibility as "the most perfect regulator of human actions" (Genard 1999: p. 32). The questions to address, then, are why and in which way responsibility has assumed such a strong role in regulating societal actions.

Capability, knowledge, will and action: A brief history of responsibility

I believe that, in order to understand the importance of responsibility and how its features have been taken up and established, it is useful to turn to those studies that, by adopting a genealogical methodology, have unveiled all the characteristics of responsibility and, most of all, the underlying reasons for interpreting it in different ways. Paul Ricoeur (2000; 2007), Jean-Louis Genard (1999) and, in a similar way, Simone Arnaldi and Luca Bianchi (2016) have provided overviews able to clarify the underlying historical drivers guiding the evolution of responsibility as well as some implicit answers to the current ambiguity about the meaning of responsibility.

According to their findings, we can detect the first occurrence of responsibility in Europe already in Roman law, where the term was used to identify the juridical figure able to contract a debt for someone who was not entitled to do so. The etymological origin of the term refers to the meaning of *spondere*, to engage or to promise, and it used to define the relation between a juridical status and the commitment to guaranteeing a freedom to a non-free subject. The 'sponsor' was a free citizen able and willing to assume the debt of a non-free subject. According to

Genard (1999), Villey (1977) and Arnaldi and Bianchi (2016), within Roman law the conceptual core of responsibility did not refer to the idea of guilt or blame, as we might think, but rather to one of defending and ensuring a fair redistribution of goods, something resembling what we would call liability. It was embedded in a cultural background concerned with the necessity to compensate any loss in an objective manner.

A general idea resembling the one of responsibility was also already present in ancient Greece, where both the interpretation of tragedies and Aristotle's ethics tried to detect and describe the different sources of action. However, according to Eric Robertson Dodds (2004) and Ernst Cassirer (1965), at that time the idea of a responsible subject could not have been present for two main reasons. The first is that they did not have the reflexive development of a subject conceived as a (moral) judge. The second, consequent one is that they could not have even posed themselves the choice between free will and determinism because such dualism only emerged with modernity. The figure of the 'daimon' captures the cultural belief that all actions were considered the inextricable outcome of individual actions and the influence of irrational forces (Dodds 2004; Cassirer 1965).

According to Genard, both Greece's and Rome's sense of responsibility belonged to an objective external register, meaning that judgements concerning an action did not fall under the personal reflexive framework in which an actor is nowadays embedded (Genard 1999, Forst 2012, Apel 1990). Even in Roman law, where the focus of the juridical realm was already raising the role of individuals, the opening towards a subjective reason was still germinal. As already understood by Paul Fauconnet (1925), the responsibility that in archaic societies was objective, communicable or collective started, then, to become individualized, but was still conceived in a strongly objective fashion. Also, Jürgen Habermas pointed out that in these kinds of juridical orders we cannot detect any trace with regard to the intentions of a subject (1986). The gravity of a crime referred to the consequences of an action, and the sanction had the purpose of refunding damage, not of inflicting a punishment. Similarly, within a 'primitive' juridical mentality, we can see a mixture of normative judgements, interests and verification of facts that almost always integrate the contribution of natural and supernatural forces (Habermas 1986: p. 60).

The passage from ancient Greece and Rome to modernity through the Middle Ages is interesting for the radical shift in the understanding of agency. Genard has proposed an interesting scheme that we can follow to continue our investigation (1999). By using the focal lenses of what he calls the 'modalities' of responsibility, i.e. knowledge, will, power and duty, he has defined the different passages that concurred to form a complementary conception of responsibility.

We have said that seemingly, in Greece or during the Roman Empire, nothing like a reflexive relation of a subject to himself and his intentions was pertaining to the parameters used to evaluate an action. Genard identifies the cornerstone of an intimate relation of an actor with his own acts only with the initial development of the concept of reason in medieval theology. To begin with, as seen in particular with Boethius (1999), who was relying on a neo-platonic framework, the possibility to act in a good or bad way was simply identified with the knowledge an agent possessed. Having a certain degree of knowledge meant that an action would have been performed accordingly. Here, we do not find any particular concern with regard to the will of an actor, but only about his reason, which was supposed to be the necessary and sufficient guidance for someone's actions.

However, starting with Duns Scotus (1997), and then continuing with Thomas Aquinas (2000), the coincidence of knowledge and will started to be questioned, moving the latter to the realm of freedom because of its unpredictability. The will rapidly became the crucial factor for judging an actor because, in the conceptual framework of that time, external reality intended as scientific development started to play an important and independent role. Thus, reason could have only provided the necessary knowledge to act, making the spectrum of external options among which to choose a matter of the personal will of individuals. If an agent had a set of possibilities, it was up to him to choose the 'right' one. In this sense, it was not simply by following or not following a rational indication that an actor could oscillate between right and wrong, but it was necessary to take into account his will in order to retrospectively judge the traits of his conduct.

With the will becoming increasingly considered as the criterion to interpret an action, we witness, according to Genard, the first occurrence of modern imputation. An act could have been imputed to an actor if that actor wanted to act in such a way. In this sense, the liberation from duty, as understood under the medieval Catholic framework, also played a crucial role, favouring a process where individuals could have, and increasingly should have, explored their preferences within themselves.

In summary, Genard has shown us that the seeds of the modern understanding of responsibility are traceable in the emergence of conscience as first developed in medieval theology, and then with the crisis of deterministic perspectives during the Renaissance. The role of confession has often been recognized as a formidable example in the development of this private form of deliberation (Genard 1999; Foucault 2014).

It is difficult to delineate a clear demarcation between the medieval and the modern understanding of agency because, as with every historical process, this crucial shift was not only based on a series of theoretical inputs, but was also and mainly possible because of changes at the political and economic levels. The first passage that distinguishes modernity from the Middle Ages is that an individual's actions passed from being performative of a status to being performative of engagement (Genard 1999: p. 101). The mould of given, fixed organization of society on the basis of inherited roles was shattered by a new interpretation of identity, promoting the idea that subjects were figures to be constructed and determined in a free manner. The breakdown of feudal societies opened up a series of new possibilities that were previously inconceivable. The passage from a deterministic perspective to one enhancing the freedom of individuals was the evidence of a radical shift in the interpretation of agency (Taylor 1992). An actor was no longer defined by his predetermined and fixed status but rather by his choices among a set of possible options. Actors needed to build their own identities through the dynamic and undetermined relation with other individuals on the basis of rational features. If before they were only created, now individuals became also creators. Accordingly, this innovative understanding of the subject, free in his will to actualize his rationally chosen preferences, required a new form of regulation from those embedded in the given, external and extraneous orders of the past.

The role of 'responsibility'[4] thus became crucial for providing individuals with a framework able to regulate different determinations of the self. The shift that responsibility had to support is that from an individual who finds the ground and the interpretation of his actions in unearthly sources to an individual called to respond to the requests through reasons, able to distinguish between his intentions and external rules (Genard 1999).

According to Ernst Cassirer, it is precisely with the Renaissance that we find the first concrete references to reflexivity as the dualistic relation between the intentions underlying an act (morality) and the objective traits of a conduct (right) (Cassirer 1965).

This opening to the self-determination of individuals on the basis of reason(s) was of course still at a very early stage, but it was at this point that the first understanding of responsibility entered into history as a subjective effort to respond to others' requests. However, the dialectics between subjective and objective features, between free acts and causal influences as well as the development of subjectivity, still had a long path to tread.

This important focus on the will and the concomitant insurgence of a new societal framework opened up another aspect of the general theory of the interpretation of actions, that of power. The passage from a predetermined, providential social framework to the contingency of historical events generated the moral and practical problem of a powerless will (Lenoir 2016). The rise of a different conception of human action and the development of natural sciences highlighted the need to address the institutional availability of concrete tools and measures to actualize a free choice. As shown by Philippe Pettit, if an agent wants to operate a choice, he needs to "have the room and the resources to enact the option he prefers" (Pettit 2014: p. 34). The basic presupposition of a choice is the possibility of having at least two options. Accordingly, these options become real when the agent is put in the condition to freely choose, meaning that he *can* actualize what his will tells him to do.

However, Genard highlights that the different meanings inherent in the term power were not yet fully acknowledged and the *possibility* of an actor was a minor aspect with respect to his *capacities* (Pufendorf 2008; Ricoeur 2000; Genard 1999). Thus, the responsibility of an individual was still tied to an epistemic dimension, focused on defining the cognitive traits by which reason, will and power were connected. All attempts to produce an exhaustive theory for the interpretation of actions were concentrated on designing the inner side of an individual that slowly became the modern subject. This effort required not only a strong epistemic effort but also a political protection of the self from external hindrances. Any external factor was in fact conceived as an obstacle to, or a deviation from, the self-determination of a free subject.

It is not surprising, then, that in the 17th and 18th centuries, we can witness a whole series of works trying to foster these two connected aspects (Genard 1999: p. 55). If an individual was supposed to self-regulate himself, it was necessary to understand the identity of the individual able to do so and the necessary related rules. Therefore, modern natural law on the one hand, and the philosophy of consciousness on the other, went hand in hand in trying to produce such frameworks (Habermas 1986). In this historical period, we can recall the role of Thomas Hobbes' political philosophy (1996), and the strong development of 'negative' freedom (Berlin 2002) promoted by philosophers as well as jurists.

It is worth noticing that in Western countries, the term 'responsibility' as such did not enter the dictionaries before the French Revolution and did not occur in political discussion until the end of the 19th century (Ricoeur 2000; Villey 1977; Kaczmarek 2012). Until then, the terms usually adopted to define the conditions and rules for individual action were mostly those of imputability and accountability (Locke 1988; Ricoeur 2000). These two terms were used to define the epistemic and juridical features according to which an action could be imputed to an agent, who then had to account for it.

The greatest exemplification of this initial interpretation of responsibility as imputability and accountability can be detected in the epistemology developed by Immanuel Kant. The contribution made by Kant throughout his works is crucial to understanding the epistemological features of responsibility and their role in law and morality.

In his *Critique of Pure Reason* (1998), Kant had been clear in defining the possibility of attributing an action to an agent by the presence of certain rational features that make the subject able to act in a human way. It is the sole presence of rationality that identifies an actor as an individual among individuals. However, in his first *Critique*, Kant stated the logical concomitance between reason and action mediated by external reality but did not assign any moral value to such a relation. As rightly noticed by Paul Ricoeur, at this stage Kant not only avoided overloading a free agent with moral considerations, but also maintained the antinomy of causal influence and free will in the interpretation of an action (Ricoeur 2000).

> Thesis: Causality in accordance with laws of nature is not the only causality from which the appearances of the world can one and all be derived. To explain these appearances it is necessary to assume that there is also another causality, that of freedom.
>
> Antithesis: There is no freedom; everything in the world takes place solely in accordance with the laws of nature. (A444–45, B472–73)
>
> (Quoted in Ricoeur 2000: p. 17)

The ascription of an action to an agent prescinded from moral considerations and could not have been imputed to the actor solely because of the influence of natural laws. As Ricoeur has highlighted, Kant was inclined to think of a possible conciliation of these two equally valid sources of action through a two-fold dimension.

This meant that for Kant, at least in the *Critique of Pure Reason* (1997), the two sides should have not been separated, but have been conceived as complementary in the definition of agency.

This point is also really important for the development of responsibility. How can we attribute the whole responsibility of an action to an agent if his actions are often, if not always, the result of different influences, also, but not only, of a necessary nature? We cannot think of any total responsibility of an individual because we need to keep in mind the 'casualty' involved when it comes to the consequences of an action.

It is with the *Critique of Practical Reason* (1997) that the presence of rational traits started to imply a moral respondence and a consequent moral judgement. Kant introduced the notion of imputability as the judgement of attribution to someone of a blameworthy action. What was earlier an epistemic and ontological trait was then developed to become "the conjunction of two more primitive ideas: the attribution of an action to an agent, and the moral and generally negative qualification of that action" (Ricoeur 2000: p. 16). If an individual had to behave as a moral subject, he needed to follow maxims and imperatives traceable in his rational faculties.[5] In this way, the agent, by being a rational individual, is automatically attributed the moral imputation of his actions. Responsibility became the response to rational abstract indications that an agent must have followed in order to act morally.

This moral absolutism was further extended with the *Metaphysics of Morals* (2009), where morality was not only defining the imputability of an agent by identifying him as a person, but also became predominant by overarching law and ethics. Kant went so far, in establishing the importance of morality in the determination of 'responsible' actions, as to blur the necessary distinction from right (Habermas 1986).

Kant had perfectly understood the necessity of legitimizing the possibility of an imputation on an impartial and universal basis. He detected this ground in the imperative actualization of a reflexive process pertaining to all rational human beings. Kant was concerned with defining a conception of imputability that could match the understanding of a universal and rational human being, and based morality on sources different from those of metaphysics (Ripstein 2010).

However, according to some criticisms, there are some main issues occurring with Kant's framework which undermine the possibility of thinking an overall, complementary conception of responsibility able to match the needs of RRI.

One general aspect is that, in his second *Critique*, Kant identified 'responsibility' with imputation, conflating its sense to a deontological, negative understanding (Ricoeur 2000; Pellé & Reber 2015; Gianni 2016). In this sense, responsible actions are only those enacted according to abstract, universal rules by an independent and isolated individual. This understanding leaves out all historical, intersubjective dynamics that need to have contingently shaped forms of regulation.

A second aspect accompanying such a strong conception of morality conceived as a rational duty is that it disregards all extra-rational factors, failing to integrate a whole series of actual 'reasons' for action (Williams 1984; Raz 2014;

Ferry 1991). Besides, this framework obscures the independent role of right, reducing it to an "insufficient modality of morality" (Habermas 1986; Kant 2009; Kervegan 2015).

These two main problems, the strong role of morality and the lack of consideration of contextual dynamics in the definition of agency, were only addressed during the 20th century by the two independent fronts, juridical positivism and existentialism, which we have mentioned as the two main interpretations of responsibility.

A particular reinterpretation of Kant's deontology and the fragmentation of morality occurred at the beginning of the 20th century and are at the basis of Hans Kelsen and H. L. A. Hart's juridical understanding of responsibility (Paulson 1992; Ricoeur 2000). The main aim driving legal positivism during the 20th century was to distinguish legal rules from moral and thus political assumptions in order to construct a conception able to overcome the dangers connected to moral pluralism and relativism when inserted into the realm of right (Kelsen 2005; Hart 1994; Hart 2008). As clearly stated by Kelsen, "uncritically, the science of law has been mixed with elements of psychology, sociology, ethics and political theory" (Kelsen 2005: p. 1).

Part of this general plan foresaw a linguistic analysis in order to distinguish terms referring to legal rules from those pertaining to a moral judgement. Thus, responsibility, a key concept within any modern legal system that had been sometimes used in ambiguous ways in order to justify single political perspectives (Ewald 1986), also needed to be analytically defined (Kelsen 2005). The outcome of this linguistic analysis was an exhaustive taxonomy of different 'senses' of responsibility and their usage across law and morality (Hart 2008: pp. 210–230; Vincent 2011; Pellé & Reber 2015). According to Kelsen and, to some extent, Hart, moral responsibility, namely actions that are blameworthy, should have been kept separate from the legal features defining the subject of rights. The legal criteria for imputing an action to an agent, his liability and accountability should have been indicated and justified according to self-referential epistemic traits. The two authors were so concerned by the negative influence of subjective positions in the realm of law that they strongly marked their ontological differences. They did admit that it might happen that moral judgements coincide with legal ones, but there is not a 'necessary' relation between the two.

Several authors have discussed the radical isolationism of this conceptual framework. Perfectly exemplified by Richard Dworkin, one of the main arguments of these criticisms is that legal systems must be developed according to some moral features if they are to obtain the necessary respondence from those who are supposed to follow them (Dworkin 1978; Dworkin 1988; Fuller 1969; Brudner 2012; Pettit 2014; Habermas 1986; Paulson 1999). Besides, the interpretations of given laws, which require a situational judgement, especially in common law, always imply the construction of additional right (Habermas 1986; Dworkin 1978).

These criticisms have unveiled a singular aspect, which appears to be important for our analysis. Adopting a clear distinction between the realm of morality and that of right surely protects our societies from dangerous moral influences in the promotion of justice. It offers the necessary procedural tools in order to avoid dangerous drifts in society. However, the argument proposed by Dworkin and others reminds us that any regulatory code needs to rely on conditions that can be potentially approved by those who are supposed to follow them.

Accordingly, the understanding of responsible or irresponsible behaviour should not be left only to the acceptance of a law, but needs to question the acceptability of a rule framing interaction.

The scope of our analysis of responsibility is to unveil a pragmatic conception able to function for the future-oriented and uncertain challenges of R&I. I wonder, then, if responsibility within such a framework could or should be reduced to its legal dimension. Or if, on the contrary, being dynamic and future-oriented, RRI is not searching for a regulatory concept that could manage to cover those spaces of action that are undetermined or undeterminable by law, as René von Schomberg once suggested (von Schomberg 2011). I am not suggesting that responsibility should be deprived of this hard core, but only that we need to construct a conception able to integrate it and go beyond it.

However, Hart already foresaw the necessity to establish certain practical preconditions in order to enable agents to adjust their behaviour to laws, constructing a bridge between his theoretical building, focused on the assumption of responsibility as a medium to obtain freedom and those instead promoting freedom as the precondition for responsibility (Hart 2008: p. 181). Unfortunately, in order not to undermine his own theoretical building, he could not go far enough to justify extra-epistemic factors as preconditions for action. The clear methodological framework, common to both Kant and the juridical positivists, is that the conditions of possibility for action and thus responsibility are identified with cognitive traits and their relation to the rationality of a rule.

This aspect has been implicitly tackled by the other group of thinkers, who, although with different arguments, share the need to highlight the existential and subjective nature of agency.[6]

At a time when environmental issues already raised the awareness that individual actions can have endless and borderless consequences, Hans Jonas felt the urge to reassert the necessity to implement responsible behaviours (Jonas 1984). He also understood that the objective individualist imputation's scheme, typical of deontological theories, was not sufficient for addressing these 'existential' concerns.

Far from being reduced to a juridical or negative understanding, existential approaches to responsibility have pointed at constructing a dynamic attitude based on elements that can be found beyond a mere cognitive approach. According to them, reducing morality to reason disregards many concrete motivations that drive an agent's actions. The kind of responsibility a subject faces in everyday life is also one based on a virtuous attitude of care towards his and others' 'environment'. These attempts share a radical perspective of responsibility, but they apply it to the vital and sentimental side of existence. In fact, the common conceptual framework is that in order to obtain and guarantee the most basic expression for any human action, i.e. life, we must act responsibly by caring for our world in all senses. The moral imperative is, in the end, an ontological (or naturalistic) one: we must guarantee the survival of the species. Unlike for Kelsen or Hart, these actions are not regulated by a set of legal rules, but by the emotional and intuitive impulse of taking care of someone. The shift is quite remarkable. Here, actions are not *attributed* or *imputed* to actors in order to evaluate their consequences. Rather, it is the actor herself that is voluntarily *assuming* the responsibility by caring. From this basic existential imperative came a whole set of more refined analyses, developing specific applications of this principle of care (Grinbaum & Groves 2013; Blok 2014; Blok 2016; Pavie Ch. 11, Gianni 2016). Existential responsibility has surely been one of the most powerful tools to contrast ecological problems exactly because of its global range and ontological depth. It has also contributed to connecting familiar models of interaction into a general dimension, representing a fruitful reference in order to actively shape social relations.

The great point of assuming responsibility as a subjective and contextual effort of care finds a concrete limit, though, if we think of it in terms of the overall concept, and its concrete application within RRI in terms of efficiency. The main shortcomings are, from what I can see, the 'unnecessary' nature of such an effort and the too-general or too-biased nature of the 'Other' to which an agent is willing to respond. The survival of the planet, or an ontological responsibility, are surely basic preconditions able to fill all those gaps in the interpretation of agency as present in a strictly juridical conception. However, they might tend to remain too abstract or too specific. The definition, extent and target of care can be highly relative and it does not always increment the general level of wellbeing.[7] Being a subjective effort, this attitude and its goals tend to be left to the free choice of an agent, which makes it contradictory to the purpose it embeds, that is, a collective one. Furthermore, we might want to ensure the possibility that a single effort finds the right external conditions, enabling individuals to provide society with realistic contributions. As noticed by Theodor W. Adorno, virtuous behaviours are conceived as such in a particular situation and in relation to specific circumstances in which they operate and that shape them. "The good is not indifferent to the conditions for its realisation" (Adorno 2005; Jaeggi 2005), but refers to a historically sound context. The 'Other' to which we ought to respond needs to be identified, and the consequent responsibilities must be promoted through concrete and stable measures.

Accordingly, I believe that existential responsibility needs to be supported by, and embedded in, a social framework where institutions promote common objectives and make them possible. In this sense, efforts based on care could not and should not ignore more objective and intersubjective criteria of responsibility.

Time and responsibility

After this brief reconnaissance, we now see the extent to which these different interpretations of action are conflictual and do not resolve the 'dilemma' of the relation between subjective efforts and objective traits. Even if they can all be considered legitimate because they address moral, legal and ontological needs, I am not entirely sure that they could be equally useful or efficient if taken separately. We need, therefore, to propose a conception of responsibility that can maintain the features of subjective efforts together with objective external criteria and merge them into a common understanding, one which is able to maintain the equilibrium between legitimacy and efficacy.

Before emphasizing a different perspective, I believe it is important to highlight a point that I will address again later. I see an underlying aspect in the current conceptions of responsibility that appears promising. Both deontological and existentialist perspectives suggest that it is the assumption of certain features and subsequent tasks that makes an agent able to be free and to self-determine his own future. If we take responsibility, then we can be free. For Kelsen, in particular, this was a crucial shift. For him, right, and therefore responsibility, had to be intended as the only way through which agents could become free because rules and norms insert them into a system that makes them free: "One does not impute a sanction to an individual's behaviour because he is free, but the individual is free because one imputed a sanction to his behaviour" (Kelsen 2005: p. 98). Also Jonas, who identified the logical necessity for such an imperative in the survival of the species, was implying that only by acting responsibly could we obtain freedom, although for future generations. These valuable perspectives focus on the will of a subject to act responsibly in order to protect and enhance his and others' freedom. However, apart from basic cognitive or emotional features, they do not eviscerate the other side of the question that we could raise on how an agent can be responsible if he is not previously free. As summarized by H. Seillan, with regard to responsibility, "Plato, Aristotle, Saint Agustin, Saint Thomas and later Kant and Durkheim have structured it around the free will of man. Freedom conditions responsibility. Man cannot be responsible if not free. A slave cannot be it" (Seillan 2016: p.293; Gianni 2016).

The relation between these two interpretations of actions can play a crucial role in a concrete understanding of what responsibility should mean for RRI. If laws are not constructed according to moral insights, they might tend to overlook particular social needs or values. Accordingly, an agent who would like to become free and thus 'accepts' that codification would probably feel an internal conflict between his capacities and his real possibilities. In a more concrete fashion, if a researcher would like to investigate in a specific direction because she considers it responsible but lacks the resources to do so, then I am not sure that the 'acceptance' of responsibility generates actual, free choices.

The answer to this tension implies a shift from the moral and epistemic dimension of responsibility to its ethical application and subsequent political governance. It means that we have to consider responsibility through the category of *time*.

What has emerged from the genealogical analyses that we have built on is that the different moral and juridical theories have tried to provide acceptable delineations of those conditions necessary to regulate human actions always on the basis of specific historical evolutions and needs. Although all those authors were defining responsibility independently of time, they all did it for reasons that were embedded within their time. If, during early modernity, responsibility was embedded in an individualistic framework defining the vertical relation of an agent with the authority and the inner relation with the self, with the 18th century also emerges the necessity to define the horizontal interaction between free individuals (Donzelot 1984; Genard 1999; Neuhouser 2000). The interpretation of action had been defined in its epistemic nature according to political reasons, meaning that institutional conditions and philosophical works focused on protecting a negative space where an individual could determine his own identity. Later on, historical developments brought the necessity for indications able to also regulate 'positive' interactions[8] (Honneth 2014; Genard 1999). What Genard calls the 'anthropology of perfectibility' was now driving individuals towards an intersubjective understanding of identity. Self-determination as the characteristic of a modern individual started to be supported and developed by the concept of self-realization in order to express and reach a satisfactory identity/life (Honneth 2014; Herder 2002). Thus, the underlying idea of freedom could also no longer be limited to (the one) avoiding interferences, but should rather point towards constructive interaction with others. Consequently, responsibility had to define the rules for regulating this new social development. With the emergence of modern economics and the rise of contemporary democracy, the conceptual framework defining power as the *capacity* to act had to be supported by a more concrete aspect of power, the *possibility* to do so. It meant acknowledging that additional aspects apart from the mere absence of obstacles for a metaphysically shaped subject were required, that is, exactly those produced and insured by a historical incarnation of social and economic nature. It was, then, for the concrete relations of an intersubjective nature that the features of responsibility needed to be redrawn.

Ethical responsibility

It is with German idealism and some recent interpretations of their concept of justice that we can detect a crucial step forward in such ethical understanding of responsibility (Maesschalck 2000; Ferry 1991; Honneth 2014; Genard 1999; Neuhouser 2000; Speight 1997).

According to these readings, both Fichte and Hegel had already indicated the importance of intersubjective and contingent relations for the establishment of rules and norms regulating individuals' actions. The epistemological conditions for understanding norms and determining our own identity, as developed by Kant, were integrated into an anthropological framework of perfectibility, which promoted identity formation through the encounter with other individuals (Genard 1999).

If Fichte defined the juridical possibility of a self on the basis of the necessary recognition of the other,[9] Hegel extended this intersubjective connection to the realization of one's identity in concrete societal domains (Hegel 1991; Honneth 1996; 2014).

This did not mean, for the two authors, that all rational features for defining the contours of imputation had to be rejected, but only that they had to be matched with a concrete, historical scenario. For Hegel, this was the necessary passage from a moral understanding of imputation to the ethical understanding of responsibility (Ritter 1982; Adorno 1993; 2005). If the rules defining the ways in which action can be regulated are reduced to fixed, abstract epistemic criteria, then not only might they lack legitimacy, but they will also miss the possibility of efficiently covering actual social dynamics. According to this perspective, then, the concept of responsibility has to be based on the possibility of referring to rational universal features, but those features should be integrated and shaped according to the historical and contextual scenario in which they are supposed to be adopted.

If responsibility aims at fulfilling its regulatory role in a legitimate and effective way, the rules, values and norms defining responsible behaviour can only be constructed by concrete partners in participatory ways (Maesschalck 2000; Honneth, 2014).

It is not surprising, then, that the first occurrences of the term responsibility only emerged with this ethical delineation of the integration of different aspects of human action and its subsequent historical actualization (Villey 1977; Kazmareck 2012). Around the middle of the 19th century, it was felt necessary to update the legal framework in order to institutionalize the increasing role of external influences on human action (Donzelot 1984). The novelty that occurred with the shift of focus in legal rules from the centrality of the guilty to that of the victim was nothing more than the juridical recognition of a more complex relation of agents with other agents in emerging industrial societies.

The concomitant presence of inner will and external forces, together with an increasingly complex division of labour, generated the need to introduce an idea able to hold these different aspects together in a balanced way. Although criticized by François Ewald because of its association with liberal policies, the idea of responsibility, as discussed in the deliberative phase of the Civil Law of 1898, was the first operation to address the social need for broadening the framework of interpretation of agency, assessing it according to the different forces at play (Ewald 1986; Donzelot 1984).

It is plausible that the development of this 'insurance regime' has had a role in the shift towards security policies and (neo) liberal strategies, but this has been, in my opinion, a historical drift that did not necessarily undermine the conceptual force of responsibility. I do not think that we need to throw the baby out with the bathwater because, as shown by Ricoeur, the application of only one of the senses of responsibility is an empirical shortcoming that proves the theoretical validity of a broader perspective.

Political responsibility

However, the measures enacting and guaranteeing such 'interconnections' among different societal domains are of a political nature (Brudney 2014). The different dissertations orbiting around responsibility have scientifically addressed aspects that are directly connected to their domains or their particular interpretations of action. But if we want to tackle the quest for a regulatory framework 'responsibly', we need to do it politically, as rightly underlined by Bernard Williams and Michiel van Oudheusden (Williams 2005; van Oudheusden 2014). This means implementing a passage from a single perspective to the comprehension of the management of their relation in a given community. Furthermore, it implies the understanding of the underlying objective of a historically situated political framework.

But, as lucidly highlighted by Hannah Arendt, the main objective of politics, especially in modernity, has always been freedom, and the ways to promote it have varied according to specific interpretations of action (Arendt 1972: p. 190).

Genard, Ricoeur and other authors who have investigated the development of responsibility have identified the different interpretations of the concept at a given historical moment, looking for conceptual interpretations of action among different domains.

What is often only implicit in their works, although it is central to the interpretation of responsibility, is the crucial role of, and the close connection with, the concept of freedom. The modern development of responsibility, in all the forms that we have briefly reported, was the necessary regulation for a concomitant historical understanding of freedom. If terms like imputation and accountability were established in order to define the limits of juridical and negative freedom, with the emergence of the social and ethical perspective promoted by German Idealism and applied during the same historical period (Donzelot 1984) the understanding of responsibility changed accordingly. It is not surprising that with a different organization of labour and the advent of particular sciences we have witnessed the need for a different understanding of responsibility.

Accordingly, we can delineate the reasons for the evolution of responsibility on the basis of the different underlying conception of freedom, which it is called upon to regulate. In order to better understand the reasons and consequences of the different theorizations of responsibility, it is always useful to integrate them or read them through the related understanding of freedom that they want to promote. Far from being an abstract or pointless erudite exercise, an identification of the kind of freedom that a concept of responsibility promotes helps us in unveiling and assessing its underlying purposes. In this way, I believe that we can emancipate the concept from its theoretical fragmentations and also protect it from the different attempts at exploitation caused by its polysemy.

In fact, there is a last passage that drives us towards an ethical and thus complementary framework of responsibility, especially for RRI. We have mentioned the limits of single perspectives of responsibility in not understanding the sense of appropriateness, which means maintaining a correct relation between legitimate and efficacious processes (Gunther 1993; Lenoir 2016). This is also the danger of freedom, which finds severe limits if reduced to one of its sides. Philippe Pettit has shown on several occasions that if an agent is to be free she needs to have the resources and the room for making her choices. These preconditions are, first of all, personal and natural, as present with the advent of modernity, but they are also social (Pettit 2014). Otherwise, according to him, we would find ourselves in a condition of domination and we would be entitled to be relieved of our responsibilities.

In a similar manner, Axel Honneth has shown us that all the rules and norms regulating our individual actions always have to presuppose a set of social institutions that makes them possible (Honneth 2014). Furthermore, Honneth has drawn attention to the potential benefits of adopting a social understanding of freedom, highlighting the necessary balance with equality and solidarity (2016). Thus, according to this perspective, promoting individual responsibility is a necessary and good indication but it cannot be isolated from other senses of responsibilities that need to be inserted into an ethical framework and driven at the political level. Besides, all these understandings of responsibility should be supported by concrete measures favouring their adoption by agents. To simply attribute responsibilities to researchers and innovators without considering if they are concretely able to choose is an unfruitful operation at best. This is the other side of the coin of justice. If we want to realistically promote responsible actions, we must ensure the concrete possibility of operating a choice.

At this point, I think that we have reached two main goals for the analysis of responsibility in the RRI framework. The first is the necessity to understand responsibility as an overall balance of its different aspects.

Elsewhere (Gianni 2016), I have argued that the only way to fulfil the purposes embedded in the concept of responsibility, to protect individuals from evil and to recognize their merits, is to conceive it in a social way, merging and integrating a reciprocal exchange between legal and moral understandings in a given space and time through social institutions.

The second goal that I believe we have achieved is that we have obtained a powerful diagnostic instrument to assess the real objectives and the overall solidity with regard to the different incitations to assume responsible attitudes that an individual receives in her daily life. Responsibility and the imperative of a responsible action are pervading our lives through different social registers. At work, in our families and in our relations with others, we are told to be responsible or we are made responsible for something or someone. Often these indications aim at recalling the necessity of protecting and promoting our reciprocal freedoms, but other times they tend to favour only a biased or interested position provoking different forms of pathologies (Laitinen 2015; Zurn 2011; Honneth 2009). It is then useful to understand, through the related concept of freedom, what kind of responsibility we are requested to carry, what is the purpose of our engagement and what are the real possibilities of fulfilling such a task or role.

I believe that this is a conception of responsibility that could be legitimate and efficacious for the RRI framework. Based on the understanding that actions are the outcomes of different sources over which an agent has limited control, we need to situate them in a regulatory framework that addresses the various expressions of freedom. Responsibility should be the overarching concept integrating all its different sides in a pondered way, offering individuals main references for acting. As is well understood by Ricoeur via Hegel, between the two extremes of a potentially infinite inner care and the objective imputability that limits the space of individual action we should choose "a concrete social morality that brings with it the wisdom of mores, customs, shared beliefs, and institutions that bear the stamp of history" (Ricoeur 2000: p. 33).

The overall argument could be summarized by the following definition: "Being responsible means responding to the guaranteed freedoms as a recognized moral agent of a given society, having the aim of preserving such freedoms and at the same time implementing them through concrete institutional arrangements" (Gianni 2016: p. 140).

It is such an 'illocutionary' and performative understanding of responsibility that could serve the purposes embedded in RRI by unveiling the common objectives of the different paradigms. We can then emphasize that not only R&I has a normative nature, but that also responsibility should not be reduced to a burden or an obstacle for R&I. On the contrary, we should intend responsible practices as the right strategy to incentivize efficient strategies without losing on legitimacy.

Conclusion

We have highlighted some of the problems connected to the ambiguity of responsibility for the implementation of RRI. We have then operated a genealogical inquiry to show that responsibility is a regulatory framework aimed at regulating human interaction. At the same time, it has emerged that responsibility cannot be understood outside its historical dimension, showing that the concept has been constantly developed according to contextual needs. Furthermore, we have emphasized the specular relation of responsibility to freedom and we have suggested that the two should be conceived in an ethical and social manner. Accordingly, the implementation of responsibility, especially within the framework of RRI, cannot be delegated to scientific or abstract criteria but should be promoted according to clear political measures.

Notes

1 I am aware of the differences between research and innovation, but for the sake of the argument of this paper, they are not as important as their similarities.
2 For a brilliant overview of these kinds of analyses, see Vincent et al. (2011).
3 For a perspective on some of the different versions and some general features, see Goodin (1995), Sen and Williams (1982) and Pettit (1997).
4 Although we cannot call it such as yet.
5 According to a critical perspective on this necessary relation, to behave irrationally means to be immoral and to be immoral necessarily implies an irrational choice (Williams 1984).
6 For a not exhausting but still important overview of some general traits of this existential conception, see E. Levinas (1998), V. Blok (2014; 2016), J. P. Sartre (1993), U. Beck (1992), H. Jonas (1979), and M. Weber (2004).
7 We can also highlight, with Habermas, the difficulties arising from a reflexive relation to the future (Habermas 2004).
8 I am referring to the distinction introduced by I. Berlin (2002).
9 Marc Maesschalck offers a more substantial perspective of Fichte's theory of recognition; see Maesschalck (2000).

References

Adorno, T. W. (1993). *Hegel: Three Studies*. Cambridge (MA): MIT Press.

Adorno, T. W. (2005). *Minima Moralia: Reflections on Damaged Life*. London: Verso.

Apel, K. O. (1990). *Diskurs und Verantwortung: Das Problem des Übergangs zur Postkonventionellen Moral*. Berlin: Suhrkamp.

Aquinas, T. (2000). *Summa Theologica*. Notre Dame (IN): Ave Maria Press.

Arendt, H. (1972). *La Crise de la Culture*. Paris: Gallimard.

Arnaldi, S. and Bianchi, L. (2016). *Responsibility in Science and Technology. Elements of a Social Theory*. Wiesbaden: Springer.

Arnaldi, S. and Gorgoni, G. (2016). Turning the tide or surfing the wave? Responsible Research and Innovation, fundamental rights and neoliberal virtues. *Life Sciences, Society and Policy*, 12(6), pp. 1–19.

Beck, U. (1992). *Risk Society: Towards a New Modernity*. London: Sage Publications.

Berlin, I. (2002). *Liberty: Incorporating Four Essays on Liberty*. Oxford: Oxford University Press.

Bessant, J. (2013). Innovation in the Twenty-First Century. In: R. Owen, Bessant, J. and Heintz, M. (Eds), *Responsible Innovation. Managing the Responsible Emergence of Science and Innovation in Society*, Hoboken (NJ): John Wiley & Sons, pp. 1–25.

Blok, V. (2014). Look who's talking: responsible innovation, the paradox of dialogue and the voice of the other in communication and negotiation processes. *Journal of Responsible Innovation*, 1(2), pp. 171–190.

Blok, V. (2016). Dealing with the wicked problem of sustainability: the role of individual virtuous competence. *Business & Professional Ethics Journal*, 34(3), pp. 297–327.

Blok, V. and Lemmens, P. (2015). The Emerging Concept of Responsible Innovation. Three Reasons Why It Is Questionable and Calls for a Radical Transformation of the Concept of Innovation. In: B.-J. Koops, J., Oosterlaken, I., Romijn, H., et al. (Eds.), *Responsible Innovation 2: Concepts, Approaches,and Applications*. Dordrecht: Springer, pp. 19–35.

Boethius, (1999). *The Consolation of Philosophy*. London: Penguin Classics.

Boltanski, L. and Chiapello, E. (2007). *The New Spirit of Capitalism*. London: Verso.

Brudner, A. (2012). Hegel on the Relation between Law and Justice. In: T. Brooks (Ed.), *Hegel's Philosophy of Right*. Oxford: Wiley Blackwell, pp. 180–208.

Brudney, D. (2014). The Young Marx and the Middle-Aged Rawls. In: J. Mandle and Reidy, D. (Eds). *A Companion to Rawls*. London: Wiley-Blackwell, pp. 450–471.

Cassirer, E. (1965). *Philosophy of Symbolic Forms, Vol. 1*. London: Yale University Press.

Dodds, E. (2004). *The Greeks and the Irrational*. London: University of California Press.

Donzelot, J. (1984). *L'invention Du Social. Essai Sur Le Déclin Des Passions Politiques*. Paris: Fayard.

Duns Scotus, J. (1997). *On Will and Morality*. Washington (DC): Catholic University America Press.

Dworkin, R. (1978). *Taking Right Seriously*. Cambridge (MA): Harvard University Press.

Dworkin, R. (1988). *Law's Empire*. Cambridge (MA): Harvard University Press.

Eagleton-Pierce, M. (2016). *Neoliberalism: The Key Concepts*. Oxford: Routledge.

Ehrenberg, A. (1998). *The Fatigue of Being Oneself: Depression and Society*. Paris: Odile Jacob.

Ewald, F. (1986). *L'Etat Providence*. Paris: Grasset et Fasquelle.

Fauconnet, P. (1925). *La responsabilité*. Paris: Felix Alcan.

Ferry, J. M. (1991). *Les Puissances de l'Experiénce*. Paris: Cerf.

Forst, R. (2012). *The Right to Justification: Elements of a Constructivist Theory of Justice*. New York: Columbia University Press.

Foucault, M. (2014). *Wrong-Doing, Truth-Telling: The Function of Avowal in Justice.* Chicago: The University of Chicago Press.

Fuller, L. L. (1969). *The Morality of Law.* Yale (CT): Yale University Press.

Genard, J.-L. (1999). *La Grammaire de la responsabilitè.* Paris: Cerf.

Gianni, R. (2016). *Freedom and Responsibility. The Ethical Realm of RRI.* London/New York: ISTE/Wiley.

Godin, B. (2015). *Innovation Contested – The Idea of Innovation over the Centuries.* London: Routledge.

Goodin, R. E. (1995). *Utilitarianism as a Public Philosophy.* New York: Cambridge University Press.

Grinbaum, A. and Groves, C. (2013). What is 'Responsible' about Responsible Innovation? Understanding the Ethical Issues. In: R. Owen, Bessant J. and Heintz M. (Eds.), *Responsible Innovation. Managing the Responsible Emergence of Science and Innovation in Society.* Hoboken (NJ): John Wiley & Sons, pp. 119–142.

Grunwald, A. (2011). Responsible innovation: bringing together technology assessment, applied ethics, and STS research. *Enterprise and Work Innovation Studies*, 7(IET), pp. 9–31.

Gunther, K. (1993). *The Sense of Appropriateness.* Albany (NY): Suny Press.

Habermas, J. (1986). Law and morality. *The Tanner Lectures on Human Values.* Available at http://tannerlectures.utah.edu/_documents/a-to-z/h/habermas88.pdf

Habermas, J. (2004). *The Future of Human Nature.* Cambridge: Polity Press.

Hart, H. L. A. (1994). *The Concept of Law* (2nd ed.). Oxford: Clarendon.

Hart, H. L. A. (2008). *Punishment and Responsibility. Essays in the Philosophy of Law.* Oxford: Oxford University Press.

Hartmann, M. and Honneth, A. (2006). Paradoxes of capitalism. *Constellations*, 13(1), pp. 41–58.

Hegel, G. W. F. (1991). *Elements of the Philosophy of Right.* Cambridge: Cambridge University Press.

Herder, J. G. (2002). On the Cognition and the Sensation of Human Soul. In *Philosophical Writings.* Cambridge: Cambridge University Press, pp. 187–244.

Hobbes, T. (1996). *Leviathan.* Cambridge: Cambridge University Press.

Honneth, A. (1996). *The Struggle for Recognition. The Moral Grammar of Social Conflicts.* Cambridge (MA): MIT Press.

Honneth, A. (2009). *Pathologies of Reason. On the Legacy of Critical Theory.* Columbia University Press: New York.

Honneth, A. (2014). *Freedom's Right. The Social Foundations of Democratic Life.* Cambridge: Polity Press.

Honneth, A. (2016). *The Idea of Socialism.* Cambridge: Polity Press.

Jacob, K. (Rapporteur); van den Hoven, J. (Chair); Nielsen, L., Roure, F., Rudze, L. and Stilgoe, J. (Members); and Blind, K., Guske, A.-L. and Martinez Riera, C. (Contributors) (2013). *Options for Strengthening RRI. Report of the Expert Group on the State of Art in Europe on Responsible Research and Innovation*, European Commission. Available at https://ec.europa.eu/research/science-society/document_library/pdf_06/options-for-strengthening_en.pdf

Jaeggi, R. (2005). Kein Einzelner vermag etwas dagegen: Adornos Minima Moralia als Kritik von Lebensformen. In: A. Honneth (Ed.), *Dialektik der Freiheit.* Frankfurt am Main: Suhrkamp, pp. 115–141.

Jonas, H. (1984). *The Imperative of Responsibility: In Search of Ethics for the Technological Age.* Chicago: University of Chicago Press.

Kaczmarek, L. (2012). *La responsabilité pour fait normal: Etude critique sur son originalité en matière civile extracontractuelle*. Paris: Publibook.

Kant, I. (1997). *Critique of Practical Reason*. Cambridge: Cambridge University Press.

Kant, I. (1998). *Critique of Pure Reason*. Cambridge: Cambridge University Press.

Kant, I. (2009). *Groundwork of the Metaphysics of Morals*. New York: Harper Perennial Modern Classics.

Kelsen, H. (2005). *Pure Theory of Law*. Berkeley: California University Press.

Kervegan, J. F. (2015). *La Raison des Normes. Essai sur Kant*. Paris: Seuil.

Kuhlmann, S., Edler, J., Ordóñez-Matamoros, G., et al. (2016). Responsibility Navigator. In: R. Lindner, Kuhlmann, S., Randles, S., Walhout, B., Gough, C. and Lindne, R. (Eds.), *Navigating towards Shared Responsibility in Research and Innovation. Approach, Process and Results of the Res-AGorA Project*. Karlsruhe: Res-AGorA, pp. 135–158. Available at https://indd.adobe.com/view/eaeb695e-a212-4a34-aeba-b3d8a7a58acc

Laitinen, A. (2015). Social Pathologies, Reflexive Pathologies, and the Idea of High-Orders Disorders. In: *Studies of Social and Political Thought*, 25(SI), pp. 44–65. Available at http://dx.doi.org/10.20919/sspt.25.2015.48

Lenoir, V. (2016). *Ethical Efficiency: Responsibility and Contingency*. London/New York: Iste/Wiley.

Levinas, E. (1998). *Otherwise Than Being or beyond Essence*. Pittsburgh (PA): Duquesne University Press.

Locke, J. (1988). *Two Treatises of Government*. Cambridge: Cambridge University Press.

MacIntyre, A. (2007). *After Virtue: A Study in Moral Theory*. Notre Dame (IN): University of Notre Dame Press.

Maesschalck, M. (2000). Provenance et Fondements de la Pragmatique Contextuelle. In: P. Coppens and Lenoble, J. (Eds.), *Democratie et Procéduralisation du Droit*, Bruxelles: Bruylant, pp. 125–154.

Moldashl, M. (2010). *Why innovation theories make no sense*. Paper provided by Chemnitz University of Technology, Faculty of Economics and Business Administration in its series Papers and Preprints of the Department of Innovation Research and Sustainable Resource Management with number 9/2010.

Neuhouser, F. (2000). *Foundations of Hegel's Social Theory*. Cambridge (MA): Harvard University Press.

Nowotny, H. (2015). *The Cunning of Uncertainty*. Oxford: Polity.

Owen, R., Bessant, J. and Heintz, M. (Eds.) (2013). *Responsible Innovation. Managing the Responsible Emergence of Science and Innovation in Society*. Hoboken (NJ): John Wiley & Sons.

Paulson, L. S. (1992). The neo-Kantian dimension of Kelsen's Pure Theory of Law. *Oxford Legal Studies*, 12(3), pp. 311–332.

Paulson, S. (1999). *Normativity and Norms: Critical Perspectives on Kelsenian Themes* Oxford: Oxford University Press.

Pavie, X. (2017). From Responsible-Innovation to Innovation-*Care*. Beyond Constraints, a Holistic Approach of Innovation. In: Gianni, R., Pearson, J. and Reber, B. (Eds.), *Responsible Research and Innovation. From Concepts to Practices*. Oxford: Routledge.

Pavie, X., Scholten, V. and Carthy D. (2014). *Responsible Innovation. From Concept to Practice*. Singapore: World Scientific.

Pellé, S. and Reber, B. (2015). Responsible innovation in the light of moral responsibility. *Journal on Chain and Network Science, Special Issue*, 15(2), pp. 107–117.

Pellizzoni, L. (2004). Responsibility and Environmental Governance. *Environmental Politics*, 13(3), pp. 541–565.

Pettit, P. (1997). The Consequentialist Perspective. In: M. Baron, Pettit, P. and Slote, M. (Eds.), *Three Methods of Ethics: A Debate*. Oxford: Blackwell.

Pettit, P. (2014). *Just Freedom. A Moral Compass for a Complex World*. New York: Norton and Company.

Pufendorf, S. (2008). *On Duty of Man & Citizen*. Cambridge: Cambridge University Press.

Raz, J. (2014). *From Normativity to Responsibility*. Oxford: Oxford University Press.

Ricoeur, P. (2007). *Reflections on The Just*. Chicago: Chicago University Press.

Ricoeur, P. (2000). *The Just*. Chicago: Chicago University Press.

Ripstein, A. (2010). *Force and Freedom: Kant's Legal and Political Philosophy*. Cambridge (MA): Harvard University Press.

Ritter, J. (1982). *Hegel and the French Revolution. Essays on the Philosophy of Right*. Cambridge (MA): MIT Press.

Sartre, J.-P. (1993). *Being and Nothingness*. Washington (DC): Washington Square Press.

Schumpeter, J. A. (1934). *The Theory of Economic Development: An Inquiry into Profits, Capital, Credit, Interest and the Business Cycle*. New Brunswick: Transaction Publishers.

Seillan, H. (2016). *Danger et précaution: le roman des mots*. Paris, Manitoba.

Sen, A. and Williams, B. (Eds.) (1982). *Utilitarianism and Beyond*, Cambridge: Cambridge University Press.

Spaapen, J. (Rapporteur); Strand, R. (Chair); Bauer, M. W., Hogan, E., Revuelta, G. and Stagl, S. (Members); and Paula, L. and Guimarães Pereira, Â. (Contributors) (2015). *Indicators for promoting and monitoring Responsible Research and Innovation. Report from the Expert Group on Policy Indicators for Responsible Research and Innovation*. European Commission. Available at http://ec.europa.eu/research/swafs/pdf/pub_rri/rri_indicators_final_version.pdf

Speight, C. A. (1997). The "metaphysics" of morals and Hegel's critique of Kantian ethics, *History of Philosophy Quarterly*, 14(4), pp. 379–402.

Stehr, N. (2008). *Moral Markets. How Knowledge and Affluence Change Consumers and Products*. Boulder (CO): Paradigm Publishers.

Taylor, C. (1992). *Sources of the Self: The Making of the Modern Identity*. Cambridge (MA): Harvard University Press.

van de Poel, I. (2011). The Relation Between Forward-Looking and Backward-Looking Responsibility. In: N. Vincent, van de Poel, I. and Van den Hoven J. (Eds.), *Moral Responsibility, Beyond Free Will & Determinism*. Dordrecht: Springer NL.

Van Den Hoven, J. (2013). Value Sensitive Design and Responsible Innovation. In: R. Owen, Bessant J., Heintz M. (Eds.), *Responsible Innovation. Managing the Responsible Emergence of Science and Innovation in Society*. Hoboken (NJ): John Wiley & Sons, pp. 75–83.

Van den Hoven, J., Doorn, N., Swierstra, T., Koops, B. J., and Romijn, H. (Eds.) (2014). *Responsible Innovation 1. Innovative Solutions for Global Issues*. Dordrecht: Springer.

Van Oudheusden, M. (2014). Where are the politics in responsible innovation? European governance, technology assessments, and beyond. *Journal of Responsible Innovation*, 1(1), pp. 67–86.

Villey, M. (1977). Esquisse historique sur le mot responsible. *Archives de philosophie du droit*, XXII, La responsabilité, pp. 45–58.

Vincent, N., van de Poel, I. and Van den Hoven J. (Eds.) (2011). *Moral Responsibility, beyond Free Will & Determinism*. Dordrecht: Springer.

von Schomberg, R. (2011). *Science, Politics, and Morality: Scientific Uncertainty and Decision Making*. Dordrecht: Springer.

Weber, M. (2004). *The Vocation Lectures: 'Science as a Vocation'; 'Politics as a Vocation'*. Indianapolis: Hackett.

Williams, B. (1984). *Moral Luck*. Albany (NY): Suny Press.
Williams, B. (2005). *In the Beginning Was the Deed: Realism and Moralism In Political Argument*. Princeton (NJ): Princeton University Press.
Zurn, C. F. (2011). Social Pathologies as Second-Order Disorders. In: D. Petherbridge (Ed.), *Axel Honneth: Critical Essays with a Reply by Axel Honneth*. Leiden: Brill, pp. 345–370.

2 Responsibility beyond consequentialism

The EEE approach to responsibility in the face of epistemic constraints[1]

Armin Grunwald

Introduction and overview

The very idea of responsibility and responsibility ethics is, following Max Weber's distinction between *Verantwortungsethik* and *Gesinnungsethik*, usually related to a consequentialist approach. Taking over responsibility or assigning responsibility to other persons, groups or institutions indispensably requires, in this paradigm, the availability of valid and reliable knowledge, or at least of a plausible picture of the consequences and impact of decisions to be made or of actions to be performed. The familiar approach of discussing responsibilities is to consider future consequences of an action (e.g. the development and use of new technologies) and then to reflect on these consequences from an ethical point of view (e.g. with respect to the acceptability of technology-induced risk). Thus, without a rather clear picture of those future consequences, any ethics of responsibility falls under the suspicion either to fail, or to lead to mere arbitrary conclusions (Hansson 2006), or to end up in mere political rhetoric.

The RRI (responsible research and innovation) debate (e.g. von Schomberg 2012, Owen et al. 2013) emerged out of the reflections on new and emerging technologies (NEST) such as nanotechnology (e.g. Fiedeler et al. 2010; Grunwald 2014a), nanobiotechnology (e.g. Paslack et al. 2012) and human enhancement (e.g. Jotterand 2008). The clue, with respect to the issue of this chapter, is that there is only little if any reliable knowledge about future consequences available in this field (e.g. Nordmann 2007, Coenen and Simakova 2013, Nordmann 2014). Because of the early stage of development in those fields, there is no valid knowledge about specific innovation paths and products or about consequences and impacts of production, use, non-intended side-effects and disposal of future products. The rationale of this chapter is to explore how responsibility could be conceptualized and made operable in this situation which renders the traditional consequentialist approach impossible (Grunwald 2013a).

While RRI has been focusing predominantly on procedural aspects and participation so far, frequently taking the notion of responsibility as a self-explanatory phrase, a theoretical debate on how to understand responsibility is still lacking. There have been only a few papers in this direction so far (e.g. Grinbaum and Groves 2013; Grunwald 2012). First reflections based on earlier concepts within the ethics of responsibility showed, however, that the notion of responsibility is far more complex than being a merely ethical term. Responsibility comprises at least three dimensions (following Grunwald 2014b; see Sect. 2): the empirical, the ethical and the epistemic one.

In the early stages of development of any R&D (e.g. in the above-mentioned NEST fields), the epistemic dimension of responsibility becomes decisive (Sect. 3). The lack of knowledge limits the possibility of drawing valid conclusions on responsibility assignments. Ethical debates in this situation mostly consider narratives about possible future developments involving visions, expectations, fears, concerns and hopes which can hardly be assessed with respect to their epistemological validity (this was the main line of criticism against the 'speculative nanoethics'; see Nordmann 2007). Questions arise such as: What could be subject to responsibility debates in the absence of valid knowledge about consequences of NEST developments? Is it possible to identify sources of providing orientation for responsibility debates and assignments beyond consequentialism?

My proposal to cope with the situation mentioned and to give at least partial answers to those questions is to suggest a *hermeneutic turn* (Grunwald 2014c). If it is no longer possible to provide orientation by exploring NEST or other R&D fields within the consequentialist paradigm, we could try to explore the narratives being debated in a different, non-consequentialist way. Changing the perspective could help to provide at least weak forms of orientation based on hermeneutic analysis. Concluding remarks will address the possible impacts of this 'hermeneutical turn' on ongoing RRI debates (Sect. 5).

The EEE concept of responsibility[2]

By using the notion of responsibility in everyday communication, a more or less clear meaning of this notion is usually supposed. However, this supposition is often not fulfilled in more complex fields, e.g. in responsibility debates on future science and technology. Concerns have been expressed that responsibility could be a void phrase without substantial meaning, that it would merely show the character of an appeal and of the moralization of conflicts, that it would perhaps not be able to contribute substantially to problem-solving, that the uncertainty of knowledge about future consequences of today's decisions (Sect. 3) would render any responsibility considerations ridiculous (Bechmann 1993), and that the complex governance of modern science and technology involving many actors would lead to the effect of 'thinning' responsibility and even to its vanishing.

These concerns must be taken seriously and require a more in-depth scrutiny of the concept of responsibility (following Lenk 1992). Having responsibility or not having it is the result of social processes, namely of *assignment acts*, either if actors assign responsibility to themselves or if the assignment of responsibility is made by others. The process of assigning responsibility takes place according to social rules based on ethical, cultural and legal considerations and customs (Jonas 1984: p. 173). Assignments of responsibility take place in concrete social and political spaces involving and affecting concrete actors in concrete constellations – therefore emphasis must be given, on the one hand, to the socio-political dimension of responsibility which can be investigated empirically by social and political sciences. On the other, light must be shed on the rules and criteria for assigning responsibility which opens up the bridge to ethics. Thus, assignments of responsibility, *ex post* as well as *ex ante*, are part of life-world practices and of the governance of the respective area. Often those processes are implicit and rely on established and recognized practices and customs; in cases of ambiguity, indifference or conflict, however, they must be made explicit. Because controversies and conflicts are not the exception but the rule in debates about new sciences and technologies and their future impacts (Brown et al. 2000), the meaning of responsibility must be made transparent in order to prevent misunderstanding.

The notion of responsibility often is characterized by reconstructions making explicit the places in a sentence which must be filled in to cover the intentions valid in a particular responsibility context (Lenk 1992). A four-place reconstruction generally seems to be suitable for discussing issues of responsibility in scientific and technical progress:

- *someone* (an actor assumes responsibility or is made responsible – responsibility is assigned to her/him) for
- *something* (such as the results of actions or decisions, e.g. on the R&D agenda in a specific field or on risk management) relative to
- *rules and criteria* (in general, the normative framework governing the respective situation, e.g. rules of responsible behaviour given in a Code of Conduct) and relative to the
- *knowledge available* (knowledge about the impacts and consequences of the action or decision under consideration).

The first two places are, in a sense, grammatically trivial in order to make sense of the word 'responsible'. However, semantically, they indicate the fundamental social context of assigning responsibility which inevitably is a process among social actors and thus constitutes the *empirical dimension* of responsibility. The third and fourth places open up further essential dimensions of responsibility: the dimension of rules and criteria comprise principles, norms and values that are decisive for the judgment, whether a specific action or decision is regarded responsible, less responsible or irresponsible – this constitutes the *ethical dimension* of responsibility. The knowledge available and its quality, including all the uncertainties, form its *epistemic dimension*. My thesis is that relevant questions in responsibility debates on NEST developments arise in *all* of these three dimensions and that *all* three dimensions must be considered in prospective debates in this field (following Grunwald 2014b).

- The *empirical dimension* of responsibility takes seriously that the assignment of responsibility is an act done by specific actors and affecting others. It refers to the basic social constellation of assignment processes. Attributing responsibilities must, on the one hand, take into account the possibilities of actors to influence actions and decisions in the respective field. Issues of accountability and power must be involved. On the other, attributing responsibilities has an impact on the *governance* of that field. Shaping that governance is the ultimate goal of debating issues of assigning and distributing responsibility *ex ante*. Relevant questions are: How are capabilities, influence and power to act and decide distributed in the field considered? Which social groups are affected and could or should help decide about the distribution of responsibility? Do the questions under consideration concern issues to be debated at the 'polis' or can they be delegated to groups or subsystems? What consequences would a particular distribution of responsibility have for the governance of the respective field and would it be in favour of desired developments?

- The *ethical dimension* of responsibility is reached when the question is posed for *criteria and rules* for judging actions and decisions under consideration as responsible or irresponsible, or for helping to find out how actions and decisions could be designed to be (more) responsible. Insofar as normative uncertainties arise, e.g. because of ambiguity or moral conflicts, ethical reflection on these rules and their justifiability is needed. Relevant questions are: What criteria allow distinguishing between responsible and irresponsible actions and decisions? Is there consensus on or controversy about these criteria among the relevant actors? Can the actions and decisions in question (e.g. about the scientific agenda or about containment measures to prevent risks) be regarded as responsible with respect to the rules and criteria?
- The *epistemic* dimension asks for the knowledge about the subject of responsibility and its epistemological status and quality. This is a relevant issue in debates on scientific responsibility in particular, because statements about impacts and consequences of science and new technology frequently show a high degree of uncertainty. The comment that nothing else comes from "mere possibility arguments" (Hansson 2006) is an indication that, in debates over responsibility, it is essential that the status of the available knowledge about the futures to be accounted for is determined and is critically reflected from an epistemological point of view (Nordmann 2007, Grunwald 2014c). Relevant questions are: What is really known about the prospective subjects of responsibility? What could be known in case of more research, and which uncertainties are pertinent? How can different uncertainties be qualified and compared with each other? And what is at stake if worse comes to worst?

Debates over responsibility in technology and science frequently focus on the *ethical dimension* while considering issues of assignment processes and epistemic constraints as secondary issues. However, regarding the analysis given so far, the ethical dimension is important but is only part of the game. It might be that the familiar criticisms towards responsibility reflections (see above) of being simply appellative, of epistemological blindness and of being politically naïve are related to narrowing responsibility to its ethical dimension. Meeting those criticisms and making the notion of responsibility work is claimed to be possible by considering all the three EEE dimensions of responsibility together.

Techno-visionary communication and epistemic constraints

In the past decade, there has been a considerable increase in visionary communication on future technologies and their impacts on society. In particular, this has been and still is the case in the fields of nanotechnology (Fiedeler et al. 2010; Arnaldi et al. 2014), human enhancement (Jotterand 2008; Coenen 2010) and synthetic biology (Giese et al. 2014). Visionary scientists and science managers have put forward far-ranging visions which have been disseminated by mass media and discussed – among other issues, with respect to chances, risks and responsibility – in science and society. There is no distinct borderline between the futuristic visions communicated in these fields and other imagined futures such as *Leitbilder* or guiding visions which have already been analysed with respect to their usage in policy advice (Grin and Grunwald 2000). However, the following characteristics may circumscribe the specific nature of futuristic visions (Grunwald 2013b):

- Futuristic visions refer to a more distant future, some decades ahead, and exhibit revolutionary aspects in terms of technology and in terms of culture, human behaviour and individual and social issues.
- Scientific and technological advances are regarded in a renewed techno-determinist fashion as by far the most important driving force in modern society (technology push perspective).
- The authors of futuristic visions are mostly scientists, science writers and science managers such as Eric Drexler and Ray Kurzweil, but NGOs and industry are also developing and communication visions.
- Milestones and technology roadmaps are to bridge the gap between today's state and the visionary future state (e.g. Roco and Bainbridge 2002).
- High degrees of uncertainty are involved; this leads to severe controversies with regard not only to societal issues but also to the feasibility of the visionary technologies.

Futuristic visions address possible scenarios for techno-visionary sciences and their impacts on society at a very early stage in their scientific and technological development. As a rule, little if any knowledge is available about how the respective technology is likely to develop, about the products which such development may spawn and about the potential impact of using such products. According to the Control Dilemma (Collingridge 1980), it is then extremely difficult, if not impossible, to shape technology because lack of knowledge could lead to a merely speculative debate, followed by arbitrary communication (Hansson 2006, Nordmann 2007).

Recently it has been discussed whether anticipatory stories about futures in this field might narrow our thinking in a techno-morph way (Nordmann 2014). This debate is obviously also relevant to the issue of responsibility. One crucial aspect would be, following the critics of anticipation, to ask not only for the responsibility for anticipated specific developments based on technological advance but also to ask for a broader view on future developments not narrowed by looking through the 'lens' of projected technologies and their anticipated consequences.

What could be sensible subjects of responsibility debates in such constellations strongly depends on the epistemological dimension. The following quote taken from a visionary paper of synthetic biology allows serious doubt about the possibility of responsibility debates at all:

> Fifty years from now, synthetic biology will be as pervasive and transformative as is electronics today. And as with that technology, the applications and impacts are impossible to predict in the field's nascent stages. Nevertheless, the decisions we make now will have an enormous impact on the shape of this future.
>
> (Ilulissat Statement 2007, p. 2)

This statement expresses (a) that the authors expect synthetic biology to lead to deep-ranging and revolutionary changes, (b) that our decisions today will have a high impact on future development but (c) we do not know at all what those future impacts will look like. If this were true, there wouldn't be any chance to assign responsibilities; even to speak about responsibility wouldn't be without any purpose because there wouldn't be any valid subject to talk about. Analogously, the critics of speculative nano-ethics (Nordmann 2007, Grunwald 2010) pointed out that no legitimate conclusions could be drawn if the ethical reflection would address merely speculative and arbitrary futures ("mere possibility arguments", cf. Hansson 2006). This constellation is valid not only for synthetic biology but also holds true for many debates on future science and technology. By definition, it is the case in all of the NEST fields but also applies to future-oriented questions of the transformation of the energy system towards more sustainability or to future developments in the area of robotics or the future Internet.

A (too) quick conclusion could be: okay, it simply might be too early to seriously think about chances and risks of synthetic biology or any other NEST development. Let the researchers do their work and come back with questions for responsibility as soon as better knowledge is available – and then discuss in the familiar consequentialist manner. Nordmann's criticism on the so-called speculative nano-ethics (Nordmann 2007) might be interpreted in this sense. But in spite of the early stage of development, including the lack of knowledge, there are good arguments to not wait (Grunwald 2014c). While futuristic narratives often appear somewhat fictitious in content, it is a fact that such narratives can and will have a real impact on scientific and public discussions (Brown et al. 2000). Even a narrative without any scientific plausibility at all can influence debates, opinion-forming, acceptance and even decision-making. For example, visions of new science and technology can have a major impact on the way in which political and public debates about future technologies are currently conducted, and will probably also have a great impact on the results of such debates – thereby considerably influencing the pathways to the future in two ways at least:

- Futuristic narratives are able to change the perception of present and possible future developments. The societal and public debate about the chances and risks of new technologies will revolve around these narratives to a considerable extent, as was the case in the field of nanotechnology (cf. Schmid et al. 2006). Futuristic narratives motivate and fuel public debate, independent of their epistemic quality. For example, negative visions and dystopias could mobilize resistance to specific technologies while positive ones could create acceptance and fascination.
- Visionary narratives have a particularly significant influence on the scientific agenda (Nordmann 2004) which, as a consequence, partly determines which knowledge will be available and applicable in the future. Directly or indirectly, they influence the views of researchers, and thus ultimately also have a bearing on political support and research funding. Visionary communication therefore influences decisions about the support and prioritization of scientific progress and are an important part of the governance of knowledge (Selin 2008).

The factual power of futuristic narratives in public debate and for decision-making on funding is a strong argument in favour of already carefully and critically analysing and assessing these narratives in the early stages of development. But how can we debate issues of responsibility beyond consequentialism?

Orientation beyond consequentialism

Issues of responsibilities are debated not as an end in itself but in order to overcome orientation problems. The scientific-technological advance results not only in unanimously welcomed progress but also in the raising of new questions concerning e.g. justice and equity, the balance or risks and chances, impacts on human rights and possible shifts of the relation between humans and nature, or between humans and technology. Debates on issues of responsible research and innovation shall help in responding to those questions in an ethically reflected way. Thus, the question for responsibility beyond consequentialism is simultaneously a question of how to provide orientation beyond consequentialism (Grunwald 2013a).

Beyond established Technology Assessment

Technology Assessment (TA) is an example of an established type of consequentialist thinking that makes use of prospective research for providing policy advice and contributions to public dialogue (Grunwald 2009) but also for meeting the goal of creating and communicating knowledge- and science-based orientation for shaping technologies due to societal values and expectations (Rip et al. 1995). It inquires at an early stage as to the *consequences* of the development and the use of new forms of technology, including the unintended consequences of technology. Orientation among the consequences is inherent in core concepts of TA, such as in the *early warning* of dangers resulting from technology, but also in the *early recognition* of the opportunities in technology so that we can take advantage of them to their utmost. The study of consequences must be *prospective*. TA creates and assesses prospective knowledge as the basis for drawing conclusions for today's decision-making (Figure 2.1).

TA usually aims at weighing risks and opportunities and at providing an integrated, comprehensive and balanced consideration. In the field of human enhancement and other techno-visionary debates, however, this balancing is not possible because it is not even clear yet which possible technical developments should be considered as risks or as opportunities. On the contrary, the same technical issues can be taken as motivation to express fascination and euphoria, on the one hand, and considered a threat to humankind, on the other. Extremely contradictory conclusions may be derived. Compare, for example, the different pictures painted by Harris (2010), based on a liberal position, and by Sandel (2007), taking a more communitarian one. Thus, the different interpretations and assessments of the future prospects related to 'converging technologies for improving human performance' (Roco and Bainbridge 2002) exhibit the *maximally imaginable disorientation*: they oscillate between expectations of paradise and of catastrophe (Grunwald 2007), and they may end up with both in different respects. The divergent nature of many NEST futures and their assessments seems to destroy any hope of gaining orientation by reflecting on future developments, as is the usual business of TA. Thus, it is not absolutely clear what the subject of an assessment should be.

An implication of this result is that we have to go beyond the established consequentialist approaches to TA. A first attempt was to postulate and design a new approach called 'Vision Assessment' (Grunwald 2007). The major aim was to take the visions proposed and communicated in many NEST debates as subjects to study and to scrutinize, e.g. in the field of human enhancement (Ferrari et al. 2012). The question should no longer be about what the visions could tell us about future developments, but about we could learn from them for today without

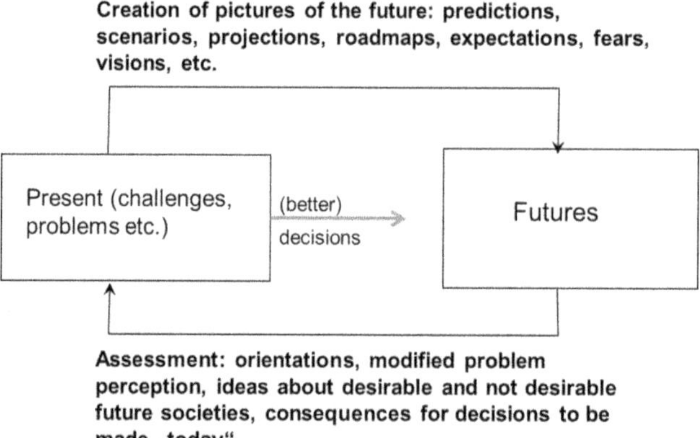

Figure 2.1 Technology Assessment: Providing orientation for the present by deliberating and assessing futures.

Source: Grunwald 2012: p. 313, modified.

Table 2.1 The three modes of orientation

	Prognostic	*Scenario-based*	*Hermeneutic*
Approach to the future	one future	corridor of sensible futures	open space of futures
Spectrum of futures	convergence as ideal	bounded diversity	unbounded divergence
Preferred methodology	quantitative, model-based	quantitative or qualitative; participatory	narrative
Knowledge used	causal and statistical knowledge	models, knowledge of stakeholders	associative knowledge, qualitative arguments
Role of normative issues	low	depends on case	high
Orientation provided	decision-making support, optimization	robust action strategies	self-reflection and contemporary diagnostics

Source: Grunwald 2013a, modified.

assigning any anticipatory power to them. Vision Assessment has meanwhile been integrated into the TA toolbox.

Modes of orientation

However, the relation of Vision Assessment to other approaches seeking orientation should be better clarified. Obviously, the possibilities to extract or derive orientation out of 'stories about the future' differ with regard to the quality of the prospective knowledge available. This was the reason for thinking more fundamentally about the possibilities of taking techno-futures of different kinds and different epistemic quality as a basis for providing orientation. According to different degrees of quality of knowledge about future developments, it was recently proposed (Grunwald 2013a) to distinguish between three methods of providing orientation by reflecting on the knowledge of the consequences (see also Table 2.1):

- *Mode 1 (i.e. prognostic) orientation*: The prognostic imagination of future technologies and their consequences is supposed to produce a reliable basis for decision-making. For instance, knowledge about future developments may be taken in this mode as information on boundary conditions within the Rational Choice paradigm in order to optimize decisions. Experience and theoretical analyses have shown, however, that as a rule, this mode does not work in considering the consequences of technology (e.g. Grunwald 2009). Instead of hoping for certain knowledge about the future, substantial uncertainty of different kinds is the rule (see below).

- *Mode 2 (i.e. scenario-based) orientation*: Scenarios have become the established means in many areas of prospective analyses, e.g. in sustainability studies (e.g. Heinrichs et al. 2012). In this mode, we reflect systematically on a future that is in principle open and thus cannot be prognosticated. The necessary precondition for mode 2 orientation to be applicable is the existence of well-founded corridors of the envisaged future development, or at least an imagination of such corridors agreed upon by relevant persons or groups. Frequently, the space of plausible futures is imagined between a 'worst case' and a 'best case' scenario.
- Mode 3 (*i.e. hermeneutic) orientation*: This mode comes into the play in the case of overwhelming uncertainty, which means that if the knowledge of the future is so uncertain or if the images of the future diverge so strongly, there are no longer any valid arguments for employing scenarios to provide orientating structure of the future (which corresponds to the 'great uncertainty' [Hansson 2006]). For this situation, rendering any form of consequentialism non-applicable – which is the case in the field of synthetic biology as has been shown above – a *hermeneutic turn* was proposed (Grunwald 2014c). Instead of trying to get a better knowledge of future development, the change of perspective consists of raising the question of what could be learned by analyzing the visionary narratives *about the contemporary situation*. The techno-visionary narratives could be examined for what they mean and under which diagnoses and values they originated. Out of this, we cannot learn anything about future developments for deriving orientation in the consequentialist paradigm, but the expectation is that we could benefit from a hermeneutic analysis and assessment of those narratives for and about our present situation.

Because the epistemological quality of knowledge comprises a continuum between full and certain knowledge at the one end (mode 1) and full ignorance at the other (mode 3), the distinguished modes of orientation overlap with gradual transitions between them. Thus, the distinction is not a logical one but rather shall orientate different approaches of providing orientation and provide an umbrella view.

While mode 1 and mode 2 orientation follows the consequentialist paradigm, this does not hold for mode 3. In the NEST debates, neither the mode 1 nor the mode 2 approach are applicable, as has become apparent (Nordmann 2014; see also above). Therefore, we have to focus on the hermeneutic mode (3). This focus leads to the necessity for us to concern ourselves with the hermeneutic constellation and to look for an adequate methodology.

Hermeneutic analysis of techno-futures

Techno-futures (e.g. in the NEST field, but also beyond) are images of the future development of society in which technology and scientific-technical progress play a perceptible role. They can include elements from specific areas of technology such as future mobility, energy supply, water management or the regulation of complex technical, social or virtual systems, such as with regard to the transformation of the energy system. They can also extend to more general issues such as the future of the nature of humans; the impact of technology's becoming increasingly autonomous; or developments in the relations between humanity, technology and nature. Techno-futures which cannot be classified with respect to epistemic quality – that means, which are more or less speculative – can only be made subject to hermeneutical analysis. This type of analysis asks for the *meaning* that is given to new technology by relating it to techno-futures (Grunwald 2014c).

Compared with the consequentialist paradigm, with its central focus on questions about the possible impacts of new technologies, how we assess these and whether and under what circumstances we welcome or reject these implications, this perspective places the focus on entirely different questions (following Grunwald 2014c):

- What are the implications of the new developments in science and technology for the present and future of man and society, which fundamental constellations (man/technology, man/nature, etc.) do they change and 'what is at stake?' e.g. in ethical, cultural and social terms?
- How is a philosophical, ethical, social, cultural etc. significance attributed to scientific-technological developments, which after all are nothing initially but scientific-technological developments? What role do e.g. (visionary) techno-futures play in this context?
- How are attributions of meaning being communicated and discussed? What roles do they play in the major technological debates of our time? What forms of communication and linguistic resources are being used and why? What extra-linguistic resources (e.g. movies, works of art) play a role in this context and what does their use reveal?
- Why do we discuss scientific-technological developments in the way we do and with the respective attributions of meaning rather than in some other way?
- How does man as a historical being see himself in discourses about techno-futures? What future concepts are being applied if the future is presented either as though it were possible to shape it technically or politically, or as what will contingently come about and will never be quite adequate in terms of a historical responsibility to bring about a better world?

The structuring of this complex field of questions begins with an almost trivial thought. Futures in general and techno-futures in particular do not exist per se, but rather are 'made' and constructed in a more or less complex manner. Techno-futures, whether they are forecasts, scenarios, plans, programs or speculative fears or expectations, are produced using a whole range of ingredients such as the available knowledge, value judgments and suppositions. They are made by specific authors who always pursue specific purposes and intentions, for example, supporting political decisions, sensitizing the public for problematic developments, mobilizing support for research, creating a vision for regional development, warning at an early stage about potential problems etc. Thus, inseparably linked with the hermeneutical analysis of techno-futures is, on the one hand, an understanding of their origin and construction and, on the other, an understanding of their diffusion in communicative processes and the consequences of these processes.

The hermeneutic analysis of pictures of the future hardly tells us anything about the future in the sense of a present in the time to come, but rather *about us today*. If projections of the future are interpreted in a way that makes it clear why we aggregate certain current ingredients to specific futures and argue dedicatedly about them, then we have learned something *explicitly* about ourselves, our societal practices, subliminal concerns, implicit hopes and fears and their cultural roots. By investigating alternative approaches to the future of humans and society with or without different techno-visionary developments, such reflection may ultimately promote democratic debate on scientific-technical progress.

Concluding remarks: What follows for RRI?

The answers to the questions above, related to a hermeneutical approach (and further ones, to be sure), will make it possible to add meta-information to RRI debates and should thus be able to enrich those debates. The added value should consist of information about *the respective current world* in which techno-futures are created and communicated. This meta-information should heighten a debate's reflection and transparency and thus help make the debate open and unbiased in the sense of a deliberative democracy. This is what a hermeneutic orientation can achieve (Grunwald 2014c) – a modest contribution.

What this could mean at the occasion of a specific RRI debate, perhaps in a specific NEST field, depends on the context. However, it seems possible to propose at least three more general lines of thinking which could enrich and orientate ongoing RRI debates:

a *Focus on present developments instead of trying to anticipate the future*
If the epistemological dimension of responsibility does not allow for applying consequentialist patterns of deriving orientation, the first conclusion is that responsibility considerations should focus on what's already going on in the present and on its ethically relevant aspects. Considering synthetic biology, for example, the subject of responsibility should be seen more in the processes of current research rather than in speculative future products. Taking over responsibility therefore means being responsible for current processes of research, defining the research agenda, determining objectives and goals and supporting current societal debates on synthetic biology instead of talking about responsible or irresponsible future outcomes of synthetic biology. In spite of the fact that it will often be impossible to completely renounce the thinking about possible future outcomes and developments, the major awareness is then given to more up-to-date questions of e.g. risk of today's research, of elements of the research process (e.g. whether animal experiments really would be helpful or even necessary) or of the allocation of resources and budgets in current research. This idea is in line with Nordmann's criticisms against a too-speculative 'nano-ethics' (Nordmann 2007) and his warning against a possible misleading allocation of the resources of ethics.

b *Avoidance of narrowing future development through a technocratic lens*
Recently, Nordmann (2014) warned against a specific aspect of approaches to anticipate the future. His concern is that anticipations could set up a kind of self-fulfilling process in approaching the future. Insofar as anticipations are usually based on today's models, today's knowledge and today's assessments – and indeed, there is no alternative to making anticipations according to the current state of the art – and on current anticipation techniques, Nordmann is afraid that the anticipated futures will merely be a prolongation of present time. If we would narrow our minds by looking at anticipations of this type we are, according to Nordmann, in danger of losing critical potential and new ideas for improving futures. Thus his plea is not to anticipate but more to think about wishful futures (Nordmann 2010). Nordmann thus makes us aware of a specific risk associated with anticipatory thinking. To take his concern seriously meets the case of the hermeneutic mode of orientation (see above). In this case, anticipation is not possible on any sound epistemic ground – and the thesis of this chapter is that we should accept this and look for a type of orientation beyond consequentialism. Doing this leads to the hermeneutical turn which avoids considering techno-futures as anticipations. Their analysis should provide us with insight into their premises and biases, and thus helps to avoid a too-narrow focus on future possibilities, but should contribute to opening up the field in order to not only take anticipations of the current world into focus but also other possible 'worlds' (Nordmann 2014). By this, the subjects to be reflected in an RRI debate should also be widened in order to cover a broader picture of possible developments.

c *Contributing to a more transparent democratic debate*
The hermeneutic analysis of techno-futures can contribute to societal orientation, public debate and decision-making in a modest manner which, however, should not be underestimated. Beyond consequentialism, the remaining way of providing orientation is by uncovering the 'ingredients', the premises and presuppositions, the knowledge but also the hopes, assumptions, cultural biases, Zeitgeist issues and concerns included in the respective techno-futures. This 'meta-knowledge' about those futures then could inform and enlighten democratic debate and deliberation and thus contribute to more transparency and a more rational debate.

Notes

1 This chapter is based on the keynote presentation given at a project meeting in Paris.
2 The notion of an EEE concept builds on recent work by the author (Grunwald 2014b).

References

Arnaldi, S., Ferrari, A., Magaudda, P. and Marin, F. (Eds.) (2014). *Responsibility in Nanotechnology Development*. Dordrecht: Springer.

Bechmann, G. (1993). Ethische Grenzen der Technik oder technische Grenzen der Ethik? *Geschichte und Gegenwart. Vierteljahreshefte für Zeitgeschichte, Gesellschaftsanalyse und politische Bildung*, 12, pp. 213–225.

Brown, J., Rappert, B. and Webster, A. (Eds.) (2000). *Contested Futures. A Sociology of Prospective Techno-Science*. Burlington: Ashgate Publishing.

Coenen, C. (2010). Deliberating visions: The case of human enhancement in the discourse on nanotechnology and convergence. In: Kaiser, M., Kurath, M., Maasen, S. and Rehmann-Sutter, C. (Eds.), *Governing Future Technologies. Nanotechnology and the Rise of an Assessment Regime*. Dordrecht: Springer, pp. 73–87.

Coenen, C. and Simakova, E. (2013). STS Policy Interactions, Technology Assessment and the Governance of Technovisionary Sciences. *Science, Technology & Innovation Studies*, 9(2), pp. 3–20.

Collingride, D. (1980). *The Social Control of Technology*. London: Pinter.

Ferrari, A., Coenen, C. and Grunwald, A. (2012). Visions and Ethics in Current Discourse on Human Enhancement. *Nanoethics*, 6(3), pp. 215–229. doi:10.1007/s11569-012-0155-1.

Fiedeler, U., Coenen, C., Davies, S. R. and Ferrari, A. (Eds.) (2010). *Understanding Nanotechnology: Philosophy, Policy and Publics*. Heidelberg: Akademische Verlagsgesellschaft.

Giese, B., Pade, C., Wigger, H. and von Gleich, A. (Eds.) (2014). *Synthetic Biology. Character and Impact*. Heidelberg: Springer.

Grin, J. and Grunwald, A. (Eds.) (2000). *Vision Assessment: Shaping Technology in 21st Century Society*. Heidelberg: Springer.

Grinbaum, A. and Groves, C. (2013). What is 'responsible' about responsible innovation? Understanding the ethical issues. In: R. Owen, Bessant J., Heintz M. (Eds.), *Responsible Innovation. Managing the Responsible Emergence of Science and Innovation in Society*. Hoboken (NJ): John Wiley & Sons, pp. 119–142.

Grunwald, A. (2007). Converging Technologies: Visions, increased contingencies of the *conditio humana*, and search for orientation. *Futures*, 39(4), pp. 380–392.

Grunwald, A. (2009). Technology assessment. In: Meijers, A. (Ed.), *Philosophy of Technology and Engineering Sciences*. Amsterdam: North-Holland, pp. 1103–1146.

Grunwald, A. (2010). From Speculative Nanoethics to Explorative Philosophy of Nanotechnology. *NanoEthics*, 4(2), pp. 91–101.

Grunwald, A. (2012). *Responsible Nanobiotechnology. Philosophy and Ethics*. Singapore: Panstanford.

Grunwald, A. (2013a). Modes of Orientation Provided by Futures Studies: Making Sense of Diversity and Divergence. *European Journal of Futures Studies*, 15(30), doi 10.1007/s40309-013-0030-5.

Grunwald, A. (2013b). Techno-visionary Sciences: Challenges to Policy Advice. *Science, Technology and Innovation Studies*, 9(2), pp. 21–38.

Grunwald, A. (2014a). Synthetic biology as technoscience and the EEE concept of responsibility. In: Giese, B., Pade, C., Wigger, H. and von Gleich, A. (Eds.), *Synthetic Biology. Character and Impact*. Heidelberg: Springer, pp. 249–266.

Grunwald, A. (2014b). Responsible research and innovations: An emerging issue in research policy rooted in the debate on nanotechnology. In: Arnaldi, S., Ferrari, A., Magaudda, P. and Marin, F. (Eds.), *Responsibility in Nanotechnology Development*. Dordrecht: Springer, pp. 191–205.

Grunwald, A. (2014c). The Hermeneutic side of Responsible Research and Innovation. *Journal of Responsible Innovation*, 1(3), pp. 274–291.

Hansson, S. O. (2006). Great uncertainty about small things. In: Schummer, J. and Baird, D. (Eds.), *Nanotechnology Challenges – Implications for Philosophy, Ethics and Society*. Singapore: World Scientific, pp. 315–325.

Harris, J. (2010). *Enhancing Evolution: The Ethical Case for Making Better People*. Princeton: Princeton University Press.

Heinrichs, D., Krellenberg, K., Hansjürgens, B. and Martínez, F. (Eds.) (2012). *Risk Habitat Megacity*. Heidelberg: Springer.

Ilulissat Statement (2008). Synthesizing the Future. A vision for the convergence of synthetic biology and nanotechnology. Views that emerged from the Kavli Futures Symposium 'The merging of bio and nano: Towards cyborg cells', 11–15 June 2007, Ilulissat, Greenland.

Jonas, H. (1984). *The Imperative of Responsibility*. Chicago: University of Chicago Press.

Jotterand, F. (2008). Beyond Therapy and Enhancement: The Alteration of Human Nature. *Nanoethics*, 2(1), pp. 15–23.

Lenk, H. (1992). *Zwischen Wissenschaft und Ethik*. Frankfurt: Suhrkamp.

Nordmann, A. (2004). *Converging Technologies – Shaping the Future of European Societies*, High Level Expert Group "Foresighting the New Technology Wave", Brussels. https://www.philosophie.tu-darmstadt.de/media/institut_fuer_philosophie/diesunddas/nordmann/cteks.pdf (accessed 9 May 2018).

Nordmann, A. (2007). If and Then: A Critique of Speculative Nanoethics. *Nanoethics*, 1(1), pp. 31–46.

Nordmann, A. (2010). A Forensics of Wishing: Technology Assessment in the Age of Technoscience. *Poiesis & Praxis: International Journal of Technology Assessment and Ethics of Science*, 7(1–2), pp. 5–15.

Nordmann, A. (2014). Responsible Innovation, the Art and Craft of Future Anticipation. *Journal of Responsible Innovation*, 1(1), pp. 87–98.

Owen, R., Bessant, J. and Heintz, M. (Eds.) (2013). *Responsible Innovation. Managing the Responsible Emergence of Science and Innovation in Society*. Hoboken (NJ): John Wiley & Sons.

Paslack, R., Ach, J. S., Luettenberg, B. and Weltring, K. (Eds.) (2012). *Proceed with Caution? Concept and Application of the Precautionary Principle in Nanobiotechnology*. Münster: LIT Verlag.

Rip, A., Misa, T. and Schot, J. (Eds.) (1995). *Managing Technology in Society*, London: Pinter.

Roco, M. C. and Bainbridge, W. S. (Eds.) (2002). *Converging Technologies for Improving Human Performance*. Arlington (VA): National Science Foundation.

Sandel, M. (2007). *The Case against Perfection. Ethics in the Age of Genetic Engineering*. Harvard: Harvard University Press.

Schmid, G., Ernst, H., Grünwald, W., Grunwald, A., Hofmann, H., Janich, P., Krug, H., Mayor, M., Rathgeber, W., Simon, B., Vogel, V. and Wyrwa, D. (Eds.) (2006). *Nanotechnology – Perspectives and Assessment*. Berlin: Springer.

Selin, C. (2008). The Sociology of the Future: Tracing Stories of Technology and Time. *Sociology Compass*, 2(6), pp. 1878–1895.

von Schomberg, R. (2012). Prospects for technology assessment in a framework of responsible research and innovation. In: M. Dusseldorp and R. Beecroft (Eds.), *Technikfolgen abschätzen lehren: Bildungspotenziale transdisziplinärer Methoden*, Wiesbaden: Springer, pp. 39–62.

3 Taking moral responsibility seriously to foster Responsible Research and Innovation

Bernard Reber

Introduction

Observers of change in the financing of European research have witnessed the introduction of a new notion within the research program H2020, that of responsible research and innovation (RRI). Moreover, this transversal research topic has also reconfigured the Science and Society research program. This new concept has surprised many researchers and potential applicants in general, and those involved in Sciences and Society programs in particular. Evidence of this is provided by the growing number of new requests addressed to researchers working on RRI from research call applicants during the drafting of European projects: there is a growing demand to know more about RRI from applicants. Furthermore, a number of researchers, institutions, museums and civil society organizations have expressed their disappointment with the appearance of the (highly normative) concept of responsibility in this area. However, many of these researchers are sociologists, political scientists, anthropologists or historians. Considering the underdevelopment of ethical sociology (or moral sociology) (Pharo 1985; 1990; 2000; 2004a; 2004b; Reber 2011), for example, the effects of such a reconfiguration can be understood.

RRI has emerged suddenly as a new research requirement in the European Research Area, and the concept suffers from being ill-defined. This lack of clarity may make it more of an obstacle than an international comparative advantage for research and innovation if it is not clearly defined and contextually translated. Strictly speaking, RRI is not a concept, unlike moral responsibility, which has had this status for a long period of time. RRI is rather a general research and innovation policy perspective that promotes and continues to be a collection of heterogeneous elements.

This first part of the book focuses mainly on ethics. For this reason, we shall concentrate on the problem of ethics in research, in the Ethics Review (ER), as a key (N° 5, as it will be presented; 2012, 2013)[1] of the European Commission (EC)'s expression of Responsible Innovation and Research, taking the different understandings of responsibility in moral philosophy into account.

Ethics and responsibility are not new in EU-funded projects. ERs have been in place for a long time, which has led to research communities taking ownership of them and integrating them into their work. Compared with ERs, RRI remains more enigmatic. One original feature of this chapter is the comparison it provides between RRI and ERs and other responsibilities central to research and innovation projects (parts 1 and 2). Although these two activities encompass convergences and specificities, the focus will mainly be on research. Nevertheless, we will not neglect the fact that both are connected in funded research. Indeed, it is common in presentation requirements for research projects to mention potential spin-offs for the economy, society and innovation. However, beyond ERs themselves, scientific work entails more central responsibilities. Researchers must comply with rules specific to their practices (epistemic norms related to their specific discipline, and common epistemic norms related to scientific work) and ethical norms (e.g. integrity). They are thus entrusted with responsibilities. What is first and foremost expected from them is scientific as well as moral responsibility in the conduct of their work. This implies achieving good quality research that respects both procedures and colleagues. We will then discuss the six different keys used by the EC to depict RRI and the relationships between them and moral and political responsibility (part 3). Indeed, the use of the six keys as a starting point, thus establishing a logical link with responsibility, is not immediately obvious. We will then propose a pluralist cartography of the 10 existing understandings of moral and political responsibility (part 4) and consider different ways to compose them, contributing to different lines of moral innovation (part 5). The conclusion will compare ethics in ER and RRI seeking cross-fertilization as a means to contribute to the development of European scientific policy.

RRI does not land in an empty space regarding responsibilities and norms

Several possible areas or perimeters for the identification and correct handling of ethical issues exist. Different approaches can be taken to ethics in research, or the observance of norms in broader terms. On the one hand, these areas are very different and, on the other, RRI does not enter an empty or unexplored field. Other fields of norms, to use this polysemic image, already exist. The question of possible conflict between them is important, not least because of the importance and attention that should be given to a particular group of norms for various research actors.

Epistemic and ethical research norms

Similarly to any other professional activity, research observes norms. Some of these norms are *specific to disciplines* (specific epistemic norms) and others are *shared* by all scientific communities (common epistemic and ethical norms). Defining what might be seen as an object of research is already an issue for every discipline.

For example, regarding specific research objects and norms, voting behaviours in political science are not analysed in the same manner as fluid flows in chemical engineering. The methods and background theories on which interpretations, constraints and constructions of scientific objects and presentations of results are based, just to mention these few elements, help to identify and distinguish these two examples as belonging to two specific and different fields. A distinction might be made between epistemic norms concerning knowledge and those specific to practices within a given discipline.

With regard to shared and transdisciplinary epistemic norms, there is a need, for instance, for the researcher to be subject to peer reviews in order to be published in related refereed journals. Researchers must make a demonstrable effort to present their results in order to make them shareable and reproducible. Relating to the appropriate exercise of scientific practice, normative norms, aimed at defining expected ethical behaviour among researchers, also exist. In fact, falsifying results is subject to punishment. These norms belong to the normative area and – in contrast to the epistemic area – can be legal and/or moral.

Epistemic and normative norms are often linked to the aforementioned meaning. For example, falsifying results is as detrimental to the progress of scientific knowledge as it would be to colleagues, were they to use such falsified results in their own work. However, these two types of norms are distinct. The harm done not only includes misleading colleagues, but also cheating and enjoying undue advantages (publication in reputable and prestigious journals and career advancement). These behaviours may also have an impact beyond the scientific community – for example, in the case of assessing the risk of a particular product or understanding environmental phenomena such as climate change.

Research integrity

If compliance with this ethical type of norms has always been somehow consubstantially committed to scientific activity, more recently, concern about ensuring the integrity of research has required more explicit and rigorous forms of institutionalization (Sutour and Lorrain 2013: p. 49). Integrity codes exist in research. In Europe, this includes *The European Code of Conduct for Research Integrity*,[2] co-edited by the European Science Foundation (78 research institutions from 30 countries), and the *All European Academies* (53 academies from 40 countries) in 2011. Researchers must therefore comply with rules specific to their practices (epistemic norms) and ethical norms (e.g. integrity). They are thus entrusted with responsibilities. Taking on these responsibilities would seem obvious in work on RRI. However, this is not really the case, a fact which should equally be borne in mind.

What is first and foremost expected from researchers is scientific as well as moral responsibility in the conduct of their work. This implies achieving good quality research (i.e. creative, accurate), and respecting a number of procedures and also research colleagues. These responsibilities are not actually dealt with in most work on RRI research, perhaps because they are taken for granted. However, they may at times have been problematic or neglected since the opinions of ethics committees and Academies have only surfaced recently,[3] emanating from scientific institutions now discussing what appears to be a prerequisite for the appropriate conduct of research.

Research ethics at large

We shall now address more external and distant ethical issues in scientific practice. In effect, research is not only a solitary activity. It needs society and money to develop. Even philosophy and mathematics require interaction with peers or instruments, be they access to databases or computer applications. Although researchers and, most often, lecturer-researchers[4] are the main actors of research, other professionals are often involved (assistants, doctoral and post-doctoral students and administrative staff are sometimes closely associated on account of their initial training as lecturer-researchers). Moreover, research also involves institutions and funding, and thus the choices that govern them.

In order to thrive in appropriate conditions, research must be protected as much as possible from other spheres of influence, such as the economic or political. However, it cannot be completely detached from these spheres and indeed from society as a whole. Given the current tendency to consider the impact of research on society and the economy, job creation has become more and more prevalent. *Accountability* that is not strictly scientific is even more explicit when research funding is project based. European research projects are the most demanding regarding the popularization and provision of results to any interested citizen, stakeholder or economic or political decision-maker. Research is frequently expected to assist in the promotion of European policies. This is the case with projects on the ethics of emerging technologies or on RRI.[5]

Although this quest for solidarity between research, scientific policy and society is understandable, research can also permanently change social interactions, security, the economy and the world of work as well as the environment. Research results initiate future uses that will be extended, transformed and disseminated in society, sometimes over several generations. Such changes can also frequently be expected in the relationship between research and innovation. The utility of research, in various forms, both economic and social, including to solve problems following a common form of pragmatism, has long featured in formulating arguments in favour of funding projects. Proponents must demonstrate how their research could be useful, not only in advancing knowledge in their field, but also in other disciplines, for application and economic benefits. Does the vulgate of scientific policy not consider that research exists to solve problems and mainly to create jobs and stimulate growth?

Two problems exist around the concern for *accountability*[6] with regard to scientific activity. The first is upstream of research activity; the second is downstream. On the one hand, private or public funding resources are not unlimited, and on the other, developments as a result of research do not only have positive effects. Research results can also be hijacked or lead to unexpected collateral effects.

For the first problem (funding), it frequently occurs that projects are considered priorities. This decision falls under scientific policy or even politics *per se*. This priority is oriented either for reasons related to scientific developments or specific to new technical possibilities, or in relation to challenges recognized as vital issues for present or future society. The *Societal Grand Challenges* for European research[7] might be cited. Indeed, one of the main forms of responsibility (*responsiveness*) is to respond to these societal and environmental challenges through the sciences.

Regarding the second problem (unexpected impacts and consequences of research), it often happens that controversies arise regarding a particular piece of research, both on the scientific and normative (ethical and/or legal) levels. This, for example, is the case with genetically modified organisms (GMOs), nanotechnology and information and communications technology (ICT). Research on these topics have supporters and opponents; most importantly, they have significant potential but are characterized by doubts regarding their effects and certain risks (*suspicions*) of causing damage that might be associated with them. Moreover, the more technological innovations are a breakthrough in comparison with existing technologies, and are therefore potentially more innovative, the more they undermine the moral intuitions of individuals. Such intuitions are variable depending on the individual, who might welcome a certain technology (*praiseworthiness*), while others deem the researchers and those who finance them to be suffused with uncertainty and sometimes with distant horizons (*blameworthiness*) (Reber 2011).

"Ethics" in European ERs

The EC retained an intermediate and more confined situation to ensure that the projects it finances are ethically sound. The EC also finances projects that are divided between research and innovation. This justifies the association of research and innovation in the conception of RRI. This is the case, for example, with projects called *Fast Track to Innovation Pilot Project*. Projects that lead to innovation must meet the same requirements as research projects. The EC mentions ethical compliance.[8] Such compliance approaches, subdues or even pads out ethics in the law and leaves little interpretative margin or room for ethical reflexivity. As shall be seen later in this text, reflexivity is part and parcel of moral responsibility.

A detailed focus on the various ethical issues considered and sub-issues associated with ERs now follows. For a complete explanation of the governance and the assessment cycle used by ethical experts, we refer to *From Ethical Review to Responsible Innovation* (Pellé and Reber 2016). Answers to the Ethical Questionnaire (EQ) are pre-filled, if positive, to the previous questions. Thus, with regard to each issue, it is clear whether the ethical issue considered applies to the project or not and, where appropriate, shows the pages relating thereto in *Part A* and the *Technical Annexes* of the projects. For each issue, a box is reserved for comments. Answers to every ethical issue reported are followed by requirements. It is worth noting that the requirements are attached to short and pre-filled comments, which may also be accompanied by experts' remarks. The 10 possible ethical issues are the following:

1 *Human embryo/fetus*: 1. this first entry seeks to know whether the project involves Human Embryonic Stem Cells. If so, the following questions are formulated: 1.1. Will the stem cells be taken from embryos within this project? 1.2. Are they previously established cell lines? 2. Does this research

involve the use of human embryos? 3. Does this research involve the use of human foetal tissues/cells?

2 *Humans*: the issues are as follows. 1. Does this research involve human participants? 1.1. Are they volunteers for social or human sciences research? 1.2. Are they persons unable to give their informed consent? 1.3. Are they vulnerable individuals or groups? 1.4. Are they children/minors? 1.5. Are they patients? 1.6. Are they healthy volunteers for medical studies? 2. Does this research involve physical interventions on the study of participants? 2.1. Does it involve invasive techniques? 2.2. Does it involve collection of biological samples?

3 *Human cells/tissues*: the questions include: 1. Does this research involve human cells or tissues (other than from "Human Embryos/Foetuses", as in the first question)? 1.1. Are they available commercially? 1.2. Are they obtained with this project? 1.3. Are they obtained from another project, laboratory or institution? 1.4. Are they obtained from a bio-bank?

4 *Protection of personal data*: 1. We ask whether the research involves the collection/processing of personal data. 1.1. Whether the research involves the collection/processing of sensitive personal data such as health, sexual lifestyle, ethnicity, political opinions, religious or philosophical convictions. 1.2. Whether the research involves the processing of genetic information. 1.3. Whether it involves tracking or observation of participants. 1.4. Whether it involves further processing of previously collected personal data (secondary use). The last box is reserved for "other".

5 *Animals*: the issues are as follows: 1. Does this research involve animals? What species? 1.1. Are they vertebrates? 1.2. Are they nonhuman primates (NHPs)? 1.3. Are they genetically modified? 1.4. Are they cloned farm animals? 1.5. Are they endangered animals?

6 *Third countries*: 1. If non-EU countries are involved, do the research related activities undertaken in these countries raise potential ethics issues? 2. Will local resources be used (e.g. animal and/or human tissue samples, genetic material, live animals, human remains, material of historical value, endangered fauna or flora samples etc.)? 3. Will any material – including personal data – from non-European countries be imported into the EC? 3.1. If yes, specify the material and countries involved. 4. Will any material – including personal data – be exported from the EU to non-EU countries? 4.1. If yes, specify the material and countries involved. 5. Does this research involve low and/or medium resource countries, and in this case, is a benefit-sharing action planned? 6. Could the context in the country in question put the individuals taking part in the research at risk?

7 *Environmental protection and security*: the issues are as follows: 1. Does this research involve the use of elements that could cause harm to the environment, to animals or to plants? 2. Does this research deal with endangered fauna and/or flora protected areas? 3. Does this research involve the use of elements that may cause harm to humans, including research staff?

8 *Dual use*:[9] 1. Does the research have the potential for military applications?

9 *Misuse* (misappropriation): 1. Does this research have the potential for malevolent/criminal/terrorist abuse? After this question, there is a space reserved for comments.
10 *Other ethical issues.*

This section is particular as it might include various dimensions. Practically, it is very rarely used.

The requirements associated with the EQ could include responsibilities that are particular to ordinary research and innovation practices and that have been mentioned in part 1. Nevertheless, they are focused on entities directly affected by the projects. Despite the value of these ERs – their stability and legitimacy – they do not cover the entire scope of ethics. They almost entirely portray ethical principles inherited from bioethics. They are also close to the ethical threshold, more broadly to deontological ethics, if these assessments are considered from the point of view of moral theories. Indeed, deontologism is understood here as one moral theory faced with a pluralistic set of options and not as professional ethics (21Pellé and Reber 2016; 33Reber 2016). The applicants, in their ethical self-assessment, and the experts are mainly guided by the following requirements: informed consent, protection of privacy and sensitive data, protection of the environment and animals (minimizing suffering), sharing of benefits (for third countries outside the EU) and avoidance of dual use.

These ethical issues applicable to every research project are more relevant to such research and discipline. In the same way, if the *Societal Grand Challenges* are a form of responsibility, the research projects intending to meet them must conform to this ethical framework.

Comments on the RRI list of keys and relationships between them

In several documents, including tenders, aimed at specifying the concept of RRI (e.g. EC 2012 p. 16), the EC has presented RRI on the basis of five (or six) keys. The RRI keys are: (1) *Participation* (and commitment) of *Stakeholders*, (2) *Scientific Education* (or literacy, science literacy), (3) *Gender Equality* in the research process and content, (4) *Openness* to scientific knowledge (data and results), and, as written in the first generation of EC documents, *Governance* (*Ethics*). *Ethics* (5) is now distinguished from (6) *Governance*, a sixth key, or one that integrates the five others.[10]

The order in which the keys are presented does not really matter. After mentioning[11] the various keys, a number of comments can now be made and the relationships between them examined. In effect, this can be done in different ways.

General remarks on the list of keys:

1 The list may seem arbitrary. Why these keys and not others? For instance, the expert report (Exp 2015), which combines keys, criteria and indicators,

extends the list with two other "additional aspects": sustainability and social justice.

1' On the contrary, if we do not observe all the five keys, are we not RRI compatible? Could it be said that we are only partly responsible? There is no clear answer here.

2 There is no justification for the inclusion of these requirements, no matter how laudable they may be. However, discussions on political theory exist; in particular, on the legitimacy of a broader inclusion of citizens or the affected public (i.e. three different perspectives with participative democracy, deliberative democracy, protection or compensation to affected people).

3 These keys are empty. Admittedly, this leaves room for different interpretations, but it could quickly become a problem if criteria or indicators for each must be observed. This requires having an idea of their contents or at least their contours. The expected justifications (2) could help to interpret the keys.

4 One might wonder whether these keys are so new compared with current practices in research and innovation. Indeed, as we have seen in the first part of this chapter, researchers are already required to anticipate the consequences of their expected results on the economy or society at large. Participative science is already at work for ornithology or vegetal biology. Open science is a new trend through different platforms and open access articles, given that, for example, a science dissemination plan is required for every European project. As a result of the prioritization of the *Societal Grand Challenges*, research is open to the future needs of society in the long term. In the same way, every European project must provide a detailed explanation of the governance plan that will be implemented (work packages and task attributions, insurance quality, clear definition of the participants and so on). The issue of gender has long been a priority and has not waited for the emergence of RRI. The name of the department in charge of ERs is (astonishingly) *Unit B.6. – Ethics and Gender, Directorate-General for Research and Innovation. Directorate B – European Research Area*. Innovation often involves the participation of stakeholders (e.g. focus groups to test products, norms or labels). The two more recent and perhaps new areas are the participation key and the ethics pillar. The former not only includes participation by stakeholders but also by citizens. Ethics is a little different from ethics in ethical reviews in terms of perimeter and reflexivity as we have presented above. The *participation of stakeholders* is not only one of the most innovative keys compared with ERs, but also one of the most destabilizing, as shall be seen afterwards.

5 These keys are not of the same order. Whether Participation, Governance and Openness are procedural, ensuring such cooperation, Gender equality, Scientific Education and Ethics are rather more substantial. Gender equality could very well be a part of the ethics questionnaire of the ERs, for example. Some project consortia already include it.

6 Some keys could be incorporated into each other or are redundant. For example, this is the case with Open Science and Science Education. It could also be argued that participation involves Open Science. Similarly, governance

could include and organize the other keys. This is the approach used by the authors of the report (Exp 2013), contrary to that of Robert Gianni (2016), who believes that ethical governance is the keystone of the entire system.

7 We could also look at possible tensions, and even contradictions, that may exist between the keys. For example, could it be possible to promote Open Science and restrict the participation of a number of stakeholders to be able to seriously deliberate?

Different types of convergence among RRI keys

Setting aside the contradictions, let us now see the types of possible convergence between the EC RRI keys.

8 RRI can be understood as an *accumulation* of demands, that each one interprets itself.

9 It can, on the contrary, imagine *solidarity* between all these demands, or even complementarity. This should be achieved so that research becomes an open system of knowledge, educating stakeholders on scientific and ethical aspects as well as equality in gender relationships.

10 The example of the expert report on indicators (Exp 2013; Spaapen et al. 2015) might be copied, or even that of Robert Gianni's book (2016), where *priority* is given to ethical governance as the backbone for restructuring RRI. Other keys might take a leadership position; for example, *participation* – which could be seen as preferable to technocratic governance. The priority given to the participation key seems to be the scenario for the future of RRI because the EC Directorate-General for Research and Innovation can only select one criterion and one indicator. The indicator will probably be the number of stakeholders.

This priority might only draw on some of the six keys, (see remark (1') above).

11 Extending the *priority* option, the following questions about governance can be asked: Should there be governance for each key? Or, should there be one governance for all the keys (i.e. Exp 2013 or Gianni 2016)? Or, better still, should there be many types of governance so that all of the keys should be held together?

12 A more complex intermediary version requires that *the demands of each key are considered by all the keys*. For example, scientific opening and education, gender equality, governance and ethics can be questioned through participation. The same can then be done with ethics for participation, scientific education and opening, gender equality and governance and so on, for each pillar.

13 Last but not least, the *relationships between these keys and responsibility* must be considered. As mentioned in (4), this is crucial for the interpretation

of the keys. These relationships are not immediately obvious. First of all, there is a need to define what responsibility means. Has the concept only one meaning, or several? Is it simple or composite? Secondly, different ways exist to match the keys with the responsibility concept. Are they to be taken as a whole or separately? If they are to be taken as a whole, points 5–12 must be clarified. If responsibility is perceived as a composite concept, there is space for more combinations in answering the question. Indeed, this will depend on the number of definitions of the responsibilities and of their various elements, should recognition of responsibility be seen as a composite concept. These two ways of understanding responsibility must be distinguished. I will develop this point in part 4.2.

Is scholarly work on RRI better shaped to answer the remarks above, and especially the last one? The proposals of some analysts to replace the EC RRI keys with five conditions (transparency, anticipation, inclusion, responsiveness, reflexivity) do not provide an answer to the remarks and problems cited above (See Pellé and Reber 2016; Reber 2018). Moreover, their connections, with responsibility understood as a pluralistic concept, are not recognized. Indeed, the fact that responsiveness is only one of the meanings of responsibility, without any justification, neglects the other ones.

The *Res-Agora Navigator Index*[12] is interesting, but selects responsibility as capacity and capability. It does not cover the core of moral responsibility.

The last comment is the most sensitive one. More clarification is needed on responsibility and its different understandings and/or components.

Moral responsibility: A conceptual constellation

The text above has included a rapid overview and comment on the RRI keys proposed by the EC. We have done the same in detail for the RRI academic literature (Pellé and Reber 2016). As yet, however, none of these approaches has explored all the possible conceptions of "responsibility" in detail, nor do they distinguish between legal, ethical (or moral), social or political responsibility. Some of this academic research fails to address the definition of responsibility, running the risk of neglecting the issue of responsibility, while other research chooses only one definition, often with limited justification. This is the case with respect to responsibility understood as *responsiveness*, *care* or *capacity* (Owen et al. 2012; Grinbaum and Groves 2013; Res-Agora 2016). In order to move toward the creation of a complete map of responsibility, several other meanings have to be explored.

Using political and moral philosophy, in particular (see, for example Hart [1968], Jonas [1984], Thompson [1980], Ricoeur [2000], Bovens [1998], Bovens *et al.*, [2014], Fischer [1999], Cane [2002], Williams [2008], Vincent [2009], Vincent et al. [2011], McKenna [2012], Dworkin [2013] and Richardson [1999]), to which we have added more recent work on RRI (Owen et al. 2012; Owen et al 2013;

Grinbaum and Groves 2013), a more complete cartography of responsibility is presented below. Its different conceptions are contained in the following, along with examples to highlight the differences between them. It is possible to identify responsibility as:

1 *cause*: for example, human activities are partly responsible for climate warming. They are a cause of it.[13]
1' *consequences*:[14] for example, hail storms that damaged vineyards in Burgundy last year doubled the cost of a bottle of wine.
2 *blameworthiness*: for example, the individual who did not make an effort to reduce ignorance is blameworthy.
2' *praiseworthiness*:[15] for example, Walter Benjamin's statement that, of all the ways to acquire books, writing them oneself is regarded as the most praiseworthy method.
3 *liability*: for example, the determination of a level of moral culpability that should be required for criminal liability in the case of HIV transmission.
4 *accountability*:[16] decision-makers are accountable for their decisions and the ways in which they have managed public finances.
5 *role*:[17] in this European project, the CNRS research team plays the leading role.
5' *task*: The role is wider than the task. It is often made up of several tasks. For example, George welcomes the guest. This role has been assigned to him, but he also has other tasks to complete.
6 *authority*: for example, the EU member States can trigger a safeguarding clause allowing any of them to prevent a vote being taken because of national policy and good reasons they see as important, for example, regarding the importation of UK meat during the mad cow disease epidemic.
7 *capacity*: for example, Alexander has the ability to be a great author.
8 *obligation*: for example, every researcher has to mention his or her conflicts of interest to be published in this peer-reviewed journal.
9 *responsiveness*: for example, well-prepared students can participate in this interactive seminar.
10 *virtue* (i.e. care): for example, Nelson Mandela's life journey has been recognized as a tendency to act in a responsible way, even when he was in jail. It is as if he had trained himself to be responsible.

A more sophisticated approach could be adopted. On accountability, McKenna writes of a "constellation of interconnected concepts" (McKenna 2012: p. 8). However, I will not dwell further on this idea as it is outside the remit of this chapter.

Different organizations of the constellation

Some forms of responsibility are more descriptive (1), (1'), (3), (4), (5), (5'), (6), (7), (9), while others imply a more normative assessment.

Based on this list, we can provide an answer to remark no. 13 regarding the keys-responsibility relationships above. Responsibility could be *simple* or *composite*. Or to express this differently, some of its components alone could represent the whole concept of responsibility. For example, responsibility can be limited to a question of capacity, authority or task. However, understood normatively, no one element of this conception is sufficient. For instance, for (2) or (2'), we need (1) and/or (1') to see if somebody is responsible or not, and she/he has to be able (7) to be responsive (9) and (4) accountable. For more complex cases, the attribution of responsibility will depend on task (5'), role (5) or authority (6). Thus, this list draws on different conceptions when responsibility is descriptively understood and different components when responsibility is normatively interpreted. This means that, frequently, more than one component is needed to describe and assess responsibility. The probability of being in this situation is higher in research and innovation processes.

The normative conceptions are related to different scientific spheres. (3) is closer to legal responsibility, while (2), (2)' and (10) are closer to moral responsibility, and (6) and (8) are at the intersection of both domains. (4) might be situated in political responsibility (Bovens, Gooding and Schillemans 2014; Rosanvallon 2015).[18]

Following the logic of this chapter, we shall focus on the concept of moral responsibility as this is the concept that best fits the RRI framework. If it is law that prevails, the actors involved have no other options but to obey, as is the case for ERs (ethical compliance) presented above. In the same way, sanctions are backward looking, in that they are applied after an act has been committed or serve as a motivation grounded in threat.

Thus, moral responsibility best fits the RRI framework. To be ethical is not simply a question of respecting the law, like in the European ERs. This is even truer for RRI in which ethics and responsibility go further than the law (Pellé and Reber 2016).

On the basis on these remarks and a number of readings in moral philosophy, a minimalist (McKenna 2012) version of moral responsibility and a maximalist one must be recognized. The latter corresponds to the map above, while the former selects some of its possibilities, minimally conceptions (2) and (2)', sometimes adding (7), (9) and (10). It would be easier to opt for the minimalist approach as it would help with prioritizing and remaining focused on the core of moral responsibility.

Nevertheless, we will not adopt this solution for three reasons. First of all, because this map comprises all the different conceptions of responsibility, and second, because all of them have been mentioned in the RRI literature. A third reason may be added: we shall also focus on the concept of political responsibility that matches individuals and collectives. Indeed, as described in the first part of this chapter, research is not an autarkic activity. The "coming rationalism" (Saint-Sernin 2007) calls for complex collaboration. This is true for innovation too. Therefore, RRI needs to combine individual moral responsibility with collective political responsibility.

Keys and understandings of responsibility

The need to interpret the RRI keys is important, as is the need to make the connection between them and responsibility. Indeed, the way in which responsibility is understood has the potential to renew the keys rather than to allow them to become nothing more than a validation of current practices or a mere communication strategy.

In an attempt to analyse the relationships between the EC's RRI keys and conceptions of responsibility, the first point is that certain conceptions of responsibility are easily and differently attracted by each key.

With regard to participation, one priority is responsiveness (9), in order to ensure that participation is effective. Capacity (7) can be added as a criterion for selecting participants or as a goal to achieve; virtue (10) for both aspects, if the desire is to attain excellence and the distribution of roles (5) and tasks (5').

Scientific education is more problematic. It depends on the content of education and the type of science considered. For the natural and engineering sciences, (1) and (1') are central to the understanding of the phenomenon or research expectations. The capacity to explain or to teach these (7) is also an issue.

If education is open to the normative sciences, especially ethics, all the above conceptions of responsibility regarding the ethics key can be included.

We have to add that, nowadays, education is bidirectional (interactive) and requires responsiveness (9).

It is difficult to match the gender equality key with one specific conception of responsibility. Accountability (8) is probably the closest as it provides figures and evidence of gender equality in the process, the selection of some research objects and the scientific design of the products.

The same difficulty occurs with openness. The closest understandings of responsibility are responsiveness (9) and accountability (4).

The governance key attracts, first and foremost, authority (6) and accountability (4).

Finally, we may match this connection between RRI keys and understandings of responsibility with the main moral theories in moral philosophy. For the sake of simplification, I will only take the relationships between moral theories and responsibility. The ethical theory of consequentialism (and its sub-family, utilitarianism) conveys (1'), obligation (8), not as legal but as deontological ethical theory; virtue (10), the third main ethical theory; and conceptions (2)[19] and (2'), operating as moral sanctions. Capacity (7), accountability (4) and responsiveness might be incorporated into this key too. Capacity and responsiveness could be requisites to trigger responsibility when an agent (or an institution) is accountable and has to justify his/her/its behaviour.

Beyond providing clarifications on the roots of responsibility, one of the most interesting results of this analytical inquiry is that participation and ethics are the keys which attract the highest number of conceptions of responsibility. This reinforces the line of this chapter, guided by an ethical approach extended by participation recognized as a novelty compared with existing institutions or procedures typically dedicated to assessing ethical issues.

Moral innovation according to different combinations of responsibilities

These remarks and analytical distinctions can be used to present the different steps involved in moral innovation. This is original in that it goes straight to responsibility as a moral concept rather than looking to offer certain components that can be united, as in the strategy implemented by the EC (keys of RRI) or by the academic literature (conditions of RRI) – a strategy which is, in fact, of great interest. The spectrum opened up in our cartography of responsibility not only allows the vagueness of a polysemic term to be avoided, but also prevents moral responsibility being bypassed by focusing on legal obligations alone. These different components or understandings of responsibility constitute a kind of colour palette that makes up the different tones of responsibilities.

The different steps of moral innovation are the following:

1 *Recognizing pluralism*: The first form of moral innovation depends on the benefits of the responsibility list and on the defence of ethical pluralism, applied here to understandings of responsibility. It is neither a monistic defence, which would only favour one understanding as the valid point, nor relativism, which would define moral responsibility by relying on considerations and conditions that are outside the normative domain (Reber and Sève 2005; Reber 2016). This seems to be the strategy chosen by composite understandings of responsibility, which indicate foundations of responsibility without providing definitions.

   By thinking of the understandings of responsibility pluralistically, innovators and researchers can avoid making arbitrary choices and, even better, can make appropriate choices aided by this cartography.

2 *Seeking complementarity*: A second form of ethical innovation in research and innovation lies in the complementarity between some understandings of responsibility, understood as elements or meanings. Each of the 10 forms of responsibility presented above can be seen as containing an *element* of responsibility, at least normatively (and not descriptively[20]) comprehended. For example, one portion of the burden is individual (obligation, virtue) and one portion falls to the organization and is therefore collective or systemic (relating to the organization taken as a whole). This is the case for responsibility as accountability.

   In the same way, responsibility as liability or as blameworthiness focuses on consequences, i.e. on the results that could directly or insidiously create harmful consequences, while responsibility as responsiveness concentrates on the aptitude of individuals for understanding and responding to the demands of others.[21]

3 *Selecting according to context sensitiveness*: Third, we shall implement a more sophisticated form of moral innovation. This is based on different combinations of the pluralistic understanding of responsibility. They can be combined in order to reach fruitful interpretations that can be adapted to the specific context in which they are applied. Faced with their polysemic nature, choices can be made to implement one understanding over the others, or even to combine several of them.
4 *Connecting responsibility with research and innovation*: This pairing focuses on the *connection* between responsibilities (and the different conceptions of responsibility in the list) and norms (epistemic, practical and specific to what ought-to-be) found within these fields (i.e. the first part of this text).
5 *Promoting positive understandings of responsibility*: Another benefit of the responsibility cartography is the identification of its negative and positive understandings. This relates to a form of ethical innovation, too, allowing the stumbling block, formed by the viewpoint that responsible innovation is an oxymoron, to be removed. This last assertion relies on the limitation of responsibility to the legal level, and sometimes also on the interpretation of moral responsibility. This combination of responsibilities relies partially on the sensitiveness to the context and also on normative considerations. To be more precise, among the 10 different meanings, a distinction can be made between negative and positive interpretations of responsibility. Negative interpretations – responsibility as blameworthiness (2), as liability (3) or as accountability (4) – are essentially retrospective. Responsibility is noted after the fact, once the harmful event has occurred. This negative understanding includes two different aspects: temporal (*ex post*) and negative assessment because of a harmful action. On the other hand, (2'), (6), (7), (9) and (10) are positive. The latter types of responsibility include a prospective element (*ex ante*), reassuring those identified as responsible that an action is carried out (or avoided) and that one or several goals are met. In this case, there is a projection toward the future in order to determine morally desirable goals. Such projection determines the possible actions and decisions that will allow the person to work toward these goals in the best way possible. However, positive decisions do not exclude a retrospective aspect. In the same way, responsibility as accountability, or as an obligation to repair damages (3), also includes prospective elements. This means that an individual must consider the future. Indeed, CEOs who follow the instructions of their shareholders see their present actions being conditioned by the future obligation to justify their choices and decisions. Likewise, an individual's current recognition of his or her responsibility as liability determines future actions, for example to repair damage caused or to offer financial compensation.

To better understand the difference between positive and negative distinctions regarding responsibility, a third element should be mentioned.

The philosopher Paul Ricoeur (2000) notes an understanding of responsibility linked to the idea of *imputation*, meaning the act of attributing an action or a result to a person. However, the case of responsibility as *response* also exists. Indeed, looking at the etymological roots of the word "responsibility", it seems that the initial meaning comes from the Latin term *respondere* (to respond). In French *répondre* (to respond), as in German with (*Verantworten*), responsibility refers both to the idea of communicating a response and to the idea of being accountable for one's actions (*répondre de ses actes*) by taking on responsibility. We focus most of all on the *intention* of the actor, whereas with the idea of *imputation* the overriding factor is the causal relationship linking actors to their acts within a particular chain of events (Pellizzoni 2004). Therefore, in one case, the individuals are responsible in so far as they must be aware of their actions, justify them and defend them, whereas in the other case, the individual's responsibility stems from the ability to attribute an action they are recognized to be the author or authors of. These two interpretations open up two different paths of reflection and two different worlds.

Moreover, the communicational conception of responsibility implies different components: other people or a forum in front of whom the actors must justify their behaviours.

To summarize, unlike negative understandings of responsibility, positive interpretations highlight an unbreakable link between the individual's actions and responsibility. This link is expressed through the ability to respond, to care or to take on the consequences of one's actions. Responsibility does not emerge after the fact, in light of the possible harmful consequences; it is intrinsic to action and to the fact that human beings are tied into networks of relationships.

6 *Broadening and deepening responsibility*: Moving from one understanding of responsibility to another can provide more depth or density to the concept of responsibility. For example, responsibility as a task is less demanding than responsibility stemming from authority. Likewise, relying on individual cognitive and moral capacities to act and make decisions introduces an extra step when it comes to the responsibility related to tasks (or roles), or from authority, whether this is allocated by a flow chart or by experience. Finally, responsibility as virtue is one of the most demanding types and requires excellence. The increased depth that comes from moving away from simple definitions of responsibility, toward interpretations that are more morally demanding, is a step toward increased reflexivity. In responsibility as virtue, for example, practising, training and, therefore, learning are what makes the difference. This is an implicitly perfectionist way of seeing. This perfectionism might be connected to moral perfectionism.

7 *Responsible sharing of responsibilities.* In this version of moral innovation, the aim is to offer the most effective[22] and coherent presentation possible. Yet, with so many understandings, we very quickly catch sight of the scope of possible choices we face if we choose to compound them.[23] Indeed, we could choose to present just one understanding of responsibility. For example, when

> only addressing the people involved in a project, we can simply allocate roles to each of them. The limit will be that responsibility relating only to their role engages participants less than if they are given authority or if they are there because of their abilities, or if their decisions have real consequences for which they must be held accountable. We shall therefore simply offer a few comments on the possible associations between these interpretations of responsibility. The various contexts, for example with regard to research projects that must meet the expectations of RRI, can allow us to select the most relevant and effective definitions. For example, it can be counterproductive to class everything as accountability understood as cumbersome controls that fall within ERs. In certain cases, these devices (and the associated understandings of responsibility) will, in theory, be less appropriate than offering training in ethics to students, which places them in a position of responsibility and provides them with ways to understand the meaning of their research in these various contexts. These three types of association – increase in depth, complementarity and relevance – allow us to share out responsibility in the most responsible way possible.

On the basis of these modes of composition of responsibilities, anyone with projects or interests, any institution or decision-maker, can select one of these precise definitions in order to introduce it and embody it within a process of research or innovation. It remains to be seen how participants, procedures and processes take charge of, use and share the chosen understanding of responsibility.

The different options for this part of the chapter to match understandings of responsibility with different forms of moral innovation echo the options presented above for the keys (part 3, 8–11).

Conclusion: The most responsible sharing of responsibilities: ethics and subsidiarity

To conclude, we will compare the devices of ERs, debated at the beginning of this chapter, and RRI. In each of these, ethics plays a pivotal role. Indeed, both propose ethics and endeavour as an essential element of the framing of research and innovation practices and in such a way that research and innovation benefit from these demands. Of course, there is no proposal as yet to replace the ERs with RRI. However, we can legitimately question the two in unison. If ERs are mandatory and evolutionary, how are RRI and ERs different, compatible, competitive and/or substitutable? Could the ERs be more responsible, providing more room for the creativity of applicants in research projects? Can they help them to assume responsibilities?

To start, we shall indicate a few differences which will allow a parallel evolution of both conceptions to be imagined.

The first difference, in length, is that of the era between one and the other. The compass of RRI's scope of consideration is much more open to research, both upstream and downstream. If we consider the *European Code on Integrity in*

Research, mentioned in part 1, which did not want to include "ethics" understood in what it calls a "social context", RRI might, on the contrary, embrace this "social context". It embraces the same territory for ethics as part of this context.

More precisely, at least three contexts need to be distinguished: the first, that is research-related; the second, that takes persons, animals and plants involved in research into consideration; and the third, that this code calls "ethical context", which resembles social context, but includes scientific policy. The territory metaphor invites the implementation of a subsidiarity principle to find a more relevant way to deal with ethics according to the perimeters. This concern is relevant to responsibility and also to the sharing of responsibilities.

The second difference is that ERs do not consider the scientific or technical part of the selected projects. They usually come into play after scientific assessment. RRI does consider the scientific and technical side through the opening and education keys. Of course, with some questions from the EQ related to the involvement of animals, one should be able to say why it is impossible to achieve the project without sacrificing animals, in order to respond to research issues, and to show what benefits other animals and human beings derive from these experiments.

The third difference is that ERs propose delimited lists of questions and principles, which are longer than the definitions of the RRI keys. The transition to RRI could be problematic in the case of a dissolution, a removal and finally a non-consideration of these problems and principles which are expected to help in responding to them.

The fourth and more sensitive difference is that some RRI keys can become problematic points of attention for the EQ in ER. For example, the RRI participation key is an issue in part 2, that concerns the involvement of humans in research. Therefore, in a bid to do well and to involve stakeholders following the RRI impetus, we are faced with an additional demand to anticipate templates for the appropriate collection of informed consent. Nevertheless, and in order to push this argument further, one can ask if the participants in the two instances have the same status. The answer may be negative if we estimate that the human beings involved in ERs are subjected to experiments, while the stakeholders can participate in the development and modifications of experiments. The case of research – and therefore open data – is also fraught with the requisites on data and their protection, especially when they are sensitive.

The fifth difference stems from the fact that different perspectives are taken by ERs, through the inclusion of experts and ethical instances, in the form of enlarged ethical committees, while extended participation promoted by RRI opens up different types of participation that are less specific. The crossing between the broad participation of heterogeneous actors (RRI) and ethical specialists or those acting as ERs has existed in certain rare experiments, similar to the one brought up by the bioethics general assemblies (*Etats généraux de la bioéthique*) in France (Reber 2010).

The sixth difference stems from a difference in perspectives. Although the word ethics is found recurrently in ERs, it is only one of the RRI keys and it does not have the same concerns. In RRI, ERs could lose their specific attention to persons, animals and plants that research must guarantee. On the contrary, RRI discusses things more widely, from different points of view.

In cases where the two come closer, one should think of destabilization or decentering of research-related tasks if this spectrum was opened to what the Code related to integrity in research calls “ethical context”.

The disparity, indeed the oppositions, between research in moral philosophy and applied ethics, on the one hand, and in political sociology or even the sociology of science and technology, on the other hand, echoes these two directions.

Nevertheless, a number of RRI demands are already included in the general, scientific and ethical assessment of projects in the process. In effect, in certain projects, several keys have already been taken into account. As we have seen, gender is considered by some proponents without them being asked to do so. In the same way, benefit sharing (justice proposed as a new key) of research for the work done in a third and poorer country figures in one of the sub-questions of the EQ. With regard to participation, one could depend on the numerous norms guiding human experiences which reveal a concern for the ethical validity of inclusion.

Without raising all the questions posed by the EQ with respect to the keys and the conditions for RRI, one could suggest that governance provides an opportunity to instil more reflexivity in ERs. More precisely, evaluators could consider the manner in which the project initiators associate the governance modes for ethical issues, with the entire implementation of the process which is relocated in research teams, how they are taken care of and their response to it.

The decompartmentalization permitted by RRI will provide another opportunity, but also a risk. Actors other than ethics experts could also have a say in it. But it will also be good to know which title and responsibilities each person will be invited to formulate, but above all to react to.

The first RRI key, pertaining to participation, concerns citizens and stakeholders. The two are not equal and do not have the same concerns. For example, a citizen can consider the common good or future generations, while stakeholders will want to promote the research in which they have invested and from which they expect economic benefits.

A form of complementary association between ERs and RRI does not necessarily imply relocating or processing the question through a partly dedicated axis (work package) or an ethics committee, as is usually the case now.

When comparing ERs and RRI, relevant governance in response to ethical issues which occur in research must be taken into consideration. Some analysts (Owen et al. 2013) describe this as deliberation. Here, the notion of deliberative democracy (Steiner 2012; Stevenson and Dryzek 2014, Parkinson and Mansbridge 2012) might be reintroduced. To be precise, deliberation should go beyond merely providing the conditions for collaboration between participants. The type of deliberation involved should teach ethical evaluation itself, leading to ethical pluralism. A certain amount of tension is involved in the passage from ERs to RRI as a result of RRI’s implicit proceduralism and ER’s substantialism.

The intertwining of a double form of deliberation (moral and political) should reduce this tension (Pellé and Reber 2016; Reber 2012, 2016).

Once again, the time is not ripe for the convergence of ERs and RRI or the replacement of one with the other. Nevertheless, if RRI should become a new requirement for every research project, as its omnipresence in the presentation of H2020 might suggest, the questions raised above will require answers. Depending on the answers, one could reduce the number of requirements. However, this might be difficult because the questions asked in the EQ appear inescapable for legal reasons linked to the various forms of protection in existence. RRI might be used in order to better respond to the EQ in a reflexive and sustainable manner throughout the projects. RRI cannot serve as a mere pretext, as such usage would incur the risk of these protection requirements being forgotten or dispersed. The role played by RRI is not limited to protection as it paves the way for the involvement of various stakeholders and broadens the spectrum by considering ethical problems. Nevertheless, this step raises a number of questions, the first of which is to ascertain who bears what responsibility. If researchers constitute just one type of stakeholder, they no longer have to bear these new responsibilities alone.

To put it succinctly, a longer list of requests could have the collateral effect of attracting attention far away to what lies at the core of a given research project, which already respects the normative requirements discussed at the beginning of this chapter. RRI therefore has numerous challenges to meet to avoid losing these responsibilities specific for research that may be hidden by new ones that are less specific.

By setting out the various interpretations of responsibility, we hope to help the many individuals who show an interest in innovation and research (public decision-makers, scientists, innovators, members of sponsoring institutions and members of civil society) to fashion understandings of responsibility adapted to their contexts. The sharing of responsibilities must be decided on the basis of the priority given to each actor, taking new understandings of subsidiarity related to ethics into account (Reber 2014).

Notes

1 https://ec.europa.eu/research/swafs/pdf/pub_public_engagement/responsible-research-and-innovation-leaflet_en.pdf presents five keys and one dimension as an umbrella for the five other ones. For six keys, see: European Commission (2013). Call for Tender, N0 RTD-B6-PP-00964-2013. *Study on Monitoring the Evolution and Benefits of Responsible Research and Innovation*, Brussels.

2 See: http://www.esf.org/fileadmin/Public_documents/Publications/Code_Conduct_ResearchIntegrity.pdf

3 See, for example, the opinion of CNRS Ethics Committee (COMETS; 2012), *Need for the establishment within the CNRS of procedures to promote research integrity*. See: http://www.cnrs.fr/comets/spip.php?article45 (website accessed on 2 June 2016).

4 We do not distinguish between researchers and teachers-researchers, knowing that it is rare to be only a researcher. Even when this is the case, as at the National Centre for Scientific Research (CNRS), for example, many researchers are teaching, especially in Humanities and Social Sciences.

5 See, for instance, the conference on RRI hosted by the European Economic and Social Committee on 14–15 January, 2016: http://www.eesc.europa.eu/?i=portal.en.press-releases.37999.

6 The word in italics indicates different understandings of responsibility that we will consider below (part 4).

7 See https://ec.europa.eu/programmes/horizon2020/en/h2020-section/societal-challenges #Article (website accessed on 15 July 2016).The European Union is focusing on seven *Grand Challenges*: Health, demographic change and wellbeing; Food security, sustainable agriculture and forestry, marine and maritime and inland water research and Bioeconomy; Secure, clean and efficient energy; Smart, green and integrated transport; Climate action, environment, resource efficiency and raw materials; Europe in a changing world- inclusive, innovative and reflective societies; Secure societies – protecting freedom and security on Europe and its citizens.

8 See: http://ec.europa.eu/research/participants/fp7documents/funding-guide/8_horizon talissues/ 3_ethics_en.html (website accessed on 15 July 2016).

9 The issue here is military use, given that the EC does not finance such research.

10 For a discussion on the differences between ethics and governance, see Pellé and Reber (2016).

11 For a detailed presentation of the keys and some examples of research on them, see Pellé and Reber (2016). Each refers to a rich scientific literature, and the interpretation of them is a prerequisite to their implementation in research and innovation projects.This is also one of the effects of the implementation of research on RRI: to join different research communities through a funding policy which is equally voluntary and important. This obviously occurs with some problems. Certainly, the EC-funded projects also call for the structuring of research institutions, but are also not involved in research. This is the case with a tender seeking to structure the ethics committees in European countries and researchers working on scientific integrity. Nevertheless, we have many theoretical and methodological problems to solve to make these forms of collaboration truly responsible regarding the epistemic responsibilities attached to good quality and creative science, satisfying each discipline involved. For the elaboration of unsolved interdisciplinary epistemology, we refer to Reber (2016).

12 See: http://responsibility-navigator.eu/navigator/ (website accessed on 10 July 2016).

13 This example shows that causality imputation is not always easy to determine.

14 It would be possible to understand responsibility as a consequence or a result. We thus distinguish it from cause, for example through the (temporal) angle from which the action is seen, between before and after the action, between what causes the action and what the action causes. Consequence is more partial and particular than result.We know that the problem of causality is huge. See, for example, Kordon (2009).

15 We do not discuss the fact that praiseworthiness and blameworthiness are not symmetrical. Praiseworthiness is associated with the evaluation of an agent rather than an act. See Heyd (2015), and: http://plato.stanford.edu/entries/supererogation/Therefore praiseworthiness is close to virtue.

16 We do not add the distinction here between accountability as a virtue or as a mechanism (see Bovens, Goodin and Schillemans [2014], Pellé and Reber [2016]).

17 We may distinguish two different ways to connect individuals with their roles, going from very important (its own role) to disconnected, as in theatre.

18 For links between moral and political responsibilities, and moral and political deliberations see Reber (2012, 2016).

19 For a presentation of all these theories and their relationships with RRI or responsibility, see Reber (2016).

20 As we have said before, this list concerns different conceptions when responsibility is descriptively understood and concerns components when responsibility is normatively interpreted.

21 For a more in-depth discussion, see Pellizzoni (2004).
22 On the link between ethics and efficiency, efficacy and effectiveness, see Lenoir (2015).
23 This complete range of possibilities goes beyond the intended scope of this chapter, so we shall contain ourselves to pointing out its existence. For a more detailed presentation, see Pellé and Reber (2016) and Reber (2016).

References

Bovens, M. (1998). *The Quest for Responsibility. Accountability and Citizenship in Complex Organisations*. Cambridge: Cambridge University Press.

Bovens, M., Goodin. R. E. and Schillemans, T. (Eds.) (2014). *The Oxford Handbook of Public Accountability*. Oxford: Oxford University Press.

Cane, P. (2002). *Responsibility in Law and Morality*. Oxford: Hart Publishing.

CNRS Ethics Committee (COMETS) (2012). *Need for the establishment within the CNRS of procedures to promote research integrity*. Available at: http://www.cnrs.fr/comets/spip.php?article45 (accessed 2 July 2016).

Dworkin, R. (2013). *Justice for Hedgehogs*. Cambridge (MA): The Belknap Press of University Press.

European Commission (2013). Call for Tender, N0 RTD-B6-PP-00964-2013. *Study on Monitoring the Evolution and Benefits of Responsible Research and Innovation*, Brussels.

European Science Foundation (2011). *The European Code of Conduct for Research Integrity*, Strasbourg. Available at: https://www.google.com/search?q=European+Science+Foundation+%282011%29.+The+European+Code+of+Conduct+for+Research+Integrity%2C+Strasbourg.+&ie=utf-8&oe=utf-8&client=firefox-b-ab (accessed 13 May 2018).

Expert Group (chair: van den Hoven J.; members: Nielsen L., Roure F., Rudze L., Stilgoe, J.; rapporteur: Jacob K. (2013). *Report on the State of Art in Europe on Responsible Research and Innovation: Options for Strengthening Responsible Research* and *Innovation*. Brussels: European Commission. Available at: https://ec.europa.eu/research/science-society/document_library/pdf_06/options-for-strengthening_en.pdf

Fischer, M. (1999). Recent Work on Moral Responsibility. *Ethics*, 110(1), pp. 93–140.

Gianni, R. (2016). *Responsibility and Freedom: The Ethical Realm of RRI*. London/New York: ISTE/Wiley.

Grinbaum, A. and Groves, C. (2013). What is 'Responsible' about Responsible Innovation? Understanding the Ethical Issues. In: R. Owen, Bessant J., Heintz M. (Eds.), *Responsible Innovation. Managing the Responsible Emergence of Science and Innovation in Society*. Hoboken (NJ): John Wiley & Sons, pp. 119–142.

Hart, H. L. A. (1968). *Punishment and Responsibility: Essays in the Philosophy of Law*. Oxford: Clarendon Press.

Heyd, D. (2015). *Superogation*. In: Stanford Encyclopedia of Philosophy (Spring 2016 Edition), Edward N. Zalta (ed.). Available at: https://plato.stanford.edu/archives/spr2016/entries/supererogation/ (accessed 13 May 2018).

Jonas, H. (1984). *The Imperative of Responsibility: In Search of an Ethics for the Technological Age*. Chicago: University of Chicago Press. Available at: http://plato.stanford.edu/entries/supererogation/

Kordon, C. (Ed.) (2009). *Sciences de l'homme et sciences de la nature*. Paris: Editions de la Maison des sciences de l'homme.

Lenoir, V. C. (2015). *Ethical Efficiency. Responsibility and Contingency*. London/New York: ISTE/Wiley.

McKenna, M. (2012). *Conversation and Responsibility*. Oxford: Oxford University Press.

Owen, R., Bessant, J. and Heintz, M. (Eds.) (2013). *Responsible Innovation. Managing the Responsible Emergence of Science and Innovation in Society*. Hoboken (NJ): John Wiley & Sons.

Owen, R., Macnaghten P. and Stilgoe, J. (2012). Responsible Research and Innovation: From Science in Society to Science for Society, With Society. *Science and Public Policy*, 39(6), pp. 751–760.

Owen, R., Macnaghten, P., Stilgoe, J., Gorman, M., Fisher, E. and Guston, D. (2013). A Framework for Responsible Innovation. In: R. Owen, Bessant J., Heintz M. (Eds.), *Responsible Innovation. Managing the Responsible Emergence of Science and Innovation in Society*. Hoboken (NJ): John Wiley & Sons, pp. 27–50.

Parkinson, J. and Mansbridge, J. (Eds.) (2012). *Deliberative Systems. Deliberative Democracy at the Large Scale*. Cambridge (UK): Cambridge University Press.

Pellé, S. and Reber, B. (2016). *From Ethical Review to Responsible Innovation*. London/ New York: ISTE/Wiley.

Pellizzoni L., (2004). Responsibility and Environmental Governance. *Environmental Politics*, 13(3), pp. 541–565.

Pharo, P. (1985). Problèmes empiriques de la sociologie compréhensive. *Revue Française de Sociologie*, 26(1), pp. 120–149.

Pharo, P. (1990). Les conditions de légitimité des actions publiques. *Revue Française de Sociologie*, 31(3), pp. 389–420.

Pharo, P. (2000). Perspectives de la sociologie de l'éthique. In: S. Bateman-Novaes, Ogien, R. and Pharo, P. (Eds.), *Raison pratique et sociologie de l'éthique. Autour des travaux de Paul Ladrière*. Paris: Editions du CNRS, pp. 207–221.

Pharo, P. (2004a). Ethique et sociologie. Perspectives actuelles de la sociologie morale. *L'Année sociologique*, 54(2), pp. 414–426.

Pharo, P. (2004b). *Morale et sociologie. Le sens et les valeurs entre nature et culture*. Paris: Gallimard.

Reber, B. and Sève, R. (Eds.) (2005). *Le Pluralisme*. Archives de philosophie du droit, vol. 49. Available at: http://www.philosophie-droit.asso.fr/old.php

Reber, B. (Ed.) (2010). La Bioéthique en débat. In: *Archives de philosophie du droit*, vol. 53, pp. 274–510.

Reber, B. (2011). *La démocratie génétiquement modifiée. Sociologies éthiques de l'évaluation des technologies controversées*. Québec: Presses de l'Université de Laval.

Reber, B. (2012). Argumenter et délibérer entre éthique et politique. In: Reber B. (Ed.), *Vertus et limites de la démocratie délibérative, Archives de Philosophie*, 74(2), pp. 289–303.

Reber, B. (2014). De l'écologie sociale à l'écologie institutionnelle. In: P.-A. Chardel and Reber, B. (Eds.), *Ecologies sociales. Le souci du commun*, Lyon: Parangon, pp. 183–205.

Reber, B. (2016). *Precautionary Principle, Pluralism and Deliberation. Sciences and Ethics*. London/New York: ISTE/Wiley.

Reber, B. (2018). RRI as Inheritor of Deliberative Democracy and the Precautionary Principle. *Journal of Responsible Innovation*, 5(1), pp. 38–64.

ResAgora Project (2016). Kuhlman S., Edler J., Ordonez-Matamoros O., Randles S., Walhout B., Gough C., Lindner R. (Eds.). *Responsibility Navigator*. Available at: http://responsibility-navigator.eu/wp-content/uploads/2016/01/Res-AGorA_Responsibility_Navigator.pdf

Richardson, H. S. (1999). Institutionally Divided Moral Responsibility In: E. F., Paul, Miller, F. D. and Paul, J. (Eds.), *Responsibility*. Cambridge (MA): Cambridge University Press, pp. 218–249.

Ricoeur, P. (2000). *The Just*. Chicago: Chicago University Press.
Rosanvallon, P. (2015). *Le bon gouvernement*. Paris: Seuil.
Saint-Sernin, B. (2007). *Le rationalisme qui vient*. Paris: Gallimard.
Spaapen, J. (Rapporteur); Strand, J. (Chair); Bauer, M. W., Hogan, E., Revuelta, G. and Stagl, S. (Members); and Paula, L. and Guimaraes Pereira, Â. (Contributors) (2015). *Indicators for Promoting and Monitoring Responsible Research and Innovation. Report from the Expert Group on Policy Indicators for Responsible Research and Innovation*. European Commission. Available at: http://ec.europa.eu/research/swafs/pdf/pub_rri/rri_indicators_final_version.pdf (accessed 13 May 2018).
Steiner J. (2012). *The Foundations of Deliberative Democracy. Empirical Research and Normative Implications*. Cambridge: Cambridge University Press.
Stevenson, H. and Dryzek, J. (2014). *Democratizing Global Climate Governance*. Cambridge: Cambridge University Press.
Sutour, S. and Lorrain, J.-L. (2013). *Rapport d'information fait au nom de la commission des affaires européennes sur la prise en compte des questions éthiques à l'échelon européen*, 67, Session ordinaire de 2013–2014, Paris: Sénat.
Thompson, D. F. (1980). Moral Responsibility and Public Officials. *American Political Science Review*, 74(4), pp. 905–916.
Vincent, N., van de Poel, I. and Van den Hoven J. (Eds.) (2011). *Moral Responsibility, Beyond Free Will & Determinism*. Dordrecht: Springer.
Vincent, N. (2009). Responsibility: Distinguishing Virtue from Capacity. *Polish Journal of Philosophy*, 3(1), pp. 111–126.
Williams, G. (2008). Responsibility as a Virtue. *Ethical Theory and Moral Practice*, 11(4), pp. 455–470.

Part II

The political dimension of Responsible Research and Innovation

4 Technocracy versus experimental learning in RRI

On making the most of RRI's interpretative flexibility

Pim Klaassen, Michelle Rijnen, Sara Vermeulen, Frank Kupper and Jacqueline Broerse

Introduction

Although, in many respects, Research and Innovation (R&I) has ameliorated the human condition, they also give rise to social, ethical and environmental concerns. One just has to think of the environmental impact of combustion engines or of controversies surrounding genetically modified crops, fracking, UMTS-signals or preimplantation genetic diagnostics to realize that not all R&I is ethically or socially acceptable or responsive to societal needs. To promote socially desirable, ethically acceptable and environmentally and economically sustainable R&I, the European Commission (EC) has promoted the governance framework of *Responsible Research and Innovation* (RRI) since 2010.[1] RRI is a form of anticipatory governance aimed at modulating R&I trajectories towards the 'right impacts', while strengthening the inclusive nature and democratic legitimacy of the R&I enterprise and stimulating the economy via the deliverance of better innovations.[2]

Although RRI, or its close relatives, can be recognized in a number of national funding schemes in both European countries[3] and the United States, it is hardly an exaggeration to say that the EU is RRI's habitat and the EC its genuine patron. Several years after its nominal launch, however, what RRI precisely entails is still under negotiation. The lack of a univocal definition of RRI becomes especially clear if one juxtaposes the way in which the EC defines RRI with the ways in which scholars of science policy and science and society interactions discuss RRI. Where the former is centred around a core of five internally heterogeneous 'keys' that arguably are best thought of as normative policy agendas, the latter are concerned more with designing ways to contribute to R&I following inclusive democratic processes with an increased chance of harvesting ethically sound and societally pertinent outcomes and achieving desirable impacts.

This observation is at this chapter's basis, as it aspires to narrow the gap between how RRI is conceived of in EC policy circles and how it is conceived of in scholarly circles. As we see it, the policy view of RRI and the scholarly view of RRI each have their strengths and weaknesses and both would be better off if coupled to the other. Major strengths of the policy concept of RRI are its focus on impact and its institutional support, whereas the academic view of RRI shows more conceptual coherence and displays more openness to the heterogeneous world in which, and for which, R&I takes place. Because, arguably, RRI is first and foremost a policy concept, our entranceway into this issue consists of an analysis of the policy concept of RRI—from now on, pRRI.

When looking at how pRRI has come about and has found its way into policy, we see that it embodies a clear tension. Although it presents a response to bottom-up societal resistance to R&I triggered by ethical and privacy issues surrounding, for instance, genetically modified organisms or electronic patient records (Von Schomberg 2013), in itself it constitutes a top-down policy-driven push on R&I. To complicate matters even more, this push directs R&I towards inclusive practices that are ethically acceptable, societally responsive and sustainable (and, hence, responsible), but the delineation of what it means to be societally responsive appears to be substantiated to a large degree in the EC's pRRI, of which it is unclear precisely how it is informed by bottom-up societal voices.[4] Ultimately, by taking the responsibility of Europe's R&I system to the next level, the latter should produce ethically sound, marketable innovations that simultaneously advance Europe's competitive edge and contribute to the battle against the EC-defined Grand Challenges of our times (von Schomberg, 2011; Lund Declaration, 2009). But whether that is also how Europe's citizens see responsibility, or whether they consider RRI a legitimate framework for governing R&I, is largely unknown.

At the core of this chapter are this and associated tensions in the concept of pRRI as embodied in EC literature. It will be argued, though, that it does not necessarily form an obstacle to reaching RRI's ultimate aims of making R&I more responsive to societal needs, more democratically accountable and delivering more beneficial innovations. To this end, we will, on the one hand, build on the intellectual resources on which RRI has been constructed. On the other hand, the authors' build on their experience in the project *RRI Tools*,[5] a support action funded by the EC's Seventh Framework Programme to contribute to fostering RRI.[6]

In section 2, the chapter discusses pRRI in more detail. Section 3 further elaborates on the tensions in pRRI. In section 4, we discuss how RRI is described in the academic literature on science governance, ethics, science and technology studies (STS) and philosophy of science—what we call aRRI, for *academic* RRI. After this, section 5 confronts pRRI with aRRI, articulating where they differ, followed by a description in section 6 of how in the *RRI Tools* project we have worked around the tensions inherent to pRRI. Finally, in section 7, we draw our conclusions, arguing that anyone's aims with RRI are best served if pRRI and aRRI join forces rather than further develop into two separate fields that run their own independent course.

pRRI: Where it comes from and what it is

Use of the concept of RRI in a policy context seriously took off after the EC gave it a central role in its Horizon 2020 framework program of 2014. Its use in the context of R&I policy is slightly older than that, though, with first signs of life in 2010.[7]

Owen et al. (2012: pp. 752–754) discuss the history of RRI as an EC-policy concept, and elaborate on the indistinct policy motivations behind the concept. These include both instrumental economic considerations, normative democratic considerations and considerations having to do with the substance of innovation. The latter can be best discerned in the work by 'EC philosopher' Renee Von Schomberg, who, building on work in STS and the philosophy of science, suggests that in cases where highly inclusive and deliberative processes are part of R&I trajectories, better innovations are brought forth (i.e., innovations with the 'right impacts' and smaller chances of technological lock-in) (Von Schomberg, 2011; 2013).

As can be read on Horizon 2020's Science With and For Society webpage,[8] today the EC defines RRI as follows:

> RRI is an inclusive approach to research and innovation (R&I), to ensure that societal actors work together during the whole research and innovation process. It aims to better align both the process and outcomes of R&I, with the values, needs and expectations of European society. In general terms, RRI implies anticipating and assessing potential implications and societal expectations with regard to research and innovation. In practice, RRI consists of designing and implementing R&I policy that will:
>
> - engage society more broadly in its research and innovation activities,
> - increase access to scientific results,
> - ensure gender equality, in both the research process and research content,
> - take into account the ethical dimension, and
> - promote formal and informal science education.

By governing R&I such that it meets this description of pRRI, R&I would allegedly help steer science and innovation towards addressing societal problems, and would do so in such a way as to optimally forestall controversies and deadlocks. The definition of pRRI reflects the EC's position that these goals will be achieved where R&I manages to engage society, grant access to its results, promote gender equality, accommodate ethical concerns and integrate R&I with science education. To achieve this, the EC uses a variety of policy measures, including the adaptation of funding schemes, offering guidelines and codes of conduct and implementing standards.[9] These five items have come to be known as what the EC sees as RRI's so-called key dimensions.

That the EC would delineate RRI in terms of such a fixed set of key dimensions was not yet clear in 2012, when Owen *et al.* wrote their history of the EC-policy concept of RRI. In the short history of the concept, some meandering in its conceptualization is visible. Specifically, in the original definition of RRI, the EC had operationalized it in terms of six rather than five such keys. In addition to the five visible in the definition quoted here, *governance* was also originally seen as a key to RRI. Recognizing that RRI is, in fact, a governance framework for R&I, the EC has decided not to mention this as an isolated and independent key anymore.

What immediately stands out when looking at this list of items is that it constitutes a rather motley collection. *Public engagement* arguably concerns the design of R&I processes such that so-called RRI outcomes might be achieved; *ethics*, like *gender* in R&I, specifies the nature of the content of RRI outcomes, but insofar as it relates to gender equality in R&I organizations, *gender* has more the appearance of a framework condition that the R&I system ought to have met before a responsible R&I process can take off in the first place. And no matter how important both arguably are in and of themselves, we hypothesize that looking at the definition given above up until the itemization of what RRI entails in practice, very few people will, for instance, see either Open Access or Science Education as essentially implicated herein.

More generally, one might even wonder whether this first part of pRRI's definition warrants *any* substantial delineation of what should be done to make R&I RRI—one would expect a procedural indication at best. With its identification of five mandatory points of passage, each with potency in one or more different departments in the governance of R&I, all in all, the pRRI definition separates out substantive content for RRI. It is our fear that, by giving such a definition as the EC offers now, with pRRI's five key dimensions, the EC runs the risk of *preliminarily* prescribing in too much detail what it means "to ensure that societal actors work together during the whole research and innovation process [such that] both the process and outcomes of R&I [better align] with the values, needs and expectations of European society" (see note 8). Rather than conceiving of RRI as space for collaborative experimentation, in which all actors engaged and interested in R&I together with societal actors investigate what RRI's first *R* stands for, pRRI presents something like an action plan that is to be implemented.

Tensions in pRRI

No matter what the definitive and complete set of motivations behind pRRI precisely is, pRRI has obviously been formulated to improve R&I and, through that, to add to the solution of environmental, social and economic problems. In that sense, in its ambitions, pRRI arguably resembles other well-known and large-scale schemes for the improvement of the human (and planetary) condition—ventures traditionally undertaken by states (Scott, 1998), but not always successfully.

In his majestic *Seeing Like a State. How Certain Schemes to Improve the Human Condition Have Failed* (1998), James Scott draws a very detailed picture of what has gone wrong in a number of High Modernist planning efforts, including Russian agricultural collectivization and urban planning in Brasilia. In each such case, the aims with which the planners set out were not reached, and instead, social or ecological disaster ensued. Though there is no reason to think pRRI shall suffer a similar faith—which in this context might, for instance, mean that by attempting to steer R&I through RRI policies, basic research is curtailed, knowledge production stymied and radical innovation impeded—neither do we have any reason not to learn from such grandiose failures to steer clear of that faith. To do so, let us first briefly sum up some likenesses between, on the one hand, the familiar disasters elaborated on by Scott, and on the other hand, pRRI.

First, good intentions are at the basis of both. Or at least, there is no reason to think the "actions [by pRRI's advocates are] cynical grabs for power and wealth," as the policymakers at issue clearly appear to be "animated by a genuine desire to improve the human condition" (Scott, 1998)—just as were the planning schemes described by Scott that failed so miserably in their goal to ameliorate man's condition. Second, just like state-planned economies, it is hard to deny that pRRI is a top-down effort that comes from 'visionary intellectuals and planners'—although those employed by the EC are not likely to be as 'guilty of hubris' as were Soviet economists or Brazilian urban planners (Scott, 1998: p. 342). Third, and perhaps most important, we can observe that both Scott's cases and pRRI are rooted in the firm belief that scientific knowledge provides the firmest basis upon which policies can be built. For example, when looking at RRI as a vital element in the EC's strategy to meet a contemporary grand challenge such as demographic ageing, it appears that the latter is targeted with an idea in mind of science and innovation as providing technical fixes. This focus might distract attention away from thinking about dealing with some of the challenges of demographic ageing through, for instance, a reorganization of labour policies. The latter could, for instance, entail such policies as cutting down working hours in order for working people to be able to take care of their elderly parents, or, on the opposite side of the spectrum, creating jobs especially for the elderly to keep them as engaged and fruitful members of society for longer parts of their lives.

Large and pertinent differences between Scott's High Modernist projects and pRRI, however, perhaps weigh heavier than do the aforementioned similarities. We will discuss two of these. First, the European Commission and its Member States do not govern with the 'stick-type' authoritarianism we associate with the Soviet Union, for instance, and hence RRI is not catapulted at those who have a stake in R&I as were the aforementioned planning disasters. Instead of forcing scientists to engage in RRI, those working in R&I are rather induced into becoming more responsible, more in the way of carrots (Dix, 2014). Changing funding schemes[10] (e.g. Horizon2020, SWAFS, MVI, EPSRC and Vinnova) and instituting awards,[11] on top of raising awareness (e.g. through support acts like *RRI Tools*), are means through which RRI is spread.

A second difference has to do with (some of) the science(s) that so much trust is invested in. And this is where we can clearly discern the central tension constitutive of pRRI. For although hope for the improvement of man's condition intrinsic to RRI concerns, to a large extent, life and natural sciences, the governance concept of RRI itself has its roots in various strands of academic thinking and doing that played no role in Brazil's urban planning or Russia's agricultural reorganizations. These include everything from STS to (constructive) *Technology Assessment (TA)*, from the science of science policy to *Ethical, Legal and Social Aspects (ELSA)* research and (more traditional) research ethics, and from the political theory of deliberative democracy to the science of science communication.

The variety of lessons pertinent to RRI that can be drawn up from these fields of research basically point in the same relatively restricted number of directions (which will be elaborated on in the next section).

- For normative democratic, substantial and instrumental reasons, diverse publics should be involved upstream in programming and performing R&I—even if *how* best to organize such engagement is not always a clear-cut issue (see e.g. Wynne, 1993; Owen *et al.*, 2012; Stilgoe *et al.*, 2014; Te Kulve and Rip, 2011).
- Responsible governance systems share responsibilities among a variety of actors, without thereby organizing irresponsibility (Beck, 1995: p. 24).
- On the one hand, governance of R&I should be robust and sufficiently familiar to be compatible with existing arrangements, and on the other hand, it should be adaptable to the unpredictable development and outcomes of R&I.

Arguably, taking on board all these lessons would capacitate one to bypass the mistakes of High Modernism in the context of science and innovation governance. Bruno Latour (2007) succinctly described what all those failures Scott that elaborated on have in common. In Latour's words, they failed because the 'common good' and the 'public good' were not supposed to be produced by experimental and carefully accountable procedures of inquiries. The 'public', the 'common', the 'disinterested' is supposed to be *by nature and once for all*, radically different from the 'private', the 'commercial', the 'selfish', the 'interested'. There are people who claim, because they are in the position of surveying those accounts, that they know what is for the public good without any *additional* empirical work of inquiry about the consequences of their remedies (Latour, 2007).

Part of the very idea of aRRI, of course, is that this mistake should be avoided. From the perspective of aRRI, doing so would entail more than just engaging various unusual suspects in, for instance, R&I agenda-setting, in research practices through midstream-modulation and for ensuring technology uptake or valorization. It would also entail that the very governance framework of RRI itself be opened up to the collective scrutiny of stakeholders in R&I. This would help secure that the public goods that RRI is supposed to serve emerge from empirical experimentation—instead of being presumed known. The tension we see here, though, relates to an often-observed democratic deficit in European policy-making, especially as concerned with so-called 'input legitimacy' (i.e., the democratic accountability of EU institutions to the electorate) (Pollack, 2015: p. 40). It is insufficiently clear how citizen or stakeholder consultation feeds into the decision-making processes that have determined that what is being captured under the rubric of pRRI indeed amounts to delivering socially responsive R&I. Put somewhat provocatively, pRRI is pushed onto the European R&I system and European community without clear indications that this is precisely what wide audiences of societal stakeholders in R&I consider the answer to the societal question for better R&I governance that, for instance, Eurobarometers have revealed.[12]

In the remainder of this chapter, this tension in pRRI will be further investigated. It will be argued, however, that also in the case of pRRI, things are not as bad as they might seem. On the contrary, the thesis will be defended that, if its proponents are to make RRI into a success, they should really nurture pRRI's essential tension.

pRRI's counterpart: aRRI

At the basis of pRRI, we can identify the recognition that R&I not only offers solutions to the major challenges of our time, but at the same time creates new risks, dilemmas and concerns. This insight, however, is not as new as pRRI is. Since the 1960s and 1970s, observations along these lines have led to the proliferation of approaches attempting to take the societal and ethical aspects of science and innovation into account at increasingly earlier stages of the R&I process. Approaches ranged from an early warning system for negative impacts (Smits and Leyten, 1984) to more participatory forms of TA such as constructive TA (Rip *et al.*, 1995; Schot and Rip, 1997), real-time TA (Guston and Sarewitz, 2002), anticipatory governance (Barben *et al.*, 2008) and public and stakeholder engagement (Stirling, 2007; Wilsdon *et al.*, 2005). No less than is the case for aRRI, this is at the foundation of pRRI, too.

But although these initiatives have certainly opened up science and technology for public scrutiny, the focus has often remained on staging discussions regarding possible consequences of science and technology and facilitating the mitigation of their negative impacts. What aRRI offers, in addition to that, is a vision of R&I according to which the scope of assessing R&I should be much broader than such impacts alone.

Thus, not only in R&I policy but also in circles of scholars studying science and innovation in society, predominantly in Europe and the United States, RRI has become a hot topic of late. What distinguishes the RRI discourse from previous academic work concerning such matters as mentioned just now is its encompassing nature and 'activist' spirit: aRRI scholars build on lessons from a very wide variety of research fields pertinent to understanding the science and society interface and do so with the ambition not only of describing *what is*, but of truly making R&I more responsible.

A rapidly increasing number of scholarly accounts of RRI have been published since the term emerged on the scene. Scholars more or less continued the participatory-deliberative turn that was increasingly made from the 1990s onwards. RRI is sketched as a new governance framework to integrate ethical reflection, public engagement and responsive change (Stilgoe *et al.*, 2013). Recent accounts of RRI that have emerged in the scholarly literature involve a common set of interrelated features: (1) a focus on socio-ecological challenges; (2) active engagement of a range of stakeholders; (3) anticipation of problems, solutions and alternatives and reflection on underlying values, assumptions and beliefs; and 4) a willingness to be responsive, act and adapt (Stilgoe *et al.*, 2013; von Schomberg, 2013; Wickson and Carew, 2014).

What is also very clear in the aRRI literature is that it is fairly conceptual (e.g. Ribeiro *et al.*, 2016). Even when claiming to aid in making RRI more amenable to implementation, aRRI texts tend to a large extent to revolve around conceptual issues concerning, for instance, the concept of innovation (Blok and Lemmens, 2015) or the many meanings of 'responsibility' (Pelle and Reber, 2015). In that sense, such texts—and we do not necessarily claim to rise above them or provide an alternative to them with this chapter—run the risk of becoming, through their *disinterested* academic stance, *uninteresting* for policy actors or other change agents in the world of R&I.

The risk that this is indeed the case is probably further increased by the emergence of a veritable community of RRI scholars, for whom the development of ever-more nuanced, detailed and theoretically rich accounts of RRI has become something of an industry in and of itself, and which is perhaps best illustrated with reference to the installation in 2014 of the *Journal of Responsible Innovation*. The risk hereof is, of course, that aRRI never reaches the policy-makers, natural and life scientists, engineers, medical scientists and the like, whose R&I supposedly can and should become (even) more responsible, because the community of aRRI-ers is too busy with its internal communication efforts and associated quality standards. Indeed, although much of the aRRI work certainly strives to avoid the sterility that comes with too much disciplinarity—as witnessed by the journals of (applied) science that it is often published in (e.g., Pelle and Reber, 2015)—the possibility of the emergence of a distinct aRRI discipline sounds to us more like something that might jeopardize RRI than something that might accelerate its normalization.

pRRI versus aRRI

As can already be tentatively gathered from the brief descriptions above, aRRI and pRRI can be seen as differently placed on a number of axes. Each of these will be briefly discussed below.

Top-down versus bottom-up

Just looking at the chronology of publications that together make up the RRI discourse, one sees that RRI is pushed onto the world of R&I by policy much more than that it has emerged as a bottom-up movement by engaged scholars. Thus, the very idea of RRI, as an empty shell, can be said to have emerged as a topic for discussion in a somewhat top-down way. However, the same holds for the *contents* of the idea. For indeed, this form of top-down advocacy can also be recognized in the way in which what it means to do responsible R&I is elaborated in pRRI. For although in pRRI literature, inclusive and deliberative processes are also referred to when explaining what distinguishes RRI from R&I *simpliciter*, in the EC definition of RRI given above, it is manifest that pRRI already pre-defines that R&I should contribute to the EC's keys if it is to count as RRI. In other words, to a reasonable extent, it is already beyond negotiation what the so-called 'values, needs and expectations' of the European people *are*.

Much of the aRRI literature is critical of both ways of top-down interventions. With regard to the first and more overarching issue, it has, for instance, been argued that through this mode of governance, the politics *of* and *in* deliberation are being neglected (van Oudheusden, 2014; Lövbrand *et al.*, 2010). aRRI criticism of the top-down push of the contents of 'responsibility' in the form of the EC-defined *keys*, which in fact are normative agendas beyond deliberation, will be discussed below.

Before we turn to that, though, a not-so-minor qualification concerning this way of relative placement of aRRI and pRRI is in place. For following the line of reasoning, section 4 ended with, it could well be argued, that aRRI is not at all a bottom-up alternative to the top-down approach to RRI that pRRI stands for. Rather, aRRI exists in parallel to the R&I that it studies and aspires to impact on. As it is, it is more in what it argues for than in what it factually realizes that much aRRI work can be described as bottom-up, and it would take (more) natural and life scientists, engineers and the like who *practice* RRI and write about it academically for aRRI to truly make aRRI pRRI's bottom-up alternative.

Universalist versus contextualized

In the policy literature, we see that a straightforwardly optimistic approach to RRI can be found, which simultaneously is very explicit and universalist about what it means to be responsible—see the definition of RRI cited in section 1. 'Doing' engagement, gender, open access, ethics and science education, in this view, is practicing RRI. Full stop. The pRRI concept of RRI gives us RRI's constitution, so to say.

Central to many of the academic publications on RRI, on the other hand, is a critical analysis of what RRI is and what RRI might mean for the improvement of the responsiveness of the R&I system to societal needs or challenges. More than a once-and-for-all definition of what constitutes RRI, aRRI gives us ideas on what we should do to better understand the meaning of responsibility in the context of R&I. And indeed, this entails that, from aRRI, some criticism can be heard concerning pRRI. For instance, regarding the type of normative orientation often found in policy documents, Macnaghten and Chilvers. (2014) write that

> Such attempts at universalism can produce unhelpfully thin normative frameworks which may mask, under the guise of universalism, culturally specific narratives regarding what the full range of stakeholders in different cultural contexts judge to be the aspects of innovation processes and outcomes that matter to them.
>
> (p. 196)

The alternative would be to be more open and responsive to locally identified and prioritized needs in articulating what constitutes a societal challenge R&I should address and what constitutes the right way of doing so.

In the making versus once-and-for-all

A further way in which the internal complexity of pRRI plays out is that, with its once-and-for-all definition of what societal responsiveness looks like, it foregoes the fact that not only is scientific knowledge constantly changing, but so too are the societies whose values, needs and expectations R&I is supposed to answer to. With its focus on ways of organizing inclusive R&I processes, again, this is less visible in aRRI.

Making sense of these distinctions

Arguably, most of these discrepancies between aRRI and pRRI above can be explained in terms of two more parameters, along which the two can be differentiated—one somewhat philosophical, and one very down-to-earth. To start with the latter, it helps to see aRRI and pRRI as apart in terms of their focus point. pRRI is generally much more focused on *outcomes* or *impacts*, whereas aRRI acknowledges that the *processes* through which these are achieved are at least as important and indeed largely definitive of its success—at least insofar as the definition of what desired outcomes and impacts *are* should be part of what responsibly undertaken R&I processes lead to.

As for the more philosophical parameter: to make sense of these differences collectively, it helps to interpret them in terms of a distinction originally developed in the context of the history and philosophy of science to describe the different roles 'things' can play in an experimental system (Rheinberger, 1997)—i.e., we propose to rephrase this issue in terms of Rheinberger's distinction between 'epistemic things' and 'technical things'. These concepts were crafted in the context of Rheinberger's investigations into the history and epistemology of molecular genetics, but arguably they are also suitable for understanding the science *of* science and innovation and the policy *concerning* science and innovation.

On first sight, epistemic things may appear simply as 'things' in the colloquial sense of the word—examples Rheinberger discusses include physical structures, chemical reactions and biological functions. Such things, however, are epistemic things only to the extent that they are defined by what has been called a "constitutive vagueness" (Klaassen, 2013). Epistemic things "embody what one does not yet know" (Rheinberger, 1997: p. 28), and in this role, they are the objects of scientific research and "have the precarious status of being absent in their experimental presence" (ibidem). This distinguishes them from the things of our ordinary life and experience.[13] As we see it, only as long as we agree that RRI, too, is only experimentally present will it be capable of living up to its promises. For that, its interpretative flexibility is more of an asset than an obstacle.

In Rheinberger's view, something that at one point in time was an epistemic thing can come to function as a 'technical thing.' To make this happen, epistemic things have to become sufficiently stable—so stable that they can become part of the armoury of experimental systems. Temperature is a good example again: once a matter of much scientific controversy, its stabilized and standardized measurement later became a routine part of all sorts of experimental systems.

When epistemic things are sufficiently stabilized, they are no longer 'unknowns,' but rather become things about which all sorts of facts can be stated uncontestably. In the context of our present discussion, pRRI can be said to be used as a technical thing, albeit in the context of science governance rather than in science practice. As we have been arguing here, however, it is vital to RRI that pRRI continues to have to same constitutive and productive vagueness that characterizes epistemic things. Put differently, our suggestion is that in order for RRI to succeed as a governance framework for the promotion of environmentally, socially and economically valuable R&I, pRRI should never diverge too far from aRRI, because its own interpretative flexibility—in the sense elaborated above—is vital to RRI's potential success. Even in its role as a technical thing, thus, RRI should still *also* continue in its role as an epistemic thing. Only then can it fulfil its role as a catalyst for continuous learning and a driving force of responsible R&I.

Releasing the tension

In this section, we display how, in the FP7 project *RRI Tools*, we have attempted to get the most out of pRRI and aRRI by releasing the tension in our work towards a conceptualization of RRI. As a preparatory step, the next section first briefly describes the project.

RRI Tools

RRI Tools, a support action funded under the European Commission's Science in Society program of the Seventh Framework Programme, aimed to promote RRI among five different stakeholder groups involved in R&I—researchers, policy-makers, science educators, Civil Society Organizations (CSO's) and business and industry. In order to succeed in doing so, *RRI Tools* built a toolkit with various types of instruments that can be used by these stakeholders in R&I to add the extra R of responsibility.

RRI Tools had a duration of three years, and in these three years it attempted simultaneously to preach RRI, and to practice what it preached. The project was carried out by a multidisciplinary consortium of 26 partners working in 19 so-called *hubs* and was overseen by an Advisory Board with members whose expertise immediately relates to the RRI keys identified by the EC. Every hub was active in one to three countries and together the19 hubs covered 30 European countries. With a budget of 6.9 million Euro, the hubs advanced RRI and established a European *community of practice* that brought together people and organizations engaged in R&I.

It was *RRI Tools*' task to provide stakeholders in R&I with tools for learning about and implementing RRI, and for training stakeholders in using these tools and in *doing* RRI. Theoretically, this could have meant that little more would have been done than setting up working groups to make an inventory of what tools were available for furthering the aforementioned RRI keys, and to go on promoting and training on these. Although that would probably have been relatively simple, it is not all that has been done. Instead, *RRI Tools* itself tried—to the extent permitted by constraints, including the areas of manpower, time, capacities and project mandate—to engage in an RRI process, finding out about the path we were walking on as we went along. The next section illustrates this process.

RRI Tools as an experimental attempt at understanding and fostering RRI, responsibly

Four main steps characterized *RRI Tools*' methodology to find out what responsible R&I means in concept and in practice. Although these individual steps were largely taken consecutively, they allowed for an iterative trajectory towards our contemporary understanding of RRI.

The first step was to develop a working definition of RRI. An early version of the definition was the result of an extensive study of both policy documents and scientific literature on RRI at that time (i.e., 2013). The initially proposed definition combines ideas well-represented in Von Schomberg (2011) and Owen *et al.* (2012) and was optimized during meetings with consortium partners and experts in (aspects of) RRI, including members of our Advisory Board. It ran as follows:

> Responsible Research and Innovation is a dynamic, iterative process by which all stakeholders involved in the R&I practice become mutually responsive and share responsibility regarding both the outcomes and process requirements.
>
> (*RRI Tools*, 2014)

To give this definition more substance, we then identified four clusters of process requirements and a tripartite categorization of types of RRI outcomes, again based on both academic and grey literature as well as expert consultation. Box 4.1 presents brief descriptions of all four process requirements; Box 4.2 does the same for RRI outcomes. Especially in the third type of outcome that we distinguished, one recognizes that EC policy was taken very seriously in our work, as *RRI Tools* adopted the EC's prioritization of challenges that R&I should address.

As for the keys defined by the EC, our thoughts were that by classifying everything from ethics to gender and from science education to open access in one and the same category of key dimensions, the EC suggests that they all relate similarly to each other and to R&I, and that each should be addressed in a similar way. However, the keys defined by the EC differ from each other considerably. For instance, ethics is something that applies much more generically and structurally to R&I processes than does open access. The very predicate of *key* suggests that when doing R&I while taking into account the key dimensions, this will automatically lead to RRI practices—as if they are literally the key to unlocking RRI.

There is, however, little reason to agree on this. If one looks at science education, for instance, one immediately observes that communicating about and teaching science can be done, and in fact is often done, in ways that do not reflect the standards of and general motivation behind RRI. And gender is perhaps best thought of as something like a mind-set crosscutting RRI.[14] For these and comparable reasons, we think that the EC's keys are better thought of as *policy agendas*. Approaching them as such enables us to deal with the differences between them in a constructive way. That is to say, without equating RRI with the policy agendas, we can still recognize that they each have their own RRI potential, and are conducive to realizing RRI.

Box 4.1 RRI's process requirements

Diversity and inclusion

Diverse and inclusive RRI processes call for the involvement of a wide range of stakeholders in all phases of R&I—from agenda-setting to implementation. Optimization of diversity and inclusion can be argued for on normative democratic grounds, instrumental grounds having to do with building public trust and acceptance of outcomes and impacts of R&I, as well as substantial reasons concerning R&I quality.

Openness and transparency

Openness and transparency are conditions for accountability, liability and thus responsibility. This is, among other things, an important aspect for the public to establish trust in science and innovation.

Anticipation and reflexivity

Anticipation concerns both understanding how the present dynamics of R&I practices shape the future, and envisioning the future. This enables R&I to act on future challenges. In order to act adequately and be open to changes in direction, reflexivity is also required. This reflexivity implies learning about the definitions of the problem(s) at issue, commitments, practices and individual and institutional values, assumptions and routines.

Responsiveness and adaptive change

Responsiveness means responding to emerging knowledge, perspectives, views and norms. Responsiveness is a condition for adaptive change. RRI requires a capacity to change or shape existing routines of thought and behaviour but also the overarching organizational structures and systems in response to changing circumstances, new insights and stakeholder and public values.

Box 4.2 RRI outcomes

Learning outcomes

RRI should lead to empowered, responsible actors across the whole range of our socio-technical systems (citizens, scientists, policymakers, NGOs, CSOs, educators, businesses and innovators). Structures and organizations where these actors function should create the opportunity for and provide support to actors to be responsible, ensuring that RRI becomes (and remains) a solid and continuous reality.

R&I outcomes

RRI practices should strive for ethically acceptable, sustainable and socially desirable outcomes. Solutions are found in opening up science through continuous meaningful deliberation with societal actors. In the end, the incorporation of societal voices in R&I will lead to relevant applications of science.

Solutions to societal challenges

Today's societies face several challenges. The European Commission has formulated seven 'Grand Challenges' as one of the three main pillars of the Horizon 2020 programme. In order to support European policy, R&I endeavours should contribute to finding solutions for these societal challenges, which are:

1 Health, demographic change and wellbeing
2 Food security, sustainable agriculture and forestry, marine and maritime and inland water research and the bio-economy
3 Secure, clean and efficient energy
4 Smart, green and integrated transport
5 Climate action, environment, resource efficiency and raw materials
6 Europe in a changing world—inclusive, innovative and reflective societies
7 Secure societies—protecting the freedom and security of Europe and its citizens.

Because the conceptualization of RRI should not only be appealing to experts in RRI but to all R&I stakeholders, the second step entailed that the proposed definition was scrutinized by a wide range of stakeholders during 27 Stakeholder Consultation Workshops held during the fall and winter of 2014 in 22 European countries, with a total of 411 participants.[15] From these workshops, we learned, among many other things, that many stakeholders required more practicable guidelines on how to operationalize RRI and that it should be explicated that RRI requires institutional and operational changes on many levels of action.

The third and fourth steps in our work on RRI were taken in close harmony, and to a large degree answer this need expressed by stakeholders during the workshops. These steps entailed the formulation of criteria for RRI process requirements in Deliverable 1.3 (Kupper et al., 2015a), making these much more accessible to work with, as well as a test for those criteria in the form of the composition of a catalogue of good RRI practices (Kupper et al., 2015b). As for the criteria, we again built on academic literature in the process dimensions we had identified in our working definition, inputs from the Stakeholder Consultation Workshops and feedback from *RRI Tools* consortium partners and from RRI experts in the Netherlands. The catalogue of good practices we built using existing R&I practices in Europe were already regarded as RRI by consortium partners and participants in the aforementioned workshops held across Europe. The guiding ideas behind this step were that lessons learned in these practices could help improve the proposed definition of RRI and that analysing promising and good practices in RRI could help the translation of abstract notions into practical standards, tools and training modules. The final catalogue of good examples of RRI practices also included analyses that fed back into our initial conceptualization of RRI. In Box 4.3, one finds a concise description of the methodology used to develop this catalogue.

Box 4.3 Building a catalogue of good practices in RRI

Phase I: invitations

In June 2014, a training on RRI for *RRI Tools*' Hub members took place. Here it was collectively decided that, as part of the work to be done towards the organization of the Stakeholder Consultation Workshops planned for the autumn of 2014, all workshop participants would be prompted to suggest what they conceived to be a promising practice in doing RRI. Also, the Hubs were asked to seek and suggest promising practices. Hub coordinators made a selection of about ten RRI practices that were described in some detail and sent to the Athena Institute for analysis.

Phase II: first selection

Subsequently, the Athena Institute analysed the descriptions of the promising practices sent in and discussed these with the Hub coordinators who had made the initial selection. Based on process requirements and challenges covered, selections were then made in dialogue between the Athena Institute and the individual Hub coordinators. The selected practices were analysed more thoroughly using an online survey.

Phase III: data collection

Hubs filled in an online survey for the selected practices using SurveyMonkey. The design of the survey was based on the working definition used in the *RRI Tools* project. Basic practical information about the practices was gathered, as well as anything relevant to estimate the practices' RRI-potential. E.g., the relation to the EC keys was queried (i.e., ethics, gender, governance, open access, public engagement and science education). In many cases, Hubs used the survey as an interview guide and filled in the questions with the direct help of people involved in the specific practices (see annex 2). The survey was open from January 26th to April 30th 2015, during which 51 surveys were completed.

Phase IV: data analysis

Analysis of the survey data proceeded as follows:

a Structuring. To analyse the 51 received and completed surveys, the project details of the practices were ordered in a table: name of the practice, leading organization, country where the practice is implemented, language in which information about the practice is available, starting date, (expected) end date and type of practice.
b Analysis. The good practices were analysed with regard to:

    1 Each of the four pairs of process requirements. For this, the quality criteria formulated for the process requirements in *RRI Tools* Deliverable 1.3 were used. Each individual criterion of the process requirements received a mark representing any of the markings *business as usual*, *on its way*, *promising*, *good* or *exemplary*.
    2 The outcomes (i.e., learning outcomes, R&I outcomes and solutions to societal challenges). The three types of outcomes were valued in a similar way to the process requirements: *absent*, *formulated in the aims*, *explicitly addressed*, *reached* or *evaluated*.

c Additional considerations involved in the final selection of practices:

    1 Whether or not practices (aim to) contribute to solutions for grand challenges
    2 The extent to which practices address both the research and the innovation component of RRI
    3 The level of information available.

To minimize researcher bias, four researchers were trained in advance of engaging in these steps. Each analysis was checked by one other team member. In the case of disagreement, analyses were discussed until researchers reached a shared interpretation. This collaborative analysis by four researchers from the Athena Institute resulted in the exclusion of 20 out of 51 practices.

Phase V: results

Thirty-one practices were included in the Catalogue. Short summaries of each practice are provided herein, as are project details, most interesting lessons learned, their relationships with EC keys, grand challenges, process requirements and information about the outcomes of the practice. The texts and information presented in the Catalogue have been approved by the Hub coordinators and representatives of the good practices selected.

Phase VI: analysis II—conclusion and discussion

Several lessons were drawn from the analysis of this collection of practices. Most pertinent in the present context are the conclusions that practices do not (have to) incorporate all RRI processes and outcomes to be considered RRI, that soft skills are vital to engaging in RRI and that including only a pre-defined set of societal challenges as a criterion for societal relevance is too narrow.

The many analytical steps we went through as we took the steps elaborated on above have motivated us to slightly adjust our conceptualization of RRI. Also, discussions with the Advisory Board played into this, as the Advisory Board stimulated us to devote more explicit attention in our conceptualization of RRI to the keys the EC has identified as being central to it.

The core idea that distinguishes Responsible R&I from R&I *simpliciter* is that the starting point of the former is the realization that science and technology have an impact on the lives of all of us, and not just on those working in R&I or explicitly and knowingly using R&I for achieving their own goals. Given this realization, in RRI, R&I is done with an eye to *societal challenges*, and inclusive and deliberative processes to query what those challenges are and what values are at the basis of the required solutions to them are vital to this. In this sense, RRI stands for a kind of *democratization* of R&I, in which through so-called hybrid forums (Callon *et al*., 2009) space is made for technical deliberation with stakeholders of all types.

Thus, as a result of the iterative investigative and analytic processes we have gone through in the *RRI Tools* project, we can now conceptualize RRI as

- a trait of the collectives involved in doing, implementing and, to an extent, using R&I
- that pertains to such collectives when R&I practices aim for *the right outcomes* (i.e., those that help solve complex societal problems) and
- on condition that those practices incorporate a certain measure of diversity and inclusion, deliberation, openness, anticipation and reflection, responsiveness and adaptive change and
- taking place in an environment that is conducive to responsible behaviour in the first place—i.e., an environment in which the policy agendas (or the EC's keys) are heeded.

RRI, in other words, is all about deliberating on ends, means and wanted and unwanted consequences of R&I among a wide variety of stakeholders, in such a way that R&I delivers ethically acceptable, environmentally sustainable and socially desirable outcomes and innovations, the implementation of which helps solve the challenges society faces. In this reconceptualization of RRI, the four dimensions of responsible R&I processes we classified earlier are still central, as are the learning outcomes and ethical, sustainable and socially desirable R&I outcomes. But it is more explicitly acknowledged that RRI requires institutional and operational changes on various levels of action and that what constitutes socially desirable outcomes should not exclusively be specified in terms of the EC's Grand Challenges. What is socially desirable is something that inclusive R&I practices are to tell us, rather than something being decided up front. In this novel conceptualization, the EC's keys receive a more central place, too, be it that they are framed as policy agendas, the deliverance of which is conditional for engaging in RRI today, and that an open mind should be kept as regards other possible agendas that might emerge in the future. Each of the EC's keys gives us something like a normative baseline, a way of stating conditions that somehow have to be met on a systemic level in order for R&I to be able to take the shape of RRI, to become responsible throughout. But rather than implying that doing RRI equals furthering these agendas, this implies that furthering these agendas is a condition for truly responsible RRI processes to be practicable.

Conclusion

The first public sign of EC support for RRI, according to Owen *et al.* (2012), ran as follows:

> Research and innovation must respond to the needs and ambitions of society, reflect its values and be responsible… our duty as policy makers (is) to shape a governance framework that encourages responsible research and innovation.
> (Marie Geoghegan-Quinn, cited in Owen *et al.* (2012): p. 753)

In our view, this is a better conceptualization of RRI than the one that is now featured on the EC website. The reason it is so much better is that it is less specific and restrictive and more interpretatively flexible. Simultaneously, it succeeds in articulating the distinctive feature of RRI by stating that science and innovation are to have a positive impact on society and to be consistent with societal values if they are to be eligible for carrying the predicate 'responsible'. The interpretative flexibility characterizing the view of RRI given here suffers less from the tension that threatens to stymie pRRI—for this conceptualization leaves open much more space for defining what the needs, values and ambitions are which R&I is to contribute to. What we have argued throughout the chapter is that what the governance framework encouraging RRI should further specify are not primarily the ends that are supposed to constitute the solution to societal problems, but rather the means requisite to meeting those societal needs.

That being said, it has to be acknowledged that pRRI has much going for it. Its focus on impact, even if perhaps too much filled in qua substance, is certainly a strength. And the same indubitably holds for the institutional support it has. Nonetheless, we can only express our hope that the latter does not weigh in pRRI's advantage when it comes to bringing the interpretative flexibility thus far inherent to RRI to an end.

RRI Tools, on the other hand, could potentially play a pivotal role as regards the realization of RRI and in bringing interpretative closure. For indeed, given the functional role the EC envisioned for the project (i.e., providing the community of stakeholders in R&I with tools for thinking about and training and engaging in RRI), it is arguably in a better position than anyone else to do so. It is our hope that, if *RRI Tools* indeed proves to be capable of fulfilling that role, what will be implemented and become stable is an RRI that is itself construed as never more than the temporary product of a continuous process of experimentation, as something akin to a continuous and collective experimental learning process in which technical things will always also remain epistemic things. If RRI becomes what we envisage it to be, then it ought never to appear as a ship in a bottle, but always at best as one in the process of entering it.

Notes

1 https://ec.europa.eu/research/swafs/pdf/pub_public_engagement/responsible-research-and-innovation-leaflet_en.pdf.
2 The Rome Declaration on Responsible Research and Innovation in Europe (2014) translates this to a call for action on many fronts. See: https://ec.europa.eu/research/swafs/pdf/rome_declaration_RRI_final_21_November.pdf.
3 For instance, the MVI-funding scheme from the Netherlands Organization for Scientific Research comes to mind (with MVI standing for Societally Responsible Innovation).
4 Moreover, this is not the only tension in RRI. See MacNaghten *et al.* (2015, pp. 195–196) for the paradox of shared versus individual responsibility and their complex relationship with hierarchical distributions that RRI embodies.
5 http://www.rri-tools.eu/.
6 Although this article presents interpretations of how the *RRI Tools* project has been organized and what it has resulted in, its contents are not themselves a product of or mandated by *RRI Tools*. The authors of this article, though indebted to all they have worked with in the context of this project, take full responsibility for the claims made here. This especially concerns the conceptualization of RRI as it is presented at the end of section 6.
7 Again, see https://ec.europa.eu/research/swafs/pdf/pub_public_engagement/responsible-research-and-innovation-leaflet_en.pdf.
8 See http://ec.europa.eu/programmes/horizon2020/en/h2020-section/science-and-society; last accessed 27 November 2016.
9 See, for example, Lund Declaration 2009, Rome Declaration 2014 and EC 2015.
10 Horizon 2020 (https://ec.europa.eu/programmes/horizon2020/), SWAFS (http://ec.europa.eu/research/swafs/index.cfm), MVI (http://www.nwo.nl/en/research-and-results/programmes/responsible+innovation), EPSRC (https://www.epsrc.ac.uk/research/framework/) and Vinnova (http://www.vinnova.se/en/).
11 For example, the European Foundations Award for RRI: http://www.rri-tools.eu/european-foundations-award-for-rri.
12 See especially the 'Eurobarometer qualitative study Public opinion on future innovations, science and technology' (2015): http://ec.europa.eu/public_opinion/archives/quali/ql_futureofscience_en.pdf and 'Special Eurobarometer 401. Responsible Research and Innovation (RRI), science and technology' (2013): http://ec.europa.eu/public_opinion/archives/ebs/ebs_401_en.pdf.
13 Moreover, they also differ from ordinary things in that they are constituted by what Rheinberger calls 'experimental systems' (i.e., the smallest unit in terms of which scientific research can be understood). Experimental systems, in turn, are built up of

technologies, techniques, tacit and explicit knowledge, assumptions, theories, skills and so on.

14 As many have argued, when keeping to the logic of pRRI, gender should perhaps be replaced by a more general notion of diversity, such that in addition to all the complex realities of gender, those of, for instance, social economic, religious, and ethnic diversity are also taken into account in R&I, both qua personnel and qua content.

15 Not only *RRI Tools*' working definition of RRI was discussed with participants of the workshops, but also any needs, obstacles and opportunities they envisioned in practicing RRI (Smallman et al., 2015).

References

Barben, D., Fisher, E., Selin, C. and Guston, D. H. (2008). Anticipatory Governance of Nanotechnology: Foresight, Engagement, and Integration. In: E. J. Hackett, O. Amsterdamska, M. E. Lynch and J. Wajcman (Eds.), *Handbook of Science and Technology Studies*. Third edition. Cambridge (MA): MIT Press, pp. 979–1000.

Beck, U. (1995). *Ecological Politics in an Age of Risk*. Cambridge: Polity Press.

Blok, V. and Lemmens, P. (2015). The Emerging Concept of Responsible Innovation. Three Reasons Why It Is Questionable and Calls for a Radical Transformation of the Concept of Innovation. In: *Responsible Innovation 2*. Dordrecht: Springer International Publishing, pp. 19–35.

Callon, M., Lascoumes, P. and Barthe, Y. (2009). *Acting in an Uncertain World*. Cambridge (MA): MIT press.

Dix, G. (2014). *Governing by carrot and stick: A genealogy of the incentive*. PhD thesis, Amsterdam: Ipskamp.

EC. (2015). Horizon 2020 Work Programme 2014–2015, 16. *Science with and for Society* (revised). Retrieved 17 March 2016, from http://ec.europa.eu/research/participants/data/ref/h2020/wp/2014_2015/main/h2020-wp1415-swfs_en.pdf.

Guston, D. and Sarewitz, D. (2002). Real-time technology assessment. *Technology in Society*, 24(1–2), pp. 93–109.

Klaassen, P. (2013). Hans-Jörg Rheinberger. In: R. Celikates, R. Gabriëls, J. F. Hartle, P. Lemmens and T. Lijster (Eds.), *De nieuwe Duitse filosofie : denkers en thema's voor de 21e eeuw*. Amsterdam: Boom, pp. 388–396.

Kupper, F., Klaassen, P., Rijnen, M., Vermeulen, S. and Broerse, J. (2015a). Deliverable 1.3. Report on the quality criteria of good practice standards in RRI. Available online at: http://tinyurl.com/h29ml5n.

Kupper, F., Klaassen, P., Rijnen, M., Vermeulen, S., Woertman, R. and Broerse, J. (2015b). Deliverable 1.4. Catalogue of good RRI practices. Available online at: http://tinyurl.com/z8c9x7d.

Latour, B. (2007). How to think like a state. Unpublished manuscript. Available online at: http://www.bruno-latour.fr/sites/default/files/P-133-LA%20HAYE-QUEEN.pdf.

Lövbrand, E., Pielke, R. and Beck, S. (2010). A democracy paradox in studies of science and technology. *Science, Technology and Human Values*, 36(4), pp. 474–496.

Lund Declaration. (2009). Conference: New Worlds – New Solutions. Research and Inno vation as a Basis for Developing Europe in a Global Context. Lund, Sweden, 7–8 July 2009. Available online at: https://www.vr.se/download/18.249c421a1504ad6d28144942/1444391884365/Lund_Declaration_2009.pdf.

Macnaghten, P. and Chilvers, J. (2014). The future of science governance: Publics, policies, practices. *Environment and Planning C: Government and Policy*, 32(3), pp. 530–548.

Owen, R., Macnaghten, P. and Stilgoe, J. (2012). Responsible research and innovation: From science in society to science for society, with society. *Science and Public Policy*, 39(6), pp. 751–760.

Pollack, M. (2015). Theorizing EU Policy-Making. In: H. Wallace, M. A. Pollack and A. R. Young (Eds.), *Policy-Making in the European Union*. Oxford: Oxford University Press.

Pelle, S. and Reber, B. (2015). Responsible innovation in the light of moral responsibility. *Journal on Chain and Network Science*, 15(2), pp. 107–117.

Rheinberger, H. J. (1997). *Toward a History of Epistemic Things: Synthesizing Proteins in the Test Tube*. Stanford, CA: Stanford University Press.

Ribeiro, B. E., Smith, R. D. and Millar, K. (2016). A mobilising concept? Unpacking academic representations of responsible research and innovation. *Science and Engineering Ethics*, 23(1), pp. 81–103.

Rip, A., Misa, T. J. and Schot, J. (1995). Constructive Technology Assessment: A New Paradigm for Managing Technology in Society. In: A. Rip, T. J. Misa and J. Schot (Eds.), *Managing Technology in Society* London: Pinter Publishers, pp. 1–14.

Rome Declaration on Responsible Research and Innovation in Europe (2014). Retrieved 17 March 2016, from https://ec.europa.eu/research/swafs/pdf/rome_declaration_RRI_final_21_November.pdf.

RRI Tools (2014). Deliverable 1.1. Policy Brief. RRI Tools: Towards RRI in action. Available online at: http://tinyurl.com/j2tlup5.

Schot, J. and Rip, A. (1997). The past and future of constructive technology assessment. *Technological Forecasting and Social Change*, 54(2), pp. 251–268.

Scott, J. C. (1998). *Seeing Like a State: How Certain Schemes to Improve the Human Condition Have Failed*. Cambridge (MA): Yale University Press.

Smallman, M., Lomme, K. and Faullimmel, N. (2015c). Deliverable 2.2. Report on the analysis of opportunities, obstacles and needs of the stakeholder groups in RRI practices in Europe. Available online at: http://tinyurl.com/jtcbk8w.

Smits, R. and Leyten, J. (1984). "Technology Assessment: Op Zoek Naar een Bruikbare Aanpak. 1. Mogelijkheden en Beperkingen. Den Haag: Staatsuitgeverij.

Stilgoe, J., Owen, R. and Macnaghten, P. (2013). Developing a framework for responsible innovation. *Research Policy*, 42(9), pp. 1568–1580.

Stilgoe, J., Lock, S. J. and Wilsdon, J. (2014). Why should we promote public engagement with science? *Public Understanding of Science*, 23(1), pp. 4–15.

Stirling, A. (2007). A general framework for analysing diversity in science, technology and society. *Journal of the Royal Society*, Interface/the Royal Society, 4(15), pp. 707–719.

Te Kulve, H. and Rip, A. (2011). Constructing productive engagement: Pre-engagement tools for emerging technologies. *Science and Engineering Ethics*, 17(4), pp. 699–714.

Van Oudheusden, M. (2014). Where are the politics in responsible innovation? European governance, technology assessments, and beyond. *Journal of Responsible Innovation*, 1(1), pp. 67–86.

Von Schomberg, R. (2011). The Quest for the "Right" Impacts of Science and Technology. An Outlook Towards a Framework for Responsible Research and Innovation. In: M. Dusseldorp and R. Beecroft (Eds.), *Technikfolgen abschätzen lehren. Bildungspotenziale transdisziplinärer Methoden*. Wiesbaden: Springer Verlag.

Von Schomberg, R. (2013). A Vision of Responsible Research and Innovation. In: R. Owen, J. Bessant and M. Heintz (Eds.), *Responsible Innovation: Managing the Responsible Emergence of Science and Innovation in Society*. West Sussex: John Wiley and Sons Ltd., pp. 51–74.

Wickson, F. and Carew, A. L. (2014). Quality criteria and indicators for responsible research and innovation: learning from transdisciplinarity. *Journal of Responsible Innovation*, 1(3), pp. 254–273.
Wilsdon, J., Wynne, B. and Stilgoe, J. (2005). *The Public Value of Science: Or how to ensure that science really matters*. London: Demos.
Wynne, B. (1993). Public uptake of science: a case for institutional reflexivity. *Public Understanding of Science*, 2(4), pp. 321–337.

5 Ever deeper research and innovation governance?

Assessing the uptake of RRI in member states' research and innovation programmes

John Pearson

Introduction

This chapter investigates the possibilities for the European Commission to encourage European member states to implement Responsible Research and Innovation in their own research and innovation governance structures.

The chapter has three main aims: to outline and make more explicit some of the reasons for encouraging the member states to take up RRI, to provide a survey of some of the existing measures for implementing RRI among some member states and to argue for a better theoretical framework to be used in the process of encouraging the implementation of RRI.

The structure of the chapter corresponds to these three main aims: after an introductory discussion of the European Union's strategy regarding RRI at the member-state level, three subsequent sections provide an outline of the reasons for encouraging the member states to adopt RRI, a survey of the existing research systems at the member-state level and an argument for a more coherent theoretical framework for the institutionalisation of RRI across the EU and member-state levels.

European strategy?

Since the Rome Declaration of 2014 (Council of the European Union 2014), the European Union's official position on RRI has become somewhat more clear and explicit. The declaration, made as part of the Italian Presidency of the Council of the European Union, provides an explicit call on European Institutions, *Member States*, Regional Authorities and Research and Innovation Funding Organisations to build capacity for RRI. Specifically, the declaration calls on these different actors to build capacity for RRI through a number of different measures (including securing resources and building networks of existing initiatives), and at the same time to review and adapt metrics for research and innovation (Council of the European Union 2014).

Despite this statement of general aims, it is harder to identify a precise overall strategy with regard to encouraging RRI among member states. One plausible possibility is that the Commission is following a more general approach that some commentators have identified, namely to operate on the assumption that the positive connotations of the RRI concept are by themselves enough to (perhaps gently) encourage wider adoption of RRI-type initiatives beyond the Commission's own programmes. As Owen, Macnaghten and Stilgoe put it, with regard to RRI, "As a term it seems hard to argue against – few would argue for irresponsible research and innovation" (Owen, Macnaghten and Stilgoe 2012, 755)" Adopting a programme that is defined in terms of a normative concept – responsibility – that few could reject seems to be a move that should by itself encourage member states to follow the Commission's lead and develop their own programmes. However, as some commentators have argued, this general strategy is not without its problems. More specifically, as van Oudheusden argues in a paper on the politics of RRI (Van Oudheusden 2014), there seems to be both a general tendency in RRI as an overall framework and within individual RRI initiatives to place an emphasis on normatively positive concepts (such as deliberation, participation, co-operation and collaboration) but not to pursue the definition and elaboration of such concepts.

Van Oudheusden goes on to identify two major risks connected with this approach (Van Oudheusden 2014, 80–81): first, there is a risk that the appeal to generally acceptable normative concepts may serve to mask less positive phenomena such as conflicts, disruptive behaviour, domination and exploitation of power inequalities. Masking these less positive elements of co-ordination and collaboration processes carries the risk that there will not be adequate mechanisms to manage them when they occur.[1] The second risk is that, by appealing to positive normative concepts and terminology, RRI initiatives will fall into assumptions about the meaning and content of those terms and thus take their meaning for granted. This in turn entails the risk that explicit criteria and standards for measuring the success of the initiatives will be difficult to define. It also raises the possible risk that participants in RRI programmes will feel compelled to accept (implicit or explicit) goals of those programmes rather than approaching RRI on their own terms, contributing to the definition of the basic terms of engagement, and potentially broadening the agenda. In brief summary, van Oudheusden's key point is that the use of apparently acceptable normative terms to motivate participation in RRI programmes may ultimately be counterproductive if it masks potential conflicts, if it prevents the definition of clearer goals and aims or if it leads to an implicit imposition of a particular agenda. These risks may not be insurmountable, but it is helpful to acknowledge them and bear them in mind in the subsequent implementation and assessments of RRI.

Bearing this key point in mind, the remainder of this section attempts to develop some possible outline arguments that could justify the further extension of RRI programmes to the member-state level. The aim is not to provide a full justification of such a policy approach, or to provide a full specification of the normative and other assumptions that might underpin such an approach. Instead, the aim is to initiate further discussion on the possible justifications for such an approach so that other contributors can criticise, develop, extend or add to the outline arguments that are presented here.

Key arguments for extending RRI to member state level

Why would EU member states want to adopt RRI at the national level? This section identifies the key reasons for doing so: mutual learning (adopting RRI would allow the EU and its member states to learn from one another's experiences of innovation governance); parallel issues (the concerns addressed by RRI are applicable at member-state level as well as at the EU level – this is especially the case for the public rejection of certain innovations); creating a common language (converging frameworks for research and innovation governance could make communication and diplomacy around research and innovation easier); and uneven member-state performance.

Mutual learning: One of the most compelling arguments for extending RRI to member-state level is that doing so would strengthen the opportunities for mutual learning between the Commission and member states with regard to research and innovation governance. Mutual learning approaches[2] build on the basic idea that it is possible to make a virtue of the diversity of political and institutional structures within the EU by treating this diversity as a laboratory for institutional and governance innovations. On this view, one of the key functions of the main EU institutions, and perhaps above all of the European Commission, is to serve as a communication and dissemination point for experiments and innovations in governance, both to facilitate learning among member states and to enable the Commission itself to learn in order to fulfil its role as a form of executive branch of the European Union. Indeed, RRI itself forms a limited example of this type of mutual learning.

The intellectual origins of RRI lie to a significant extent in research and innovation governance practices and theories that were developed and applied in the Netherlands, partly through different variants of technology assessment. Technology assessment came to play a very significant role in the methodological and theoretical and institutional development of RRI at the level of the Commission, with several influential figures in the Commission drawing on technology assessment as part of the development of the initial conceptual framework for RRI – see, in particular, Von Schomberg (2013) and Fisher and Rip (2013). Directly prior to the development of the European Commission's RRI programme, the Dutch national research and innovation funding institution (the NWO) began to adopt its own new research and innovation framework – *Maatschappelijk Verantwoord Innoveren*, or Socially Responsible Innovation (Nederlands Organisatie voor Wetenschappelijk Onderzoek 2016) – motivated by similar concerns to those that drove the adoption of RRI. This simple outline of one of the processes that influenced the development of RRI is in some ways a classic example of a mutual learning 'boomerang' process: practices developed at one level (in this case, a member state) influence practices at another level (in this case, the Commission), only to return to further influence practices at the original level. However, while the Dutch MVI programme is an interesting example of this kind of boomerang effect, it is also a rather isolated example. As we will see below, the Dutch adoption of an RRI-inspired research and funding programme is rather distinctive. This rather limits the potential for mutual learning, even if it does demonstrate quite clearly how such mechanisms can work in practice.

Parallel issues: One of the most important reasons for encouraging national-level RRI programmes is that individual member states have faced similar or analogous problems to the problems that seem to have motivated RRI at the Commission level. The problems of genetically modified organisms (GMOs) led to a crisis for the regulation of research and innovation at the European level (Dabrowska 2010). Similarly, there have been cases of strong public and/or professional opposition and rejection of some technological and science-based initiatives at member-state level. A particularly striking example is the case of the Dutch Electronic Patient Dossier – a national system that would have allowed doctors and other medical practitioners to share information about patients electronically (van der Graaf 2012). In this case, a combination of legal and technical concerns about data security, and opposition from doctors, led to rejection of the legislative basis for the system by the Dutch parliament (NU 2013). Another example is fracking: public opposition to this practice has led to intense public protests and (temporary) bans on the practice in several member-state countries (Howarth, Ingraffea and Engelder 2011) – although public opinion on fracking has been divided, with a majority (58%) of people in the UK supporting the practice in 2013, a situation which had reversed by 2016, with only 36% support (*The Guardian* 2016).

This argument for adopting RRI at the member-state level is perhaps one of the most compelling for the member states themselves, because it offers an approach to addressing the potentially problematic public responses to research and innovation. In particular, RRI may offer a way to address divided and often changeable public opinion, both by providing better information about the implications of innovations, and by better enabling the public to assess those implications (particularly via science education).

Creating a common language: Many of the issues generated by science, technology and innovation have a strong cross-border dimension. To give a clear example: if one country promotes experiments with genetically modified crops, it is possible that the pollen and seeds from these crops could find their way into neighbouring countries that have banned GMOs.[3] Situations such as this can lead to tensions and conflicts between member states; developing a shared methodology and a common approach to addressing societal challenges (in this case, food security) through research and innovation could enable the member states to handle these conflicts and tensions more smoothly. Dabrowska offers a similar argument to this point by stressing the need to improve deliberative and institutional capacities in the EU as well as regulation itself (Dabrowska 2010).

Uneven member-state performance: There is some evidence that the performance of member states with regard to some of the key RRI action points is uneven and in some cases unsatisfactory. A special Eurobarometer survey from 2013 followed up on previous surveys that indicated knowledge gaps and a lack of science education among citizens (DG Comm Research and Speechwriting Unit 2013). Although the survey did not cover all the RRI keys, it revealed some interesting points relevant to engagement and science education. With regard to engagement, a majority of citizens felt interested in science and technology

(53% said they were either interested or very interested, p. 5). However, only in one in five of the member states did more than half of respondents feel well-informed about science: Denmark (65%), Sweden (61%), Luxembourg (58%), the UK (56%) and France (51%). In several countries, as few as 25% of those surveyed said they felt very well or fairly well-informed: Hungary (25%), Bulgaria (25%) and Romania (25%) (DG Comm Research and Speechwriting Unit 2013, 8). Furthermore, there was a geographical divide, with citizens in Southern and Eastern countries tending to feel less informed than those in the North and West. A similar pattern emerges with regard to the role of governments in an important element of science education – their stimulation of young people's interest in science. A majority of citizens across the EU (65%) felt that their governments do not do enough to stimulate young peoples' interest in science, and again this tendency was particularly pronounced in Southern and Eastern countries: 83% of Spanish, 78% of Greek, 76% of Croatian and Latvian and 75% of Italian respondents agreed that their governments were not doing enough in this area – however, the survey also suggests that scientists working in the public sector are more trustworthy sources than government representatives or politicians: 66% of those surveyed thought scientists working at universities or government laboratories are best qualified to explain the impacts of scientific and technological developments, compared with 6% who thought government representatives are best qualified and 4% who thought politicians were best qualified (DG Comm Research and Speechwriting Unit 2013, 126).

While this data does not cover all aspects of public engagement or science education, it does reveal some important patterns and variations among member states. There is a general tendency among citizens of member states to feel under-informed about science – 58% of respondents said they feel they are not very well-informed or not at all informed about developments in science. Being well-informed is a pre-requisite for meaningful engagement. There is also a strong tendency to feel that governments are not doing enough to stimulate young peoples' interest in science (an issue that relates to science education). Furthermore, there are geographical divides on both issues. This uneven performance can be taken as the basis for an argument for a more consistent approach to the RRI keys among the member states, and thus for a stronger set of national initiatives to address the RRI keys (at a minimum, in the areas where member states have already been shown to be under-performing through surveys such as the Eurobarometer).

The aim of developing the various arguments above has not been to provide a comprehensive or complete justification for promoting the extension of RRI to the member-state level. Rather, the aim was twofold: first, to motivate the rest of this chapter by identifying some explicit arguments for the extension of RRI to the member-state level (rather than simply assuming that such an extension can and should occur), and second, to try to respond to van Oudheusden's concerns about the apparent lack of politics in the development and extension of the RRI framework. As discussed above, the core of van Oudheusden's critique is that the implementation of RRI up to now seems to rely quite heavily on an assumption that the positive-sounding, broadly acceptable guiding RRI norms (such as transparency, openness, social desirability or inclusion) are enough by themselves to drive further adoption and implementation of RRI (Van Oudheusden 2014, 81). This critique can be extended to the implementation of RRI at the national level: there has been relatively little explicit discussion of why or how RRI should be extended to the member-state level, even though there are some signs that this is an important path for its further development. This lack of open discussion of co-ordination is the result of the sensitivity and complexity surrounding the subsidiarity principle – the principle that the "EU does not take action (except in the areas that fall within its exclusive competence), unless it is more effective than action taken at national, regional or local level" (EUR-Lex 2016). Significant areas of research and innovation policy remain the responsibility of the member states – this is particularly the case with higher education policy, for example, so RRI initiatives that intervene directly in national higher education policies could potentially come into conflict with the subsidiarity principle.[4]

In order to respond to van Oudheusden's critique, this section has taken some very small steps towards developing the possible arguments for this approach, mainly in order to try to motivate a debate around the various requirements for achieving this (in particular, the necessary normative justifications and institutional structures). In the next section, the chapter will investigate the current situation with regard to RRI at the level of the member states.

Responsible Research and Innovation: Member state initiatives

This section provides an initial overview and survey of the current situation regarding RRI in several of the EU's member states. The section draws mainly on the ResAGorA project's RRI Trends Report, which is at present the only attempt to provide a systematic overview of the adoption and implementation of RRI by EU member states (ResAGorA 2015). The RRI Trends reports only cover fifteen of the twenty-eight EU member states, plus Iceland.[5] However, they do attempt to represent the different geographical areas of the European Union: Southern Europe/Mediterranean (Greece, Italy, Spain); Central and Eastern Europe (Czech Republic, Hungary, Lithuania, Poland); North-West Europe (Austria, France, Germany, Ireland, Netherlands and the UK), and Scandinavia (Denmark and Finland). Furthermore, they follow a methodology that is intended to select representative examples of different types of economy and research and innovation cultures. This methodology was developed for a previous project, MASIS – Monitoring Policy and Research Activities on Science in Society in Europe (Mejlgaard, et al. 2008), and re-applied in the ResAGorA project.

The reports submitted for ResAGorA's RRI Trends survey are rather varied in terms of detail, content and quality. For example, there is the methodological problem that some of the reports respond directly to questions posed as part of the survey while others do not, and instead use their own structure. As a result, in order to provide a structured overview, this section will identify and examine different aspects that are common to most or all of the reports. It is intended that this structure can then be used to provide a structure further reporting on RRI at the member-state level. The reports were examined to establish whether they addressed the following elements:

- *General research and innovation cultures*: This aspect is considered because an understanding of the member states' different research and innovation cultures could be useful in assessing the likelihood of RRI uptake within the different states, as well as providing an overview of the diversity of different member states. Culture here refers to the general attitude to research and innovation that can be discerned from the statements in the country reports. These attitudes are generally discerned from the overview of policy documents provided in the reports. As an example, research and innovation culture may be characterised by different ways of justifying research and innovation: as a source of public good or of economic progress (or a combination of both). Some cultures may emphasise environmental or sustainability issues, while others may emphasise the importance of reconciling science with religious values.
- *Response to and uptake of RRI key issues and RRI norms*: This aspect addresses the extent to which member states have taken up both the RRI key issues and the background norms that have been derived from definitions of RRI, either explicitly as a response to the RRI programme or as part of existing programmes.
- *Institutional structures and RRI*: This section examines the extent to which the reports identify different national institutional structures through which RRI could be developed and implemented. Through an analysis of the reports, the following key institutions and institutional structures have been identified:
    - *National policy initiatives*: This category aims to cover policy-making processes that are relevant to research and innovation and that could thus form potential structures through which RRI could be disseminated.
    - *National legislation*: This category addresses the possible uptake of RRI-related issues in national legislation, with a particular focus on 'hard law' that relates to RRI.
    - *Research funding bodies*: This section addresses the question of whether any of the national-level research funding bodies have taken up RRI or pursued similar initiatives.
    - *Universities and higher education*: This section summarises the extent to which RRI has been taken up by universities and associations of universities in the member states.
    - *Business*: This section assesses whether there are any initiatives to involve businesses directly in RRI and RRI-related activities in the member states.
    - *Other innovation bodies*: This section discusses other governmental and non-governmental organisations that have been identified as playing a role in the development of RRI.

These different elements of RRI are addressed in turn.

General research and innovation cultures at national level

Despite the different historical, political and cultural circumstances of the member states surveyed, there is at least one common theme that recurs in almost all of the country reports: most of the countries view research and innovation primarily as drivers of economic prosperity and success, with other benefits of research and innovation (such as environmental benefits, benefits in terms of personal well-being and so on) taking a secondary role. This tendency is particularly clear in the reports from Iceland (Sveinsdottir 2013), Finland (Nieminen 2013), the Czech Republic (Filacek 2013), Germany (Hufnagl 2013), Ireland (Murphy and Hughes 2013) and Austria (Griessler 2013). In some cases, such as Germany, evidence of conflicting views of research and innovation was presented: proposals to improve participation in research and innovation policies were proposed by Green and left-wing parties, but rejected in the German Bundestag (Hufnagl 2013, 3).

However, this initial impression of a common tendency to prioritise the economic dimensions of research and innovation needs some nuance. In some countries, particularly Austria, the reports give an impression that the economic elements of research and innovation are given a strong priority at the cost of other elements. In other cases, the picture is somewhat more complex. In Ireland and Finland, for example, it could be argued that there is a slightly more 'enlightened' approach: although economic considerations are still given priority, these countries include other elements because they are seen as having an impact on the economic success of research and innovation: in the Irish case, this includes consideration of innovations that address environmental issues (Murphy and Hughes 2013). In the Finnish case, there is a tendency to emphasise participatory approaches in order to better target innovations at potential end users or customers (Nieminen 2013). Another group of countries, particularly those heavily affected by the 2007–2008 financial crisis, have tended to focus on the economic aspects of research and innovation because they see RRI approaches as a means to restore economic prosperity, and have withdrawn or reduced potentially promising RRI-related programmes. This appears to be the case in Greece, Italy and Ireland, where we see that external circumstances not connected to research and innovation policy (such as the financial crisis) can have an impact on the uptake of RRI.

One consequence of this analysis of the differing research and innovation cultures is that we need to beware of either exaggerating the differences between the member states or of reducing the motives of the different countries to a universal tendency to give priority to economic issues. It is certainly true that some countries do appear to prioritise economic issues, but they can have different motives for doing so, and different ways of doing this. For example, the Austrian report stresses that recent emphasis on the economic benefits of research and innovation has arisen in the context of the financial crisis. On the other hand, the Czech report does not suggest that the emphasis on economic efficiency in research and innovation is connected to the financial crisis. This may indicate that other factors motivate this emphasis, possibly including the general attitudes and culture of research and innovation that prevail in the Czech context. These considerations are important in building any potential approaches to promoting RRI among member states: for instance, emphasising the possible relative success of member states that take a more enlightened approach to RRI could be a way to provide guidance for member states taking a more purely economic approach.

Another area in which comparisons between the countries have to be made with care relates to the general culture of public and democratic involvement in research and innovation. The reports from Austria (Griessler 2013), the Czech Republic (Filacek 2013) and Spain (Revuelta 2013) all mention the lack of a culture of public dialogue on or democratic oversight of science and innovation policy. However, the precise reasons for this are rather different: in Austria, this tendency seems to stem from the fact that research and innovation policy is largely the responsibility of the executive branch (as is also the case in France). In both the Czech Republic and Spain, the lack of public dialogue and democratic oversight seems to stem from the still quite recent history of totalitarianism in those countries, and the fact that the democratic cultures are still relatively young – so there is a more general lack of public participation in political decision-making in these countries. These differences indicate that different approaches to building more democratic governance of research and innovation are needed in these different contexts.

Uptake of RRI keys issues in member states

In terms of objectives, the Commission's RRI programme defines a series of key action points: public engagement, gender equality, science education, open access, ethics and governance (European Commission 2014). The member-state reports are almost unanimous in their admission that this set of action points has not had much direct influence on national policies or strategies. Despite this lack of direct influence, many of the country reports do emphasise that some elements of the action points are already being addressed. In particular, several of the reports describe steps that have previously been taken with regard to gender issues, or emphasise current practices with regard to research ethics, or with regard to open access. This approach of emphasising some of the RRI keys and not mentioning the others is somewhat troubling because the keys should ideally form a coherent set of action points that should altogether be mutually reinforcing, rather than a menu of options from which actors can choose.

There are two further important observations to be made about the member states' uptake of the RRI key action points. First, several of the reports place quite heavy emphasis on environmental sustainability and environmental responsibilities, even though environmental sustainability does not appear on the Commission's list of action points. Given the apparent importance given to environmental issues by the member states, it is interesting to ask why the Commission did not include it as one of the RRI keys, or why it could not be added to the list of keys.[6]

A second observation is that the respondents often emphasise their actions with regard to research and innovation ethics. However, the content of the descriptions of the activities in this area suggests that only a rather narrow conception of research ethics is being addressed: many of the reports refer to ethics boards in quite specific scientific fields – particularly in bioethics, e.g. in the report from Hungary (Inzelt and Csonka 2013, 3). This possibly reflects an excessively narrow conception of ethics, restricting it to considerations of compliance with established norms in particular research fields.

This narrow conception of ethics contrasts quite sharply with one of the main recommendations of Owen, Stilgoe and Macnaghten's proposed framework for responsible innovation. These authors propose

> [A] far wider, systemic reconfiguration, and indeed a significant culture change in this regard. Importantly, we will argue that stewardship of science and innovation must not only include broad reflection and deliberation on their products, however uncertain these may be, but also (and critically) the very *purposes* of science or innovation: why do it, what are the intentions and motivations, who might benefit and who might not? What should the targets for innovation be – what Von Schomberg (Chapter 3) describes as the "right impacts" (see also Von Schomberg, 2011a) – and how can these be democratically defined? What values should these based on?
>
> (Stilgoe et al., 2013, p. 28)

There is a danger here that a broader conception of ethics as reflection on the ultimate goals of different activities and as mediation between different human values could be lost if too much emphasis is placed on research ethics in a narrow sense. Worryingly, only the Austrian report refers to any concern about the tendency to focus on research ethics in a narrow sense at the expense of wider reflection on goals and values (Griessler 2013, 4); some of the other reports seem to assume that reference to research ethics is adequate to address the ethics RRI action point – for example, the Finnish report (Nieminen 2013, 3), the Spanish report, (Revuelta 2013, 2), the Lithuanian report (Tauginiene and Maciukaite-Zvinien 2013) and the Greek report (Tsipouri 2013, 3).

Understanding of RRI norms in member states

RRI is defined in terms of a set of norms that go beyond the key action points discussed above, and which to some degree help to understand the meaning and purpose of the action points themselves. These norms have been developed as part of the process of defining RRI. Three of the most influential statements of the RRI norms are found in Von Schomberg's definition of RRI; Stilgoe, Owen and Macnaghten's framework for RRI; and the European Commission's report on RRI (the references to the norms are highlighted using italics):

> Responsible innovation means taking care of the future through *collective stewardship* of science and innovation in the present.
>
> (Stilgoe, Owen and Macnaghten 2013, 1570)

> Responsible Research and Innovation is a *transparent*, interactive process by which societal actors and innovators become mutually responsive to each other with a view to the *(ethical) acceptability*, *sustainability* and *societal desirability* of the innovation process and its marketable products (in order to allow a proper embedding of scientific and technological advances in our society).
>
> (Von Schomberg 2013, 39)

> Responsible Research and Innovation means that societal actors work together during the whole research and innovation process in order to better align both the process and its outcomes, with the values, needs and expectations of European society. RRI is an ambitious challenge for the creation of a Research and Innovation policy driven by the needs of society and *engaging* all societal actors via *inclusive participatory* approaches.
>
> (European Commission 2012, 3)

These definitions and frameworks are referred to in several of the country reports, but a closer examination reveals some problems regarding the actual understanding and uptake of the norms.

In particular, the various definitions emphasise norms of co-operation, interaction and deliberation – these can be understood as procedural norms that guide decision-making about research and innovation issues, in contrast to substantive norms such as social justice. While several of the reports – e.g. Finland (Nieminen 2013) and Austria (Griessler 2013) – mention that similar norms are acknowledged at the national level, it is also possible to identify concerns about these norms. Specifically, there is a tendency to conflate concepts such as deliberation, participation and engagement, and to use them interchangeably. As van Oudheusden stresses – following Mutz (2006) – deliberation and participation in particular are not synonymous: deliberation aims to develop rational-critical debate with the aim of encouraging mutual learning and, eventually, rational consensus formation, whereas participation is potentially more ambiguous: it can be understood as either encouraging broad participation or as encouraging political activism by mobilising partisan groups around a particular cause (Van Oudheusden 2014, 79). While van Oudheusden's suggestion that the two approaches are mutually incompatible is debatable,[7] his point that we need to take care in distinguishing the approaches is an important one. Perhaps more troubling still is the use of concepts such as engagement: as the Austrian report points out, 'engagement' is used to justify or legitimate activities that really amount to little more than 'selling science' – treating the public as passive recipients of the results of science and innovation. Similarly, the Finnish report expresses the worry that the supposed 'user orientation' of recent research and innovation policy is mainly aimed at treating citizens as potential customers of innovations, rather than involving them in policy processes relating to science and innovation. This suggests the need for more robust and consistent definitions of some of the key RRI concepts. An example of this more robust kind of definition is Archon Fung's concept of

Empowered Participatory Governance (EPG) (Fung 2003). EPG emphasises both the deliberative aspects of participation and the importance of linking deliberation to action. A more robust definition such as this could provide a stronger normative base to judge and criticise (and if necessary, correct) some of the misuses of key RRI norms such as participation and deliberation.

In summary, there are clear problems with the current understandings among the member states of one of the central sets of guiding RRI norms – those relating to deliberation. The main risk seems to be a potential for conflation between deliberation and other norms such as participation, inclusion and engagement, and indeed that these different terms are either not well understood or (at worst) are used superficially by member states to legitimate existing practices that fall short of the aims of RRI.

A second set of concerns arises in relation to the appeal to norms of societal relevance. The references to society, social acceptability and societal embedding in the various definitions of RRI reflect a general concern to ensure that research and innovation are aligned with social needs and values – as far as possible, given that such needs and values are neither fixed nor subject to universal agreement. This concern is also reflected in the development of the Science with and for Society programme (European Commission 2016) and the thematic approach of many of the calls in Horizon 2020 (H2020), which reflect a concern to address grand social challenges (Reillon, Horizon 2020 Budget and Implementation: A Guide to the Structure of the Programme 2015).

Turning to the member states, the focus on 'grand societal challenges'[8] and social relevance again raises a potential concern. At least two of the reporters (from the UK and the Netherlands) raise the point that the focus on grand societal challenges is seen as being sufficient by itself to fulfil the obligation to carry out RRI:

> A research focus on environmental and societal challenges is often presented as in itself to be a responsible activity as results are expected to bring a solution or an overall better society and positive environmental impact.
>
> (Sveinsdottir, UK National Policies on RRI 2013, 2)

A similar point can be found in the Netherlands report: the author expresses the concern that, although 'societal embedding' and 'tackling societal issues' are acknowledged, social sciences and humanities play only a limited 'secondary' role in the programmes, with the aim of informing, raising awareness and analysing research and innovation, rather than playing a more active role in criticising and shaping research and innovation processes and governance.

This focus on societal issues is problematic because the Commission's RRI approach clearly aims to go beyond simply focusing on grand social challenges or societal relevance: accompanying this focus is a concern to improve the processes of research and innovation through the introduction of deliberative practices (as discussed above in this section). Focusing on societal challenges and expecting this focus to do the work of legitimising research and innovation could lead to a one-sided approach in which the accompanying changes in governance processes (towards more deliberative governance) are neglected.

The previous two sections examined the uptake and understanding of both the key RRI action points and some of the guiding RRI norms among the member states. It is important to stress that the point of the analysis is not to assess whether the member states have already directly taken up the Commission's norms and action points, but rather to assess the understanding of similar norms and principles among the member states in order to identify potential issues in communicating and disseminating the norms. The analysis reveals two concerns: first, that member states tend to conflate key terms such as deliberation, engagement, inclusion and participation. Greater clarity is needed over the understanding of these terms to prevent this type of conflation. Second, some member states seem to use a focus on societal challenges (without accompanying changes in governance) as a means to legitimise research and innovation; this approach risks being one-sided and failing to take into account the governance side of RRI.

Institutional structures and RRI

In this section, we turn to the institutional structures that could potentially be used for the dissemination and further development of RRI. While some of these structures match the institutions that are responsible for RRI at the European Commission level, there are also other institutions that could play a role.

- *National research and innovation policy strategies*

Several of the member states' reports refer to periodic science, research and innovation policy strategy plans. These plans cover different time periods. In the case of the Italian National Research Plans (Arnaldi 2013), the period is two years. For the Greek National Strategic Framework for the Development of Research and Innovation, the period is five years (Tsipouri 2013). The Irish Strategies for Science, Technology and Innovation extend to seven years (Murphy and Hughes 2013), and the Polish government's long-term development strategy extends to 2030 (Kozlowski 2013). These policy programmes can partly be seen as the national equivalents to the European Commission's Innovation Union, which is part of the European Union's overall Europe 2020 programme.

The inclusion of RRI-related initiatives in the various member-state strategy plans has been uneven at best. The Italian and the Irish reports both mention that earlier strategies included references to RRI-related topics such as science and society, public consultation, responsibility and precaution. However, in both cases, these considerations were then withdrawn in subsequent strategies. Comparable strategies in Greece (Tsipouri 2013), France (Tancoigne and Joly 2013), Germany (Hufnagl 2013) and Spain (Revuelta 2013) make reference to issues such as responsibility, the social responsibility of scientists, social dialogue and ethical reflection. However, the various reporters observe that there are few mentions of the precise policy tools to be used in these areas, or of systems to monitor progress. The German reporter does note the implementation of citizen dialogues through the current High-Technology Strategy for Germany.

The existence of these various strategies provides an opportunity to experiment with RRI at the national level, particularly given their resemblance to the European Commission's own research and innovation strategy programmes. Two considerations arise, however. First, there is a question about how far these programmes can result in policy lock-in (or indeed 'lock-out' in some cases): How far can the programmes be changed to reflect different circumstances once they have been adapted? For instance, is it the case that the Irish seven-year strategy would exclude the possibility of adopting RRI-related initiatives at this policy level, or can the plan be changed if necessary? Second, there is a question about the relationship between the political bodies responsible for the initiatives. In the Austrian report, mention is made of the way in which political structures can influence the character of the strategic plans (Griessler 2013). In Austria, the planning is mainly carried out by an executive that is somewhat shielded from parliamentary intervention (in some ways resembling the relationship between the European Parliament and the European Commission). Unfortunately, the other reports do not discuss this issue, which is an important consideration for the dissemination of RRI: if, for example, national parliaments have strong influence over the production of the national strategies, this could positively or negatively influence the likelihood of the inclusion of RRI elements in the strategies, according to the political composition of the parliament in question.

- *National research funding bodies*

The national research funding bodies are of equal or even greater importance for the possible dissemination of RRI at national level, since they are equivalent to the H2020 funding programme, which has been the main structure through which RRI has been implemented at the European level.

At present, there is only very limited evidence of RRI-type activities that have been implemented through national funding bodies. The Irish Research Council has implemented a programme related to gender, while the Lithuanian MITA (the main funding body for innovation) has supported programmes in green and ecological innovation.

The two most important national programmes, however, are without doubt the British Engineering and Physical Sciences Research Council's (EPSRC) Framework for Responsible Innovation (EPSRC 2016) and the Dutch Nederlandse Organisatie voor Wetenschappelijk Onderzoek's (NWO) Maatschappelijk Verantwoord Innoveren (MVI) programmes (Nederlands Organisatie voor Wetenschappelijk Onderzoek 2016).

The EPSRC programme has turned out to be highly influential in the further development of RRI (despite its rather limited scope – the project took place only within one of the sections of the British government's research funding systems, and focused specifically on geo-engineering). The basic principles that were originally identified in the EPSRC project have since been widely cited in subsequent discussions of RRI. The actual content of the EPSRC programme has changed slightly. From the original focus on anticipation, reflection, deliberation and responsiveness, the EPSRC programme has now changed to 'AREA' – Anticipate, Reflect, Engage, Act (EPSRC 2016) as the guiding normative structure. The programme is also now presented on the EPSRC website as a 'soft intervention', with the emphasis on encouraging researchers to consider and implement the approach in the work. The author of the UK report observes that broader adoption of the EPSRC's framework on RRI by the UK's other research councils would be a major advance, but there does not seem to be evidence of this occurring.

The Dutch MVI programme is one of the most institutionally embedded of all the RRI-related programmes. The programme consists of research funding for small (€125,000) and large (€250–500,000) projects. The project also holds periodic conferences and has gathered its main findings in a series of publications (NWO 2010). However, there are some contrasts with the H2020 approach. Whereas the H2020 approach is thematic, in line with, for example, the grand social challenges, the NWO programme does not specify any particular research fields: it seems in principle possible to submit an MVI application for any field. In particular, while RRI is a 'cross cutting issue' (all H2020 projects are expected to account for RRI to some extent), the Dutch MVI programme seems rather more isolated: it is not clear whether there are plans to expand the programme more widely.[9] One criticism of the Dutch approach is that there does not seem to be a structured attempt to develop any guiding RRI principles or to actively try to derive such principles from the projects. The normative approaches taken within the different projects seem to be quite diverse. The periodic conferences attached to the MVI programme and the published books may help to encourage mutual learning, but beyond these initiatives there does not seem to be a structured effort to develop an overarching set of RRI principles from the projects.

Looking at these two main national initiatives together, they can appear to be two sides of one coin. On the one hand, the UK Responsible Innovation programme represents an attempt to develop a set of basic RRI norms and principles that researchers can apply in their projects, but does not provide a lot of financial or institutional support to facilitate this. On the other hand, the Dutch programme provides financial support for projects under a broad RRI umbrella, but does not appear to be designed to develop a general normative framework or set of generally applicable methods and principles on the basis of the projects. Both of these approaches then contrast further with the European Commission's H2020 approach, which attempts to do both: providing support for RRI projects across H2020 while at the same time developing RRI methods and principles through projects in FP7 and H2020's Science in Society and Science with and for Society programmes.

- *Other innovation bodies*

Besides national research and innovation funding bodies, most member states have (often quite complex) networks of institutions that share general responsibilities for science, research and innovation governance, or whose mandate covers areas relevant to research and innovation. Clear examples include the British Royal Society, Department for Business, Innovation and Skills, and Technology Strategy Board; the German Advisory Council on Global Change and Council of Science and Humanities; the Danish Board of Technology; and the Austrian Council. It is important to note the existence of such bodies, which could potentially serve as alternative or supporting players in the national development of RRI. An interesting point to note is that these types of institutions seem to be more prominent in North-West European and Scandinavian countries; there are fewer references to these kinds of institutions among Central and Eastern and Southern and Mediterranean reporters.[10] This could be an important factor if the existence or absence of such institutions has an impact on the effective dissemination of RRI.

Besides these general advisory and governance bodies, many countries refer to specialised bodies with a role in ethical or other RRI-relevant fields. Boards and organisations dealing with bioethics are particularly common; here, the geographical divide mentioned above is less prominent. In some cases, these specialised bodies may be even more important than either general research funding bodies or general advisory bodies. For example, the Irish Environmental Protection Agency is, according to the Irish report, the main funder of RRI-related projects, even though the body has not yet adopted RRI as part of its strategy (Murphy and Hughes 2013).

As with the general advisory bodies, these more specialised organisations could form an important supporting or alternative route for the development of RRI (for example in the case of 'policy lock out' due to long-term strategies at government level, or due to partisan opposition in highly politicised research and innovation systems). However, it is important to be aware that these bodies operate in more narrowly defined fields, so that extra work may be necessary to draw more general conclusions from any initiatives taken by them.[11] Similarly, attention must be paid to avoiding a situation in which these institutions only deal with narrow issues specific to their field and fail to respond to the more expansive conception of ethics discussed above.

- *National legislation*

Several of the reports make reference to national legislation that relates to RRI and RRI-related issues. For example, both the Hungarian (Inzelt and Csonka 2013) and Austrian (Griessler 2013) reports refer to legislation banning genetically modified crops. Some of the reports mention national legislation relating to gender equality that has impacted on careers in research – e.g. the Austrian report (Griessler 2013, 6). Perhaps most notable is the French *Charte de l'environnement*, which was an environmental charter adopted by the French Parliament and integrated into the French Constitution (Tancoigne and Joly 2013, 2). French law on bioethics is also regularly revised, and one of the recent revisions was preceded by an organised public debate (Tancoigne and Joly 2013, 2). However, there are various reasons to be very wary of using legal rules to promote RRI. First, RRI norms and standards can be interpreted as addressing issues for which 'hard' legislation is, for various reasons, ineffective, or as addressing cultural changes that may be necessary to reinforce or supplement legal changes. For example, 'hard' laws on gender equality may need to be supplemented with 'soft' laws to address background features of academic or research culture that create additional obstacles to gender equality. Second, RRI aims at deliberative conceptions of its guiding norms. An over-reliance on legal rules could lead to a 'compliance' culture that is in conflict with this deliberative approach. Indeed, some authors have even argued for the adoption of legal standards (as opposed to legal rules) that are *not* precisely defined, specifically in order to foster this more deliberative attitude among citizens – see, for example, Shiffrin (Shiffrin 2010). Finally, the use of or encouragement of national legal instruments to encourage RRI raises complex questions about subsidiarity and the legal authority of the European institutions over national research and innovation policies (as noted above, p. 5).

- *Universities and higher education*

Universities can play a key role in the dissemination and implementation of RRI and are clearly among the main targets and beneficiaries of the existing RRI instruments. Despite this, there are relatively few references to independent RRI-related initiatives that have been taken by universities or associations of universities in the member states. At least one of the reports (Sveinsdottir 2013) complains of vaguely worded mission statements regarding ethics and social responsibility from its universities. There are only a couple of exceptions to this. The Austrian report describes the successful implementation of a gender equality policy through a long-term combination of hard and soft law measures (Griessler 2013), while the French report refers to some university initiatives such as master's programmes in responsible innovation (Tancoigne and Joly 2013). At least one French university (Lyon) has set up a training programme that draws on responsible innovation methodologies (University of Lyon 2016), and ESSEC Business School has integrated RRI into its teaching programmes on business strategy (ESSEC Business School 2017). A few of the reports also refer to associations of universities that could be dissemination channels for RRI (Griessler 2013) (Murphy and Hughes 2013).

- *Business, civil society and non-governmental actors*

Besides the various institutions, bodies, processes and actors described above, there are also some indications of the uptake of RRI among national business actors. The French report notes that a few French companies have taken up RRI as a term for their social responsibility activities (Tancoigne and Joly 2013, 3). There is also some evidence of companies operating in the field of responsible innovation consulting in both France (SoScience 2016) and Spain (Eticas 2016). Several of the reports, for example Poland and the Czech Republic, mention strong corporate social responsibility (CSR) cultures (Kozlowski 2013; Filacek 2013). However, the relation between CSR and RRI has yet to be fully clarified, and it is not clear if CSR serves more as a 'trojan horse' (opening businesses to a wider range of responsible practices), or more as a barrier to RRI (with CSR providing a reason for companies to argue that they are already acting responsibly and do not need to take further action).

A few of the reports also make reference to civil society. Where this issue is discussed, it is mainly to address the prevailing civil society culture in the country: in Spain, public engagement in science is still underdeveloped, and this is attributed to a general lack of public participation in mainstream politics due to the country's status as a relatively young democracy (Revuelta 2013), whereas in both Austria (Griessler 2013) and Poland (Kozlowski 2013), civil society actions relating to innovations with environmental impact are apparently more noticeable. There is little or no mention of initiatives to include civil society actors in responsible innovation or indeed in innovation policy more generally. Similarly, there is little discussion of any possible non-governmental organisations dealing with RRI. The Italian Bassetti Foundation – one of the most prominent non-governmental organisations dealing with responsible innovation – is not mentioned in the Italian report (Bassetti Foundation 2016).

In summary, this survey of the country reports on RRI has demonstrated that there is quite a wide range of different types of institutions that could be included in efforts to further spread RRI at the member-state level. This summary has attempted to classify the different types of member-state institutions that were covered in the surveys published by RES AGORA in order to provide a clearer overview, and to provide a structure that could be built on for future surveys.

A few points can be made in conclusion. First, the institutional diversity reveals a wider range of possible options for disseminating RRI among the member states than are currently found at the level of the European Union institutions At present, the main institutional structures the EU has used to disseminate RRI are the Commission's H2020 funding programme and its research projects. Second, although this diversity provides a wide range of potential opportunities for developing RRI programmes at national level, a method for coping with and understanding the diversity of possible institutions and structures needs to be found. For example, it would help to have an understanding of which institutions are likely to be more effective: Are national research funding bodies more likely to be able to influence other RRI actors because they ultimately determine which type of research gets done, or are they too inflexible and subject to national research strategies that could 'lock out' RRI for considerable periods of time? Similarly, can smaller advisory bodies exercise more flexibility, or are they likely to struggle to exert adequate influence? As a further point, the differing levels of development of national research infrastructures could be an issue that needs to be addressed. As mentioned, some countries such as the newer member states seem to lack the variety of advisory and policy bodies found in countries like the UK.[12] An understanding of whether or how to develop these types of institutions, and to do so in a way that could further RRI, would be helpful.

Developing an institutional approach to RRI

In this section, an argument for the next steps for the development of RRI is proposed. Specifically, it is argued that it is necessary to develop a more detailed institutional theory of RRI: by an institutional theory, we mean here a theory that can help us understand how "schemes, rules, norms, and routines, become established as authoritative guidelines for social behaviour" (Scott 2004, 408). We start by using the analysis from the previous sections to provide a sketch of the current situation regarding RRI – this will help justify the choice of institutional approach that we will then advocate: namely, the 'Architecture of Experimentalist Governance' that has been developed over the past few years by Charles Sabel and Jonathan Zeitlin.

An outline of the institutional context of RRI

From the two sections above, we can identify two key features of the context in which RRI has emerged and developed. The first we will label 'normative uncertainty'. The second will be labelled 'institutional diversity'.

Normative uncertainty is intended to label a series of observations about the context of RRI. To a certain extent, the vagueness of the RRI concepts may have been a deliberate move by the designers of the RRI programme, with the vagueness being used to prompt reflection on the norms by those responsible for implementing them – in contrast to the 'tick box' or compliance approach that characterises some of the formal procedures of research ethics. There is a cluster of norms that characterise the RRI approach (including, among others, deliberation, anticipation, transparency, social acceptability and embedding within the European Union's common legal and ethical traditions). However, these norms tend to be vaguely specified, and the implications of their translation into practice are unclear. Furthermore, the subject matter of RRI does not generally lend itself to the specification of strong authoritative legal standards: the uncertainties around new technologies and innovations make it hard to specify precise legal norms regarding their practical application.

Institutional diversity is intended to label the observation that there is a wide range of institutions that are or could be implicated in the further development of the RRI framework. This is perhaps most clearly illustrated by the variety of responses to the ResAGorA survey: the respondents picked out a wide range of different institutions and they were also rather inconsistent in their responses. Some included businesses and universities in their surveys, for example, whereas other did not. This inconsistency is perhaps inevitable given the relatively recent emergence of RRI – the respondents were to some extent required to interpret the meaning of the concept and its practical implications for themselves. It is quite clear that the range of institutions that could be used in developing RRI is not at present being put to full use. There are also questions about which institutions are best suited to developing RRI: for example, national funding bodies play a similar role to the H2020 programme, but they may be subject to restrictions and inflexibilities imposed by national research strategies.

These two key features of RRI help to justify the choice of Sabel and Zeitlin's experimentalist governance approach as a theoretical framework, for several reasons.[13] Before justifying this choice, a brief outline of the experimentalist governance approach is necessary. The approach is characterised by what Sabel and Zeitlin term "a recursive process of provisional goal-setting and revision based on learning from the comparison of alternative approaches to advancing them in different contexts" (Sabel and Zeitlin 2012b, 169). That is, the approach consists in setting goals, but periodically revising those goals in the light of information that results from (experimental) attempts to implement those goals in different practical contexts. This approach is relevant as a theoretical framework for RRI for the following reasons:

First, Sabel and Zeitlin's approach is not structured by a focus on any one specific set of institutions. As Eckett and Boerzel state (2012), experimentalist governance is not structured by a divide between public and private institutions, and neither does it distinguish between actors on the basis of whether they have an electoral mandate. This opens the scope of their framework to the wide range of actors discussed above.

Second, Sabel and Zeitlin's approach is framed by a commitment to general deliberative principles: they emphasise the importance of mutual reason-giving and justification between different actors as the deliberative core of their approach, but also stress that this process is not necessarily aimed at achieving consensus: "Practices and institutions are expected to evolve, but not to converge to a single consensus" (Sabel and Zeitlin 2010, 4).

Third, the approach is intended to address situations in which hierarchies between different actors are either practically or normatively inappropriate. Sabel and Zeitlin reject a principal-agent approach in which agents lower down a hierarchy are expected to conform with clear rules set out by principals at the top (Sabel and Zeitlin, Learning from Difference: the New Architecture of Experimentalist Governance in the EU 2010, 13). Instead, they advocate a combination of peer review-inspired practices and destabilisation regimes. Peer review-inspired practices are intended to reflect the non-hierarchical practice of mutual reason-giving and accountability, while destabilisation regimes refers to a range of formal and informal measures designed to incentivise participants to engage in these processes of mutual accountability (Sabel and Zeitlin 2010, 30).

Eckert and Boerzel neatly summarise the key elements of Sabel and Zeitlin's proposed methodology in terms of the following iterative cycle:

- setting broad framework goals
- granting discretion to lower levels when implementing the goals
- practices of regular reporting and assessment
- periodical revision of framework goals.

(Eckert and Boerzel 2012, 37)

It can be argued that the current implementation of the RRI approach partly implements some of these key elements, but that the implementation could be reinforced in a number of ways. This point can be developed by looking at the four elements in turn:

1. Setting broad framework goals: The RRI keys and the normative principles can be seen as providing a basis for framework goals, but not a specific definition of targets or outcomes. The keys and normative principles do not generally define specific goals. For example, the guidance for evaluators of H2020 projects explains that evaluators should assess proposals for 'gender balance' in the research team, but does not specify any targets or precise definitions for this balance (European Commission 2014, 5). Similarly, the indicators for RRI mention percentages of women involved in different parts of the research and innovation process, but does not specify precise targets – and the indicators are not as yet included in the guidance for evaluators (Strand 2015, 28). Similarly, the indicators mention activities such as visits to museum exhibitions as examples of public engagement outcomes, but these are clearly suggestions for those responsible for designing projects, rather than strictly defined goals (Strand 2015, 25). This is perhaps justifiable given the nature of the RRI approach, which is still at an early phase. In these conditions, the lower-level actors could perhaps be better encouraged to set and justify their own goals and to provide justified interpretations of the outline principles.
2. Granting discretion to lower levels: The inclusion of lower levels has increased, particularly with the inclusion of national-level research organisations in projects such as RRI Tools (RRI Tools Project 2017). The current calls for H2020 in 2016–2017 extend this programme further, e.g. with support for developing RRI in research funding organisations (European Commission 2016). However, it seems important at this stage to develop a clearer taxonomy of different types of institution in order to identify which actors could potentially be included, and to allow for practices such as the matching of different peers. The above discussion has attempted to make a first step towards developing a possible taxonomy. Also, as implied in the previous section, considerable space is granted to the project consortia themselves to define the key RRI action points and develop activities to put the action points into practice. For example, with regard to public engagement, the guidance for evaluators states:

    > Where relevant, evaluators should consider whether or not the engagement process is methodologically sound, includes the appropriate expertise and resources to design and implement the engagement process, and likely to lead to a positive and real impact during and after the project.
    >
    > (European Commission 2014, 4)

    However, the appropriate methodologies for public engagement are not specified further, leaving a lot of space for the project consortia to decide how to put the action point into practice.

3 Practices of regular reporting and assessment: The current H2020 framework, and particularly the SWAFS programmes, are structured by reference to the RRI keys, which creates a certain pressure to show how the projects respond to the key action points (European Commission 2016). However, there seems to be less attention paid to explaining how projects understand and fulfil the normative principles that guide RRI.
4 Periodical revision of framework goals: It is not clear at present how the current RRI framework, including the RRI key action points, could be revised. As noted above, the frequent references to environment and sustainability in the various member-state reports suggest that revisions to take account of this goal (or to explain why it is not included) could be made.

In summary, the RRI framework could be restructured to take more account of the peer-review approach to mutual justification that Sabel and Zeitlin advocate. This would require attention to the definition and understanding of how the concept of 'peers' is understood. For example, if projects frequently choose museum exhibitions as one of their public engagement activities, it makes sense to involve other museums and exhibition spaces in providing realistic guidelines for such activities – not just for individual projects, but for the broader guidance for the framework programmes. It therefore also requires attention to which lower-level institutions should be included if extending RRI to the member-state level. Furthermore, better methodologies and requirements could be developed to encourage reflection and review in relation to the framework goals of RRI (which are at present defined in terms of the key action points and the looser set of normative guidelines).

Before concluding, it is also important to reflect on and provide an initial response to some of the main criticisms of the experimental governance approach, and to put these responses in the context of the further implementation of RRI. The criticisms are as follows: democratic deficit and technocracy, lack of a detailed theory of learning and lack of attention to background conditions. A brief outline and response to the criticisms is provided below – this discussion is intended as a prompt to further reflection rather than a definitive set of responses.

Democratic deficit: a general and frequently recurring criticism of experimentalist governance is that it is undemocratic and potentially technocratic because it focuses on decision-making among peers with no inherent connection to representative and electorally mandated institutions. A number of responses can be developed as a reaction to this point. First, as Sabel and Zeitlin stress, one aim of the experimental governance approach is to try to reinforce the deliberative practice of mutual reason-giving and justification. In principle, reinforcing this practice could in fact contribute to the quality of democratic decision-making by improving the processes and substantive content of public discussion. However, more attention needs to be paid to how this improvement might come about – for example, in the RRI case, whether better links between RRI projects and parliamentarians could contribute to better deliberation. At present, different member states have their own national offices for technology assessment that contribute to parliamentary decision-making – compare the French Office parlementaire d'évaluation des choix scientifiques et technologiques and the Danish Board of Technology, for example (Assemblée Nationale 2017; Danish Board of Technology Foundation 2017). However, it is not clear if there are institutional structures for these different entities to collaborate or engage in the peer review of one another's activities. A second response could be to stress theories that make clearer distinctions between different locations for political and democratic debate and action. For example, the institutional side of Habermas's discourse theory identifies three different discursive arenas: the dispersed discursive interaction of citizens in civil society, the mass communication in the political public sphere and the institutionalised legislative processes (Habermas 1998, 452; 99–109; Finlayson and Freyenhagen 2011, 11). Part of the RRI programme could then focus on the role of the experimentalist governance approach in the different spheres, and how it could contribute to improving communication within them.

Finally, we could emphasise the point from the RRI and related studies (such as the Eurobarometer surveys) which tend to show that scientists generally tend to enjoy higher levels of public legitimacy than elected officials, and ask what this phenomenon implies for both the place of scientists in public debate, and for the contribution of peer review and scientific deliberation to this legitimacy: in short, how (if at all) do the processes of scientific debate themselves contribute to the legitimacy of scientists, and what does this imply for the proposed extension of peer review and similar techniques to other fields? To put the point in a different way: Could involving politicians and other public figures in open processes of peer review of policies help to address the low level of public trust in their ability to explain scientific issues (DG Comm Research and Speechwriting Unit 2013, 44)?

Mutual learning: A second frequently recurring criticism of experimentalist governance is that it lacks a fully elaborated theory of mutual learning. Some critics go so far as to argue that some of the phenomena that Sabel and Zeitlin attribute to mutual learning are in fact simply imitation by one actor of another's actions. While it is not possible to give a detailed response here, one possible way to address this criticism could be to introduce possibilities for reflection among the participants in experimental governance projects with regard to their own learning processes. This could include requiring participants in RRI projects that implement peer review of the type proposed to reflect not only on what was actually learned during the project, but also to think about how the learning process came about. This is intended as a more pragmatic approach than trying to identify and specify a complete learning process for implementation in the RRI framework – such a pragmatic approach may be appropriate, given that it is not obvious what kind of learning theory would be most appropriate.

Background conditions: A third criticism is that the experimentalist governance approach pays too little attention to the range of background conditions that are necessary for its implementation. This includes a set of cultural perspectives (risking an assumption of shared commitments to certain values) and institutional conditions (broadly, institutions that are willing and able to identify and provide a range of material and other conditions for a particular approach). Rather than answering this question directly, it is possible to respond in the context of the possible extension of the RRI programme to the increasingly sophisticated and varied empirical research regarding experimentalist governance. From a position in which a few idealised cases were examined, the research programme has extended to a wider range of empirical studies. This increasing range gives us a better opportunity to examine the problems and potential of the experimental governance approach in a range of different circumstances that may be more or less analogous to the RRI approach. For example, recent contributions by von Homeyer (2010) Vos (2010) and Dabrowska (2010) examine the role of experimentalist governance in environmental governance, food safety and GMOs, all of which are fields that are connected in some way to RRI and can thus provide lessons about the prerequisites for the implementation of an experimentalist governance approach in practice. Lessons can also be drawn from well-established practices such as participatory technology assessment (Reber 2012). Although a comprehensive overview is not possible here, it can be argued that the general tone of the contributions referred to suggests that the experimental governance approach can be applied in a range of different contexts, with varying scope and success according to the nature of the case in question – even in a relatively difficult context, such as the politically charged discussions around GMO, it was possible for some elements of the experimental governance approach to emerge, for example. A similar situation is beginning to emerge with regard to RRI. RRI was originally developed in the context of some specific pioneering case studies – Owen and Goldberg's study of geo-engineering is a notable example (Owen and Goldberg 2010). With the ongoing development of both the H2020 programme and national initiatives such as the Dutch MVI programme, the range of empirical evidence regarding the practical implementation of RRI is steadily increasing, which provides an opportunity to investigate the background conditions necessary for successful implementation.

Conclusion

This chapter has investigated three aspects of the implementation of RRI in national research and innovation programmes and governance structures: first, the reasons for encouraging this implementation; second, the state of RRI in several member states, as described in the ResAGorA reports; and third, the need for an overall theoretical conception of the implementation of RRI, and eventual improvements on current RRI practices. The main contributions of the reflection on these three considerations can be summarised as follows. First, there is a need to be more clear and explicit about the reasons for encouraging the adoption of RRI at the member-state level. While the normative considerations that motivate RRI have been summarised in the Rome Declaration, stronger arguments for the more practical policy reasons for co-ordination between the different research and innovation governance regimes at the EU and at the member-state level could be made. This could in turn improve the implementation itself by providing a clearer rationale. Second, the general picture of current RRI implementation by member states reveals a low level of actual implementation of RRI in terms of the adoption of specific RRI programmes (with the exceptions of the UK and the Netherlands). Furthermore, the situation is characterised by normative uncertainty (lack of certainty about the meaning of key RRI norms and the connections between those key norms) and institutional diversity (a wide range of different national institutions and structures that are at different levels of evolution). This situation emphasises the potential difficulties that any programme to encourage national adoption of RRI will face. Third, the theory of experimentalist governance that Sabel and Zeitlin have developed is well suited to providing a theoretical framework for co-ordinating the implementation of RRI principles at national level – for example, because the framework is intended to deal with institutional diversity, and because it does not require a strong hierarchical relationship between different types of actors.

As a final conclusion, some practical suggestions for the integration of an experimentalist governance approach to RRI are offered:

1 Setting clearer practical framework goals for RRI. This could be done within the framework of the existing RRI key action points (as outlined above). At present, there is little clarity on specific aims for the keys, such as raising levels of public participation. Neither is there clarity on the level of funding that individual projects should devote to RRI activities, or on the level of funding that research programmes should devote to RRI-type activities. Nevertheless, examples such as the Dutch MVI programme could be used for guidance in this area.
2 Clearer delegation of responsibility for RRI. Responsibility for national-level research governance still rests with national governments and their agencies, in line with the principle of subsidiarity. However, reporting mechanisms within national research and innovation agencies could be established to better monitor and assess the implementation of RRI at national level – for example, to improve the quality and frequency of reports such as those gathered for the ResAGorA project.
3 Stronger mechanisms for sharing experiences. As noted above, there is increasing empirical evidence on the practical application of RRI and similar concepts, as a result of the increased number of ongoing or completed projects. However, better mechanisms for sharing the experiences of these projects could be devised. The periodic Dutch MVI conference (NWO 2016) and the publication of summaries of the MVI projects are good examples of actions that could be taken to improve the sharing of knowledge and experience. These knowledge-sharing activities could constitute a less-formal type of reporting and information-sharing exercise.
4 Better mechanisms for revising and assessing framework goals. At present, the setting of the RRI key action points has been rather opaque and inflexible. It is not clear how these key elements of RRI are defined, or how they could be changed. As noted above in the first point, there are also few practical goals associated with the action points. This situation could be

improved by involving a wider range of stakeholders (including national research governance organisations) in the definition and eventual revision of the key action points.

In summary, several practical steps could be taken to implement a more coherent institutional framework for encouraging the implementation of RRI at the national level, and to do so in a manner that is informed by the insights of theories of experimentalist governance.[14]

Notes

1 This is not to say that RRI cannot cope with such conflicts, or that RRI is not an improvement over a situation where no such framework exists. Rather, the most pressing concern could be that mechanisms to deal with conflicts would be more effective if they are included more explicitly in the institutional design of RRI. Without such mechanisms, RRI may operate sub-optimally, and it may be necessary to work with ad hoc solutions that are inefficient to implement.

2 The approaches will be discussed further below with regard to Sabel and Zeitlin's theory of experimentalist governance as it is applied to the European Union.

3 See van den Hoven et al. for a discussion of genetically modified organisms in the context of Responsible Research and Innovation (Expert Group on the State of the Art in Europe on Responsible Research and Innovation, 2013, p. 14).

4 Although there are various calls for better co-ordination of research and innovation policy to tackle the fragmentation of such policy in the EU; see Reillon (2016); Technopolis Group (2014).

5 Iceland has requested to not be considered as a candidate member state and its application for EU membership is thus currently on hold, but it is a member of the European Economic Area.

6 The 2015 report *Indicators for Promoting and Monitoring Responsible Research and Innovation* does advocate including both sustainability and social justice as additional RRI indicators (Strand 2015). However, these additional indicators have not as yet been integrated into the Commission's public definitions of RRI – for example, they do not appear on the H2020 RRI page (European Commission 2016).

7 One could, for example, argue that deliberative methods could be used to mitigate the partisanship that attaches to some forms of participation.

8 https://ec.europa.eu/programmes/horizon2020/en/h2020-section/societal-challenges

9 At present, the funding for the MVI programme represents 4% of the total NWO funding budget. The author of the Dutch report points out that this figure is difficult to put into context because the Dutch MVI programme is the only national programme of its type at present.

10 This does not of course mean that such institutions do not exist in such countries, but they may be less visible, play a less active role or be perceived as not having a role to play by the reporters from these areas.

11 The EPSRC's Responsible Innovation initiative is a confirmation that this is possible.

12 The UK report was written before the June 2016 vote to leave the European Union. It remains to be seen whether and how the UK would continue to participate in the Framework Programmes. Even if the UK does not exit the Framework Programmes, its influence over the governance of the programmes will be diminished (e.g. if it continues as some kind of associate member), and it is also possible that other member states would be less inclined to look to the UK as an example of RRI governance.

13 Marc Maesschalck also expresses regret at the absence of a properly elaborated theory of governance to underpin the RRI framework – see Maesschalck (2016) – and advocates a reflexive theory of governance as an alternative to Sabel and Zeitlin's experimentalist approach.
14 Many thanks to Bernard Reber and Robert Gianni for their helpful and constructive comments on this paper.

References

Arnaldi, S. (2013). *MORRI 1st Country Report Italy.* Brussels: ResAGorA.

Assemblée Nationale. (2017). *Office Parlementaire d'évaluation des choix scientifiques et technologiques.* Accessed 29 March 2016. http://www2.assemblee-nationale.fr/14/les-delegations-comite-et-office-parlementaire/office-parlementaire-d-evaluation-des-choix-scientifiques-et-technologiques.

Bassetti Foundation. (2016). *Fondazione Giannino Bassetti.* Accessed July 7, 2016. www.fondazionebassetti.org/en.

Council of the European Union. (2014). *Rome Declaration on Responsible Research and Innovation in Europe.* Rome: European Commission.

Dabrowska, P. (2010). "EU Governance of GMOs: Political Struggles and Experimentalist Solutions?" In: *Experimentalist Governance in the European Union: Towards a New Architecture*, by Charles Sabel and Jonathan Zeitlin. Oxford: Oxford University Press, pp. 171–214.

Danish Board of Technology Foundation. (2017). *Creating Society Together.* Accessed March 29, 2017. http://www.tekno.dk/?lang=en.

DG Comm Research and Speechwriting Unit. (2013). *Special Eurobarometer: Responsible Research and Innovation, Science and Technology.* Directorate General for Communication. Brussels: European Commission.

Eckert, S., and T. A. Boerzel. (2012). "Experimentalist Governance: An Introduction". *Regulation and Governance* 6 (3), pp. 371–377.

EPSRC. (2016). *Framework for Responsible Innovation.* Accessed July 7, 2016. https://www.epsrc.ac.uk/index.cfm/research/framework.

ESSEC Business School. (2017). *Responsible Innovation Department.* Accessed 29 March 2016. http://www.isis.essec.edu/responsible-innovation-departement---rid/Our-actions.

Eticas. (2016). *Eticas: Where Social Science Meets Technology and Security.* Accessed July 7, 2016. http://www.eticasconsulting.com.

EUR-Lex. (2016). *Glossary of Summaries.* 29 March. http://eur-lex.europa.eu/summary/glossary/subsidiarity.html.

European Commission. (2014). *Guidance for Evaluators of Horizon 2020 Proposals.* Brussels: European Commission.

European Commission. (2016). *Horizon 2020.* Accessed March 29, 2017. https://ec.europa.eu/programmes/horizon2020/en/h2020-section/responsible-research-innovation.

European Commission. (2016). *Horizon 2020 Work Programme 2016-17: 16 Science and Society.* Brussels: European Commission.

European Commission. (2014). "Responsible Research and Innovation". *Horizon 2020.* Accessed 19 March, 2016. ec.europa.eu.

European Commission. (2012). *Responsible Research and Innovation: Europe's Ability to Respond to Societal Challenges.* Science in Society, European Commission. Brussels: Publications Office of the European Union.

European Commission. (2016). *Science with and for Society*. Accessed July 7, 2016. https://ec.europa.eu/programmes/horizon2020/en/h2020-section/science-and-society.

Expert Group on Policy Indicators for Responsible Research and Innovation. (2015). *Indicators for Promoting and Monitoring Responsible Research and Innovation*. Brussels: European Commission.

Expert Group on the State of the Art in Europe on Responsible Research and Innovation. (2013). *Options for Strengthening Responsible Research and Innovation*. Directorate B – European Research Area, Directorate General for Research and Innovation, Brussels: European Commission.

Filacek, A. (2013). *Brief Analysis Addressing the RRI Situation and Policies in the Czech Republic*. Brussels: ResAGorA.

Finlayson, J. Gordon, and F. Freyenhagen. (2011). “Introduction”. In: J. Gordon Finlayson and F. Freyenhagen (Eds.) *Habermas and Rawls: Disputing the Political*. London: Routledge, pp. 1–25.

Fisher, E., and A. Rip. (2013). *Responsible Innovation: Multi-Level Dynamics and Soft Intervention Practices*. Chichester: Wiley.

Fung, A. (2003). *Deepening Democracy*. London: Verso.

Griessler, E. (2013). *RRI in Austria – Preliminary Observations*. Brussels: ResAGorA.

Habermas, J. (1998). *Between Facts and Norms: Contributions to a Discourse Theory of Law and Democracy*. Boston: MIT Press.

Howarth, R., A. Ingraffea and T. Engelder. (2011). “Natural Gas: Should Fracking Stop?” *Nature: International Weekly Journal of Science* 477, pp. 271–275.

Hufnagl, M. (2013). *MORRI 1st Country Report Germany*. Brussels: ResAGorA.

Inzelt, A. and L. Csonka. (2013). *Responsible Research and Innovation in Hungary*. Brussels: ResAGorA.

Kozlowski, J. (2013). *Responsible Research and Innovation in Poland: First Results*. Brussels: ResAGorA.

Maesschalck, M. (2016). *Reflexive Governance for Research and Innovation Knowledge*. London: Wiley.

Mejlgaard, N., C. Bloch, L. Degn, T. Ravn and M. W. Nielsen. (2008). *Monitoring Policy and Research Activities on Science and Society in Europe – Final Synthesis Report*. European Commission, Luxembourg: Publications Office of the European Union.

Murphy, P. and S. Hughes. (2013). *The Beginnings of RRI in Ireland*. Brussels: ResAGorA.

Mutz, D. (2006). *Hearing the Other Side: Deliberative versus Participatory Democracy*. Cambridge: Cambridge University Press.

Nederlands Organisatie voor Wetenschappelijk Onderzoek. (2016). *NWO-MVI (Maatschappelijk Verantwoord Innoveren)*. Accessed July 4, 2016. http://www.nwo.nl/onderzoek-en-resultaten/programmas/maatschappelijk+verantwoord+innoveren.

Nieminen, M. (2013). *RRI Policy in Finland – Overview Based on Selected Documents*. Brussels: ResAGorA.

NU. (2013). “Moeizame weg naar e-patiëntendossier”, *NU.nl*. 2013 February. Accessed March 29, 2017 http://www.nu.nl/gezondheid/3123666/moeizame-weg-e-patienten dossier.html.

NWO. (2016). *NWO-MVI Conference 2016*. Accessed July 7, 2016. www.nwo.nl/en/research-and-results/programmes/responsible+innovation/meetings/nwo-mvi+conference+2016.

NWO. (2010). *Responsible Innovation: Project Summaries*. Humanities Division, The Hague: Netherlands Organisation for Scientific Research.

Owen, R., P. Macnaghten, and J. Stilgoe. (2012). "Responsible Research and Innovation: From Science in Society to Science With Society, For Society". *Science and Public Policy* 6, pp. 751–760.

Owen, R. and N. Goldberg. (2010). "Responsible Innovation: A Pilot Study with the UK Engineering and Physical Sciences Research Council". *Risk Analysis* 30 (11), pp. 1699–1707.

Reber, B. (2012). *La démocratie génétiquement modifée.* Paris: Presses Université Laval.

Reillon, V. (2016). *EU Innovation Policy: Part II.* Brussels: European Parliamentary Research Service.

ResAGorA. (2015). *RRI Trends.* July. Accessed July 4, 2016. https://rritrends.res-agora.eu/reports.

Revuelta, G. (2013). *Overview on Spanish National Policies towards Responsible Research and Innovation.* Brussels: ResAGorA.

RRI Tools Project. (2017). *RRI Tools.* Accessed March 29, 2017. https://www.rri-tools.eu/.

Sabel, C. and J. Zeitlin. (2012a). "Experimentalism in the EU: Common Ground and Persistent Differences". *Regulation and Governance* 6 (3), pp. 410–426.

Sabel, C. and J. Zeitlin. (2012b). "Experimentalist Governance". In: D. Leiv-Faur (Ed.), *The Oxford Handbook of Governance.* Oxford: Oxford University Press, pp. 169–187.

Sabel, C. and J. Zeitlin. (2010). "Learning from Difference: the New Architecture of Experimentalist Governance in the EU". In: C. Sabel and J. Zeitlin (Eds.), *Experimentalist Governance in the EU: Towards a New Architecture.* Oxford: Oxford University Press, pp. 1–28.

Scott, W. R. (2004). "Institutional Theory". In: G. Ritzer (Ed.), *Encylopedia of Social Theory.* Thousand Oaks, CA: SAGE, pp. 408–414.

Shiffrin, S. (2010). "Inducing Moral Deliberation: On the Occasional Virtues of Fog". *Harvard Law Review* 123, pp. 1214–1246.

SoScience. (2016). *SoScience – Driving Responsible Innovation.* Accessed July 7, 2016. www.soscience.org.

Stilgoe, J., R. Owen and P. Macnaghten. (2013). "Developing a Framework for Responsible Innovation". *Research Policy* 42 (9), pp. 1568–1580.

Strand, R.(Chair), Spaapen, J. (Rapporteur); Bauer, M. W., Hogan, E., Revuelta, G. and Stagl, S. (Members); and Paula, L. and Guimarães Pereira, Â. (Contributors) (2015). *Indicators for Promoting and Monitoring Responsible Research and Innovation.* Brussels: Directorate General for Research and Innovation.

Sveinsdottir, T. (2013). *Responsible Research and Innovation in Iceland: Review of National Policies.* Brussels: ResAGorA.

Sveinsdottir, T. (2013). *UK National Policies on RRI.* Brussels: ResAGorA.

Tancoigne, E. and P.-B. Joly. (2013). *RRI in France – First Report.* Brussels: ResAGorA.

Tauginiene, L. and S. Maciukaite-Zvinien. (2013). *RRI in Lithuania.* Brussels: ResAGorA.

Technopolis Group. (2014). *European Added Value of EU Science, Technology and Innovation Actions.* Brussels: Directorate General for Research and Innovation.

The Guardian. (2016). *British public support for fracking sinks to lowest ever level.* 13 October. Accessed March 29, 2017 https://www.theguardian.com/environment/2016/oct/13/british-public-support-for-fracking-sinks-to-lowest-ever-level.

Tsipouri, L. (2013). *MORRI 1st Country Report Greece.* Brussels: ResAGorA.

University of Lyon. (2016). *Universite de Lyon.* Accessed July 7, 2016. www.universite-lyon.fr/sciences-societe/.

van der Graaf, P. (2012). *EPR in the Dutch Hospitals: A Decade of Changes.* University of Twente, Enschede: University of Twente.

Van Oudheusden, M. (2014). "Where Are the Politics in Responsible Innovation? European Governance, Technology Assessment and Beyond". *Journal of Responsible Innovation* 1 (1), pp. 67–86.

von Homeyer, I. (2010). "Emerging Experimentalism in EU Environmental Governance". In: C. Sabel and J. Zeitlin (Eds.), *Experimentalist Governance in the European Union: Towards a New Architecture*. Oxford: Oxford University Press, pp. 121–150.

Von Schomberg, R. (2013). "A Vision of Responsible Research and Innovation". In: R. Owen, J. Bessant and M. Heintz (Eds.), *Responsible Innovation: Managing the Responsible Emergence of Science and Innovation in Society*. Chichester: Wiley, pp. 34–48.

Vos, E. (2010). "Responding to Catastrophe: Towards a New Architecture for EU Food Saftey Regulation?" In: C. Sabel and J. Zeitlin (Eds.), *Experimentalist Governance in the European Union: Towards a New Architecture*. Oxford: Oxford University Press, pp. 151–176.

6 Policy relevance and the concept of responsible research and innovation

Anna-Lena Guske and Klaus Jacob

Introduction

We live in a world of increasing interdependencies and uncertainty, which poses a challenge to society and decision-makers in particular. Societal issues that need to be addressed by policy-making are complex: on the one hand, decisions are often pressing and time for decisions is limited; on the other hand, the impacts are often unclear and far-reaching. As the example of climate change shows, decision-makers have to take decisions considering several types of uncertainties:

- future drivers of climate change are unclear
- the responses of the climate system to the past, current and future drivers of climate change are uncertain
- the models and methods of scientists for developing future climate scenarios are limited

At the same time, decisions may affect not only the intended target group, but may also cause side-effects with negative and/or positive impacts on other societal groups, the economy or the environment. Similarly, the development and implementation of new technologies is often fraught with uncertainty about its effects on society and is therefore often contested in societies as examples like geoengineering or nanotechnologies show. Hence, decision-makers are interested in reducing the associated risks with these uncertainties as much as possible (Stilgoe *et al.* 2013). Therefore, at European Union level, but also in the member states, the question of how to assess research and innovation's impact on society is gaining momentum. Two distinct yet related discourses are particularly relevant in this context:

First, transdisciplinary research approaches, such as sustainability science, have the aim of integrating multiple scientific disciplines as well non-academic stakeholders to jointly work on pressing societal issues with the aim of producing knowledge that is relevant in societal decision-making. It is a demand-driven research approach that puts societal relevance at the heart of the research process (Kates *et al.* 2001; Brandt *et al.* 2013; Jahn *et al.* 2012; Klein *et al.* 2001).

Secondly, the discourse on responsible innovation also focuses on the societal implications of research and innovation with a focus on, but not limited to, the ethical dimension of (technological) innovations. In this context, responsibility is conceptualized as an active forward-looking modality, which aims at proactively steering the innovation process in a participative way (Arnaldi *et al.* 2016, Owen *et al.* 2012).

The topic has also been taken up by the European Commission (EC) and manifests in the concept of Responsible Research and Innovation (RRI), which has been developed at the EC since 2010 with the purpose of involving society and integrating societal needs and demands more strongly in future research funding programmes (Owen *et al.* 2012). In this context, Rene von Schomberg (2011) proposed a now widely used definition of RRI: "Responsible Research and Innovation is a transparent, interactive process by which societal actors and innovators become mutually responsive to each other with a view on the (ethical) acceptability, sustainability and social desirability of the innovation process and its marketable products (in order to allow a proper embedding of scientific and technological advances in our society)" (von Schomberg 2011: 9).

The uptake of RRI in European research and innovation policy contexts reflects an increasing awareness of profound impacts of innovations on society and the increased willingness to challenge traditional models of science and research as proposed in both the discourse on policy-relevant research and responsible innovation. However, the implementation of such participatory research approaches faces several challenges: researchers fear that their credibility will be questioned if they engage in societal decision-making, there are no agreed quality criteria for societally relevant research yet and additional resources for scientists and stakeholders are needed to engage in joint research projects.

In the following, we examine which implications this shift towards the increased societal relevance of research has for research, how it is reflected in research policies and which steps are needed to further promote these research approaches.

Changing expectations? New requirements for research

Science for society – the demand for policy relevant research

Many current societal issues have in common that they are complex in nature and are characterized by their long-term and large-scale impacts, entrenched interests, compounding risks and uncertainties – so called "wicked problems" (Balint *et al.* 2011; Blok *et al.* 2016; van den Hove 2007; Head 2008; Rockström *et al.* 2009). These include maintaining economic prosperity despite the challenges of increasing and intensifying competition in a globalized economic world, or demographic change and an ageing population in most European countries, etc. However, economic growth and prosperity is not the only goal pursued by governments and society. At the same time, societies aim for sustainable development, keeping in mind not only economic prosperity but also social cohesion and environmental protection. Integrating the economic, environmental and social dimensions into decision-making is often a challenge as the impacts on the different dimensions are manifold and often intertwined, which makes it difficult to have an overview of all effects on society and the environment at large. Therefore, expectations emerge regarding a policy-relevant sustainability science that would help in achieving sustainable development.

Also, in the context of innovation, expectations for integrating societal demands are increasing. Research and innovation will – at least to some extent – always be unpredictable and associated with uncertainties about their impacts on society or the environment. To avoid unwanted side-effects and to improve acceptance of innovation, technologies are to be assessed against not only the economic potentials but also the social, environmental and ethical implications.

Such expectations are highly visible in areas such as nanotechnology, genomics or geoengineering. But also, increasingly, questions with regard to privacy in the development of Information and Communication Technologies (ICT) are high on the agenda, which has both an ethical dimension as well as a security dimension (Stahl *et al.* 2010; Van Schomberg 2011; Quigley 2005). This is also reflected in the emerging concept of RRI (Karinen and Guston 2010; Owen *et al.* 2012, van den Hoven et. al. 2013; von Schomberg 2012; von Schomberg 2011).

Against this background, not just applied research but also basic science are expected to support shedding light on these complexities and to point out ways of how to handle the issues at stake. The evidence base of decision-making is perceived as a major source of legitimacy for decision-making. There are at least three major areas in which science is expected to contribute to societal needs and demands:

First, science is increasingly involved in identifying the need for action to achieve set objectives such as sustainable development. One example is the Intergovernmental Panel on Climate Change (IPCC), which has developed scenarios to better understand the future impacts of climate change since 1988. In its reports, the IPCC sets out the technical and socio-economic information that is relevant to understand the risks associated with climate change and its potential impacts (e.g. IPCC 2014). Another example of science informing about the need for action is the Intergovernmental Science-Policy Platform on Biodiversity and Ecosystem Services (IPBES). IPBES has the objective to synthesize and critically assess knowledge in the context of biodiversity loss and ecosystem (e.g. IPBES 2016).

Secondly, knowledge on possible societal goals is demanded. Science is requested to develop and to justify the goals to be achieved, such as, for example, the goal of not exceeding global temperature rise beyond 2°C or 1.5°C. The definition of 'planetary boundaries' (Rockström *et al.* 2009; Steffen *et al.* 2015) is another example which is gaining influence in societal debates. Science is invited to further specify and operationalize what is necessary, but also what is feasible and desirable. Given the normative core of these aspects, it is a sensitive issue, and not all scientists are willing to become engaged in this.

Yet the role of science in addressing societal challenges is not limited to pointing out needs for action and possible goals and visions for society. Third, in order to address these and other societal challenges, the development of options for actions is necessary. On the one hand, science can offer innovations, including technological solutions as well as social innovations. This may include technologies like carbon capture and storage (CCS) to address climate change, which are highly debated in society, and technologies to increase energy efficiency to decrease greenhouse gas emissions, but also education programs to foster environmentally friendly behaviour. In most cases, it is not sufficient to develop social or technological innovations. Scientists and innovators also need to keep in mind both the normative and the social acceptability of innovations and create mechanisms to ensure acceptance of the innovation and demonstrate it benefits for society and sustainable development (van den Hoven *et al.* 2013).

At the same time, adequate policies need to be implemented to support social and technological change towards sustainable development. Research is increasingly sought after to help identify adequate policy options to address complex societal issues. Hence, research is increasingly asked to support the determination of which policy option(s) out of the variety of options available is most suitable to achieve the objectives set by policy-makers. Evidence is increasingly being gathered to unravel the complexity of relationships between policies and societal issues. One example of the growing importance of evidence in policy-making is the increasing adoption and broadened requirements for policy impact assessment (IA). IA is an ex-ante method and formalized process to understand the likely impacts of decisions to advise decision-makers proactively on their potential advantages and disadvantages (Meuleman 2014). It is now a formalized instrument in all OECD (Organisation for Economic Cooperation and Development) countries, and is also spreading beyond. IA provides a framework for ensuring basic comparability of policy options while being adaptable to all policy sectors integrating all three pillars of sustainable development. In order to achieve this, an IA starts with framing the problem, which should be addressed by a new policy measure to justify the need for action. This includes the development of a baseline scenario explaining how the current situation would evolve in the future if no additional action is taken. This also sets the system boundaries and determines the framework for the assessment. In this way, complexity is reduced and the analysis becomes manageable. Based on this, different policy options are developed that may be suitable to address the problem. To come to a conclusion on which policy option is most suitable for achieving the set objectives, decision-makers include scientific information that takes into account the complex relationships between the different dimensions of sustainable development and their impacts on society. The analysis points out the cause-and-effect-relationships between a policy and the system analysed by bringing together all relevant knowledge and contextualizing it with regard to the policy objectives. This analysis provides a basis for comparing the options against one another and against the status quo (Jacob 2010; Jacob *et al.* 2011).

However, not all scientific knowledge that is available is taken up by society or in policy processes, even if it is regarded as scientifically credible in the scientific community. Often, knowledge is not perceived relevant and therefore disregarded in decision-making or contested based on ethical concerns (Podhora *et al.* 2013; Turnpenny *et al.* 2009; Hertin *et al.* 2009; Macnaghten 2012; Karinen & Guston 2010). Even if developed in a participatory way, and considering ethical theories, the plurality of norms and interest is a limitation for assessing knowledge (Reber 2015). Relevancy and social acceptability are not necessarily a property of scientific knowledge, but are determined by the contexts. Hence, scientists also need to understand decision-makers and their needs and driving forces in order to provide them with relevant information to make informed decisions. However, developing policy-relevant and socially acceptable knowledge is often a challenge for researchers.

Living up to expectations – how to create policy relevance

Currently, knowledge systems are either focused on scientific discovery and publication or on the development or improvement of technologies that are successful in the markets. In the first case, science addresses questions that are defined by scientists. Quality is assessed in peer reviews by other scientists and can be measured, e.g. in citations. In the second case, programming and assessment of research is primarily by business. The success of innovation can be measured by uptake in the markets. However, this focus on scientific excellence on the one hand and innovation on the other does not necessarily meet the demand for knowledge in societal decision-making (Cash *et al.* 2003). Awareness that these 'wicked problems' cannot be solved by traditional (excellence-oriented) knowledge production is being raised. In this traditional view, science is often regarded as a linear system of knowledge production in which science is puzzle-solving and develops by accumulating accepted (by the scientific community) facts and theories ('normal science'). The way science is organized, e.g. the requirements of scientific publications or the criteria for the promotion of scientists, are reinforcing this mode of science. Scientific rationality was seen as a key to solving societal issues, which implied that decision-makers' knowledge of policy-making was replaced by a scientifically validated type of knowledge. In this view, the role of science in policy was seen as 'speaking truth to power' (Kuhn 1962; Lasswell 1971; Wildavsky 1979). This way of understanding and conducting science, however, seems insufficient to address many of the current knowledge demands of societal relevance. It has become increasingly accepted that scientists, in the context of policy-making, shape the world they study by the way they frame problems or research questions and by the assumptions underlying their research. From this viewpoint, the science policy interface is regarded as a two-way process which can be described as the 'scientification' of policy and the politicization of science. One illustration of this interplay between science and policy-making is that scientists have been the first to point out many political issues, such as environmental pollution, before they were taken up in policy-making. In this way, science shapes the way problems are perceived in society. On the other hand, scientific knowledge and innovations are necessarily judged by society when they enter the public arena, and are expected to deliver solutions to formerly identified problems. Consequently, science can no longer claim to 'speak truth to power'. Rather, this view is increasingly replaced by different modes of 'making sense together', i.e. including societies' demands in the knowledge-creation process (Hoppe 2010; Weingart 1999; Hellström and Jacob 2000).

However, living up to these expectations poses a challenge for science. In order to be relevant to societal decision-making, Cash *et al.* (2003) have developed three criteria for creating knowledge that is relevant for decision-making:

1 Credibility: Knowledge must be perceived as credible by decision-makers in order to be taken up in decision-making processes. This criterion refers to scientific adequacy, so that arguments and scientific evidence are open to scrutiny, and are developed according to current standards of scientific excellence.
2 Legitimacy: As a second criterion, knowledge has to be regarded as legitimate by the different stakeholders involved in the decision-making process. These stakeholders do not necessarily share the same values, beliefs and priorities. Legitimacy can be created by reflecting these different perceptions and being transparent about the methods used and assumptions made in the scientific process. In this way, it can be shown that the production of information or technologies has taken these diverging world views into account.
3 Salience: Even if knowledge was produced according to the criteria of scientific excellence and transparency, it is not guaranteed that it is used in decision-making processes. This is often due to a lack of awareness of the decision-makers needs in terms of the timing and/or focus, scale and scope of the information provided. Creating salience by considering the needs of decision-makers in the knowledge-production process is therefore the third crucial criterion.

While developing credible and legitimate information is less of a problem, knowledge produced in the traditional way often fails to be perceived as salient and is not used in decision-making processes as it is not relevant to decision-makers. Reasons may be that the scope of a study does not fit the policy-makers' demands or information is provided only too late, when decisions have already been taken in the political arena (Cash *et al.* 2003). One reason for this gap between the provision of scientific information and the uptake in policy-making is that salience and relevancy are aspects which are not only a property of research itself, but are attributed by the recipients or users of this information. Furthermore, there is no uniform view on the relevancy and salience of science, and as a result, science and scientists are assessed by non-scientific criteria and become part of societal debate. This imposes a risk for scientists of losing their credibility in the scientific community if their presence in societal debates leads to a situation in which their research is perceived as biased.

Science with the ambition of informing decision-makers, especially in the context of 'wicked problems', requires strong interaction with stakeholders outside the scientific community in a joint process of innovation and shared learning ('post-normal science') to be relevant for decision-making (Gibbon *et al.* 1994; Funtowicz & Ravetz 1993; Funtowicz & Ravetz 1991; Hoppe 2010). However, the aspiration of integrating societal demands and needs of decision-makers into the scientific process is often difficult because such approaches do not follow the same mechanisms as traditional knowledge production. Therefore, scientific approaches towards creating policy relevance of science are still lacking recognition in mainstream science (Jahn *et al.* 2012). Researchers who nevertheless have the aim of integrating societal needs into their research process often face the following challenges:

First, knowledge for decision-making contexts needs a specific problem orientation. In that sense, policy-relevant science has the aim of solving 'real-world problems' and is generated in a context of application from the beginning. Even if traditional knowledge production ('mode 1') can also result in practical applications, the real-world problem is usually not the starting point of the research, with some exceptions like engineering, for example. Hence, in 'mode 1' science, there is often a gap between the actual knowledge production and its practical application so that mechanisms of knowledge transfer between the two worlds are needed. In contrast to this, 'mode 2 science' is conceptualized with a specific societally relevant problem in mind (Hessels and van Lente 2008; Jahn *et al.* 2012; Nowotny *et al.* 2001).

However, as pointed out before, many current societal issues are complex in nature. They are often difficult to solve because of incomplete or contradictory knowledge, large consequences and connections with other societal challenges (Funtowicz & Ravetz 1993; van den Hoven *et al.* 2013; van den Hove 2007). Addressing these four challenges requires cross-disciplinary approaches towards knowledge production, which go beyond interdisciplinary collaboration. Rather, it is necessary to mobilize and integrate a variety of theoretical perspectives and methodological approaches from various scientific disciplines and beyond, also including practitioners' views from outside the academic world (Hessels and van Lente 2008; Jahn *et al.* 2013; Pohl 2014). Hence, the requirements for producing knowledge that is relevant in decision-making processes go beyond interdisciplinary approaches towards research. In addition to the integration of different scientific disciplines, the views of societal stakeholders need to be included as well.

Following on from the requirements of integrating society into the research process and, vice versa, of integrating science more closely into societal decision-making, it becomes clear that expertize is not a privilege of science anymore. In a close exchange with practitioners, research results are challenged not only within the scientific community but are also discussed and possibly questioned by people outside academia. This requires the researcher to develop mechanisms to establish trust and acceptance of his/her research results beyond traditional means of academic quality control (van den Hoven *et al.* 2013; Jahn *et al.* 2013; Maasen 2008).

Despite these challenges for researchers, attention to the role of scientific knowledge in strategic contexts is rising (Jansen *et al.* 2013; Richardson and Cashmore 2011; Partidário and Sheate 2013), and different approaches have been developed to accommodate these new requirements. As a response to these requests, new concepts for the production of knowledge with relevance for societal decision-making have started to evolve.

Analysis of contexts

As a starting point for increasing societal relevance, the context in which knowledge or an innovation is to be used needs to be clear. Often it is assumed that knowledge and the context in which it is used are uniform. However, both the knowledge-production process and decision-making process are complex. Hence, a shared understanding of the requirements of decision-makers is needed as well as a description of available knowledge, which contextualizes this information with regard to these requirements. This can be reached by analysing policy context from available literature, policy documents etc. This contextual knowledge can then be used to describe research and its results in a way that responds to the knowledge demands of society (Ward *et al.* 2009; Jansen *et al.* 2013).

Knowledge brokerage

While analysing the context in which knowledge is to be used is a first step in creating policy-relevant knowledge, it is also necessary to develop approaches and create mechanisms to transfer both scientific knowledge into decision-making contexts as well as decision-makers' views and demands into research processes by engaging scientists and decision-makers in a dialogue (van Kammen *et al.* 2006; Ward *et al.* 2009). Knowledge brokerage is one of these approaches for long-term learning of science and decision-making by slowly feeding information and new perspectives into decision-making processes, and the other way around. A knowledge broker or boundary worker acts as a mediator between the two worlds and facilitates the exchange by utilizing different techniques. These techniques range from disseminating targeted information to facilitating exchange between experts and decision-makers in workshops to jointly collaborating on co-managing and co-producing knowledge throughout the entire research process (Michaels 2009; Weiland 2011). In this view of the interface between science and society, decision-makers are actively participating in the learning process for sharing knowledge and are not merely passive recipients of (scientific) information. Hence, knowledge brokerage is a two-way approach towards sharing knowledge by creating dialogue between users of knowledge and its producers (Hertin *et al.* 2009; van Kammen *et al.* 2006; Ward *et al.* 2009; Partidário and Sheate 2013; Sheate and Partidário 2010).

Transdisciplinary research

A third pathway towards increasing the societal relevance of research is the application of 'mode 2' research as a way to perform 'mode 2 science'. There are different forms of 'mode 2 science', which have in common that they share a specific problem orientation with the objective of developing solution options by collaborating with scientists from different disciplines and stakeholders outside academia (Lang *et al.* 2012). For example, transdisciplinary research is defined as a research approach which includes multiple scientific disciplines as well as practitioners from outside academia who all focus on a shared problem in the knowledge-production process

(Brandt *et al.* 2013: 1). Hence, the transdisciplinary approach is a demand-driven form of research, focusing on societal problems. So, transdisciplinarity describes a new form of doing research in an inclusive way (Jahn *et al.* 2012; Klein *et al.* 2001). In the context of sustainable development, sustainability science has evolved as another concept for addressing today's complex and pressing societal issues, focusing on the dynamic interactions between nature and society (Kates *et al.* 2001). Like transdisciplinary research, this approach has the objective of integrating all relevant knowledge, making divergent values transparent and coming to an agreement on joint preferences of society, as well as creating ownership of options on how to solve these issues (Lang *et al.* 2012).

Collaborative research approaches, such as transdisciplinary research or sustainability science, are contested outside the relevant communities in academia and in parts of society that were not part of the research process. Some critics question its credibility with regard to the reliability and validity of the research; others may contest the salience or relevance of the produced knowledge in decision-making contexts (Cash *et al.* 2003; Lang *et al.* 2012). Therefore, conducting research that is relevant for societal decision-making needs different framework conditions regarding resources and evaluation criteria than traditional science for undertaking analyses of societal demands, as will be shown in the following.

Creating framework conditions – a reflection of new requirements in science policy

Changing the rules of the game – integrating societal relevance in research policies

The growing demand for policy-relevant research not only led to changes in how research is done; the new requirements for doing societally relevant research is also reflected in research policies. While scientific excellence and innovation are still major objectives of research policy, in addition, a new additional dimension is gaining importance: societal relevance and the consideration of societal concerns and demands in research.

The growing importance of innovation-oriented and applied research is reflected in high-level political agreements and strategies. For example, the Lisbon Treaty authorizes the European Union (EU) to create a European Research Area (ERA) (Art. 179 TFEU) which entails – among other measures – the adoption of multiannual research programs. This goes beyond the former European research policy as 'scientific and technological advance' now is officially a distinct objective of the Treaty (Art. 3.3 TEU). The Europe 2020 strategy again stresses the importance of research and innovation for the EU, which sets the priorities of achieving smart, sustainable and inclusive growth in Europe. Investment in research and development (R&D) activities is seen as a key instrument to achieve these policy goals (EC 2010: 10). The need for linking society and its needs and demands more closely to the research and innovation process is also reflected in the Directorate-General for Research & Innovation (DG RTD) and its Science with and for Society programme under Horizon 2020, which was designed to bridge the gap between the scientific community and society. The current programme has roots in the Science and Society Action Plan, which was introduced in 2001, and later became Science in Society (SiS) before it developed into the Science with and for Society programme in later years. In this context, DG RTD has started to develop a framework for RRI, which goes beyond addressing legal concerns connected to research and innovation activities such as genetically modified organisms (GMOs), geoengineering or privacy issues of new ICTs. Rather, it aims at including societal actors in the whole research and innovation process to align research with the needs and expectations of society. In this way, discussions on the ethical dimensions of research are broadened by the dimension of societal relevance. The aim is to increase the societal relevance of research via participatory research approaches (von Schomberg 2011; Sutcliffe 2011; Owen *et al.* 2012). Both requirements – i.e. the ethical acceptability of research and the societal relevance – can be complementary: first, from the point of view of research policies – by combining the issues under the umbrella of RRI, legitimacy and political relevance are reinforced. Second, from the point of view of organizing research – both require an opening of the black boxes of scientific inquiry and the interaction with stakeholders. There are, however, also tensions in combining the agendas: within scientific disciplines, relevance is more often an attribute of applied sciences. As a result, scientists may disregard the principles and processes of RRI, which are committed to basic research, as they may be considered not relevant.

The target of creating an Innovation Union stresses the importance of research activities' relevance for society. This is reflected, first, in re-focusing research and innovation policy on major policy challenges like climate change; health; demographic change and wellbeing; food security; sustainable agriculture; marine and maritime research and the bio-economy; secure, clean and efficient energy; smart, green and integrated transport; resource efficiency and raw materials; inclusive, innovative and secure societies ('Grand Challenges'). Second, European research policy has the aim of closing the gap between science and the market and fostering the turning of inventions into marketable products and thereby facilitating Europe's global competitiveness. So, the current research framework programme (Horizon 2020), which is funding European R&D activities between 2014 and 2020, consists of three main pillars: Excellent Science, Industrial Leadership and Societal Challenges (EC 2011; EC 2010). Also, in former research funding programmes, the support for innovation and the concern to increase European competitiveness were major objectives. And the integration of social and natural sciences in innovation processes from early on has also already been promoted in European research funding in previous framework programmes to a certain extent (Rodríguez *et al.* 2013; Andrée 2009). But the need for policy-relevant science is also reflected in European research framework programmes. For example, Podhora *et al.* (2013) analysed the variety of tools that were funded in the framework programmes FP6 and FP7 with the designated purpose of supporting IA. Out of the 7,781 projects that were funded in FP6 and FP7, 203 (2.6%) that designed tools for the IA process were identified, covering a variety of impact areas such as economic and environmental impacts and, to a lesser extent, social impacts of a proposed policy. At first sight, 2.6% seems to be a small number, especially considering that FP6 and FP7 were explicitly dedicated to providing evidence for decision-making (Annerberg *et al.* 2010; Rietschel *et al.* 2009). Nevertheless, FP6 and FP7 were mainly driven by a scientific rationale that provided researchers with a high degree of freedom regarding the design of research, while research to support policy processes is only recently emerging in many research fields. Considering this, the number of projects developing tools to support IA is high (Podhora *et al.* 2013).

The societal dimension of research is becoming more pronounced in Horizon 2020 than it has been in previous framework programs. This is shown not only in the uptake of societal challenges as thematic issues in one of the three pillars of Horizon 2020, but is also reflected in the conceptual approaches towards research promoted in this context. Research on societal challenges should bring together knowledge from different scientific disciplines and technologies, as well as supporting activities beyond the research process such as piloting or support for public procurement, etc. Which disciplines, technologies etc. should work together depends on the addressed problem and research question (EC 2011).

This shift towards integrating societal needs and policy relevance into research funding can be observed not only at the European level. In some of the member states, funding programs dedicated exclusively to research with societal relevance have also been introduced. For example, the German research-funding scheme FONA (*Forschung für nachhaltige Entwicklung* [Research for Sustainable Development]) is funding research for developing decision-making tools for future-oriented action with regard to a sustainable society. The program was developed in a collaborative process involving stakeholders from academia, policy-making, business and civil society to identify relevant research priorities. The Federal Ministry for Education and Research initiated an agenda process which brought together the relevant stakeholders in workshops and expert consultations. They identified relevant guiding questions, prioritized them and integrated these research questions into a research strategy. Later on, these were specified and translated into research funding programmes (BMBF 2015; Thorn 2015). Building on this process, three flagship initiatives were identified: Green Economy, the City of the Future and the Energy Transition in Germany. These challenges are not just specific to Germany. Hence, there are overlaps with research priorities in other contexts, such as the EU. However, the substantiation of the research questions is tied to the German context and challenges. Research as part of these flagships is designed to be application-oriented, involves researchers from multiple disciplines and requires the inclusion of stakeholders, such as businesses and local communities, in the research process. The overall objective of research under this framework programme is to support implementation processes and, by doing so, to stimulate sustainable development (BMBF 2015). But also in the Netherlands, the Dutch Responsible Innovation Programme (MVI) is funding multi-disciplinary research projects in close cooperation with stakeholders from business and society to foster innovation relating to the Grand Challenges (NOW 2016), as well as Austria, with its provision-funding scheme (Felt *et al.* 2016). Such research programmes acknowledge the need for different approaches towards research if societally relevant research addressing the Grand Challenges should be supported. They reflect the need for a close involvement of stakeholders from policy, business and society in both the design and priority-setting of funding schemes as well as in conducting the research to ensure that societally relevant results will be achieved. However, these funding programmes only account for a small fraction of the overall amount of research funding and cannot yet be considered as a mainstream approach for designing research-funding programmes (van den Hoven *et al.* 2013).

Next to funding programmes that specifically address societally relevant research and evaluate research proposals with regard to their possible contributions to the Grand Challenges, in mainstream research funding, societal impact is also gaining momentum as an additional evaluation criterion beyond scientific excellence. Not only under Horizon 2020 do applicants have to demonstrate the societal impact of their research; also in the UK, for example, applicants for grants from one of the Research Councils have to complete a 'pathway to impact' statement demonstrating the aspired economic or societal impacts of the research. The impacts that should be demonstrated are (1) fostering global economic performance, and specifically the economic competitiveness of the UK; (2) increasing the effectiveness of public services and policy; and (3) enhancing quality of life, health and creative output (RUC 2014). This approach has caused a controversial debate in the UK, as researchers in the domain of basic research are afraid of losing their independence and access to funding to define their research questions and priorities.

Furthermore, other than for scientific excellence and for the economic potential of innovation, there are no universally agreed criteria on how to measure the societal impact of research, which makes it more difficult to consider this aspect in the decisions on research funding (van den Hoven *et al.* 2013; RCUK 2014). Research that is committed to contributing to societal decision-making is more often perceived as applied science rather than basic science, and research may be considered as a consultancy type of activity. Therefore, researchers in the domain of basic research are reluctant to engage in research with a societal impact. There is a controversial debate about how far this should be a criterion for the decisions on the funding of research (Watermeyer 2016; Strohschneider 2013; Bornmann 2012; Jahn & Keil 2015; Jahn *et al.* 2013; Lang *et al.* 2012; Scholz 2011; Maasen 2008). The debate, however, hardly distinguishes between the desirability of research with an impact and the methods to actually measure such impacts. It could be argued that, besides orientation on innovation and excellence, a third target area of societal impacts is emerging that would require its own methods for evaluation and, most importantly, indicators. The mere existence of such methods and indicators would not constrain an individual researcher or a research organization to pursue research within one or the other target area.

Remaining hurdles – obstacles for increasing policy relevance of research and innovation

Although there is a growing demand for integrating societal needs and demands in research and innovation, and even though research policies are starting to reflect this new dimension, societal needs and demands are often not considered or are considered only (too) late in research and innovation processes.

In some cases, innovations are developed and research funders invest large sums in technologies, which are technically and economically feasible. Still, they might fail on the market because they are contested by society because of ethical or security concerns. Carbon capture and storage (CCS) technologies and smart metering, but also geoengineering, GMOs or nanotechnologies, are examples of such contested innovations. Other research questions are not tackled, even if societal benefits can be expected, because no immediate economic return can be expected (van den Hoven *et al.* 2013; Stilgoe 2007; Owen *et al.* 2012, etc.). Similarly, researchers with the aim of providing knowledge relevant to decision-making face the situation that their information or tools are not used in decision-making processes. Even though a number of tools with the designated purpose of informing decision-makers have been developed (Podhora *et al.* 2013), their application in practice is limited. The reasons for this are that the available knowledge does not cover the required scale or scope. Also, the timing of providing research results may not be sufficient. The process of conducting research, compiling a report and going through scientific review processes can be time-consuming. However, research results can often only be integrated into the decision-making process at specific points in time. After this window of opportunity has passed, political decisions may be taken and further information becomes irrelevant to decision-makers. A third reason may be that decision-makers are not aware of the availability of relevant knowledge or tools (Adelle 2011; De Smedt 2010; Jacob *et al.* 2008).

Therefore, although there is a vast stock of literature available on developing methods and approaches towards ensuring societal relevance (Cash *et al.* 2003; Hessels and van Lente 2008; Jahn *et al.* 2013; Pohl 2014), the interaction (in form of mutual information on demands, knowledge needs and requirements) between science and society in research and innovation processes is still insufficient. This is due to the persistent lack of incentives for researchers to engage in science–society dialogues (Felt *et al.* 2016; Jahn *et al.* 2014; van den Hoven *et al.* 2013).

First, there are no universally agreed frameworks and criteria for evaluating the quality of societally relevant research which goes beyond excellence. There have been many approaches towards developing criteria for measuring the societal impact of research (for example, Jahn *et al.* 2013; Ernø-Kjølhede & Hansson 2011; Lang *et al.* 2012; Bergmann *et al.* 2005 and Scholz 2011). Criteria for scientific excellence have been established and are widely used in review processes, which generally focus on the product dimension of science. These criteria include, but are not limited to, the number of publications in peer-reviewed journals, amount of funding obtained, number of citations in high-ranked peer-reviewed journals and the number of patents (Matthies and Simon 2007). Criteria for the societal relevance of research have not yet been established. In contrast, the proposed evaluation frameworks for this aspect of research focus on the process dimension of research that goes beyond the existing process-related formal codes of conduct of mainstream science. These process criteria include dimensions such as the systemic character and scale of the problem addressed, the methods used and the integration of stakeholders, as well as the impact orientation of the results (Jahn & Keil 2015; Maasen 2008). Also, in the context of RRI governance, frameworks are emerging to structure the research and innovation process (Stilgoe *et al.* 2013; Lindner *et al.* 2016; von Schomberg 2011). However, there is not yet a shared approach that is accepted and used in science as well as science policy to conceptualize and evaluate research projects or research funding schemes. Therefore, engaging in transdisciplinary research still holds little reward for researchers as the main evaluation criteria for science remains scientific excellence.

The second obstacle also reflects this: the lack of career opportunities for researchers with inter- or transdisciplinary backgrounds. The main criterion for evaluating research is scientific excellence, which is measured by the number of publications in peer-reviewed journals, the research funds acquired or the market success of an innovation. There are some examples of the integration of inter- and transdisciplinary competences in the curriculums to integrate the requirements for the societal relevance of research already in the education of young researchers (Schier and Schwinger 2014). In addition, management positions are, in some cases, filled with researchers with interdisciplinary profiles. The Centre National de la Recherche Scientifique is one example. Yet, the majority of career opportunities are based on disciplinary careers. In addition, the number of journals with a high impact factor that publish transdisciplinary studies is still limited. Even though there are research funds for transdisciplinary projects available, the majority of funding is still spent on traditional research projects. A multi-disciplinary background is therefore difficult for academics to achieve, so researchers concentrate on advancing in their disciplinary field (van den Hoven *et al.* 2013; Felt *et al.* 2016).

Corresponding with the lack of academic career opportunities, training for young researchers usually follows traditional, disciplinary models of research and moves mostly within the paradigm of normal science ('mode 1'). However, transdisciplinarity requires special skills, which include taking (societal) problems as a starting point for research or communication skills for integrating different scientific disciplines and non-academic stakeholders, etc. These skills receive rather limited consideration in academic teaching (Merck and Beerman 2015).

Given the high resource intensity (at both ends – researchers as well as stakeholders need the capabilities, time etc. to participate in participative research activities) that is needed to integrate various academic disciplines and engage with stakeholders throughout the research process, establishing transdisciplinary research approaches remains a challenge, both in the context of RRI and policy-relevant research.

Conclusions

Science for decision-making in society and RRI have many overlaps in terms of methods but are different in terms of their scope and intention. For both, it is of importance to include the viewpoints of non-scientific stakeholders into the processes of research. Thereby, they share a key feature of what Funtowicz and Ravetz (1993; 1991) describe as 'post-normal' science. However, they also share different challenges: additional, non-scientific criteria for assessing the quality of research are brought into the scientific process. The consideration of such criteria is typically not rewarding for scientific careers. Researchers are promoted by their peers because of the impacts of their publications or by business because of the market success of their innovation. The consideration of ethical aspects of research and innovation going beyond ethical reviews and including moral dimensions of research or the consideration of non-marketable societal needs requires resources (time, interaction with stakeholders) or even bears risks (evaluation on the basis of ambiguous criteria). There are no accepted criteria for quality in transdisciplinary methods, but there is wide consensus that the views of stakeholders on the frame of the problem to be addressed, the desired future with regard to the problem addressed and the knowledge needed to achieve these objectives need to be taken into account.

While the tools and the challenges of their applications are similar, the scope and intention of RRI and research for society can and should be distinguished. By definition, research for society is applied research. It may, and should, build on a wider stock of basic research, but ultimately it seeks application in problem-solving, which is oriented towards societal needs and demands. Furthermore, research for society is typically interdisciplinary, as societal problems and the interdependencies of societal systems typically do not fit within disciplinary boundaries.

RRI does not necessarily share these features. The principles and tools of RRI can be and in fact should be embedded not only in applied research, but also in basic as well as in mono-disciplinary research. Basic, excellence-oriented research should take into account and integrate the principles of RRI. RRI is not limited to applied research only. There are, however, unique challenges of RRI for basic research: in highly specialized fields, it is more difficult to include stakeholder views, as it would require considerable efforts to translate between laypersons and scientists. Laypersons would be required to have a basic understanding of the scientific process and expected outcomes in order to assess the ethical implications.

Keeping the principles of RRI and applied science for society apart keeps open room for critical research: the orientation on problem-solving, the struggle for relevancy and acceptance by society in research for society may hinder the researcher to take a critical view on society as this would not be supported and rewarded in this type of research. Independent research that is committed to the principles of RRI, however, could take viewpoints that challenge society, if the principles are not harmed.

An interesting overlap between research for society and RRI would be in the field of social innovation: new strategies, concepts, ideas, organizations and patterns of behaviour in the various domains of civil society. Frequently, it is argued that transition to a sustainable development cannot be achieved by improving or replacing current technologies, but instead would require social innovation as well (Rückert-John 2013). The development of such innovation, including the research and innovation policies in support of such innovation, could greatly benefit from considering the principles of RRI. The term 'social' is ambivalent in this context. On the one hand, it refers to new patterns of human interaction; on the other hand, it is used normatively as 'good for society'. Compared with technological innovations, social innovations are not necessarily based on novel technical artefacts. Just the opposite can be the case: social innovations may be based on rediscovering old techniques and using them in new contexts to achieve societal goals. In farming, for example, local, organic farming provides a means to address challenges society faces, such as loss of biodiversity, water pollution or climate change, while at the same time fostering rural development (Di Iacovo *et al.* 2014).

Social innovations are – very much like technological innovations – not free from risks: social innovations that are based on communities may entail an exclusion of services for non-members; there may be problems from scaling up social innovation – e.g. once the sharing movement became professionalized, it resulted in (self-)exploitation of service providers, etc. Applying the principles of RRI in developing and assessing these types of innovation would help to overcome such problems while at the same time contribute to addressing the challenges of sustainable development.

References

Adelle, C. (2011). *Impact Assessment Practice in Europe.* LIAISE Innovation Report No. 2. Berlin.

Andrée, D. (2009). *Priority-setting in the European Research Framework Programmes - Vinnova Analysis.* In: Vinnova Analysis VA 2009:17, VINNO VA – Swedish Governmental Agency for Innovation Systems.

Arnaldi, S., Gorgoni, G. and Pariotti, E. (2016). RRI as a governance paradigm: What is new? In: Lindner, R., Kuhlmann, S., Randles, S., Bedsted, B., Gorgoni, G., Griessler, E., Loconto, A., Mejlgaard (Eds.), *Towards Shared Responsibility: Navigating Towards Shared Responsibility in Research and Innovation Approach, Process and Results of the Res-AGorA Project.* Karlsruhe: Fraunhofer ISI.

Annerberg, R., Begg, I., Acheson, H., Borrás, S., Hallén, A., Maimets, T., Mustonen, R., Raffler, H., Swings, J.-P. and Ylihonko, K. (2010). *Interim Evaluation of the Seventh Framework Programme, Report of the Expert Group*, November 2010. Brussels.

Balint, P.J., Stewart, R.E., Desai, A. and Walters, L.C. (2011). *Wicked Environmental Problems – Managing Uncertainty and Conflict.* Washington D.C.: Island Press.

Bergmann, M., Brohmann, B., Hoffmann, E., Loibl, M.C., Rehaag, R., Schramm, E. and Voß, J.-P. (2005). *Quality criteria of transdisciplinary research. A guide for the formative evaluation of research projects.* ISOE-Studientexte, N 13, Frankfurt am Main.

BMBF – Federal Ministry for Education and Research. (2015). *Research for Sustainable development - FONA.*[3] Framework programme of the Federal Ministry for Education and Research. Berlin.

Blok, V., Gremmen, B. and Wesselink, R. (2016). Dealing with the wicked problem of sustainability: The role of individual virtuous competence. *Business and Professional Ethics Journal*, 34(3), pp. 297–327.

Bornmann, L. (2012). Measuring the societal impact of research: Research is less and less assessed on scientific impact alone—we should aim to quantify the increasingly important contributions of science to society. *EMBO Reports*, 13(8), pp. 673–676.

Brandt, P., Ernst, A., Gralla, F., Luederitz, Ch., Lang, D.J., Newig, J., Reinert, F., Abson, D.J. and von Wehrden, H. (2013). A review of trasdisciplinary research in sustainability science. *Ecological Economics*, 92(2013), pp. 1–15.

Cash, D.W., Clar, W.C., Alcock, F., Dickson, N.M., Eckley, N., Guston, D.H., Jäger, J. and Mitchell, R.B. (2003). Knowledge systems for sustainable development. *PNAS*, 100(14), pp. 8086–8091.

De Smedt, P. (2010). The use of impact assessment tools to support sustainable policy objectives in Europe. *Ecology and Society*, 15(4), p. 30.

Di Iacovo, F., Moruzzo, R., Rossignoli, C. and Scarpellini, P. (2014). Transition management and social innovation in rural areas: Lessons from social farming. *The Journal of Agricultural Education and Extension*, 20(3), pp. 327–334.

EC – European Commission. (2011). *Horizon 2020 - The Framework Programme for Research and Innovation. Communication from the Commission to the European Parliament, the Council, the European Economic and Social Committee and the Committee of the Regions*. Brussels, COM (2011) 808 final. Available at: http://ec.europa.eu/research/horizon2020/pdf/proposals/communication_from_the_commission_-_horizon_2020_-_the_framework_programme_for_research_and_innovation.pdf (15.05.2016).

EC – European Commission. (2010). *EUROPE 2020: A strategy for smart, sustainable and inclusive growth. Communication from the Commission.* Brussels, COM (2010) 2020 final. Available at: http://eur-lex.europa.eu/legal-content/en/ALL/?uri=CELEX%3A52010DC2020 (15.05.2016).

Ernø-Kjølhede, E. and Hansson, F. (2011). Measuring research performance during a changing relationship between science and society. *Research Evaluation*, 20(2), pp. 131–143.

Felt, U., Igelsbo, J., Schikowitz, An. and Volkert, T. (2016). Transdisciplinary sustainability research in practice: Between imaginaries of collective experimentation and entrenched academic value orders. *Science, Technology, & Human Values*, 0(0), pp. 1–30.

Funtowicz, S.O. and Ravetz, J.R. (1991). A new scientific methodology for global environmental issues. In: Costanza, R. (Ed.), *Ecological Economics: The Science and Management of Sustainability*. New York: Columbia University Press, pp. 137–152.

Funtowicz, S.O. and Ravetz, J.R. (1993). Science for the post-normal age. *Futures*, 25(7), pp. 735–755.

Gibbons, M., Limoges, C., Nowotny, H., Schwartzman, S., Scott, P. and Trow, M. (1994). *The New Production of Knowledge*. London: Sage.

Head, B.W. (2008). Wicked problems in public policy. *Public Policy*, 3(2), pp. 101–118.

Hellström, T. and Jacob, M. (2000). Scientification of politics or politicization of science? Traditionalist science-policy discourse and its quarrels with mode 2 epistemology. *Social Epistemology*, 14(1), pp. 69–77.

Hertin, J., Turnpenny, J., Nilsson, M., Russel, D. and Nykvist, B. (2009). Rationalising the policy mess? Ex ante policy assessment and the utilisation of knowledge in the policy process. *Environment and Planning*, 41(5), pp. 1185–1200.

Hessels, L.K. and van Lente, H. (2008). Re-thinking new knowledge production: A literature review and a research agenda. *Research Policy*, 37(4), pp. 740–760.

Hoppe, R. (2010). *The Governance of Problems – Puzzling, Powering and Participation*. Bristol: Policy Press.

IPBES. (2016). *Summary for policymakers of the assessment report of the Intergovernmental Science-Policy Platform on Biodiversity and Ecosystem Services on pollinators, pollination and food production.* S.G. Potts, V. L. Imperatriz-Fonseca, H. T. Ngo, J. C. Biesmeijer, T. D. Breeze, L. V. Dicks, L. A. Garibaldi, R. Hill, J. Settele, A. J.

Vanbergen, M. A. Aizen, S. A. Cunningham, C. Eardley, B. M. Freitas, N. Gallai, P. G. Kevan, A. Kovács-Hostyánszki, P. K. Kwapong, J. Li, X. Li, D. J. Martins, G. Nates-Parra, J. S. Pettis, R. Rader, and B. F. Viana (Eds.). Bonn, Germany: Secretariat of the Intergovernmental Science-Policy Platform on Biodiversity and Ecosystem Services.

IPCC. (2014). *Climate Change 2014: Synthesis Report. Contribution of Working Groups I, II and III to the Fifth Assessment Report of the Intergovernmental Panel on Climate Change* [(Core Writing Team, Pachauri, R.K. and Meyer, L.A. [Eds.]). Geneva: IPCC.

Jacob, K. (2010). Regulatory impact assessment and sustainable development: Towards a common framework? *European Journal of Risk Regulation*, 3, pp. 276–280.

Jacob, K., Guske, A.-L. and von Prittwitz, V. (2011). *Consideration of Sustainability Aspects in Policy Impact Assessment: An International Comparative Study of Innovations and Trends*. Study undertaken by the Freie Universität on behalf of the Bertelsmann Stiftung, Berlin. Available at: http://www.polsoz.fu-berlin.de/polwiss/forschung/systeme/ffu/files/SIA-Study_2011_Jacob_ex.pdf (15.05.2016).

Jacob, K., Hertin, J., Hjerp, P., Radaelli, C., Meuwese, A., Wolf, O., Pacchi, C. and Rennings, K. (2008). Improving the practice of impact assessment: Policy conclusions from FP6 EVIA project. *EVIA-Policy Paper*. Forschungszentrum für Umweltpolitik, Berlin.

Jahn, T., Bergmann, M. and Keil, F. (2012). Transdisciplinarity: Between mainstreaming and marginalization. *Ecological Economics*, 79, pp. 1–10.

Jahn, T. Keil, F., Petschow, U. and Jacob, K. (2013). *Policy Relevant Sustainability Research – Requirements Profiles for Research Funding Agencies, Researchers and Policymakers Regarding Improving and Ensuring Quality of Research. A Guide*. Dessau-Roßlau: Umweltbundesamt.

Jahn, T., Guske, A.-L., Jacob, K., Keil, F. and Petschow, U. (2014). *Verbesserung der strategischen umweltpolitischen Beratung im Kontext des Leitbilds Nachhaltiger Entwicklung. Studie und Fachdialog zu Ansätzen und Nutzungsperspektiven der Umwelt- und Nachhaltigkeitsforschung*. UBA Text 52/2014. Dessau-Roßlau: Umweltbundesamt.

Jahn, T. and Keil, F. (2015). An actor-specific guideline for quality assurance in transdisciplinary research. *Futures*, 65, pp. 195–208.

Jansen, J., Adelle, C., Crimi, J. Dick, J., Helming, K., Janssen, S., Podhora, A., Reis, S., Roosenschoon, O., Saarela, S.-R., Södermann, T., Turnpenny, J. and Wien, J.E. (2013). *The LIAISE approach for co-designing knowledge on impact assessment tools*. LIAISE working paper, No. 1/2013.

Karinen, R. and Guston, D.H. (2010). Towards anticipatory governance. The experience with nanotechnology. In: Kaiser, M. (Ed.), *Governing Future Technologies. Nanotechnology and the Rise of an Assessment Regime*. New York: Springer, pp. 217–232.

Kates, R.W., Clark, W.C., Correll, R., Hall, J.M., Jaeger, C.C., Lowe, I., McCarthy, J.J., Schellnhuber, H.J., Bolin, B., Dickson, N.M. and Faucheux, S. (2001). Sustainability science. *Science*, 292(5517), pp. 641–642.

Klein, J., Grossenbacher-Mansuy, W., Häberli, R., Bill, A., Scholz, R.W. and Welti, M. (Eds.) (2001). *Transdisciplinarity: Joint Problem Solving Among Science, Technology and Society. An Effective Way for Managing Complexity*. Basel: Birkhäuser Verlag.

Kuhn, T.S. (1962). *The Structure of Scientific Revolutions*. Chicago: Chicago University Press.

Lang, D.J., Wiek, A. Bergmann, M., Stauffacher, M., Martens, P., Moll, P. Swilling, M. and Thomas, C.J. (2012). Transdisciplinary research in sustainability science: Practice, principles, and challenges. *Sustain Science*, 7 (Supplement 1), pp. 25–43.

Lasswell, H.D. (1971). *A Pre-View of Policy Sciences*. New York: Elsevier.

Lindner, R., Kuhlmann, S., Randles, S., Bedsted, B., Gorgoni, G., Griessler, E., Loconto, A. and Mejlgaard, N. (Eds.) (2016). *Towards Shared Responsibility: Navigating Towards Shared Responsibility in Research and Innovation Approach, Process and Results of the Res-AGorA Project*. Karlsruhe: Fraunhofer ISI.

Maasen, S. (2008). Exzellenz oder Transdisziplinarität: Zur Gleichzeitigkeit zweier Qualitätsdiskurse. In: Hornbostel, S., Simon, D., Heise, S. (Eds.), *Exzellente Wissenschaft: das Problem, der Diskurs, das Programm und die Folgen*. iFQ-Working Paper, 4, Bonn, pp. 23–32.

Macnaghten, T. and Chilvers, J. (2012). Governing risky technology. In: Lane, S., Klauser, F., and Kearnes, M. (Eds.), *Critical Risk Research: Practices, Politics, and Ethics*. Oxford: Wiley-Blackwell, pp. 99–124.

Matthies, H. and Simon, D. (Eds.) (2007). *Wissenschaft unter Beobachtung*. Leviathan Sonderheft 24/2007. Wiesbaden: VS Verlag für Sozialwissenschaften.

Merck, J. and Beermann, M. (2015). The relevance of transdisciplinary teaching and learning for the successful integration of sustainability issues into higher education development. In: W. Leal Filho, W., Brandli, L., Kuznetsova, O. and do Paco, A.M.F. (Eds.), *Integrative Approaches to Sustainable Development at University Level*. Basel: Springer, pp. 19–25.

Meuleman, L. (2014). Owl meets beehive: How impact assessment and governance relate. *Impact Assessment and Project Appraisal*, 33(1), pp. 4–15.

Michaels, S. (2009). Matching knowledge brokering strategies to environmental policy problems and settings. *Environmental Science & Policy*, 12(7), pp. 994–1011.

NOW – The Netherlands Organisation for Scientific Research. (2016). *Responsible Innovation*. Available at: http://www.nwo.nl/en/funding/our-funding-instruments/gw/responsible-innovation/responsible-innovation.html (12.05.2016).

Nowotny, H., Scott, P. and Gibbons, M. (2001). *Re-Thinking Science: Knowledge and the Public in an Age of Uncertainty*. Cambridge: Polity Press.

Owen, R., Macnaghten, P. and Stilgoe, J. (2012). Responsible research and innovation: From Science in Society to Science for Society, with Society. *Science and Public Policy*, 39, pp. 751–760.

Partidário, M. and Sheate, W. (2013). Knowledge brokerage – Potential for increased capacities and shared power in impact assessment. *Environmental Impact Assessment Review*, 39, pp. 26–36.

Podhora A., Helming, K., Adenäuer, L., Heckelei, T., Kautto, P., Reidsma, P., Rennings, K., Turnpenny, J. and Jansen, J. (2013). The policy-relevancy of impact assessment tools: Evaluating nine years of European research funding. *Environmental Science & Policy*, 31(0), pp.85–95.

Pohl, C. (2014). From complexity to solvability: The praxeology of transdisciplinary research. In: Huutoniemi, K. and Tapio, P. (Eds.), *Transdisciplinary Sustainability Studies: A Heuristic Approach*. New York: Routledge, pp. 103–118.

Quigley, M. (2005). *Information Security and Ethics: Social and Organizational Issues*. Hershey (PA): IRM Press.

RCUK – Research Councils United Kingdom. (2014). *How to apply for research funding*. Available at: http://www.rcuk.ac.uk/funding/howtoapply/ (12.05.2014).

Reber, B. (2015) Governance: Precautionary principle and pluralism. *International Social Science Journal*, 64(211–212), pp. 75–87.

Richardson, T. and Cashmore, M. (2011). Power, knowledge and environmental assessment: the World Bank's pursuit of 'good governance'. *Journal of Political Power*, 4(1), pp. 105–125.

Rietschel, E. Th., Arnold, E., Čenys, A., Dearing, A., Feller, I., Joussaume, S., Lange, L., Langer, J., Ley, V., Mustonen, R., Pooley, D. and Stame, N. (2009). Evaluation of the Sixth Framework Programmes for Research and Technology Development 2002-2006. *Report of the Expert Group*, Brussels.

Rockström, J., Steffen, W., Noone, K., Persson, Å., Chapin, F.S., Lambin, E.F., Lenton, T.M., Scheffer, M., Folke, C., Schellnhuber, H.J. and Nykvist, B. (2009). Planetary boundaries: Exploring the safe operating space for humanity. *Ecology and Society*, 14(2), p. 32.

Rodríguez, H., Fisher, E. and Schuurbiersd, D. (2013). Integrating science and society in European Framework Programmes: Trends in project-level solicitations. *Research Policy*, 42, pp. 1126–1137.

Rückert-John, J. (Ed.) (2013). *Soziale Innovation und Nachhaltigkeit. Perspektiven sozialen Wandels*. Wiesbaden: Springer VS.

Scholz, R.W. (2011). *Environmental Literacy in Science and Society. From Knowledge to Decisions*. Cambridge: Cambridge University Press.

Sheate, W.R. and Partidário, M.R. (2010). Strategic approaches and assessment techniques—Potential for knowledge brokerage towards sustainability. *Environmental Impact Assessment Review*, 30, pp. 278–288.

Schier, C. and Schwinger, E. (Eds.) (2014). *Interdisziplinarität und Transdisziplinarität als Herausforderung akademischer Bildung Innovative Konzepte für die Lehre an Hochschulen und Universitäten*. Bielefeld: Transcript.

Stahl, B. C., Heersmink, R., Goujon, P., Flick, C., van den Hoven, J., Wakunuma, K., Ikonen, V. and Rader, M. (2010). Identifying the ethics of emerging information and communication technologies: An essay on issues, concepts and method. *International Journal of Technoethics*, 1(4), pp. 20–38.

Stilgoe, J., Owen, R. and Macnaghten, P. (2013). Developing a framework for responsible innovation. *Research Policy*, 42, pp. 1568–1580.

Steffen, W., Richardson, K., Rockstrom, J., Cornell, S.E., Fetzer, I., Bennett, E.M., Biggs, R., Carpenter, S.R., de Vries, W., and de Wit, C.A., Folke, C., Gerten, D., Heinke, J., Mace, G.M., Persson, L.M, Ramanathan, V., Reyers, B. and Sorlin, S. (2015). Planetary boundaries: Guiding human development on a changing planet. *Science*, 347, p. 6223.

Stilgoe, J. (2007). *Nanodialogues: Experiments with Public Engagement with Science*. London: Demos.

Strohschneider, P. (2013). *Vom Nutzen und der Freiheit der Forschung*. Rede des Präsidenten der Deutschen Forschungsgemeinschaft (DFG). 10th STS-Forum, Kyoto, Japan, October 2013.

Sutcliffe, H. (2011). *A Report on Responsible Research and Innovation for the European Commission*. Available at: https://ec.europa.eu/research/science-society/document_library/pdf_06/rri-report-hilary-sutcliffe_en.pdf (12.05.2016).

TEU – *Consolidated version of the Treaty on European Union*. (2012). Available at: http://eur-lex.europa.eu/legal-content/EN/TXT/PDF/?uri=CELEX:12012M/TXT&from=EN (12.05.2016).

TFEU – Consolidated version of the Treaty on the Functioning of the European Union. (2012). Available at: http://eur-lex.europa.eu/legal-content/EN/TXT/PDF/?uri=CELEX:12012E/TXT&from=EN (12.05.2016).

Thorn, M. (2015). Förderkonzept für eine gesellschaftsbezogene Nachhaltigkeitsforschung. *GAIA - Ecological Perspectives for Science and Society*, 24(4), pp. 273–274.

Turnpenny, J., Radaelli, C.M., Jordan, A. and Jacob, K. (2009). The policy and politics of policy appraisal: Emerging trends and new directions. *Journal of European Public Policy*, 16(4), pp. 640–653.

Van den Hoven, J., Jacob, K., Nielsen, L., Roure, F., Rudze, L. and Stilgoe, J. (2013). Options for Strengthening Responsible Research and Innovation. *Report of the Expert Group on the State of Art in Europe on Responsible Research and Innovation*. Luxembourg, European Union.

Van den Hove, S. (2007). A rationale for science-policy interfaces. *Futures*, 39(7), pp. 807–826.

Van Kammen, J., de Savigny, D. and Sewankambo, N. (2006). Using the knowledge brokering to promote evidence-based policy-making: The need for support structures. *Bulletin of the World Health Organisation*, 84(8), pp. 608–612.

Von Schomberg, R. (2011). *Towards Responsible Research and Innovation in the Information and Communication Technologies and Security Technologies Fields*. Brussels: European Commission.

Von Schomberg, R. (2012). Prospects for technology assessment in a framework of responsible research and innovation. In: Dusseldorp, M. and Beecroft, R. (Eds.), *Technikfolgen abschätzen lehren. Bildungspotentiale transdisziplinärer Methoden*, Wiesbaden: Springer.

Watermeyer, R. (2016). *Impact in the REF: Issues and obstacles. Studies in Higher Education*, 41(2), pp. 199–214.

Ward, V., House A., and Hamer S. (2009). Knowledge brokering: The missing link in the evidence to action chain? *Evidence & Policy*, 5, pp. 267–279.

Weiland, S. (2011). The Science-Policy Interface. *LIAISE Innovation Report*, No. 3. Berlin.

Weingart, P. (1999). Scientific expertise and political accountability: Paradoxes of science in politics. *Science and Public Policy*, 26(3), pp. 151–161.

Wildavsky, A. (1979). *Speaking Truth to Power: The Art and Craft of Policy Analysis*. Boston: Little, Brown and Co.

Part III

Avoiding the instrumentalization of Responsible Research and Innovation

7 Responsible research and innovation between "New Governance" and fundamental rights

Simone Arnaldi, Guido Gorgoni and Elena Pariotti

Introduction: Governing technologies under uncertainty conditions[1]

Academic literature and public debates alike have increasingly acknowledged the pervasiveness of uncertainty in science, technology and their governance. Uncertainty is no longer viewed as a residual area of ignorance and risk to be gradually reduced by way of increasing expert knowledge and enhancing technological control. On the contrary, uncertainty is viewed as the unavoidable consequence of the interaction of technology with its environment, that is, of technology's ecological nature (Luhmann 1993). As an effect of these limitations of our experimental knowledge, the introduction of new technologies in society becomes a form of "societal experimentation" (e.g. van de Poel 2009; Felt and Wynne 2007), and risks and possible developments can be detected only after technologies have been introduced in and have displayed their impacts on society. Notions like "manufactured risk" (Giddens 1999) or "secondary consequences" (Beck 1992) were introduced to interpret this paradoxical relationship between increased contingency and the unprecedented knowledge about and control of social life and the physical world, characterizing new and emerging technologies. Indeed, the increased manipulative knowledge of nature and society produces uncertainty rather than reducing it (Coeckelbergh 2012).

The boundaries of science and policy, knowledge and values are redesigned by this radical uncertainty. Accepting that nature and society are co-produced (Jasanoff 2006; Pellizzoni 2010) implies the acknowledgement that the reception of scientific knowledge, technology developments and their consequences "is never, and never can be, a purely intellectual process, about reception of knowledge per se. People experience these in the form of material and social relationships, interactions and interests, and thus they logically define and judge the risk, the risk information, or the scientific knowledge as part and parcel of that 'social package'" (Wynne 1992: pp. 281–282). Knowledge and technology, therefore, implicitly incorporate models, worldviews and societal patterns (Wynne 1992), and, therefore, uncertain knowledge comes with embattled consent where the governance of new technologies is concerned (Douglas and Wildavsky 1983: p. 6).

In this chapter, we argue that responsible research and innovation (RRI) can be an effective answer to this twofold uncertainty, so that responsiveness and the normative steering of research and innovation acquire more importance over risk individuation and management. Our hypothesis is that the models of governance currently in place and the governance framework that is outlined in the literature and policy documents on RRI may be suitable to address the uncertainty challenge, if some conditions are met, such as the ability of these models to properly include the reference to normative dimensions, among which fundamental rights are the edge, and to implement a *specific* idea of responsibility.

The following sections will first examine the diffusion of soft regulation as an important component of the current governance framework of science and technology. Soft regulation attempts to answer the twofold uncertainty described above, which is addressed by leveraging the knowledge pool possessed by the regulatees and by integrating the divergence of values and interests through cooperation and flexibility. After presenting some examples of soft regulatory initiatives from nanotechnologies, the chapter frames these regulatory developments in the context of the New Governance approach. A second part of the chapter briefly presents RRI in the broader context of the evolution of responsibility paradigms. By referring to their characterization in terms of time orientation (prospective, retrospective) and active/passive attitude to responsibility, three paradigms (fault, risk and precaution) are distinguished. Then, RRI is presented as a proactive, participative, multidimensional approach to responsibility in the governance of Science, Technology and Innovation (STI) that is founded on the mutual commitments of societal actors, thus constituting a distinct paradigm on its own. Drawing on these remarks, the meaning and relevance of fundamental rights in RRI is assessed. Far from being a constraint on innovation and on the public debate of its trajectories, fundamental rights are viewed as a catalyst of normative orientation *and* public participation. The conclusions observe how the reference to fundamental rights makes RRI a more comprehensive approach when compared with New Governance, as it internalizes the problem of the normative anchoring of decisions and of the consistency among different kinds of normative elements. Eventually, it is noticed that the potential of fundamental rights to successfully combine normative orientation, openness and flexibility in RRI is conditioned by the capacity to design a governance framework that can ensure the complementarity between hard and soft regulation, legal norms and voluntary commitments.

Soft regulation: General remarks and examples from nanotechnology

The notion of "soft regulation" refers to a broad range of regulatory instruments such as guidelines and recommendations, resolutions, declarations, codes of practice and conduct. Soft regulation is a set of explicit rules which have either a non-binding character or are utterly voluntary (Fredriksson et al. 2012; Skjærseth et al. 2006). While they are acknowledged as having legal relevance, soft norms lack the formal binding effects and clearly top-down delineated enforcement mechanisms that are typical of traditional "command and control" regulatory approaches (Shaffer and Pollack 2013). Definitions like "non-legislative modes of policy-making" (Hérriet, in Fredriksson et al. 2012: p. 53) or even "quasi-legal instruments" (Koutalakis et al. 2010: p. 330) have been introduced to capture this characteristic nature of soft norms. As Dorbeck-Jung and Shelley-Egan notice (2013: p. 56), soft regulation describes a shift "from direct intervention ('rowing') to indirect intervention ('steering') in terms of enabling, motivating and pressing the regulated parties to regulate and to comply with self-regulation".

The prominence of soft regulation has increased as a consequence of three intersecting processes (Arnaldi 2014). First, globalization fundamentally reshaped the general context in which soft regulation has established its significance. These changes challenged the previously uncontested role of the State in setting domestic and international regulations, through command-and-control mechanisms and the forms of international public law (Ferrarese 2000).

Second, soft regulation represents a tool that regulators have for leveraging the information advantages of those actors who are (or are being) regulated. In emerging technological fields that are characterized by a high degree of uncertainty, regulators have insufficient resources or information to define mandatory rules (Dorbeck-Jung and Shelley-Egan 2013). The effective regulation of these areas often requires "frequently changing cognitive and material resources for effective regulation, which state actors often do not have and lie with industry as the primary rule target. This is particularly the case in highly technical areas where the state depends on individual producers for crucial regulatory information related to product characteristics and production processes" (Koutalakis et al. 2010: p. 334). Third, uncertainty drives regulatory decision-making towards "a more political direction" (Falkner and Jaspers 2012: p. 30). Regulatory choices become more "political", insofar as they require "the weighing up of sometimes competing values, such as technology promotion versus harm prevention. Scientific risk assessment criteria alone cannot guide regulators and policy-makers in such situations. Instead, a wider range of factors enters the calculations that inform regulatory action, from political ideology and societal risk attitudes to national or sectoral economic interests" (Falkner and Jaspers 2012: p. 33). In this context, soft regulation is used to improve the legitimacy and sustainability of regulatory decisions when "there is the need to build consensus on legal and political decisions in a participatory manner" (Pariotti 2011: p. 516) and there is "little space for different and conflicting interests to be articulated" (Garsten and Jacobsson 2011: p. 422).

The coexistence and the combination with hard law create "hybrid" regulatory frameworks (Heyvaert 2009: pp. 649–650). "This happens when, for instance, a voluntary good practice code is used as a benchmark for compliance with a 'hard law' prescription" (Heyvaert 2009: p. 650) or, on the contrary, when soft regulatory instruments refer to hard law provisions. On the international level, soft regulatory processes are seen to combine inter-governmental, shared-sovereignty aims and non-governmental, civil society values (Hickey et al. 2006: p. 298).

In the nanotechnology field, soft regulatory solutions have been widely implemented and have been regarded with particular interest as a tool for the international harmonization and coordination of regulatory frameworks (Bowman and

Table 7.1 Examples of soft regulatory initiatives

Level of initiative			
Initiator		*National/subnational*	*International/ supranational*
	Public	Voluntary Reporting Scheme for Engineered Nanoscale Materials (UK) EPA Nanoscale Materials Stewardship Program	OECD Working Party on Nanotechnology European Commission Code of Conduct
	Private	Responsible Nanocode	ISO TC 229 Responsible Care

Source: Arnaldi (2014).

Hodge 2007; Marchant et al. 2009; see Table 7.1 for some examples based on the level of the regulatory initiatives and the type of initiator).[2] The European Commission's Code of Conduct for responsible nanosciences and nanotechnologies (European Commission 2008), the "Voluntary Reporting Scheme for Engineered Nanoscale Materials" of the UK Department of Environment, Food and Rural Affairs (DEFRA 2008a, 2008b), the voluntary "stewardship program" for nanoscale materials under the Toxic Substances Control Act (TSCA) of the US Environmental Protection Agency (EPA n.d.), the Responsible Nanocode (NIA, n.d.), the codes of conduct and assessment frameworks developed by companies like DuPont and BASF (DuPont 2012; BASF, n.d.) or broader initiatives like ResponsibleCare© for the chemical industry (Heinemann and Schäfer 2009, ICCA 2006) are all examples of initiatives fostering the cooperative and voluntary commitment of a variety of social actors, beyond mere legislative and regulatory compliance.[3]

Soft regulation and "New Governance"

This evolution in regulation has been seen as a part and consequence of the emergence of the so-called "New Governance" model. The New Governance, which is also referred to as "distributed governance" (MASIS 2009), "constructive governance" (Ozolina 2009) or "democratic experimentalism" (Szyszcak 2006), is the model of governance that inspires, for example, the "open method of coordination" among member States about the EU goals for social policies (and social rights) (cf. Trubeck and Trubeck 2007: pp. 12–16, for an illustration and a comparison with the Classic Community Method). It rests on tools such as guidelines, periodic reporting, multilateral surveillance, exchange of best practices and social dialogue. As it relies on local deliberation and stakeholder participation, it was meant to provide an answer to the democratic deficit in the EU (Kohler-Koch and Rittberger 2006). As such, it is part of the broader shift towards distributed, soft regulatory frameworks that we described in the previous section of this chapter. Indeed, it does not solely rely on experts' deliberation in European regulatory agencies or committees, but "enables stakeholders to participate directly in decision-making processes" (Eberlein and Kerwer 2004: p. 133).

As is widely acknowledged, the "governance turn" in policy-making and in regulation (Braithwaite, Coglianese and Levi-Faur, 2007) implies the following main elements: (1) a situation in which "the government is a relationship of negotiation and cooperation with private actors" so that (Chowdhury and Wessel 2012: p. 345) (2) rule/norm making, rule implementation and rule enforcement activities are dispersed "across different administrative levels both within and beyond nation state" (Chowdhury and Wessel 2012: p. 346) and (3) a central ordering of regulation is lacking. In this framework, the "New Governance model" introduces a special concern for public engagement and participation as one of its essential features.

It can be said that the New Governance model integrates principle-based regulation and outcome-oriented regulation as an alternative to rule-based regulation. It has a set of specific features, such as participation and power-sharing, integration of different levels of governance, diversity and decentralization and expansion of the space for stakeholders' deliberation. Furthermore, its features of flexibility and revisability make it experimental and tentative in nature, so that regulation can adapt to distinctive economic, environmental, social and administrative conditions that cannot be regulated through uniformly binding legislative requirements (Scott and Trubeck 2002; Pariotti 2011), thus reducing transaction costs of regulators and regulatees (Koutalakis et al. 2010: p. 330).

In general, this model is not immune from criticism and, again, nanotechnology represents a significant example. Maynard and Rejeski (2009) contest the effectiveness of voluntary reporting of nanomaterials by industry and support the adoption of mandatory measures. Marchant and Abbott (2013) point to the inconsistent and limited implementation of the existing international soft regulation initiatives for nanotechnology and of their impacts. Stokes (2013) notes that regulators prefer more conventional command-and-control methods of regulation in dealing with considerable uncertainties. From a policy perspective, two important stakeholders such as the European Trade Unions Confederations (ETUC) and the European Parliament have asked for stricter and more specific provisions, especially by applying the existing chemical or cosmetics regulations (ETUC 2008; 2010; European Parliament 2009; Ponce del Castillo 2013; Ruggiu 2013) to nanotechnologies. In the US, the EPA undertook a step in a similar direction, proposing in 2013 a mandatory reporting programme under the TSCA for several nanomaterials (EPA, n.d.).

Indeed, the crucial challenge of "New Governance" arrangements is to strike a balance between flexibility and efficacy, in terms of the behavioural orientation of the (self)-regulated parties. As the examples above show, the critics of soft regulation tend to prefer binding, rule-based regulation over the outcome-based approach that is typical of soft regulatory instruments, which measures performance against regulatory goals rather than against rule compliance.

As stated in the introduction, we maintain that this complementarity is just the kind of result that is pursued by the idea of RRI. In order to support this position, we characterize RRI in the context of the diversity and historical evolution of the notion of responsibility. This argument is preliminary to discussing the interplay of the New Governance and fundamental rights *vis a vis* the realization of RRI.

Responsible research and innovation as a new paradigm of responsibility?

RRI aims at introducing responsibility into research and innovation processes at an early stage, by involving those who are concerned with their consequences in framing innovation activities, their aims and their goals. From this viewpoint, innovation and research activities might be characterized as "responsible" according to the extent they take into consideration a broader societal perspective in their development (van den Hoven et al. 2013), rather than from the narrower perspective of liability, risk management, and compensation for damages.

As RRI claims to be a new approach to responsibility in science and innovation, the issue of whether it has new features or whether it is yet another version of responsibility paradigms we already know has to be addressed. In particular, it should be discussed whether RRI differs significantly from the Precautionary Principle (PP) or not, as the PP also adopts an anticipatory logic of responsibility in scientific and technological innovation activities.

The idea of precaution stems from the new context of scientific uncertainty highlighted above (see section 1), to which neither the preventive approach of risk management could provide acceptable answers, nor the fault paradigm would help make innovation processes more responsible. Instead, it frames responsibility in terms of a duty of anticipating the undesirable outcomes of techno-scientific activities through value-centred decisions in a context of epistemic uncertainty. The PP is based on the idea of a *preventive exercise* of responsibility rather than on its post hoc ascription (be it via fault or risk management mechanisms): within this logic, the focus of responsibility is on anticipating the potentially harmful outcomes by balancing values in context-based decisions. Indeed, precaution operates precisely where adequate guarantees against undesirable harmful consequences of scientific innovation cannot be provided by applying the general rules and standards of risk management, so that the criteria for a responsible management of innovation have to be set case by case. So it could be told that the PP operates a sort of a re-ethicization of responsibility. It does not introduce new concepts of liability (nor new criteria of risk assessment), but it shapes legal responsibility in a way which is similar to a situated ethical judgment (Papaux 2006; Gorgoni 2010), as it asks (and prompts) for decision-making in a context where the causal link between potentially harmful activities and the possible threats (be it for the human health or for the environment) is not certain, marking a major epistemic break with the epistemology underpinning typical risk management techniques (Osimani 2013).

From this perspective, RRI and the PP share the same epistemology, but RRI draws different conclusions. The lack of scientific certainty about potential harms no longer represents an obstacle for taking preventive actions (like in the PP): it rather gives way to a *proactive* appraisal of a situation characterized by both *cognitive uncertainty* and some degree of *values indeterminacy*. What, therefore, specifically differentiates RRI from the PP is, at least in principle, the *integration of responsibility within the innovation process itself.* In other words, what makes RRI different from the PP is not its inner logic (anticipation) or its underlying epistemology (as they both refer to decisions in a context of uncertainty), but rather its contexts and conditions of application. Indeed, the PP has been invoked as a safeguard against the undesirable outcomes of innovation activities, serving as a tool for correcting its path, either by inverting, diverting or blocking it (Callon, Lascoumes and Barthe 2009). Nevertheless, the PP remains linked to a context in which positions are confronted in an adversarial logic, while RRI aims at changing the context in which precaution intervenes, by shifting to a cooperative logic when decisions about the innovation trajectories are concerned. Indeed, RRI promotes a logic of *responsibilization*, which has been broadly characterized as "predisposing actors to assume responsibility for their action" (Dorbeck-Jung, Shelley-Egan 2013). More precisely, RRI predisposes societal actors to voluntarily assume an early and shared responsibility for research and innovation processes beyond merely abiding by duties or complying with rules.

For RRI to represent something new, it is necessary to give value to these features and acknowledge the consequences implied by them. RRI makes strong claims in terms of principles, but it may be translated into nothing other than a rhetorical appeal if its features are not given credit and their implications are not taken into account and fully recognized.

The novel features of RRI and existing responsibility models

In order to develop the features distinguishing RRI from other approaches highlighted above, it is necessary to frame it within the context of the existing responsibility approaches. Instead of detailing the different meanings of responsibility, as others have done (e.g. Davis 2012; van de Poel 2011; Vincent 2011; Gorgoni 2011; Ricoeur 2000; Hart 1968), we propose to take into account and examine the deep semantic underpinnings of responsibility, whose different meanings can be distinguished by the combinations between two different modes (passive and active) and two temporal directions (retrospective and prospective). We could maintain that different meanings of responsibility are built on the combinations of these modes and these time orientations. In the following pages, we will first characterize each of these aspects, and then we will analyse their combinations.

As for the first pair of concepts, the passive pole of responsibility corresponds to one of the most common understandings of responsibility, i.e. that of a sanction intended in a broad sense, as synonymous of holding someone responsible for something (typically the legal imputation of liability), while the active pole is also linked to another common understanding of responsibility, the idea of "acting responsibly", in the sense of assuming one's own responsibilities (self-ascription of responsibility), either in terms of specific duties or in terms of a caring relation for something or somebody. The passive and the active modalities of responsibility are not mutually exclusive, and it is possible to highlight some oscillations of the meaning of responsibility between those poles, which sometimes may conflict with each other.

Indeed, if we shift from the passive towards the active mode, responsibility can be equally understood in terms of 1) the *obligation* to bear the consequences of an action (liability, which is essentially passive); 2) the *capacity* to act, taking into account one's duties (combining the passive pole of obligation and the active pole of capacity); and 3) the *capacity* to act, taking into account the resulting consequences, even without necessarily referring to some pre-established duties (what could be termed as a self-ascription of responsibility). In this latter sense, the idea of responsibility has to be intended in terms of *responsiveness* more than in terms of *reaction*. Responsiveness expresses the idea of a *response* to somebody's appeal (Pellizzoni 2004: p. 557), thus characterizing the active pole of responsibility in very different terms than the passive one.

As for the second pair of concepts (retrospective and prospective), the distinction between the active and the passive modalities of responsibility entails some distinctions regarding the time orientation of responsibility, namely the retrospective (backward-looking) (Bovens 1998) and the prospective (forward-looking) ones (Cane 2002; Gorgoni 2008). Retrospective responsibility is essentially linked to the idea of an ex-post imputation of responsibility, and so to the ideas of sanction (*liability*), compensation (*damage*) or justification (*accountability*), which do shape the idea of responsibility, essentially in terms of a *reaction* to a certain state of affairs. Responsibility, in this case, is essentially backward-looking, i.e. past-oriented, and therefore can be characterized as retrospective in that its key element is the *ex post* evaluation of a situation and the subsequent judgement in terms of the imputation of the consequences.

On the other side, prospective responsibility is essentially linked to the idea of acting responsibly, both in the sense of complying with the duties associated to someone's role, but also with the broader idea of *(pro)actively* assuming responsibilities, even when the contents of duties and tasks are not or cannot be established in advance. These features make the idea of prospective responsibility more complex than the notion of duty, despite the fact that these two concepts tend to overlap in the legal field. This prospective conception defines responsibility not as a *reaction to* a certain state of affairs, but rather as a *projection over* it.

Drawing on these discussions, the different models of responsibility can be framed as combinations between the two semantic poles and the two temporal dimensions highlighted above. Drawing from the work of François Ewald (2001), it is possible to point out three main paradigms in the historical evolution of responsibility. These paradigms can be clearly distinguished only at the theoretical level, while they coexist, overlap, and sometimes compete in history. These paradigms are: 1) the paradigm of *fault*, corresponding to the traditional moral and legal idea of responsibility as a reaction to a certain state of affairs, and which is essentially *retrospective* (e.g. Hart 1968); 2) the paradigm of *risk*, which aims at guaranteeing the compensation for the damages rather than the sanction of a fault, thus disconnecting indemnification from liability (Beck 1992); and 3) the paradigm of *safety*, which is linked to the idea of *precaution* as a reaction to the residual uncertainty which cannot be domesticated by means of risk calculation. Indeed, the two former paradigms of responsibility are seriously challenged by the evolution of science and innovation, as they both presuppose either an identifiable author (fault) or the possibility of relying on statistical data (risk).

Compared with those paradigms, RRI presents some distinctive features that we should briefly analyse. While RRI is defined in different ways by the various authors dealing with the subject (von Schomberg 2013; Owen 2014; van den Hoven et al. 2013; Forsberg et al. 2015), the literature appears to have a common understanding of this notion and of its main features, which include: 1) the future orientation of responsibility, advocating for a *prospective* idea of responsibility as a mean of steering the innovation processes according to societal values and needs; 2) the focus on proaction, as RRI is intended to be mainly a *driving factor* of innovation process more than a constraint, extending responsibility beyond the strict boundaries of what is legally due; 3) the framing of responsibility as a *collective and participative* process: responsibility is not only shared by the various actors in the innovation system, but it is also seen as a result of a collaborative process between the innovators and society as a whole; and d) the crucial role of *voluntary instruments*: RRI both promotes and implies collaborative dynamics instead of typical dispute-settlement mechanisms (be it at the judicial level or not), encouraging the creation of (commonly agreed) voluntary standards and procedures. So, ultimately, responsibility should be organized through norms, which are: 1) instrumental to achieve broader societal goals such as environmental, social and economic sustainability; 2) flexible enough to adapt to technological developments; and 3) promote proactive interventions in order to avoid or reduce any potential or even unforeseeable risk in cases of scientific uncertainty.

If we give credit to its ambitions, and only if we do so, then RRI can perhaps be considered as a new paradigm of responsibility, combining in a new way the elements of other responsibility paradigms (see Table 7.2 for an unavoidably simplified comparison). As it aims at *steering the innovation process from the inside* towards societal goals rather than coping with its (actual or anticipated) unwanted and unintended externalities, RRI integrates responsibility within the innovation process itself. Despite the (at least partial) indeterminacy of societal goals and values on which this approach is based, we maintain that a distinctive feature of RRI is its normative commitment to the protection of fundamental rights

Table 7.2 RRI and the evolution of responsibility paradigms

Paradigm	*Criterion of ascription*	*Mean of realization*	*Target*	*Dimension*	*Orientation in time*	*Responsibility dimensions*	*Regulating mechanism*
Fault	Liability	Sanction	Negative outcomes	Individual	Retrospective	Liability-responsibility	Hard law
Risk	Damage	Compensation	Negative outcomes	Systemic	Prospective/ retrospective	Causality-responsibility	Hard law
Safety	Uncertainty	Expertize	Negative outcomes	Collective	Prospective/anticipative (or preventive)	Capacity-responsibility	Hard law/soft law
RRI	Responsiveness	Participation	Negative and positive outcomes	Collaborative	Prospective/proactive	Virtue-responsibility	Self-regulation/soft law/hard law

Source: Adapted from Arnaldi and Gorgoni (2016).

(Arnaldi, Gorgoni and Pariotti 2016). This commitment distinguishes RRI from the regulatory approaches based on deregulation in a purely market-driven logic (Arnaldi and Gorgoni 2016).

RRI and fundamental rights[3]

The nature of RRI as a conceptual and policy approach aimed at actors' reciprocal responsibilization creates a space for innovative forms of governance centred on the adoption and the practical implementation of (self-) regulatory instruments such as codes of conduct, guidelines, technical standards, reporting and audits. As we have seen, these types of regulatory instruments and their incorporation into hybrid regulatory schemes correspond to the features that are key to the New Governance model, such as participation and power sharing; integration of different levels of governance, diversity and decentralization; and expansion of the space for stakeholders' deliberation.

Yet, RRI directly addresses the question of defining the ultimate purposes of science, technology and innovation as an essential feature of a truly innovative and alternative approach to research and innovation governance (as indicated by the switch from the logic of "science *and* society" to that of "science *in* society", marking their reciprocal integration rather than their separation).

Under this perspective, it is therefore clear that RRI brings some strong normative requirements in order to be both a coherent and innovative way of dealing with responsibility issues of the research and innovation process.

While a significant part of the literature considers the definition of the ultimate purposes of science, technology and innovation as the result of (normative) deliberations on science and technology (Owen et al. 2013), emerging from the spontaneous interplay between science and society, the literature which is closest to the EU policy environment, explicitly refers to fundamental rights as the source of orientation of research and innovation (von Schomberg 2013; Ozolina et al. 2009: p. 3).

In our view, this latter approach is better suited for configuring RRI as a more comprehensive new approach to the governance of responsibility, as it introduces some explicit "normative anchor points" which are in line with the democratic guarantees that ultimately characterize the RRI idea.

Indeed, in one of its most cited definitions, RRI is framed as "a transparent, interactive process by which societal actors and innovators become mutually responsive to each other with a view to the (ethical) acceptability, sustainability and societal desirability of the innovation process and its marketable products (in order to allow a proper embedding of scientific and technological advances in our society)" (Von Schomberg 2013: p. 50; 2014: p. 39). From this viewpoint, ethical acceptability in the EU context "refers to a mandatory compliance with the fundamental values of the EU Charter on fundamental rights" (von Schomberg 2013: p. 40). Social desirability "captures the relevant, and more specific normative anchor points of the treaty on the European Union" (von Schomberg 2013: p. 40). Competitiveness, scientific progress, fundamental rights and environmental protection can be taken as the normative anchor points of EU research and innovation policies and, therefore, they play a role as the normative "building-blocks" of a governance framework for research and innovation activities.

Indeed, RRI comprehensively combines and integrates earlier approaches and methods, as "technology assessment and foresight, application of the precautionary principle, normative/ethical principles to design technology, innovation governance and stakeholder involvement and public engagement" in both deliberation and regulation (von Schomberg 2013: p. 41). RRI complements this interest in the design and implementation of governance frameworks, which are understood as sets of concrete processes and mechanisms, with the warranty of compliance with normative requirements. On the other hand, however, the definition of RRI we have cited emphasizes the integrated presence of multiple dimensions within the notion of RRI, such as the ethical, political, social and legal ones.

When these governance approaches are discussed, stressing the reference to fundamental rights could be regarded as a way to rigidly set values and goals, even regardless of public debate and public opinion development. From this point of view, fundamental rights could be considered as normative constraints defined in a top-down way, limiting the scope and influence of public involvement. However, this representation of fundamental rights in general and of their specific role in RRI is indeed debatable. Human rights are usually seen from two opposite perspectives and both of them should be rejected. According to a first view, human rights are abstract ideals, which easily can be reduced to rhetorical appeals. According to a second perspective, human rights are expressed by norms and, because of that, they have a closed and compelling meaning that concerns solely the relationships between citizens and their governments or judicial courts. In this understanding, fundamental rights have no relation to public opinion.

Fundamental rights can, on the contrary, be thought of as claims that are justified by strong moral reasons and supported by legal norms, suitable for regulating both the (vertical) relations between the government and the citizens and, often, the (horizontal) relations among citizens themselves and, in general, among private actors. However, it is important to note that the legal norms supporting such claims are often structurally vague, because they have to apply to as high a number of cases as possible.

In science, technology and innovation many private actors actively self-regulate and possess information and knowledge crucial to regulation, so regulation needs to reflect such a diffuse and shared nature of responsibility. As a consequence, the contents of fundamental rights should emerge in a bottom-up fashion through a diffused meaning-making process which could, and often does, also contribute to shaping self-regulatory tools.

Indeed, human rights do affect the regulation of innovation in several ways. First, on a judicial level, by referring to the sources on fundamental rights in the EU, the judicial stance contributes to the definition of their content. Second, on a policy level, the protection and promotion of rights might act as a driver for policy-making. Third, the reference to human rights plays a role also on a horizontal level, between private actors, for instance, when the most diverse organizations adopt and implement social responsibility instruments (codes of conduct, self-regulation).

Therefore, fundamental rights constitute a basic reference for a normative governance model, whose development and implementation must and can come to terms with different values and with different interpretations of the rights themselves. Especially in the European context, "human rights can help in strengthening both the legislation needed for regulating the present market and the soft instruments needed for steering research and for fostering the stakeholders' participation without sacrificing the coherence of the regulatory response" (Ruggiu 2013: p. 201).

When understood in this way, human rights might gain a central space in RRI as they could represent the "normative anchor points" for defining ethical acceptability, thus shaping what has been regarded as the main feature of a specific European approach to the ethical and regulatory challenges of innovation (Ozolina et al. 2009: p. 27). As we already mentioned, normative-flavoured definitions of RRI explicitly link the ethical acceptability of research and innovation and compliance with the EU charter on fundamental rights, besides a general reference to safety as a paramount criterion for assessing technology and innovation (van den Hoven et al. 2013: p. 58). Moreover, innovation is expected to take into account the societal needs embodied in the Treaty on European Union, as sustainable development, equality and quality of life (van den Hoven et al. 2013: p. 58). Yet, fundamental rights and societal needs are seen as explicitly and mutually linked goals of a comprehensive normative framework for the governance of science, technology and innovation. Nevertheless, despite their strong embedding within the EU Treaty and the EU Charter of Fundamental Rights, it has to be recognized that some ambiguities can exist in the "normative anchor points" themselves, as they may give rise to conflicting interpretations, uses or applications. This is the reason why RRI frameworks should give room to contestation as an unavoidable feature to be taken into account (e.g. see Res-AgorA Project, Responsibility Navigator: http://responsibility-navigator.eu/).

To sum up, two remarks here are in order to justify an integrated view of fundamental rights and governance. First, considering fundamental rights as essential elements of a governance framework does not imply any closure to public involvement, as it does not mean that both the normative standards to be complied with and the goals to be pursued are already fully set in a top-down manner. Far from it: once listed, fundamental rights have to be filled with contents and have to be detailed with regard to specific domains, contexts and cases. In this open-ended process of interpretation and application of principles, societal values and norms can find (and usually do find) a way of expression. Within this perspective, they can rather be seen as being "a public normative practice" (Beitz 2009: p. 170), as long as their content is not established once and for all in the law-making process, but it has to be shaped also in a bottom-up manner by several relevant actors during the application stage, such as judges, but also private actors, promoting tools of self-regulation. Second, fundamental rights are not mere constraints for innovation which aim at reducing or avoiding its undesirable or negative consequences by warranting the respect of human health, dignity, privacy etc. Rather, they also concern the shaping of policies, so that rights are not only respected and protected, but also promoted by way of proactive initiatives: "we should allow fundamental rights to work in a truly proactive fashion, and this is possible only in a rights based model, a system where (legal issues on) human rights are not an accident on the route of governance, but are integrated into all its phases from the outset" (Ruggiu 2015: p. 233). When their meaning is understood in this way, the reference to fundamental rights adds a significant dimension to governance frameworks such as RRI, which aim at encouraging proactive policies, as they imply and require the contribution of stakeholders and, in general, of the citizens in determining their content and the concrete goals to be pursued within the innovation process.

Conclusion

RRI can be deemed as a governance approach integrating fundamental rights with voluntary regulatory mechanisms and instruments typical of the New Governance model. The efficacy of this approach is based on just such an integrative nature, i.e. on the combination of principle-based and outcome-oriented regulation. We emphasized fundamental rights as the main "building blocks" of principle-based regulation and, more in general, of this framework.

The combination of fundamental rights with soft and hybrid regulatory instruments that are typical of New Governance seems particularly apt to cope with the situation to which RRI is called to answer. As we have said in the introduction, we might see the orientation provided by the RRI approach as "a joint product of knowledge about the future and consent about the most desired prospects", in a situation that can be properly characterized as uncertain in terms of knowledge and contested in terms of consent (Douglas and Wildavsky 1983: pp. 5–6). In the context of RRI, the reference to fundamental rights could be seen, therefore, as an important component in the constellation of elements determining the ethical acceptability of innovation and techno-scientific developments. This is the main reason for maintaining that, in the field of the governance of innovation, RRI tends to be a more comprehensive approach than the New Governance itself. In RRI, the reference to fundamental rights is one of the elements to be taken into consideration when assessing the ethical acceptability of innovation. This situation reflects the RRI focus on actors' *responsibilization* and the appeal to their capacity of committing to some goals beyond what is strictly mandated by the law: "Responsibilisation – namely expecting and assuming the reflexive moral capacities of various social actors – is the practical link that connects the ideal-typical scheme of governance to actual practices on the ground. Responsibility – in contrast to mere compliance with rules – presupposes one's care for one's duties and one's un-coerced application of certain values as a root motivation for action" (Shamir, 2008).

Our discussion suggests that the potential of fundamental rights to successfully combine a stable normative orientation with openness and flexibility in RRI should be considered with regard to how this commitment to fundamental rights can be properly adjusted into decentred and bottom-up regulation. In other words, it is a matter of how the basic requirements of the constitutional state can be preserved in the multilevel and manifold regulation that characterizes the New Governance approach. Indeed, when assessing the coherence and suitability of soft regulation according to the framework of RRI, the relationship between the New Governance approach and the (multilevel) constitutional dimension of the EU needs to be addressed. In general, the relationships between the typical tools of New Governance have been differently identified as characterized by complementarity, rivalry or transformation (i.e. the transformation of legal regulation due to the influence of governance frameworks) (Trubek and Trubek 2007: pp. 6–13). The success of referring to fundamental rights as a solution to provide "normative anchor points" for RRI requires a careful examination of the legal and regulatory framework in which STI activities are framed in the EU and, at the same time, a deliberate effort to construe a governance framework designed to ensure the complementarity between hard and soft regulation, legal norms and voluntary commitments.

RRI would be yet another recast of purely market-based approaches promoting an "'economized' language of responsibility" (Shamir 2008) instead of a "responsible" approach in the broader sense claimed by RRI (Arnaldi and Gorgoni 2016) if it is not backed by strong normative commitments towards the basic democratic values expressed by constitutionalism and the rule of law, which do represent a fundamental, specifically European, ethical-political and also legal legacy.

Notes

1 All the authors outlined the structure of the chapter. S. Arnaldi wrote sections 1 and 2; G. Gorgoni wrote section 4 and 5; E. Pariotti wrote sections 3 and 6; all authors wrote section 7. All authors have read and approved the manuscript. This chapter is based on several publications in which the authors have discussed the link between responsibilization and soft regulation, as well as between RRI and fundamental rights (Arnaldi et al. 2016; Arnaldi and Gorgoni 2016; Arnaldi 2017).

2 For further details about these and other initiatives, see Arnaldi (2014); Arnaldi et al. (2014).

3 For the purposes of this chapter we do not differentiate between "Fundamental Rights" and "Human Rights", although it is both possible and relevant to do it from a legal point of view, as they have a different legal status. The consequences of the distinction for an RRI framework are explained by Ruggiu (2015: p. 232).

References

Arnaldi S. (2014). '¿Qué tan suave debería ser la regulación nano? Identidades sociales y opiniones de los stakeholders italianos', *Mundo Nano. Revista Interdisciplinaria en Nanociencias y Nanotecnología*, 7(13), pp. 6–27.

Arnaldi S. (2017). Changing me softly: Making sense of soft regulation and compliance in the Italian nanotechnology sector, *Nanoethics*, 11(1), pp. 1–13.

Arnaldi S., Gorgoni G. and Pariotti, E. (2016). *Responsible Research and Innovation as a governance paradigm: What is new?* In: Lindner R., Kuhlmann, S., Randles, S.,

Bedsted, B., Gorgoni, G., Griessler, E., Loconto, A. and Mejlgaard, N. (Eds.), *Navigating Towards Shared Responsibility in Research and Innovation. Approach, Process and Results of the Res-AGorA Project.* Karlsruhe: Fraunhofer ISI, pp. 23–29. ISBN: 978-3-00-051709-9.

Arnaldi, S. and Gorgoni, G. (2016). Turning the tide or surfing the wave? Responsible Research and Innovation, fundamental rights and neoliberal virtues. *Life Sciences, Society and Policy*, 6, pp. 1–19. DOI : 10.1186/s40504-016-0038-2.

Arnaldi, S., Ferrari, A., Magaudda, P. and Marin F. (2014). Nanotechnologies and the quest for responsibility. In Arnaldi, S., Ferrari, A., Magaudda, P., Marin, F. (Eds.), *Responsibility in Nanotechnology Development.* Dordrecht: Springer, pp. 1–18.

BASF. (n.d.). *Nanotechnology code of conduct.* Available from: http://www.basf.com/group/corporate/nanotechnology/en/microsites/nanotechnology/safety/code-of-conduct. [accessed 30 December 2013].

Beck, U. (1992). *Risk Society: Towards a New Modernity.* London: Sage Publications.

Beitz, C. (2009). *The Idea of Human Rights.* Oxford: Oxford University Press.

Bovens, M. (1998). *The Quest for Responsibility. Accountability and Citizenship in Complex Organisations.* Cambridge: Cambridge University Press.

Bowman, D. M. and Hodge, G. A. (2007). Governing nanotechnology without government? *Science and Public Policy*, 35(7), pp. 475–487.

Braithwaite, J., Coglianese, C. and Levi-Faur D. (2007). Can regulation and governance make a difference. *Regulation and Governance*, 1, pp. 1–7.

Callon, M., Lascoumes, P. and Barthe, Y. (2009). *Acting in an Uncertain World. An Essay on Technical Democracy.* Cambridge (MA):MIT Press.

Cane, P. (2002). *Responsibility in Law and Morality.* Oxford: Hart Publishing.

Chowdhury, N. and Wessel, R. A. (2012). Conceptualising multilevel regulation on the EU: A legal translation of multilevel governance? *European Law Journal*, 18(3), pp. 335–357.

Coeckelbergh, M. (2012). Moral responsibility, technology, and experiences of the tragic: From Kierkegaard to offshore engineering. *Science and Engineering Ethics*, 18(1), pp. 35–48.

Davis, M. (2012). Ain't no one here but us social forces: Constructing the professional responsibility of engineers. *Science and Engineering Ethics*, 18 (1), pp. 13–34.

DEFRA – Department of Environment, Food and Rural Affairs. (2008a). *The Voluntary Reporting Scheme.* Available from: http://archive.defra.gov.uk/environment/quality/nanotech/documents/ vrs-nanoscale.pdf. [accessed 30 December 2013].

DEFRA – Department of Environment, Food and Rural Affairs. (2008b). *A supplementary guide for the UK Voluntary Reporting Scheme.* Available from: http://archive.defra.gov.uk/environment/quality/nanotech/documents/nano-hazards.pdf. [accessed 30 December 2013].

Dorbeck-Jung, B. and Shelley-Egan, C. (2013). Meta-regulation and nanotechnologies: The challenge of responsibilisation within the European Commission's code of conduct for responsible nanosciences and nanotechnologies research. *Nanoethics*, 7(1), pp. 55–68.

Douglas, M. and Wildavsky, A. B. (1983). *Risk and Culture: An Essay on the Selection of Technical and Environmental Dangers.* Berkeley: University of California Press.

DuPont. (2012). *DuPont Position Statement on Nanotechnology.* Available from: http://www.dupont.com/corporate-functions/news-and-events/insights/articles/position-statements/articles/nanotechnology.html. [accessed 30 December 2013].

Eberlein, B. and Kerwer, D. (2004). New governance in the European Union: A theoretical perspective. *Journal of Common Market Studies*, 42(1), pp. 121–142.

EPA – Environmental Protection Agency. (n.d.). *Control of Nanoscale Materials under the Toxic Substances Control Act.* Available from: http://www.epa.gov/oppt/nano/. [accessed 30 December 2013].

EPA – Environmental Protection Agency. (n.d.). *Nanoscale Materials Stewardship Program*. Available from: http://epa.gov/oppt/nano/stewardship.htm. [accessed 30 December 2013].

European Commission. (2008). *Recommendation on a Code of Conduct for Responsible Nanosciences and Nanotechnologies Research, 1st Revision: Analysis of results from the Public Consultation of the Public Consultation*. Available from: http://ec.europa.eu/research/consultations/nano-code/consultation_en.htm. [accessed 30 December 2013].

Ewald, F. (2001). Philosophie politique du principe de precaution. In: Ewald F., Gollier C., and de Sadeleer N. (Eds.), *Le principe de precaution*. PUF: Paris, pp. 29–44.

Falkner, R. and Jaspers, N. (2012). Regulating nanotechnologies: Risk, uncertainty and the global governance gap. *Global Environmental Politics*, 12(1), pp. 30–55.

Felt, U. and Wynne, B. (2007). *Taking European Knowledge Society Seriously. Report of the Expert Group on Science and Governance to the Science, Economy and Society Directorate, Directorate-General for Research*. Brussels: European Commission.

Ferrarese, M. R. (2000). *Le istituzioni della globalizzazione*. Bologna: Il Mulino.

Forsberg, E. M., Quaglio, G. L., O'Kane, H., Karapiperis, T., Van Woensel, L. and Arnaldi, S. (2015). Assessment of science and technologies: Advising for and with responsibility. *Technology in Society*, 42, pp. 21–27.

Fredriksson, M., Blomqvist, P. and Winblad, U. (2012). Conflict and compliance in Swedish health care governance: Soft law in the shadow of hierarchy. *Scandinavian Political Studies*, 35(1), pp. 48–70.

Garsten, C. and Jacobsson, K. (2011). Post-political regulation: Soft power and post-political visions in global governance. *Critical Sociology*, 39(3), pp. 421–438.

Giddens, A. (1999). Risk and responsibility. *The Modern Law Review*, 62(1), pp. 1–10.

Gorgoni, G. (2008). La responsabilité comme projet. Réflexions sur une responsabilité juridique "prospective". In: Eberhard, C. (Ed.), *Traduire nos responsabilités planétaires, recomposer nos paysages juridiques*. Bruxelles: Bruylant, pp. 131–146, ISBN/ISSN: 9782802726548.

Gorgoni, G. (2010). (Pre)caution improvisation area. Improvisation and responsibility in the practice of the precautionary principle. *Critical Studies In Improvisation*, 6(1), (*Lex Non Scripta, Ars Non Scripta: Law, Justice, and Improvisation)*, ISSN : 1712-0624, online [http://www.criticalimprov.com].

Gorgoni, G. (2011). Modelli di responsabilità e regolazione delle nanotecnologie nel diritto comunitario. Dal principio di precauzione ai codici di condotta. In: Guerra, G., Muratorio, A., Pariotti, E., Piccinni, M. and Ruggiu, D. (Eds.), *Forme di responsabilità, regolazione e nanotecnologie*. Bologna: Il Mulino, pp. 371–395.

Hart, H. L. A. (1968). *Punishment and Responsibility*. Oxford: Oxford University Press.

Heinemann, M. Schäfer, H. (2009). Guidance for handling and use of nanomaterials at the workplace. *Human and Experimental Toxicology*, 28(6–7), pp. 407–411.

Heyvaert, V. (2009). Levelling down, levelling up, and governing across: Three responses to hybridization in international law. *The European Journal of International Law*, 20(3), pp. 647–674.

Hickey, G. M., Innes, J. L., Kozak, R. A., Bull, G. Q. and Vertinsky, I. (2006). Monitoring and information reporting for sustainable forest management: An inter-jurisdictional comparison of soft law standards. *Forest Policy and Economics*, 9(4), pp. 297–315.

ICCA – International Council of Chemical Associations. (2006). *Responsible Care® Global Charter in English*. Available from: http://www.icca-chem.org/ICCADocs/09_RCGC_EN_Feb2006.pdf. [accessed 30 December 2013].

ISO – International Organization for Standardization. (n.d.) ISO/TC 229 Nanotechnologies. Available from: http://www.iso.org/iso/iso_technical_committee?commid=381983. [accessed 30 December 2013].

Jasanoff, S. (2006). Ordering knowledge, ordering society. In: *States of Knowledge: The Co-Production of Science and the Social Order*. New York: Routledge, pp. 13–45.

Kohler-Koch, B. and Rittberger, B. (2006). The 'governance turn' in EU Studies. *Journal of Common Market Studies*, 44, pp. 27–49.

Koutalakis, C., Buzogany A. and Börzel, T. A. (2010). When soft regulation is not enough: The integrated pollution prevention and control directive of the European Union. *Regulation and Governance*, 4(3), pp. 329–344.

Luhmann, N. (1993). *Risk: A Sociological Theory*. New Bruswick: Transaction Publishers.

Marchant, G. E. and Abbott, K. W. (2013). International harmonization of nanotechnology governance through 'soft law' approaches. *Nanotechnology Law and Business*, 9(4), pp. 393–410.

Marchant, G. E., Sylvester, D. J., Abbott, K. W. and Danforth, T. L. (2009). International harmonization of regulation of nanomedicine. *Studies in Ethics*, *Law*, and *Technology*, 3(3), art. no. 6.

MASIS – Monitoring Activities of Science in Society in Europe Experts Group. (2009). *Challenging Futures of Science in Society. Emerging Trends and Cutting-Edge Issues*. European Commission, Directorate-General for Research, Luxembourg.

Maynard, A. and Rejeski, D. (2009). Too small to overlook. *Nature*, 460(7252), p. 174.

Osimani, B. (2013). An epistemic analysis of the precautionary principle. *Dilemata*, 11, pp. 149–167.

Owen R., Stilgoe, J., Macnaghten, P., Fisher, E., Gorman, M. and Guston, D. H. (2013). A framework for responsible innovation. In: Owen, R., Heintz, M. and Bessant, J. (Eds.), *Responsible Innovation. Managing the Responsible Emergence of Science and Innovation in Society*. Hoboken (NJ): John Wiley & Sons, pp. 27–50.

Owen, R. (2014). *Responsible Research and Innovation: Options for research and innovation policy in the EU*. Available from: https://ec.europa.eu/research/innovation-union/pdf/expert-groups/Responsible_Research_and_Innovation.pdf [accessed 2 February 2015].

Ozolina, Z., Mitcham, C. and Stilgoe, J. (2009). *Global Governance of Science, Report of the Expert Group on Global Governance of Science to the Science, Economy and Society Directorate*. Brussels: Directorate-General for Research, European Commission.

Papaux, A. (2006). *Introduction à la philosophie du "droit en situation". De la codification légaliste au droit prudentiel*. Paris/Zurich/Bruxelles: L.G.D.J./Schulthess/Bruylant.

Pariotti, E. (2011). Normatività giuridica e governance delle tecnologie emergent. In: Guerra, G., Muratorio, A. Pariotti, E., Piccinni, M. and Ruggiu, D. (Eds.), *Forme di responsabilità, regolazione e nanotecnologie*. Bologna: Il Mulino, pp. 509–549.

Pellizzoni, L. (2010). Environmental knowledge and deliberative democracy. In: Gross, M. and Heinrichs, H. (Eds.), *Environmental Sociology*. Amsterdam: Springer, pp. 159–182. doi:10.1007/978-90-481-8730-0_10.

Pellizzoni, L. (2004). Responsibility and environmental governance. *Environmental Politics*, 13(3), pp. 541–565.

Ponce Del Castillo, A. M. (2013). 'The European and member states' approaches to regulating nanomaterials: Two levels of governance. *NanoEthics*, 7(3), pp. 189–199.

Ricoeur, P. (2000). *The Just*. Chicago: Chicago University Press.

Ruggiu, D. (2013). Temporal perspectives of the nanotechnological challenge to regulation: How human rights can contribute to the present and future of nanotechnologies. *NanoEthics*, 7(3), pp. 201–215.

Ruggiu, D. (2015). Anchoring European governance: Two versions of responsible research and innovation and EU fundamental rights as 'normative anchor Points'. *NanoEthics*, 9, pp. 217–235.

Scott, J. E. and Trubeck, D. M. (2002). Mind the gap: Law and new approaches to governance in the European Union. *European Law Journal*, 8(1), pp. 1–18.

Shaffer, G. and Pollack, M. A. (2013). Hard and soft law. In : J.L. Dunoff and Pollack, M.A. (Eds.) *Interdisciplinary Perspectives on International Law and International Relations*. New York: Cambridge University Press, pp. 197–222.

Shamir, R. (2008). The age of responsibilization: On market-embedded morality. *Economy and Society*, 37(1), pp. 1–19. Doi:10.1080/03085140701760833.

Skjærseth, J. B., Stokke, O. S. and Wettestad, J. (2006). Soft law, hard law, and effective implementation of international environmental norms. *Global Environmental Politics*, 6(3), pp. 104–120.

Stokes, E. (2013). Demand for command: Responding to technological risks and scientific uncertainties. *Medical Law Review*, 21(1), pp. 11–38.

Szyszcak, E. (2006). Experimental governance: The open method of coordination. *European Law Journal*, 12(4), pp. 486–502.

Trubek, D. M. and Trubek, L. G. (2007). New governance and legal regulation: Complementarity, rivalry, and transformation. *Legal Studies Research Paper Series*, University of Wisconsin Law School, Paper No. 1047.

van de Poel, I. (2009). The introduction of nanotechnology as a societal experiment. In: Arnaldi, S., Lorenzet, A. and Russo, F. (Eds.), *Technoscience in Progress. Managing the Uncertainty of Nanotechnology*. Amsterdam: IOS Press, pp. 129–142.

van de Poel, I. (2011). The relation between forward-looking and backward-looking responsibility. In: Vincent, N. A., van de Poel I., van den Hove I. (Eds.), *Moral Responsibility: Beyond Free Will and Determinism*. Dordrecht: Springer, pp. 37–52.

van den Hoven, J., Jacob, K., Nielsen, L., Roure, F., Rudze, L., Stilgoe, J., et al. (2013). *Options for strengthening responsible research and innovation: Report of the Expert Group on the State of Art in Europe on Responsible Research and Innovation*. Available from: http://ec.europa.eu/ research/science-society/document_library/pdf_06/options-for- strengthening_en.pdf. [accessed 2 February 2015].

Vincent, N. A. (2011). *A Structured Taxonomy of Responsibility Concepts*. In: Vincent N. A., van de Poel I. and van den Hoven, J. (Eds.), *Moral Responsibility: Beyond Free Will and Determinism*. Dordrecht: Springer, pp. 15–35.

Von Schomberg, R. (2013). A vision of responsible innovation. In: Owen, R., Heintz, M. and Bessant, J. (Eds.), *Responsible Innovation. Managing the Responsible Emergence of Science and Innovation in Society*. Hoboken (NJ): John Wiley & Sons, pp. 51–73.

Wynne, B. (1992). Misunderstood misunderstanding. Social identities and public uptake of science. *Public Understanding of Science*, 1(3), pp. 281–304.

8 What are the conditions for the ethical implementation of RRI?

Responsible governance and second-order reflexivity

Robert Gianni and Philippe Goujon

Introduction

In recent decades we have witnessed the increasing need for new regulatory forms that can be articulated through flexible modalities in order to be able to respond to the complex needs of current society. In this sense, Responsible Research and Innovation (RRI) is a fairly recent framework aimed at creating a meaningful and fruitful dialectic between technical and economic ambitions (R&I) and the normative claims present in or arising from society.

Although RRI is a relatively new notion, we can already find several contributions trying to define its scope, methodology and application (Owen *et al.* 2013; Von Schomberg 2013; Van den Hoven *et al.* 2014; Koops *et al.* 2015).

However, we are still far from achieving a shared understanding of what RRI should be and could do, and which tools would best suit its purposes. Most of the policy-oriented proposals suggest a set of procedural indications, flexible enough to be adapted in different circumstances and uncertain scenarios. Given their scope and nature, these indications tend to remain abstract and thus open to different interpretations, which often slows down the whole process. But the high interest in the implementation of RRI has also contributed to generating a growing literary production, which unfortunately has not always developed harmoniously. Some argue, for instance, that the distance between academic production and policies can undermine the efficacy of an implementation process (Klassen *et al.* Ch. 4). Furthermore, some analyses have shown examples of what we might empirically consider as a 'responsible' product or process, which does not match the commonly accepted theoretical indications (Blok Ch. 10). It appears that this urge for regulation, that RRI hopes to represent, has somehow flooded the process to operationalize it, raising some scepticism about its efficacy.

In order to try and fill this gap between theory and practice, between academic references and policies, we find it useful to analyse the categories of innovation and responsibility, together with the most common tools suggested in the literature and policies as measures to implement RRI.[1] In this way, we believe that we can start clarifying the epistemic nature of RRI's components as well as their moral duties and political roles.

Research and innovation (R&I) requires, nowadays, an effort and a cross-fertilization that transcends both geographical borders between countries and epistemic differences between different social domains. This scenario arises due to several concomitant factors. Among the different causes, we can surely highlight globalization, which has made their virtual operating range unlimited in space but also in time. But we could also add the overall acceleration of technologies, especially those involving informatics, causing new phenomena like the one described by Bernhard Peters as the "trans-nationalization of public spheres" (Peters 2007), which has led to new epistemic understandings of societal dynamics now defined according to a horizontal perspective instead of a vertical one. Thus, the current proliferation of sociological narrations in terms of information, reticula or media (Duff 2000; Castells 2010).

From an ecologic point of view, the scarcity of energy resources and the necessity to invert a global climate drift, the effects of which seem irreversible, represent more than a simple alert. Such awareness has also generated a parallel change in the economic sector, which has required a paradigmatic, as well as evoked, shift in the production process from a linear one to a circular one (Stehr 2008; Streeck 2014; Dardot and Laval 2016; Nathan Ch.13).

From a political point of view, the growing impact of the effects of technologies on society together with the increase in democratizing processes (Donzelot 1984) has generated a quest for more inclusive development of the role, scope and methodology of R&I.

All these changes have contributed to shining the spotlight on R&I as a field apt to fulfil all these different needs. However, general concerns over the potential effects of research and innovation have also contributed to the necessity of promoting a regulatory framework able to drive R&I towards societal goals. The emergence of a 'new' regulatory framework, RRI, is, then, called to now answer to these challenges.

The framework of RRI aims at providing researchers and innovators with new regulatory indications able to respond in an efficient and legitimate way to their needs but also to the values and claims arising from society. Most of the old regulatory forms were based on a double delegation model (Callon *et al.* 2009) where policy-makers and experts were the only depositaries of 'truth', developing their processes through a command-and-control paradigm. Also, because of the above-mentioned changes, these models are no longer perceived as legitimate and/or efficient for implementing processes or products acceptable by society (Pellizzoni 2008; Arnaldi & Bianchi 2016). Furthermore, as some recent examples have shown, to narrow the regulation of science into top-down protocols might end up in paradoxically confining all concerns into an 'anti-science' paradigm, undermining the possibility to integrate new knowledge into R&I (Von Schomberg 1993).[2] New regulatory forms are therefore required to compensate for the inefficiencies or 'injustices' caused by hard regulatory frameworks of R&I.

The main difficulty for any regulatory framework is to understand how to translate the abstract rules necessary to set in motion a process according to contextual aspects, without diluting its regulatory power into relativistic perspectives. When it comes to RRI, this translates into the necessity to make the different epistemic dimensions of facts and values interact with one another without losing sight of the necessary overall framework. In other words, the problem is not only how to pass from an abstract conception to concrete measures, but also – and especially – how to deal with the epistemic, moral and political pluralism characterizing our societies (Reber 2016). When it comes to RRI, we believe that the most sensitive issue is to understand how we can implement tools and measures which integrate into one framework the normative features belonging to responsibility with the more technical and 'objective' procedures pertaining to R&I. Furthermore, if the clashes of 'languages' at the basis of R&I can be a matter of argument, the plurality entrenched in responsibility surely requires a further and deeper analysis as rightly highlighted by some authors (Ricœur 2000; 2007; Pellé & Reber 2016).

At the crossroads of the epistemic and moral side of problems, we can detect a complex gap between what we might define as the justification of a norm, necessary to regulate the process, and its consequent application. Our claim is that the two sides of the implementation of a norm able to represent a regulatory tool, justification and application, should be kept in balance. An excessive stress on the latter can, in fact, lead to the taking into account only the acceptance of a product or a process, paving the way to several forms of instrumentalization that would endanger the credibility of the process. On the other hand, a stronger priority assigned to the former can, and often does, cause an impossibility or unwillingness to adopt the necessary norm, making the process at least inefficient (Gunther 1993; Williams 1984; Maesschalck 2000; 2017).

In addition to the epistemic divergences and moral pluralism, we can easily detect several practical and sometimes more political barriers and obstacles preventing an efficient application of RRI, like funding, institutional arrangements and standardization processes.

Once having identified these issues, we now need to address them by trying to indicate some useful countermeasures. In order to do so, it is necessary to investigate the main shortcomings and biases, propose some alternatives and try to derive indications able to respond to the double imperative of legitimacy and efficiency.

Conceptual analysis of responsible innovation

Innovation

The category of innovation is often recognized as a main conceptual and managerial methodology able to respond to the radical changes that occur in the production process (Leonard-Barthon 1995). Without the necessity to abandon certain efficient managerial procedures, it can also integrate new forms, helping the transition from a linear model to a circular one (Godin 2006; Nathan Ch. 13).

The current understanding of innovation, although conjugated according to the level of novelty as incremental or disruptive (Bower and Christensen 1995; Dewar and Dutton 1986), and surely developed in more refined ways, is still inspired by Joseph Schumpeter's famous theorization. Schumpeter thought of the category of innovation as the peculiar capacity or talent of an entrepreneur to have an intuition and to introduce to the market a new combination of existing factors (Schumpeter 1934). In fact, economic development can and should be generated through the implementation of such an innovative vision which consists, according to Schumpeter, "of the different employment of existing resources, in doing new things with them, without considering if these resources have increased or not" (1934: p. 70). Schumpeter defined innovation as the exemplification of three related figures: "a spontaneous change", within a "dynamic theoretical apparatus" incarnated in the figure of the "entrepreneur" (1934: p. 81).

However, innovation seems to carry a paradoxical objective, which becomes even stronger if assessed against the concept of responsibility.

In fact, innovation should deal with economic progress by attributing to ideas, knowledge and individual capacities what was earlier subsumed under materials and collective features. It then faces an apparent paradox because, if on the one hand, its nature and strength reside in the unpredictability of its development, on the other hand, this uncertainty jeopardizes not only its economic success, but also and especially its moral and political justness. Schumpeter was not unaware of the risks connected to the uncertainty embedded in the model of innovation: "Even with an intense preliminary work we cannot exhaustively grasp all the effects and repercussions of the plan" (1934: p. 83). But if we connect that original conception with the changes that occurred at the moral and political level in our current societies, we can easily grasp all the extent of what we might call a wicked problem. If we then subsume such perspective under a responsible framework, an innovator is in principle supposed to develop something that is going to be profitable and that should remain morally and politically justifiable without having the possibility of foreseeing its consequences. Most of the difficulties and thus scepticism with regard to RRI are connected to this apparently clashing or paradoxical logic, which involves also the relation between research and responsibility.[3]

However, our assumption is that the paradox is not entrenched in the two paradigms as such but stems from posing the question in a wrong perspective. In fact, the shortcomings in pursuing an innovation process drawing on the general features proposed by Schumpeter do not lie in some kind of moral wickedness of an economic logic but in its isolation from other societal aspects. It is the closure to such a contamination that causes what we might call an epistemic failure. By epistemic failure, we mean the incapacity to pursue specific objectives due to endemic isolated formulations. In other words, we believe that the problem pertaining to bridging innovation with responsibility does not reside in the difference between the two logics, but in an eventual short-sighted unwillingness to acknowledge the necessary intersections between them. The apparent clash between a technical and a normative logic can be overcome by opening to reciprocal fertilization through means of communicating and influencing each other. Thus, such a paradoxical perspective can be adjusted if innovation is not confined to a technical process aimed at increasing profits, or at least it is important to widen its logic, scope and methodology (Pavie *et al.* 2014; Blok & Lemmens 2015).

It becomes useful, then, to try and mitigate this clashing view by further addressing the conceptualization of innovation and confronting it with that of responsibility in the framework of RRI.

Following the extensive overview provided by Jack Stilgoe, it is possible to highlight a whole series of unwanted consequences potentially stemming from an innovation when it is not developed according to external references (Collingridge 1980; Jonas 1984; Beck 1992; Sarewitz 2004; Perrow 1970; Wynne 1992).[4] In order to avoid certain recurrent phenomena that could fossilize in what Stilgoe has called 'pathologies', innovation needs to define its scope and the necessary requirements on the basis of a wider contribution from society at large.[5]

In order to understand how to help in driving innovation towards a broader approach, it is useful to think of innovation in its different moments. The taxonomy provided by John Bessant (2013) helps us in highlighting four dimensions of innovation on which we could potentially act to modify its outcomes. According to Bessant, innovation can be defined as a product, a process, a position or a paradigm.

The product side refers to the things (products/services) that an organization offers. The position concerns the context in which the products/services are introduced. The process addresses the ways in which products and services are created and delivered. Lastly, the paradigm tackles the underlying mental (business) models, which express the objectives and the values that an organization wants to promote.

On the one hand, it is interesting to understand what different moments of innovation can be assessed as responsible by trying to identify all the different aspects of an innovation within a production flow. According to this scheme, in fact, if we want to make an innovation responsible, we can act on any of these moments. On the other hand, we think that this taxonomy can also be adopted to assess the responsibility of the whole idea of innovation in a logical and temporal flow. It would not be logically wrong to infer that an innovation is set in motion on the basis of a conceptual model, enacting and framing a process which generates a product and outlines the context in which it will be launched, although this last point might be more blurred than foreseen.

Vincent Blok (Ch. 10), for instance, has shown the importance of developing a process-oriented shift in order to have a more likely structural approach to responsibility. In other words, if it is true that a responsible as well as an irresponsible product can be the outcome of an accidental convergence of different factors, it is also plausible to think that the potential responsibility of a process will consistently increase the chances of generating responsible products.

As we might recall, the problem we have highlighted with innovation, as defined by Schumpeter, was embedded in a sort of epistemic shortcoming. If we now adopt a lexical perspective[6] on the innovation flow, as delineated by Bessant, the consequent methodological outcome is to radicalize Blok's suggestion by acting on what is at the basis of the concept of innovation: its epistemic framework, i.e. the paradigm.[7]

The insightful investigations made by O'Sullivan and Dooley (2009) and Benoit Godin (2015) provide additional support to the necessity of a broader understanding of the concept of innovation. According to their analysis, there are two main aspects at the core of innovation. The first one, as for Schumpeter, is the dynamic nature of innovation, its (inter) active side. The second one is the structural relation of an innovation to a context. Curiously enough, they underline the general tendency within innovation management theories to underestimate the importance of this second aspect. What is actually pursued instead is the development of innovation only according to 'endogenous' criteria (Blok and Lemmens 2015). O'Connor has delineated a scenario where, up to a few years ago, innovation has been narrowly managed in several established firms (O'Connor 2008). In these analyses, an isolated approach or a marketing exploitation of the process are conceived as reliable vehicles for profitable outcomes. However, some more recent contributions (Blok and Lemmens 2015) and some important distinctions (Godin 2016)[8] prove that we are assisting in a significant shift with regard to the role of contextual, external factors in those fields where the seeds have not yet sprouted up.

As has been shown by Manfred Moldashl (2010), to think narrowly about a theory of (economic) innovation undermines its basic meaning and its practical efficacy. Innovation involves too many different aspects and fields, meaning that if it is conceived only in mere instrumental terms, it will overlook the normative and moral factors necessary to achieve public acceptance,[9] transforming innovation in an inefficient or unprofitable product or process. Innovation entails the possibility of social progress that, by definition, cannot be conflated to an economic profit (Blok and Lemmens 2015).

What we should focus on is not a simple theory of innovation but, following Moldashl, the contextual, societal role that every innovation involves and, therefore, its relation with a given normative framework.

Established this epistemic necessity of dealing with external and contextual factors, of integrating alternative perspectives, we now need to understand the moral and political paths able to drive us through the complex scenario generated by plural perspectives in society. In other words, once established that plural perspectives are not only necessary but also beneficial, especially for innovation, we now need to address the ways to cope with these differences.

Some past experiences Genetically Modified Organisms (GMOs) have exemplified that the context, in this case intended as some acting minorities, is perfectly able to reject or to accept an innovative product according to features that are not technical and often not foreseeable in a technical or scientific manner. Scientific data about GMOs, for instance, are still insufficient to define the consequences stemming from all the possible interactions between natural and artificial operations, also considering intentional and unintentional instrumentalization. If some scientists have highlighted the clear benefits, others have raised several doubts with regard to the potential side-effects (Hug 2008; Bawa & Anilakumar 2013). What this and other similar debates suggest is that the choice to adopt certain products cannot be delegated to technical knowledge, not only because of clashing arguments, but most of all because of plural moral views (Frewer 2003; Reber 2016).

The intertwined relation between technical knowledge and moral features is not a ground-breaking one, although we might find a consolidated resistance to moral influences in science, especially according to a positivist tradition (Habermas 1971; Dahms 1994). What is important here is not the basic necessity to unveil existing or implicit normative perspectives in the development of R&I. This is a condition that has been accepted and exploited since a long time ago (Boltanski & Chiapello 2007). What is necessary here is rather to understand the manner in which those technical and normative features can be integrated, given the plurality characterizing European societies.

In order to find a potential answer to this question, we now need to have a look at the meaning of responsibility. If innovation suffers, perhaps, from a narrow understanding with respect to its social aspects, responsibility surely entails such a wide range of meanings generating opposite but equally important problems. However, we believe that we can find some fruitful indications in its conceptual core.

Responsibility

Responsibility is a term that started to become central to science and technology after the Second World War, and especially around the 1960s, mainly because of the emergence of technology-related problems, especially in the field of environmental issues (Grunwald 2014). The progressive evidence of the fact that science and technology are not value-neutral, or pure, independent from any societal conception (Rip *et al.* 1995), has slowly but constantly led to a corresponding rise in concerns to which the concept of responsibility appeared to be a powerful answer (Jonas 1984; Durbin *et al.* 1987; Grunwald 2014).

However, given the historical development of the understanding of responsibility, we now find ourselves with a concept that embeds several different meanings, opening the way for different and often clashing interpretations (Gianni 2016; Arnaldi & Gorgoni 2016; Pellé & Reber 2016).

According to the field, expertize and objective, different authors have emphasized different aspects of the concept (Pellé & Reber 2016; Gianni 2016; Vincent 2011; van de Poel 2011; Ricœur 2000). Responsibility is, in fact, a term that includes different understandings or acceptions.

To be responsible could mean to respond to our actions, to our role, to others, in different social spheres, contexts and dimensions. Ibo van de Poel (2011), Nicole Vincent (2011), Hannah Arendt (2005) and Pellé and Reber (2016) showed us the complexity of and variations in the concept of responsibility in its moral dimension. H. Kelsen and H. L. A. Hart (Kelsen 2005; Hart 2008) have rigorously defined the contours of juridical responsibility as distinguished from moral responsibility. Jean-Paul Sartre (1993), Ulrich Beck (1992), Hans Jonas (1984) and Grinbaum and Groves (2013), although with different backgrounds and methodologies, have emphasized the subjective–collective character and existential importance of responsibility. Xavier Pavie has unveiled also the strategic value and the potential economic applications of responsibility (Pavie *et al.* 2014). Grunwald (2014) and Arnaldi and Bianchi (2016) are the two most prominent examples among the authors pointing at the necessity and proposing a methodology to activate responsibility in the realm of science and technology.

Mark Bovens has emphasized the agency distinction in the different acceptions of responsibility (Bovens 1998) by distinguishing a passive and an active understanding of the term. Moreover, with the emergence of environmental and existential concerns, responsibility has been fully displayed within the category of time and has thus opened up to the future. Whether a future-looking responsibility is logically derived from a backwards-looking one is a matter on which the debate is still open (Cane 2002). The solution to this dilemma implies an investigation of the relation between the deontology of responsible actions and a consequentialist perspective able to integrate the causal chain of events external to a subject's power (Jonas 1984; Ricœur 2000; 2007; Kant 1998).

Another important distinction is one concerning the individual or the collective nature of responsibility and the relation between the two, which can be seen as problematic or, more optimistically, under a process of 'hybridization' (Lascoumes 1995; Grinbaum & Groves 2013, Bovens 1998).

Lastly, we cannot forget the proliferation of dissertations on the possible applications of the term to specific situations, which has generated a semantic and pragmatic inflation of the term that is difficult to summarize (Ricœur 2000).

However, it is important to briefly reconstruct the development of this concept so to be able to grasp its historical nature and its overall purpose. Arnaldi and Gorgoni (2016) (Gianni Ch. 1), via the means of a genealogical investigation, have made an original reconstruction of the different understandings of responsibility. According to them, as well as to François Ewald (1986), the different acceptions should be inserted also in a historical framework and not only in a theoretical one. The authors believe that different understandings of responsibility have been generated because of the different guiding principles ruling specific historical periods, namely the one of fault in the 19th, of risk in the 20th and of precaution in the 21st century.[10] Accordingly, they suggest that the different meanings should not be seen as opposing but as cumulative, integrating with the current polysemic sense of the term. With their political–historical retrospection, Arnaldi and Gorgoni have made explicit a crucial aspect which is often implicit in other conceptions. For them, responsibility should not only be conceived as an abstract philosophical concept but rather as a concrete action, status and attitude, entrenched in daily life and, most importantly, embedded in institutions which promote a specific understanding of it. As they explicitly mention, referring to the work of Jean-Louis Genard, "its meaning (of responsibility) also emerges from the particular institutional conditions of its exercise. There is no prior understanding of responsibility which is subsequently translated in concrete practices, because the two aspects influence each other" (Arnaldi and Gorgoni 2016; Genard 1999).

According to our knowledge, there are two aspects that appear less central in the literature, but that can help us in understanding how to deal with its polysemy by unveiling the political nature of responsibility. These two sides are closely connected and can be helpful in clarifying the connections between the different understandings of the term.

The first aspect that tends to find less space in the literature is how to handle the relation between different acceptions of responsibility, not only conceptually, but also, and especially, in practice. A fruitful path in order to offer a solution can be found in Paul Ricœur's analysis of the concept.

Ricœur has highlighted all the different aspects and issues falling under the umbrella of responsibility. External causes, epistemic capacities and will are only the agent-based picture of a framework involving two different visions of the world with regard to the concept of 'person', as lucidly described by Roberto Esposito (Esposito 2015).

Paul Ricœur's analysis touches the deepest roots of the concept of responsibility with all its problems but there is one aspect that we find particularly relevant for our analysis. In fact, in our reading it is worth noticing an interesting dichotomy highlighted by Ricœur. These two sides can be exemplified by the passive presuppositions of responsibility as a set of rules impeding individuals from harming others, and an active one where individuals should act in order to improve personal or general conditions.

On the one hand, there is the necessity to attribute an action, potentially a negative one, to an actor, which enables individuals to achieve the double objective of recognizing others but also themselves through their own actions. If an individual possesses certain basic capacities, like rationality or will, he can be identified as subject to a set of rules. Accordingly, an individual enters, or he is inserted, into a system of abstract rules where he can then decide the extent and depth of his relationship to the world. In principle, this understanding of responsibility, intended as a set of deontological rules, does not promote any active measure towards mutual dialectic but defines the limits that individuals should or must respect. In other words, this understanding is what we may identify as a legal framework of responsibility, exemplified by the terms accountability, liability and blameworthiness, entailing an individualistic and retroactive judgment of wrong or bad actions.

On the other hand, starting with the end of the 19th century, we assist in the emergence of an understanding of responsibility that aimed at protecting individuals not from the intentional interferences of others but from causal or accidental forces. The fact that this emergence was generated in a particular situation, protecting workers from accidents, does not diminish the depth of this shift in the development of responsibility. What was at stake was the necessity to finally deal with agents at the mercy of events over which they could not exercise control. This is particularly relevant for our analysis, as this novelty was meant to regulate the effects of new technologies and a new production process.

After the establishment of ideals of freedom and equality through its deontological mechanisms, responsibility was now called to answer to the social claims based on the third major ideal stemming from the Enlightenment, the one of fraternity (Honneth 2016). Conjugated in materialistic terms, the necessity to introduce such a regulatory concept was to promote measures able to protect vulnerable actors from unintended negative consequences and so to establish and increase the general level of solidarity (Donzelot 1984; Ewald 1986).[11] Here, the focus was not really on individuals as owners of a personhood capable of freely interacting on an equal ground, but rather the emergence of concrete problems generated by a new production process and a mechanical division of labour where actors were not all equally free (Karsenti & Lemieux 2017; Ewald 1986; Donzelot 1984). To summarize, we can detect two main sides in this antinomy, which generate some exegetic difficulties. On the one hand is a conception according to which individuals are 'in charge' of their actions and thus responsible for harming others. On the other hand is the fact that individuals' actions are also subject to external forces which are not controllable and/or foreseeable.

Later political and theoretical developments have mostly tended to adopt and develop either one or the other underlying framework, with few contributions seeking a bridging solution (Ricœur 2000; 2007). The outcomes of such a clashing perspective can be easily understood if we take into account how this dichotomy has resisted and been exacerbated in current times. We still find two understandings where, on the one hand, actors are immersed in an insurance regime aimed at delegating any sort of negative effect, and on the other hand, there is a widespread perception of responsibility as the omnipresent imperative of one's own life. If the former tends to detach responsibility from single actors and risks eliminating stringency from actions, the latter becomes unbearable for individuals that feel but cannot recognize the unbridgeable gap between their intentions and actual outcomes (Ricœur 2000; Ehrenberg 1998; Illouz 2013).

Ricœur has highlighted how such an 'idiosyncratic' way of dealing with the understandings of responsibility cannot describe the complex dynamics underlying human and social actions (2000). Responsibility is always at the crossroads between the free actions of an individual and their 'necessary' relation with external forces (natural events or other actors). Accordingly, as already understood by Immanuel Kant, men will always struggle with trying to solve the antinomy of human agency and causality in which any responsibility is caught (1997).

If we consider the necessity of integrating the different sides of responsibility, and its connection with a related understanding of freedom, it appears plausible to follow Paul Ricœur instead, through a different reading of the concept, tries to overcome the apparent dilemma by proposing a 'prudential' framework based on Hegel's conception of ethics (Ricœur 2000; Ritter 1982).

Ethics, in Hegel's formulation, is the application of moral principles through norms, rules, values and interests aimed at regulating in a just manner the legal, moral and social relations in a given context (Ritter 1982). By steering the dynamics among these different dimensions, according to the principle of equilibrium, we can obtain a picture that Hegel would have described as an ethical framework.

For Ricœur, then, the way to deal with the different sides of responsibility is to try and hold them together in the formulation of a judgment. However, it remains unclear in Ricœur's formulation how this can be practically justified, considering the different perspectives on responsibility. One can argue that individuals should be held accountable if causing damage and that this understanding exhausts the sense of responsibility. Or we could say that no one can ever be considered responsible for an action given the infinite influences concurring with its outcomes. These positions can be defended according to both different situations and perspectives.

A fruitful way of supporting and translating Ricœur's suggestion is to grasp what emerges only implicitly in several contributions, that is, the relation between responsibility and its conditions of possibility. It sounds reasonable to state that an individual cannot always be considered responsible for the outcome of an action. At the same time, certain outcomes are the direct consequence of one's intentions. Besides, it would be politically counterproductive, morally bad and logically wrong to eliminate any direct relation between an action and actor.

However, it is important to highlight clearly that only on the basis of certain (pre)conditions are individuals enabled to assume a responsibility or to dismiss it. Without the need to go into philosophical arguments, we can assert that these conditions can be named as the freedom an actor enjoys, allowing him to act. The concept of freedom is the condition of possibility of any understanding of responsibility. As summarized by H. Seillan, "The word (responsibility) is intrinsically intermingled with moral considerations. Plato, Aristotle, Saint Agustin, Saint Thomas and later Kant and Durkheim have structured it around the free will of man. Freedom conditions responsibility. Man cannot be responsible if not free. A slave cannot be it" (Seillan 2016: p. 293; Gianni 2016). Axel Honneth has shown that throughout modernity we encounter different conceptions of freedom, varying according to the level of cooperation and discursive practices used to promote individual needs and values (Honneth 2014a; 2016). Drawing on a pragmatic interpretation of Hegel's *Philosophy of Right*, also for Honneth, a just conception of freedom is one that develops in its historical contextual forms according to shared procedures of decision-making. Following such a historical understanding of freedom, it is not difficult to match it with a specular conception of responsibility, which has been changing according to historical developments.

Accordingly, any variation in responsibility should be understood as the expression of a related freedom. Depending on which conception of freedom we intend to assert, we would then refer to a corresponding responsibility. If, for instance, we believe that freedom should be intended as a legal, 'negative' understanding, where individuals are protected by the coercive interference of others (Berlin 2002; Nozick 2013), then we should limit our understanding of responsibility to liability or accountability.

Throughout modernity, and especially in the last century, we encounter several theorizations of freedom (Berlin 2002; Honneth 2014a; Gianni 2016) and, logically speaking, it would be a matter of freedom to choose which freedom to defend.

However, what both Honneth and Arnaldi and Gorgoni sustain from different angles is that this historical development has been a cumulative one, integrating the different aspects within one concept.

If we follow Honneth, the concept of freedom as such is logically, morally and politically a social one, which embeds and promotes all its different expressions. In a similar way, Ricoeur defined the ethical understanding of responsibility as the prudential balance of its different aspects. Our proposal is that if we adopt the adjective responsible to assess an action, we need to so according to such equilibrium between its single meanings. An actor can be defined as responsible or irresponsible only according to legal criteria or to moral ones. He should be judged according to the respect of different criteria in his decision. Especially when it comes to R&I, such an operation would allow us to operate with a greater flexibility and would avoid the shortcomings of a pure deontological approach (Pellé & Reber 2016).

What both Ricœur and Honneth suggest is that if we base a conceptual and ethical understanding of agency on a framework which disregards either individual reasons or external, social influences, then we will not be able to grasp the actual dynamics that every agent has to face when called to act. Accordingly, such an understanding of responsibility would be unable to be neither efficient, because it would be missing an important part of the concrete reasons for acting, nor legitimate, because it would be the result of a unilateral or partial vision of the world. Therefore, we believe that an efficient and legitimate theory of responsibility is one that manages to integrate all the different 'interests' at stake in the assessment of an action.

However, we need to take a step further in our analysis. In fact, we have recognized that the only reasonable understanding of responsibility for R&I where different needs, expectations, interests and regulation come into play is an ethical one. An ethical understanding means one that considers all the drivers and sources of action in a balanced way, meaning that none of the regulatory schemes, as well as the different 'interests', are disregarded.

Equilibrium, here, does not express a quantitative or mechanic ration. Instead, it should be focused on finding a qualitative correlation between different elements. What is not clear, then, is how we decide to favour one aspect over another, also considering societal plurality. In other words, if, in a decision, we need to take into account different actors as well as different regulations, and considering the potential clash between these, how do we justify the promotion of one without falling back into a pre-ethical stage?

This question will be answered in the second and last parts of this contribution by analysing which political framework can actualize a responsible approach to R&I.

The political dimension of RRI

The determination of what might be considered to be efficient and legitimate (i.e. ethical), especially when it comes to R&I, cannot be relegated to abstract or technical guidelines but has to be fed, if not decided, according to empirical, contextual features. Such importance of the contextual determination of responsible practices is crucial in order not to disregard the historical nature of societal needs, values and claims. The perspective behind the decision on what will be promoted in R&I is often, if not always, a political decision. But in order to assume the ethical traits that we have mentioned, we need to analyse which governance model, used according to which tools, is best suited to achieve such an objective.

Accordingly, by conceiving responsibility as an ethical concept, as the concrete practice of actualizing norms and values in a determined context (Shamir 2008), we need to go further in analysing the relation of responsibility and innovation to the context in which they are always actualized. In this way, we can analyse some tools in order to promote a responsible governance of RRI.

Participation

When it comes to the relation with a context in R&I, we find several different terms used to define the strategies, aims, methodologies and actors involved. An increase in knowledge, justice, discursive participation and stakeholders' engagement are only a few examples defining the aforementioned categories (Reber 2007; Delli Carpini *et al.* 2004; Owen *et al.* 2013).

However, the main underlying sense lies in the will and necessity to include external 'affected' agents into the decision-making process by means of different tools. The general objective is to make those agents 'participants' in the decision on the directions R&I should take.

Participation, inclusiveness and engagement are only the three most popular variations of a conception used to highlight the importance of opening R&I to the broader public. Nevertheless, they are different in the degree of influence they can potentially entail.

Despite their differences and shortcomings (Fung 2006; Wynne 2007; Jasanoff 2004), we will provide a brief and general overview of the issues connected to participatory processes in general, trying to propose a 'thick' (Geertz 1973) framework.

Participatory processes are crucial tools for trying to define the direction of RRI. For Owen *et al.* (2013), inclusiveness is one of the four dimensions by which we can innovate responsibly. Accordingly, the authors state that "new areas of public value for innovation should be democratically and inclusively defined and realised" (Owen *et al.* 2013: p. 35).

René Von Schomberg has highlighted how "the involvement of stakeholders and other interested parties should lead to an inclusive innovation process" (Owen *et al.* 2013: p. 65) and has showed how this also represents the main principle inspiring the European Commission's efforts, as demonstrated by the Charter of Fundamental Rights of the European Union and the Code of Conduct on Nanotechnologies (Commission of the European Communities 2008; EC 2010; 2012).

Sykes and Macnaghten (2013) have summarized the different actions taken to implement stakeholders' contributions in the assessment of R&I across Europe. For the two authors, public engagement has represented an answer able to address four main dynamics in the relation between science and society:

- *the new politics of protest about certain technological projects and visions, visible in the growth of environmental and anti-nuclear movements from the 1960s;*

- *the requirement for governments (and parliaments) to have robust knowledge of the impacts of new science and technology in order to better anticipate their societal consequences;*
- *the perceived need to extend spaces for citizen participation, typically through the involvement of organized civil society groups, to make the governance of science and technology more accountable;*
- *and the demands from science communities to improve public understanding of science (PUS) where conflicts and tensions are presumed to stem from public ignorance and misunderstanding.*

(2013: p. 87)

Also, Koops *et al.* (2015) have underlined that there are many ways to approach responsible innovation in practice, but that there is one element that "stands out as a common factor within the variety of approaches: the engagement with stakeholders" (2015: p. 5).

What participation, engagement and inclusiveness seem to have in common is the main necessity of being open to alternative positions. These alternatives can justify the existent, provide modifications or propose different perspectives. This is seen to be crucial on the three levels we are taking into account: the epistemic, the moral and the political. The epistemic framework underlying participatory initiatives suggests that a quantitative growth of knowledge can lead to an increase in the overall quality (Pavie *et al.* 2014). More perspectives lead to more knowledge, which can generate better products.

From a moral perspective, the inclusion of external actors in the development of R&I can be conceived as a laudable effort towards an opening to society's claims, and works in the direction of an enhancement of individual autonomy. Besides, being bottom-up approaches, the results of these processes might not only generate a higher level of legitimacy, but could also enhance the efficiency of a process because they can increase the successful expectations of acceptance of new products by society. And, in fact, as R&I is now embedded in a network society (Castells 2010) aimed at marketing products and processes, a growth in terms of knowledge together with a 'responsible image' may lead to better results, also in terms of efficiency (Randles *et al.* 2015). From a political point of view, a participatory process is the key tool to answer the claims for the democratization of science that have been growing for fifty years.

However, although this general overview emphasizes a general agreement on the necessity of participatory processes to avoid certain kinds of epistemic, moral and political shortcomings, it is important to keep in mind not only the quantitative side of participation but also the qualitative one. This implies that perhaps the equation according to which an increase in quantity automatically generates an improvement in quality might turn out to be questionable. Participation should not be considered as an self-standing solution and needs to be defined in terms of its objective, actual influence in the decision-making process and underlying framework.

With regard to the first point, Lee and Petts (2013), for instance, have noticed some cases where the overall objective and guiding framework appeared to be short-sighted with regard to the scope that such processes should pursue. They mention, for instance, that "in the UK, governmental views of this have still often been restricted to promoting understanding and debating fears around a potentially controversial technology in advance of significant application. [...] It is still about risk regulation, rather than a more vital discussion about science, values, and what society expects from technology-based innovation" (Lee and Petts 2013: p. 147).

If we consider the second point, Archon Fung has extensively described the potential gap between the simple inclusion of different stakeholders in a participatory process and the actual influence of those participants on the decision-making process (Fung 2006). In order to assess participation in its real scope, Fung has proposed to analyse it according to its two mains aspects, the selection of participants and the communication or influence on decision-making stemming from such processes. Selection can include eight different mechanisms, going from the most exclusive (expert administrators) to the most encompassing (mini-publics). Communication instead invests in a spectrum of six options stretching from participants as spectators to participants as technical experts, according to the level of influence that those 'external actors' exert on the decision-making process.

The estimations Fung has made tell us that "there are few public meetings in which everyone is a spectator. Almost all of them offer opportunities for some to express their preferences to the audience and officials there" (2006, p. 68). But he also recognizes that "mechanisms employing these first three modes of communication often do not attempt to translate the views or preferences of participants into a collective view or decision" (*Ibidem*). He then defines other modes of communicating and deciding between spectators and technical experts. We find "aggregation and bargaining" but also deliberation and negotiation, where "participants deliberate to figure out what they want individually and as a group" (2006: p. 69). However, it is according to another mechanism that decisions are almost always made: "Many (perhaps most) public policies and decisions are determined not through aggregation or deliberation but rather through the technical expertise of officials whose training and professional specialization suits them to solving particular problems" (2006: p. 69).

The picture described by Archon Fung suggests that promoting participation does not necessarily mean that those processes imply an effective modification in the decision-making process, undermining the scope for which participation is always claimed to be necessary.

The third point, which intersects and affects the previous two, has been analysed by Luigi Pellizzoni throughout his interdisciplinary investigations. Pellizzoni has often pointed to the different ways in which participation can be 'framed' so as to generate forms of voluntary or involuntary manipulation of the arenas. Thus, for him, a participatory process should be assessed not only for having been initiated, but also considering other thicker aspects like "the selection of participants, issues and agenda definition, role allocation, information control and 'groups' dynamics" (Pellizzoni 2005; 2008). Otherwise, the risk is that participants can remain relegated to a role of agenda-takers rather than agenda-setters (Pellizzoni 2008).

What Pellizzoni has repeatedly highlighted is the necessity to unveil the often-implicit connection between the epistemic, moral and political dimensions that form the regulatory framework of participatory processes.

The example of Corporate Social Responsibility (CSR), which exemplifies an extreme of public participation, is particularly interesting in order to grasp the potentially questionable repercussions arising from a seemingly positive operation. According to Pellizzoni, the voluntary processes of regulation as embedded in the CSR framework aim at replacing the will arising from the public sphere with the perspective of one actor (the company). In fact, by pursuing certain objectives, one company promotes specific values according to criteria that are not political in their adoption but that are in their effects (Michael 2003). In this way, the criterion of responsibility, by which companies label their ethical commitments, if not distorted, is certainly reduced to the aspect of accountability, where controlling organs and unilateral policies represent the regulators and validators of the innovation path. In this way, the 'public', says Pellizzoni, becomes represented or participates "by proxy, through the impartiality of controlling bodies and the objectivity and transparency of procedures" (Pellizzoni 2008: p. 14). The public is paradoxically still 'participating', but according to criteria and forms that are pre-decided by a private actor of society, which in this way leaves out the possibility of concretely contributing to the decision-making process.

Lee and Petts, Fung and Pellizzoni are not the only ones who are careful with regard to the supposed neutrality and goodness of participation. The political management of participatory processes in RRI has been addressed by several other authors, in a range of critiques, which can be summarized in:

- the simple absence of politics in RRI (van Oudheusden 2014)
- a demagogic and instrumental use in order to legitimize or regain trust ('responsibility wash', Randles *et al.* 2015; Wynne, 2007);
- the implicit or explicit 'threat' of neo-liberal plans and policies (Arnaldi and Gorgoni 2016; Thorpe and Gregory 2010; Sykes and Macnaghten 2013).

The general perspective seems to be that the apparently neutral epistemic dimension of inclusion cannot be assessed without considering the political origins of participatory mechanisms. Participatory efforts are always promoted with a specific aim and embedded in a conceptual framework, not to mention the rules and discourse criteria, which can set, politically, the threshold for exclusion and inclusion.

To summarize these critical analyses: although participation is often indicated as a solution for improving the legitimacy – and in the long run the efficiency – of R&I, it can also rely on instrumental kinds of dialogues or, in general, pre-framed ones, so that it can generate effects which are different from those initially claimed (Chilvers and Macnaghten 2011; Pellizzoni 2008). In other words, although participation is a fundamental part of responsible governance, we should be aware that it could also be ineffective if not enforced in a transparent way and able to influence the decision-making process.

It appears reasonable to believe that instrumental or non-transparent approaches to inclusion transcend the explicit objective of RRI as defined by the European Commission. RRI methodology calls for a collaboration of all *societal* actors who are supposed to "work together during the whole research and innovation process in order to better align both the process and its outcomes, with the values, needs and expectations of European society" (EC 2012).

However, it is important to bear in mind the gap between theory and practice to which a participatory mechanism can be subjected when its scope, structure and influence are not explicitly defined. To withhold that the presence of a participative form is sufficient to guarantee the ethical appropriateness (responsibility) of R&I can generate the risk of incrementing the mistrust about R&I within society and can generate counterproductive effects (Leach *et al.* 2006).

What this overview has enabled us to understand is that participation is a recognized necessary tool to answer the claims of society for the democratization of processes that have a potential social impact. Furthermore, several authors have highlighted its functional efficiency for increasing the available level of knowledge and the expectations of the acceptance of products. However, from an ethical point of view, it is also clear that participation needs to be integrated and supported by more active tools, able to preserve its objectives from controversial or instrumental approaches.

We will analyse what kind of support can be beneficial to participatory processes in the next section.

Reflexivity: A legitimacy tool

One of the most common strategies to substantiate the practice of participation and to which extensive references are to be found both in literature and policy indications[12] is the recourse to reflexive moments.

Reflexivity has been increasingly proposed as a strategic and legitimizing tool to overcome the limits of conventional regulations.

The logic of conventional regulations, which has often proved to be unable to respond to the two-fold imperative of legitimacy and efficiency,[13] follows a market-based or command-and-control scheme (Perez 2011; Pellizzoni 2008). Processes of self-regulation are, quite evidently, one of the answers to the mistrust that society felt (and still feels) against institutional figures perceived as unable to tackle the issues arising from an uncertain scenario (Nowotny 2015; Perez 2011). It is not surprising, then, that with the passage from a normal science paradigm to a post-normal one (Funtowicz & Ravetz 1994), reflexivity has become even more important. In fact, reflexivity potentially enables actors to make an individual or a shared assessment without the need to be strictly ruled by an external body.

The traditional model of government based on the double-delegation paradigm, where authority is retained by experts and politicians (Callon *et al.* 2001), seemingly leaves room for models of more democratic governance of R&I as regulatory tools. At the core of these governance models of R&I, we find not only the necessity to participate and to engage, but also the need to do so in a conscious and often personal way. The contents, objectives and modalities of single reflexive processes vary, but nevertheless, there is widespread trust in the positive contribution of reflexivity to the design and development of R&I.

In general, reflexivity is seen as a promising tool in the development path of self-regulatory devices because it can address the "hyper complexity" (Qvortrup 2003) of our societies by acting through the voluntary contributions of individuals and therefore reaching spaces of manoeuvre that are hard to regulate in a command–control fashion. Reflexivity is supposed to enhance the troubled balance between legitimacy and efficacy because it can operate at three different but interlaced levels.

Firstly, reflexivity acts at an epistemic level. Reflexivity can be seen as a tool for incrementing the quality of knowledge available to researchers and innovators as well as to citizens (Funtowicz & Ravetz 2008; Van den Hoven 2013; Arnaldi & Bianchi 2016). In this sense, reflection should imply a growth in terms of the quantity and quality of knowledge, which would be beneficial for the general development of R&I.

Secondly, reflexivity represents a moral imperative within the modern conception of freedom. It assumes a strong moral load by being the key operation to actualize an individual's autonomy, intended as self-determination (Kant 1997; Honneth 2014a; 2014b;) Accordingly, reflexivity is a crucial operational tool for increasing an individual's contribution to the determination of R&I's development. This aspect is also a powerful tool for overcoming logics which are paternalistic and conceive citizens as incompetent or unable to assess the outcomes of science, and it is related to a third level.

Third, reflexivity, in fact, operates at a political level by opening to a more 'democratic' process through the conscious interaction of different stakeholders (Dewey 1987). Reflexivity is often conceived as a tool for planning a correct strategy in order to evaluate practical situations and to delineate paths for action. Thus, reflexivity is supposed to add a qualitative layer to participation and to consciously steer the process of R&I, increasing its efficacy and legitimacy.

Reflexivity was already (and still is) at the core of previous assessment paradigms like, for instance, the different forms of technology assessment (TA) (Grunwald 2011; 2014; Rip *et al.* 1995; Voss *et al.* 2006). Fortunately, RRI has not disregarded the lessons learned by TA and is developing in continuity with TA[14] on the basis of this central role of reflexivity (Owen *et al.* 2013; Von Schomberg 2013; Kuhlmann *et al.* 2016).

The existing RRI literature production tries, in fact, to highlight the importance of reflexivity for developing 'appropriate' processes (Gunther 1993). René Von Schomberg's account, for instance, promotes reflexivity as the main tool defining the objectives and contents of innovation: "We make no a priori assumptions regarding the nature, trajectory, and pace of any particular area of innovation. Rather, this should necessarily be a product of the reflexive process itself, which may speed innovation up, slow it down, or change its direction accordingly" (Von Schomberg 2013: p. 39).

However, we also find more cautious positions with regard to the role of reflexivity, emphasizing the necessity to deepen its scope and to connect it to a clear normative reference.

Arnaldi and Gorgoni emphasize one of the underlying risks for RRI in adopting a blurred use of reflexivity. In fact, reflexivity *per se* can also be implemented in ways that pursue neo-liberal objectives because it is an instrument adoptable also in instrumental-driven calculations, where societal needs and values are not necessarily implied, or at least not in a legitimate way. The two authors highlight the similarities between reflexivity in RRI and "the neoliberal idea of reflexive, entrepreneurial agents maximizing the 'return on investment' of their actions and projects" (Arnaldi and Gorgoni 2016: p. 12). According to the two authors, this ambiguous resemblance can be overcome if the reflexive process is anchored in a clear normative reference, in our case the normative horizon provided by the Charter of Fundamental Rights of the European Union.

The difficulty in, and at the same time the necessity of, answering "to the epistemic and normative challenges of the neo-liberal project of social engineering" has also been urged by other authors (Braithwaite 2011; Perez 2011; Teubner 1993; Black and Baldwin 2010). These concerns point to the self-regulatory framework in which the reflexive process can be embedded, and the moral, epistemic and political shortcomings of previous and concomitant attempts (Gianni 2016; Perez 2011; Michael 2003; Mullerat 2009; Horrigan 2010; Fernando 2011).

In a more general fashion, some authors are sceptical that self-regulatory forms based on reflexivity would necessarily lead to a more efficacious model of R&I (Pellizzoni 2008). Others suggest to rather focus on the measures for institutionally integrating society in the design and development of R&I, with the aim of democratizing science (Guston 2001; Guston & Sarewitz 2002; Wynne 1993).

In other words, reflexivity, like participation, intended in a simple way, can lead to practices that are pragmatically inefficient and morally despicable.

Reflexivity is a broad concept and can imply even broader methodologies. Therefore, in order to protect reflexivity from instrumentalization or from the 'tragedy of inefficacy', we need to understand under what kind of regulatory process RRI is supposed to be framed in order to respond to the failures of 'conventional regulations' (Lee and Petts 2013; Owen *et al.* 2013, p. XIV).

As we have briefly seen, participatory processes are considered to be fundamental in order to increase knowledge, legitimacy and, to a certain extent, the efficiency of R&I at the epistemic, moral and political level. However, we have found several analyses warning against the risks connected to a formal and abstract approach to participation. We have seen how a 'thin' participatory process does not necessarily lead to an improvement in terms of legitimacy or efficiency. Ordinary participation can turn out to be weak in terms of its substance, running the risk of being manipulated, or kept from being influential in the decision-making process. As highlighted by several authors, to invoke participation as the panacea for the legitimate and efficient development of R&I is not only naïve but could also be counterproductive, legitimising not a public scope but rather those private purposes that John Dewey called 'vested interests'.

Consequently, we have suggested integrating participatory practices with reflection exercises able to increase the autonomous and voluntary influence of the stakeholders called to participate. Reflexivity can also be considered as increasing the efficiency and legitimation for the design and development of R&I. It can favour an autonomous expression of free will and help in overcoming top-down approaches based on command-and-control schemes. Reflecting can improve the legitimacy and the efficacy at the epistemic, moral and political level. However, if we rely on formal procedural rules and do not foresee the presence of a normative shared reference, how can we be sure that it will really be legitimate? How do we construct a reflexive methodology that can overcome the limits and weaknesses embedded in a non-substantive and individualistic process?

By answering these questions, we believe we could move forward in the development of an ethical governance of RRI.

Second-order reflexivity

In order to reach our objective, we need to operate a radicalization of reflexivity by shifting the focus to reflexivity itself. As for responsibility, it is useful to reflect on what the conditions of possibility enabling and driving reflexivity are.

As introduced earlier, in the RRI literature we already find the need to question reflexivity in a deeper way. Owen *et al.* (2013) conceive reflexivity as one of the four central dimensions of RRI. Interestingly enough, though, they make an important step forward by pointing to the underlying premises of a reflexive process. They specify that in order to innovate responsibly, we need "reflecting on underlying purposes, motivations, and potential impacts, what is known (including those areas of regulation, ethical review, or other forms of governance that may exist) and what is not known; associated uncertainties, risks, areas of ignorance, assumptions, questions, and dilemmas" (2013: p. 38). For Owen *et al.*, it is not sufficient to address what is known but also to unveil what is not known. Following this suggestion, we will try to question and extend the concept of reflexivity by proposing a two-fold model of reflexivity or two orders of reflexivity.

A first-order reflexivity is one focused on assessing specific issues that may arise in a given scenario. In this sense, it is easier to define the necessary features of a reflexive process in practice, so as to increase its efficacy for R&I. However, it would be disputable to indicate one methodology or another without questioning the basis of those indications. The legitimacy of a reflexive operation should be achieved by questioning the underlying framework enacting or facilitating reflexivity itself. This questioning can operate at different levels according to the depth of the analysis, but even at the most simple one, reflecting is a fundamental passage in order to avoid manipulation or inefficient processes.

Therefore, we believe it sensible to also operate an analysis of the second order. A second-order reflexivity is one that questions the reflexive process itself by indicating the epistemic framework in which a specific reflection is regulated and the empirical settings enacting the reflexive process (Perez 2011; Lenoble and Maesschalck 2003; Maesschalck 2017). As we have noticed, the supposedly neutral epistemic framework is often established according to a political plan, so turning reflexivity to itself can unveil this strategy. It is this second-order reflexivity that contributes to guaranteeing the efficacy of a first-order reflection because it makes visible a series of prejudices, preconceptions and presuppositions that always frame the reflexive process and that are often implicit or hidden. Accordingly, making these epistemic, moral and politic presuppositions explicit can substantially improve the efficacy of a participatory reflexive process (Brandom, 1998).

A second-order reflexivity has two potential exemplifications. The first one addresses the epistemic weaknesses in a theoretical way. In this sense, different ways of posing the problem, or ways to address it, can be implemented. A second application is instead a more pragmatic one, applicable to stakeholders when called to participate in a reflexive process by asking themselves what the framing conditions driving the participation are, and what the objectives, the methodology and the influence they are going to exert on the decision-making process are. Oren Perez, for instance, is confident about the impact of second-order reflexivity which, according to his opinion, can improve the process in different ways: "not merely to be able to learn from your mistakes at the first order level of the policy parameters, but also to be able to reflect on your learning procedures and improve them as independent objects of inquiry" (Perez 2011: p. 777).

We will now analyse this aspect further so as to understand what the essence and role of reflexivity should be and how we can steer it in order to use it to drive the RRI paradigm. From such a conception, we will draw a responsible or co-regulatory governance which will be based on these epistemic assumptions.

In order to inquire into the concept of reflexivity and propose a version that could overcome the practical limits mentioned above, we need to address its epistemic basis. We can move further in this attempt by following parts of the analysis operated by Marc Maesschalck (2000; 2017).

The conceptual framework proposed by Maesschalck tries to overcome the epistemic limits of most common reflexive theories in ethics by addressing its relation to the context when constructing a norm. According to Maesschalck, the main limit of what he names 'rationalistic' approaches is that reflexivity is intended as a discourse that the subject operates within himself, without opening to the concrete otherness, but according to universal and rationalistic principles. It is understood as a sort of solitary confession that does not enter into an intersubjective relation. In this way, though, the reflexive process is conflated to the procedural development of a justification, which limits the structures of capacitation, or the discursive competences, to the possession of rational capacities, re-proposing a strong naturalistic and deontological framework. Maesschalck emphasizes, however, that the rational validity of a norm, based on a 'rationalistic'[15] scheme, does not necessarily imply the successful application of the same norm in a context, undermining the scope of the norm itself. The design of a norm according to a theoretical, universalistic validation falls short because it focuses on the justification and ignores the practical, intersubjective nature of the application of a norm, which embeds not only rational abstract criteria but also their modelling in a context.

The shortcomings of such a reductive approach, underestimating the context and the application of a norm, can be highlighted according to the three levels we have proposed as a plan of analysis for reflexive participatory processes.

At the epistemic level, what these conceptions tend to undermine in the first place is a wider or deeper understanding of the structures of 'capacitation' and the application of a norm (Maesschalck 2000; Lenoble and Maesschalck 2003; Williams 1984; Sen 1999; Taylor 1992). Reflection considered as a private exercise according to universalistic criteria is surely a crucial aspect of the whole reflexive process. However, reflexivity, at least in RRI, is supposed to overcome the epistemic and axiological clashes arising from a pluralist society, which are at the basis of the difficulty in finding a common understanding of a responsible development of R&I.

When deprived of further implementation, a conception of reflexivity as the expression of a self-conscious individual encounters two main shortcomings, at least for its adoption in a pluralist society. One limit is at the theoretical level (Esposito 2015) and the other is at the *de facto* level, although they are interlaced.

In fact, this interpretation does not take into account the distance between an ideal situation, where an actor is supposed to reflect and change his perspective, and the *actual circumstances* where reflexivity does not necessarily provoke a change, but, rather, often helps to radicalize beliefs and values and thus exacerbates clashes. Furthermore, considering the idiosyncrasy present in societies, the adoption of this kind of reflexivity as a solution would presuppose a rationalistic prejudice, understanding conflict as the mere expression of irrational clashes (Williams, 1984). As suggested by Jean Ladrière (1994; 1997), Paul Ricœur (2000) and Bernard Williams (1984), among others, this explanation cannot be exhaustive of a theory of agency and would not enable us to grasp other 'reasons' at the basis of social dialectics (Reber 2005; Williams 1984). Such a perspective of rationality would be reductive because it underestimates the importance of beliefs, values or 'reasons', and would hardly be efficacious in practice. It is not clear, in fact, why actors should be inclined to change their perspectives, considering that those perspectives are surely reasonable for them, and that they possess a strong motivating power for action.

This understanding of reflexivity, which Maesschalck detects in many attempts to develop a system of procedural ethics, might underestimate the role, impact and general importance of extra-rational factors for the acceptance, and most of all for the adoption, of a norm. If reflexivity aims at being a crucial tool for regulatory frameworks, it should seriously consider the values and beliefs that concur to motivate agents to act. Because, if it is true that not all values and beliefs have a normative power, it is also true that all norms owe their actual power to the values and beliefs they incarnate (Ferry 2002; Dworkin 1978; 1985; 1988; Habermas 1986).[16]

The great influence of pluralist societal values concurring to shape R&I has often been recognized as a crucial one. Whether nature and society are co-produced

(Jasanoff 2004; Pellizzoni 2010), or whether they influence each other to different degrees (Wynne 1992; 1993), several authors have agreed that science and society must develop according to features that cannot be reduced to the 'rationalistic', technical or objective, but rather need to cope with "the intermingling of facts and values" (Funtowicz & Ravetz 1993; 2008; Nowotny 1999).[17] Accordingly, as lucidly summarized by Arnaldi & Bianchi (2016), R&I should be generated and evaluated on the basis of a pragmatic integration of "extended facts" (Funtowicz and Ravetz 2008), tacit knowledge (Wynne 1992) and "worlds of relevance" (Limoges 1993).

This aspect leads us to the second disputable issue concerning a reductive conception of reflexivity. By maintaining an introspective reflexive stance, we run the risk of not moving too far from a conception where the future is assessed and managed *a priori* according to available data, which is at the core of risk-based regulation (Arnaldi & Bianchi 2016).

These criticisms highlight the importance, for RRI as a participatory reflexive process, to consider not only individual actors or single perspectives, like social spheres, groups and institutions, as parts of a bigger circle. What needs to be pointed out within our pluralist (Reber 2005) network-based (Castells 2010) and hyper-complex (Qvortrup 2003) societies is the epistemic, moral and sociological difficulty of isolating a single perspective from its relations, in this case reflexive, with those other parts concurring to generate an idiosyncratic scenario.

It is not difficult to deduce how this epistemic shortcoming implies moral and political consequences for reducing the role of agency to some rational(istic) features.

From a moral and ethical perspective, in fact, as introduced above, the rational legitimacy of a norm does not determine its usage by an actor (Lenoble and Maesschalck 2003; Ferry 2002). Thus, the regulatory role and scope of morality and ethics fades, thereby undermining the purpose and efficacy of an ethical frame.

According to Maesschalck (2000), the two main branches of moral theory, deontology and consequentialist ethics, have in common the equal disinterest about the actualization of a normative framework in the name of a 'holism of justification'. What Maesschalck means with such a definition is that both positions prioritize the theoretical justification of the whole to the detriment of single, contingent and concrete aspects. They both tend to project their principles onto reality without taking into account any contextual application. On the one hand, deontology must abstract from reality (and thus appear ineffective) in order to fulfil the conditions of legitimacy embedded in a universalistic posture. On the other hand, consequentialism encounters a severe limit because it also ignores the effectiveness of a norm. "It transcends", says Maesschalck, "acts and consequences by gathering them together" (2000: p. 152). By dismissing the performative role of a norm, its insertion and its functionality into a context, the context appears as an 'occult power' that largely escapes from the rational mediation it tries to extract from it. Consequentialists and deontological positions remain blind to the contextual requests that norms always imply. "In this way 'ethics' cedes to a radical formalism of the norm which confines itself to the inventory of rational procedures for validating a maxim of action" (2000: p. 153). A reflexive ethics of this sort, and Maesschalck has Habermas in mind, not only appears ineffective in motivating for action, but it also entails a dangerous threshold for including or excluding participants from the discourse (Honneth 1991). It is here that the connection between a self-centred epistemic paradigm, a deontological process of justification and their effects on practices clearly emerge.

Such reduction, in fact, also affects the efficacy of a norm at the political level. If R&I is designed and developed without a substantial influence from society in its different expressions, then policy-makers are not answering the calls for the democratization of R&I, undermining their own mission. Besides, the products and processes generated by R&I are doomed to remain in a state of uncertainty and ineffectiveness because they will lack all the insights, information and inputs helping to develop it according to the needs, values and beliefs arising in society.

Another aspect on which a self-centred, individualistic reflexivity appears to be questionable is the necessity to unveil the integration of a single operation in a more complex net of relations and epistemic frames. According to the reading of Maesschalck, following Searle and Bourdieu, in order to demonstrate his point, the structures of capacitation of an agent need to address the relation that a norm maintains with action, and thus they shall include references to an institutional context which embeds the structural components of a life-world (Maesschalck 2000: p. 142; 1998).

When such an attempt is operated at the political level, trying to develop self-referential approaches for society, we fall back on those criticisms moved to self-regulatory models such as CSR, which is accused of overcoming public conflict by deciding unilaterally what values and beliefs are worth promoting (Michael 2003; Gianni 2016). In this way, the political decision of the path to be taken by a specific context is decided by one of its members. Similarly, other attempts to adopt a self-regulatory framework based on universalistic reflexivity have also shown concrete limits with regard to the practical implementation of such a tool (Teubner 1993; Perez 2011).

We find some experiments to support reflexive practices with external criteria, like, for instance, the one mentioned by Perez (US Office of Information and Regulatory Affairs, OIRA), aimed "at providing different social subsystems with a centralized, external interface so as to detect or assess intrinsic flaws and mutual inconsistencies in proposed regulations" (2011: p. 771). The problem highlighted by Perez with such an example is the lack of stable moral criteria, apart from merely technical ones, according to which decisions can be taken. If it is deprived of a clear normative reference, a judgment will have difficulty in finding a legitimate justification, ending in what we might call 'technical overload' or moral relativism.

This interesting aspect suggests again that a decision on the design and development of R&I should not be left to technical criteria, not only because they entail a political perspective but also because technology does not always reduce the complexity of reality, but, on the contrary, can increase it (Arnaldi & Bianchi 2016).

Responsible governance and co-regulation

We can detect two main challenges or aspects that responsible governance should address if it does not want to undermine its capacity to attain the objectives of legitimacy and efficiency.

The first one concerns the axiological plurality of current societies. When it comes to responsible actions within society, we need to adopt measures and ethical references able to integrate the plural values and beliefs of a society (Weber 2004; Arnaldi & Bianchi 2016; Reber 2005). This aspect is even stronger if we consider not only the axiological and normative clashes in Europe but also the recent attempts to 'export' RRI outside its European cradle.[18]

A second challenge concerns plurality with regard to the epistemological point of views that can jeopardize or open for instrumentalization the project of a responsible governance. Different social dimensions can follow different epistemic features and actors actually belong to different 'worlds' with different drivers (Dewey 1954). The necessary intersections, which unveil the plural and often conflictual nature of a context, require a special sensitivity for different languages and different 'levels' of rationality. The main shift is to try and transform these intersections into interconnections where the reflexive participation in R&I is developed through communicative processes based on reciprocal recognition (Brudney 2014; Maesschalck 2000; Parsons 1991; Dewey 1987).

According to Marc Maesschalck, we can do this if we reverse the understanding of the relation between a norm and its context of application. Instead of focusing on the justification of a norm according to rationalistic and thus abstract features, we must concentrate on the operationality (*opérativité*) of a norm; in other words, a norm can be shaped in a context that models it and makes it effective. This implies going beyond a dualistic perspective where the legitimacy of a norm or rule is detached from the efficiency of a process, and finding a third position trying to balance the two, i.e., the efficacy by which a norm is activated (Maesschalck 2000; Lenoir 2016).

The first step is then to rethink the category of capacitation.

Borrowing Searle's understanding of the structures of capacitation, Maesschalck emphasizes the role of the background (Searle 1995) or habitus (Bourdieu 1990) in the adoption of a norm. A norm must always be integrated into a context provided with its implicit practical culture formed by values, beliefs, desires and other expressions of one's freedom (Ricœur 2000; Ferry 2002; Honneth 2014a; Taylor 1985: pp. 211–229). Furthermore, the capacitation of an actor cannot prescind from a series of material conditions that determine the possibility of his contribution to the 'discourse' (Honneth 1991; 2014a). This aspect calls for a grounded or materialist ethics aiming to use participatory practices on the basis of a "pondered equilibrium between the discursive competences of an actor and the components of its life world" (Maesschalck 2000: p. 142).

The uncertainty embedded in the design and development of R&I can be addressed by a principle of analogy that connects past experiences with new needs and desires. It is clear that the adoption of contextual features implies the need to assess a norm according to a historical perspective, trying to adapt it to a current scenario. In this sense, then, the first point is to widen the understanding of capacitation in order to integrate historical, material and extra-rational features that converge in an actor's background.

Once those background aspects and extra-rational presuppositions are integrated into the reflexive participation, we need to connect it to a different 'spatial' methodological grounding. Otherwise, in principle, we could impute this conception with the same criticisms moved to those self-validating approaches that have been previously mentioned.

However, the self-comprehension of the context as a means to 'responsibilize' actors is here framed by the fact that such 'reflexivity' has an intersubjective nature. For Maesschalck, this presupposition is evident exactly because the whole structure of contextual pragmatics rests on the active side of a norm, its contextual *opérativité*, and not on its justification. Maesschalck bases his version of a pragmatic ethics on the basis of a reinterpretation of Fichte's conception of intersubjectivity, in terms of the material recognition of two individuals. Through the experience of a choc (*Anstoss*), a displacement, generated by an external body and the subsequent recognition of the 'other' as setting in motion the recognition of the self, Maesschalck strongly underlines the necessity of overcoming the limits of a self-referent subject still present in mentalist philosophies. By trying to demolish the theological-political understanding of the person as an isolated self, owning his consciousness and executor of an abstract norm, he unveils the conceptual paradoxes of such isolation: "A formal rule of morality as self-realisation is senseless if it is not conceived in function of the realisation of a concrete community of codetermination" (2000: p. 148; Esposito 2015).

Accordingly, Maesschalck connects this material and cultural framework with the role of reflexivity. Reflexivity is an *activity* that emerges from the awareness of a double self-limitation, which is called upon to mediate. On the one hand is the restraint of moral individualism, where single perspectives are inserted into formal and informal networks. On the other hand is the limitation of the formalism of legislation by its historical applications. The main objective of a reflexive process is then to connect these two sides, the different values and beliefs with a shared normative framework, in order to modify or shape a normative framework according to the historical developments arising from the context.

It appears clear now that the different logical systems in the RRI framework should be conceived according to this balanced relation. The concept of responsibility, as the term suggests, should be applied following a 'reflective equilibrium' and a practical translation between its different acceptions. The nature of responsibility, in some ways, also defines its meta-function within the framework of RRI. By being a concept that embeds a plurality, it can be an example of how to manage the plurality to which RRI is called to respond.

In this way, we are able to overcome the two main weaknesses of a dualistic perspective. On the one hand, we can avoid the risk of remaining in a rationalistic conception. The 'adaptation' process that we have described cannot, in fact, be associated with a mentalist methodology because it is not stemming from rationalistic procedures but from the practical adjustment generated by a contextual interaction. It is this intersubjective nature of a pragmatic ethics that represents the second main characteristic of co-regulatory or responsible governance.

On the other hand, we can also avoid the risk of running into a relativist position, because there is always the need to rely on a shared normative framework. This framework also differs from the one that tries to isolate different social domains. The fragmentation of morality into applied forms of ethics, which focus on specific matters without a broader picture, often falls into conflictual positions with other domains. On the contrary, we believe that ethics should represent the contextual translation of shared principles and norms into single domains. It is true that it is challenging to succeed in such attempts. But it is also true that we cannot prescind from the research of hypotheses that aim at connecting the different domains or social sectors rather than distinguishing them.

In addition to circumventing the risk of falling back into a partial conceptualization, we also moved forward by enabling a practical proposal for a co-regulatory governance to emerge. Such a model of governance would be appointed to actively favour co-regulation, i.e., the reflexive adjustments of norms and context, and to facilitate this process by pursuing two main tasks. As stated by Maesschalck, a responsible governance cannot simply be "another justification register for regulatory devices, but must rather engage responsibly with a view on the transformation of life forms that those devices bring about" (2000: p. 151).

The first is to develop mechanisms and procedures able to identify problems: collective uncertainties (Maesschalck 2000), and structural and contingent weaknesses of actors, or to remove communicative barriers (Dewey 1987; Honneth 2016). This action can also be taken through soft regulation like the one represented by codes of conduct (Von Schomberg 2014; Wilms 2014).

A second task is to implement new methodologies for concerted actions based on reflexive approaches. As proposed by J. Ladrière (1994) and followed by Maesschalck, such a governance should promote reflexivity not as an "effort of the self-representation of a reflecting reason, but rather like the possible opened by the self-experimentation of a community as a game of incorporation of rules of actions" Maesschalck 2000: p. 149). Reflexivity should be encouraged as the practical means to opening for alternatives in given situations. It should be focused on seeking creative and experimental solutions to given problems, as it is in the nature of innovation. "The linkage between creativity and reflexivity lies first in their common rejection of dogmatic frameworks, and second in the capacity of creative thinking to enable non-linear crossing between reflexive hierarchies" (Perez 2011: p. 774). Tensions or clashes emerging in the assessment of R&I and its directions can often be solved by formulating problems in a different manner or imagining different ways to cope with them. "In many cases, creativity emerges in response to the need to bring together apparently incompatible representations or interpretations" (*Ibidem*). A similar approach, far from being abstract or unfeasible, has been adopted by scholars who, puzzled by the frequent moral overload in R&I, decided to address the problem by displacing its initial or common understanding through collaboration and experimentation. Jeroen Van den Hoven is probably the most exemplary author to have shown how, for instance, a value-sensitive design methodology can help in solving these kinds of tensions, not by pursuing a unilateral perspective but by making the actors rethink the terms of the problem in a dialectical way (Van den Hoven *et al.* 2012; 2013; Van den Hoven *et al.* 2014).[19]

Accordingly, the understanding of responsible governance in these terms cannot be reduced to its liability or accountability but shall be seen as a practice that goes beyond, an active engagement to promote innovations by constructing them with a context. Such governance shall be able to 'seek an equilibrium' between existing norms and the novelties arising with the uncertain fruits of R&I.

Conclusion

Our contribution has tried to provide an extensive analysis of the framework of RRI from an analytical point of view. We have investigated the conceptual roots of innovation and of responsibility so to show some potential solutions to actual barriers and obstacles. Initially, we proposed a broader understanding of innovation following some recent literature. We have then highlighted the historical and plural nature of responsibility in a double sense. On the one hand, responsibility must deal with a plurality of social dimensions. On the other hand, responsibility is itself a plural concept. In order to solve the puzzle stemming from its polysemy, we have connected it to the concept of freedom to which responsibility is always connected. By supporting responsibility with an ethical and social understanding, we have proposed a complementary and balanced reading of its features. We have shown how this concept should seek to keep a balance between its different layers and meanings so to exploit its enormous potential.

In this way, we have understood that such an ethical, pragmatic framework could also be beneficial to improve the current common tools adopted to implement an efficient and legitimate process of R&I. In fact, participation and reflexivity, despite their positive role, are often developed in ways that are inefficient or counterproductive. Accordingly, not only participation should be implemented through influential engagement of different stakeholders, but also reflexive processes should be questioned regarding their background and scope. Therefore, not only do participation and reflexivity have to be integrated with one another, but they also have to be enforced according to a substantial ethical perspective. This means seeking a balance among different actors potentially affected with the objective of implementing freedom. As for responsibility, RRI should represent the adaptable ethical connection between abstract, established standards and new, plural normative claims. At the end of our path, we have proposed the model of a responsible, co-regulating governance where different actors should be put in the position to communicate and act together towards new horizons.

Notes

1 We will focus only on innovation and not on research in order to avoid confusion, and also because the scope of this paper is not necessarily to address the epistemic differences between research and innovation.

2 For an exemplary case in the U.S., see http://www.slate.com/articles/technology/future_tense/2017/04/the_aquadvantage_salmon_debate_and_skepticism_about_biotechnology.html.
3 Although we will not go through an analysis of research, there is an understanding of research, at least basic research, that conceives it as being developed for the sake of knowledge without the necessity of considering any other aspects apart from technical ones. As the argument we want to develop questions this dichotomy between different social paradigms, it is sufficient here to analyse the category of innovation to prove our thesis.
4 Although these authors do not always refer to innovation as such, the underlying process and its outcomes can be seen as very similar.
5 Presentation given at a Great project workshop, Paris 2013.
6 Ricoeur gives this clear explanation of a similar methodology used by John Rawls: “Rawls calls this order lexical or lexicographic for a simple reason. In a dictionary, the first letter is lexically first, in the sense that no compensation at the level of the subsequent letters can wipe out the negative effect that would result from substituting any other letter for this first letter. This impossible substitution gives an infinite weight to the first letter. Nevertheless the following order is not denuded of sense since the subsequent letters make the difference between two words having the same first letter without making them mutually substitutable for one another”.
7 We can, for instance, detect the differences in paradigms by understanding whether a process refers to risk management and risk assessment or what its overall relation to society is.
8 Benoit Godin has shown how technological innovation has represented a countertrend aiming at including external knowledge.
9 This ‘spiritual’ or social aspect of new processes has for a long time been highlighted by sociologists; for an example of the concrete role of a normative discourse in the development of societies, see Boltanski and Chiapello (2007).
10 See also François Ewald (1986).
11 Ewald offers a different reading of the purposes of such an understanding of responsibility, related to a liberal discourse.
12 https://ec.europa.eu/programmes/horizon2020/en/h2020-section/europe-changing-world-inclusive-innovative-and-reflective-societies.
13 For what concerns R&I, several examples can be found in Owen *et al.* (2013) and Van den Hoven *et al.* (2014).
14 On the relation between TA and RRI, see Grunwald (2011) and Gianni (2016).
15 From now on, we will use this term to summarize the categories adopted by Maesschalck, namely mentalist, intentionalist and schematist, because from our perspective, these three acceptions have in common the construction of a norm according to predetermined and stable rational features.
16 This statement does not of course consider neo-positivist perspectives.
17 For a general overview of the development of the relation between science and society, see the brilliant contribution made by Simone Arnaldi in Arnaldi and Bianchi (2016), *Responsibility in Science and Technology. Elements of a Social Theory* (Springer, Ch. 4).
18 http://www.progressproject.euhttp://ec.europa.eu/research/participants/portal/desktop/en/opportunities/h2020/topics/swafs-14-2017.html.
19 Although this approach deals with values and not with norms.

References

Arendt, H. (2005). *Responsibility and Judgment*. Berlin: Schocken.

Arnaldi, S. and Bianchi, L. (2016). *Responsibility in Science and Technology*. Wiesbaden: Springer.

Arnaldi, S. and Gorgoni, G. (2016). Turning the tide or surfing the wave? Responsible Research and Innovation, fundamental rights and neoliberal virtues. *Life Sciences, Society and Policy*, 12(6), pp. 1–19.

Bawa, A. S. and Anilakumar, K. R. (2013). Genetically modified foods: safety, risks and public concerns—a review. *J Food Sci Technology*, 50(6), pp. 1035–1046.

Beck, U. (1992). *Risk Society: Towards a New Modernity*. London: Sage Publications.

Berlin, I. (2002). *Liberty: Incorporating Four Essays on Liberty*. Oxford: Oxford University Press.

Bessant, J. (2013). Innovation in the twenty-first century. In R. Owen, J. Bessant and M. Heintz (Eds.), *Responsible Innovation. Managing the Responsible Emergence of Science and Innovation in Society*. Hoboken (NJ): John Wiley & Sons, pp. 1–25.

Black, J. and Baldwin, R. (2010). Really responsive risk-based regulation. *Law & Policy*, 32(2), pp. 181–213.

Blok, V. (2019). The ideal of transparency as a process and as an output variable of Responsible Innovation: The case of 'The Circle'. In R. Gianni, J. Pearson and B. Reber (Eds.), *Responsible Research and Innovation. From Concept to Practices*. Oxford: Routledge.

Blok, V. and Lemmens, P. (2015). The emerging concept of responsible innovation. Three reasons why it is questionable and calls for a radical transformation of the concept of innovation. In B. J. Koops, I. Oosterlaken, H. Romijn, Swierstra, T. and Van den Hoven, J. (Eds.), *Responsible Innovation 2: Concepts, Approaches, and Applications*. Dordrecht: Springer International Publishing, pp. 19–35.

Boltanski, L. and Chiapello, E. (2007). *The New Spirit of Capitalism*. London: Verso.

Bourdieu, P. (1990). *The Logic of Practice*. Stanford: Stanford University Press.

Bovens, M. (1998). *The Quest for Responsibility: Accountability and Citizenship in Complex Organizations*. Cambridge: Cambridge University Press.

Bower, J. L. and Christensen, C. M. (1995). Disruptive technologies: Catching the wave. *Harvard Business Review*, 73(1), pp. 43–53.

Braithwaite, J. (2011). The essence of responsive regulation. *UBC Rev.*, 44(3), pp. 475–520.

Brandom, R. B. (1998). *Making it Explicit: Reasoning, Representing and Discursive Commitment*. Cambridge (MA): Harvard University Press.

Brudney, D. (2014). The young Marx and the middle-aged Rawls. In J. Mandle and D. Reidy (Eds.), *A Companion to Rawls*. Oxford: Wiley-Blackwell, pp. 450–471.

Callon, M., Lescoumes, P. and Barthe, Y. (2001). *Agir dans une monde incertain. Essai sur la démocratie technique*. Paris: Editions du Seuil.

Callon, M., Lascoumes, P. and Barthes Y. (2009). *Acting in an Uncertain World. An Essay on Technical Democracy*. Cambridge (MA): MIT Press.

Cane, P. (2002). *Responsibility in Law and Morality*. Oxford (PO): Hart Publishing.

Castells, M. (2010). *The Rise of the Network Society. Economy, Society and Culture. Vol. 1: The Information Age: Economy, Society and Culture*. 2nd Revised Edition. Oxford: Wiley-Blackwell.

Chilvers, J. and Macnaghten, P. (2011). *The future of science governance. A review of public concerns, governance and institutional response*. BIS/Sciencewise-ERC.

Collingridge, D. (1980). *The Social Control of Technology*. New York: Frances Pinter.

Commission of the European Communities. (2008). Commission Recommendation of 7 February 2008, on a Code of Conduct for Responsible Nanosciences and Nanotechnologies Research, 7 February 2008. Available at: http://ec.europa.eu/research/science-society/document_library/pdf_06/nanocode-apr09_en.pdf.

Dahms, H.-J. (1994). *Positivismusstreit. Die Auseinandersetzungen der Frankfurter Schule mit dem logischen Positivismus, dem amerikanischen Pragmatismus und dem kritischen Rationalismus*. Frankfurt am Main: Suhrkamp.

Dardot, P. and Laval, C. (2016). *The New Way of the World. On Neoliberal Societies*. London: Verso.

Delli Carpini, M., Cook, F. L. and Jacobs, L. R. (2004). Public deliberation, discursive participation, and citizen engagement: A review of the empirical literature. *Annual Review of Political Science*, 7(1), pp. 315–344.

Dewer, R. and Dutton, J. (1986). The adoption of radical and incremental innovations: An empirical analysis. *Management Science*, 32(11), pp. 1422–1433.

Dewey, J. (1954). *The Public and Its Problems*. Athens (OH): Swallow Press.

Dewey, J. (1987). Liberalism and social action. In J. A. Boydston (Ed.), *The Later Works of John Dewey, 1925–1953, Vol. 11*. Carbondale (IL): Southern Illinois University, pp. 5–41.

Donzelot, J. (1984). *L'invention du social. Essai sur le déclin des passions politiques*. Paris: Fayard.

Duff, A. (2000). *Information Society Studies*. New York: Routledge.

Durbin, P. and Lenk, H. (Eds.) (1987). *Technology and Responsibility*. Boston: Reidel Publishing.

Dworkin, R. (1978). *Taking Right Seriously*. Cambridge (MA): Harvard University Press.

Dworkin, R. (1985). *A Matter of Principle*. Cambridge (MA): Harvard University Press.

Dworkin, R. (1988). *Law's Empire*. Cambridge (MA): Harvard University Press.

Ehrenberg, A. (1998). *The Fatigue of Being Oneself: Depression and Society*. Paris: Odile Jacob.

Esposito, R. (2015). *The Machine of Political Theology and the Place of Thought*. Oxford: Oxford University Press.

European Commission. (2012). *Science with and for Society*. Available at: https://ec.europa.eu/programmes/horizon2020/en/h2020-section/science-and-society.

European Commission. (2012). Charter Of Fundamental Rights Of The European Union. Available at: http://eur-lex.europa.eu/legal-content/EN/TXT/?uri=CELEX%3A12012P%2FTXT.

European Commission. (2010). Communication from the Commission. Europe 2020. A Strategy for Smart, Sustainable and Inclusive Growth. Available at: http://ec.europa.eu/eu2020/pdf/COMPLET%20EN%20BARROSO%20%20%20007%20-%20Europe%202020%20-%20EN%20version.pdf.

Ewald, F. (1986). *L'Etat Providence*. Paris: Grasset et Fasquelle.

Fernando, A. C. (2011). *Business Environment*. Chennai, India: Pearson.

Ferry, J. M. (2002). *Valeurs et Normes*. Bruxelles: Université Libre Bruxelles.

Frewer, L. (2003). Societal issues and public attitudes towards genetically modified foods. *Trends Food Sci Technol*. 14, pp. 319–332.

Fung, A. (2006). Varieties of participation in complex governance. *Public Administration Review*, 66(Special Issue 1), pp. 66–75.

Funtowicz, S. O. and Ravetz J. R. (1993). Science for the post-normal age. *Futures*, 25(7), pp. 739–755.

Funtowicz, S. O. and Ravetz, J. R. (1994). The worth of a songbird: Ecological economics as a post-normal science. *Ecological Economics*, 10(3), pp. 197–207.

Funtowicz, S. O. and Ravetz, J. R. (2008). Beyond complex systems: Emergent complexity and social solidarity. In D. Waltner-Toews, J. J. Kay and N.-M. Lister

(Eds.), *The Ecosystem Approach: Complexity, Uncertainty, and Managing for Sustainability*. New York: Columbia University Press, pp. 309–322.

Geertz, C. 1973. *The Interpretation of Cultures*. New York: Basic Books.

Genard, J. L. (1999). *Grammaire de la Responsabilité*. Paris: CERF.

Gianni, R. (2016). *Freedom and Responsibility. The Ethical Realm of RRI*. London/New York: ISTE/Wiley.

Godin, B. (2006). The linear model of innovation. The historical construction of an analytical model. *Science, Technology and Human Values*, 31(6), pp. 639–667.

Godin, B. (2015). *Innovation Contested – The Idea of Innovation over the Centuries*. London: Routledge.

Godin, B. (2016). Technological innovation: On the origins and development of an inclusive concept. *Technology and Culture*, 57(3), pp. 527–556.

Grinbaum, A. and Groves, C. (2013). What is 'responsible' about responsible innovation? Understanding the ethical issues. In R. Owen, J. Bessant and M. Heintz (Eds.), *Responsible Innovation. Managing the Responsible Emergence of Science and Innovation in Society*. Hoboken (NJ): John Wiley & Sons, pp. 119–142.

Grunwald, A. (2011). Responsible innovation: Bringing together technology assessment, applied ethics, and STS research. *Enterprise and Work Innovation Studies*, 7(IET), pp. 9–31.

Grunwald, A. (2014). Technology assessment for responsible innovation. In J. Van den Hoven, N. Doorn, T. Swierstra, B. J. Koops and H. Romijn (Eds.), *Responsible Innovation 1. Innovative Solutions for Global Issues*. Dordrecht: Springer Science and Business Media, pp.15–31.

Guston, D. H. (2001). Integrity, responsibility, and democracy in Science. *SciPolicy. A Journal of Science and Health Policy*, 1(2), pp. 168–189.

Gunther, K. (1993). *The Sense of Appropriateness: Application Discourse in Morality and Law*. Albany (NY): Suny Press.

Guston, D. H. and Sarewitz, D. (2002). Real-time technology assessment. *Technology in Society*, 24(1–2), pp. 93–109.

Habermas, J. (1971). Technology and science as ideology. In J. Habermas (Ed.), *Toward a Rational Society: Student Protest, Science and Politics*. London:Heinemann, pp. 81–122.

Habermas, J. (1986). Law and morality. *The Tanner Lectures on Human Values*. Available at http://tannerlectures.utah.edu/_documents/a-to-z/h/habermas88.pdf.

Hart, H. L. A. (2008). *Punishment and Responsibility. Essays in the Philosophy of Law, 2nd Edition*. Oxford: Oxford University Press.

Honneth, A. (1991). *The Critique of Power: Reflective Stages in a Critical Social Theory*. Cambridge (MA): MIT Press.

Honneth, A. (2014a). *Freedom's Right. The Social Foundations of Democratic Life*. Cambridge: Polity Press.

Honneth, A. (2014b). *De la reconnaissance à la liberté*. Lormont: Le Bord de l'Eau.

Honneth, A. (2016). *The Idea of Socialism*. Cambridge: Polity.

Horrigan, B. (2010). *Corporate Social Responsibility in the 21st Century: Debates, Models and Practices Across Government, Law and Business*. Cheltenham (UK): Edward Elgar.

Hug, K. (2008). Genetically modified organisms: Do the benefits outweigh the risks? *Medicina (Kaunas)*, 44, pp. 87–99.

Illouz, E. (2013). *Why Love Hurts: A Sociological Explanation*. Cambridge: Polity Press.

Jasanoff, S. (2004). *States of Knowledge. The Co-Production of Science and Social Order*. London: Routledge.

Jonas, H. (1984). *The Imperative of Responsibility: In Search of Ethics for the Technological Age*. Chicago: University of Chicago Press.

Kant, I. (1997). *Critique of Practical Reason*. Cambridge: Cambridge University Press.

Kant, I. (1998). *Critique of Pure Reason*. Cambridge: Cambridge University Press.

Karsenti, B. and Lemieux, C. (2017). *Socialisme et sociologie*. Paris: EHESS.

Kelsen, H. (2005). *Pure Theory of Law*. Berkeley: California University Press.

Koops, B. J., Oosterlaken, I., Romijn, H., Swierstra, T and Van den Hoven, J. (2015). *Responsible Innovation 2: Concepts, Approaches, and Applications*. Dordrecht: Springer International Publishing.

Kuhlmann, S., Edler, J., Ordóñez-Matamoros, G., Randles, S., Walhout, B., Gough, C. and Lindner, R. (2016). Responsibility navigator. In R. Lindner, S. Kuhlmann, S. Randles, B. Bedsted, G. Gorgoni, E. Griessler, A. Loconto and N. Mejlgaard (Eds.), *Navigating Towards Shared Responsibility in Research and Innovation. Approach, Process and Results of the Res-AGorA Project*. Karlsruhe: Fraunhofer ISI, pp. 135–158.

Ladrière, J. (1994). La déstabilisation de l'éthique. In *Variations sur l'éthique, Hommage a Jacques Dabin*. Bruxelles: Saint-Louis, pp. 57–73.

Ladrière, J. (1997). *L'éthique dans l'univers de la rationalité*. Québec-Namur: Artel-fides.

Lascoumes, P. (1995). L'Eco pouvoir. *Revue Française de Science Politique*, 45(3), pp. 491–493.

Leach, M., Scoones, I. and Wynne, B. (Eds.) (2006). *Science and Citizens: Globalization and the Challenge of Engagement*. London: Wiley.

Lee, R. J. and Petts, J. (2013). Adaptive governance for responsible innovation. In R. Owen, J. Bessant and M. Heintz (Eds.), *Responsible Innovation. Managing the Responsible Emergence of Science and Innovation in Society*. Hoboken (NJ): John Wiley & Sons, pp. 143–160.

Lenoble, J. and Maesschalck, M. (2003). *Toward a Theory of Governance: The Action of Norms*. The Hague: Kluwer Law International.

Lenoir, V. (2016). *Ethical Efficiency: Responsibility and Contingency*. London/New York: Iste/Wiley.

Leonard-Barthon, D. 1995. *Wellsprings of Knowledge: Building and Sustaining the Sources of Innovation*. Boston (MA): Harvard Business School Press.

Limoges, C. (1993). Expert knowledge and decision-making in controversy contexts. *Public Understanding of Science*. 2(4), pp. 417–426.

Maesschalck, M. (2000). Provenance et Fondements de la Pragmatique Contextuelle. In P. Coppens and J. Lenoble (Eds.), *Democratie et Procéduralisation du Droit*. Bruxelles: Bruylant, pp. 125–154.

Maesschalck, M. (2017). *Reflexive Governance for Research and Innovation Knowledge*. London/New York: ISTE/Wiley.

Michael, B. (2003). Corporate social responsibility in international developments: An overview and critique. *Journal of Corporate Social Responsibility and Environmental Responsibility*, 10(3), pp. 115–128.

Moldashl, M. (2010). *Why innovation theories make no sense*. Paper provided by Chemnitz University of Technology, Faculty of Economics and Business Administration in its series Papers and Preprints of the Department of Innovation Research and Sustainable Resource Management with number 9/2010. https://www.econstor.eu/obitstream/10419/55370/1/684996685.pdf.

Mullerat, R. (2009). *International Corporate Social Responsibility*. Netherlands: Kluwer Law International.

Nowotny, H. (1999). The place of people in our knowledge. *European Review*, 7(2), pp. 247–262.

Nowotny, H. (2015). *The Cunning of Uncertainty*. Oxford: Polity.

Nozick, R. (2013). *Anarchy, State and Utopia*. New York: Basic Books.

O'Connor, G. C. 2008. Major innovation as a dynamic capability: A systems approach. *The Journal of Product Innovation Management*, 25(4), pp. 313–330.

O'Sullivan, D. and Dooley, L. (2009). *Applying Innovation*. London: Sage.

Owen, R., Bessant, J. and Heintz, M. (Eds.) (2013). *Responsible Innovation. Managing the Responsible Emergence of Science and Innovation in Society*. Hoboken (NJ): John Wiley & Sons.

Parsons, T. (1991). The integration of economic and sociological theory. The Marshall lectures. *Sociological Inquiry*, 61(1), pp. 10–59.

Pavie, X., Scholten, V. and Carthy, D. (2014). *Responsible Innovation. From Concept to Practice*. Singapore: World Scientific.

Pellé, S. and Reber, B. (2016). *From Ethical Review to Responsible Research and Innovation*. London/New York: ISTE/Wiley.

Pellizzoni, L. (2005). Cosa significa deliberare? Promesse e problem della democrazia deliberative. In L. Pellizzoni (Ed.), *La deliberazione pubblica*, Roma: Meltemi.

Pellizzoni, L. (2008). Politiche Pubbliche e nuove forme di partecipazione. *Partecipazione e Conflitto*, 0, pp. 93–116.

Pellizzoni, L. (2010). Environmental knowledge and deliberative democracy. In M. Gross and H. Heinrichs (Eds.), *Environmental Sociology: European Perspectives and Interdisciplinary Challenges*. Dordrecht: Springer.

Perez, O. (2011). Responsive regulation and second-order reflexivity: On the limits of regulatory intervention. *UBC Law Review*, 44(3), pp. 743–778.

Perrow, C. (1970). Departmental power and perspectives in industrial firms. In M. N. Zald (Ed.), *Power in Organizations*. Nashville: Vanderbilt University Press.

Peters, B. (2007). *Der Sinn von Öffentlichkeit*. Frankfurt am Main: Suhrkamp.

Qvortrup, L. (2003). *The Hypercomplex Society*. New York: Peter Lang.

Randles, S., Edler, J. and Gee, S. (2015). Governance and the Institutionalisation of Responsible Research and Innovation in Europe. Transversal Lessons from an Extensive Programme of Case Studies. Stakeholder Report. *Deliverable of the Res-AGorA project D3.6*. Karlsruhe; http://res-agora.eu/assets/Res-AgorA_321427_Del_3-6_final.pdf.

Reber, B. (2005). Pluralisme moral: les valeurs, les croyances et les théories morales. *Archives de Philosophie du Droit*, 49, pp. 21–46.

Reber, B. (2007). Technology assessment as policy analysis: From expert advice to participatory approaches. In F. Fischer, G. J. Miller and M. S. Sidney(Eds.), *Handbook of Public Policy Analysis: Theory, Politics, and Methods*. New York: CRC Press, pp. 493–512.

Reber, B. (2016). *Precautionary Principle, Pluralism and Deliberation: Science and Ethics*. London/New York: ISTE/Wiley.

Ricouer, P. (2000). *The Just*. Chicago: Chicago University Press.

Ricœur, P. (2007). *Reflections on The Just*. Chicago: Chicago University Press.

Rip, A., Misa, T. J. and Schot, J. (Eds.) (1995). *Managing Technology in Society. The Approach of Constructive Technology Assessment*. London: Pinter Publishers.

Ritter, J. (1982). *Hegel and the French Revolution. Essays on the Philosophy of Right*. Cambridge (MA): MIT Press.

Sarewitz, D. (2004). How science makes environmental controversies worse. *Environmental Science & Policy*, 7(5), pp. 385–403.

Sartre, J. P. (1993). *Being and Nothingness*. Washington: Washington Square Press.

Schumpeter, J. (1934). *The Theory of Economic Development: An Inquiry into Profits, Capital, Credit, Interest and the Business Cycle*. New Brunswick: Transaction Publishers.

Searle, J. R. (1995). *The Construction of Social Reality*. New York: The Free Press.

Seillan, H. (2016). *Danger et precaution. Le roman des mots*. Paris: Les Belles Lettres-Manitoba.

Sen, A. (1999). *Development as Freedom*. Oxford: Oxford University Press.

Shamir, R. (2008). The age of responsibilization: On market-embedded morality. *Economy and Society*, 37(1), pp. 1–19.

Stehr, N. (2008). *Moral Markets. How Knowledge and Affluence Change Consumers and Products*. Boulder (CO): Paradigm Publishers.

Streeck, W. (2014). *Buying Time. The Delayed Crisis of Democratic Capitalism*. London: Verso.

Sykes, K. and Macnaghten, P. (2013). Responsible innovation – Opening up dialogue and debate. In R. Owen, J. Bessant and Heintz, M. (Eds.), *Responsible Innovation. Managing the Responsible Emergence of Science and Innovation in Society*. Hoboken (NJ): John Wiley & Sons, pp. 85–107.

Taylor, C. (1985). *Philosophy and Human Sciences*. Cambridge: Cambridge University Press.

Taylor, C. (1992). *Sources of the Self: The Making of the Modern Identity*. Cambridge (MA): Harvard University Press.

Teubner, G. (1993). *Law as an Autopoietic System*. Oxford: Blackwell.

Thorpe, C. and Gregory, J. (2010). Producing the post-Fordist public: The political economy of public engagement with science. *Science as Culture*, 19(3), pp. 273–301.

Van de Poel, I. (2011). The relation between forward-looking and backward-looking responsibility. In N. Vincent, I. van de Poeland J. Van den Hoven (Eds.), *Moral Responsibility, Beyond Free Will & Determinism*. Dordrecht (NL): Springer.

Van den Hoven, J., Lokhorst, G. J. C. and van de Poel, I. (2012). Engineering and the problem of moral overload. *Science and Engineering Ethics*, 18(1), pp. 1–13.

Van den Hoven, J. (2013). In R. Owen, J. Bessant and M. Heintz (Eds.), *Responsible Innovation. Managing the Responsible Emergence of Science and Innovation in Society*. Hoboken (NJ): John Wiley & Sons.

Van den Hoven, J., Doorn, N., Swierstra, T., Koops, B. J. and Romijn, H. (2014). Dordrecht: Springer Science and Business Media.

Van Oudheusden, M. (2014). Where are the politics in responsible innovation? European governance, technology assessments, and beyond. *Journal of Responsible Innovation*, 1(1), pp. 67–86.

Vincent, N. van de Poel, I. and Van den Hoven, J. (Eds.) (2011), *Moral Responsibility, Beyond Free Will & Determinism*. Dordrecht (NL): Springer.

Von Schomberg, R. (Ed.) (1993). *Science, Politics and Morality: Scientific Uncertainty and Decision Making*. Dordrecht: Springer.

Von Schomberg, R. (2013). A vision of responsible research and innovation. In R. Owen, J. Bessant and M. Heintz (Eds.), *Responsible Innovation. Managing the Responsible Emergence of Science and Innovation in Society*. Hoboken (NJ): John Wiley & Sons, pp. 51–74.

Von Schomberg, R. (2014). The quest for the 'right' impacts of science and technology: A framework for responsible research and innovation. In J. Van den Hoven, N. Doorn, T. Swierstra, B. J. Koops and H. Romijn (Eds.), *Responsible Innovation 1. Innovative Solutions for Global Issues*. Dordrecht: Springer Science and Business Media.

Voss, J.-P., Bauknecht, D. and Kemp, R. (Eds.) (2006). *Reflexive Governance for Sustainable Development.* Cheltenham, UK: Edward Elgar.

Weber, M. (2004). *The Vocation Lectures: 'Science as a Vocation'; 'Politics as a Vocation'.* Cambridge: Hackett.

Williams, B. (1984). *Moral Luck.* Albany (NY): Suny Press.

Wilms, H.-C. (2014). The assumption of scientific responsibility by ethical codes – A European dilemma of fundamental rights. In J. Van den Hoven, N. Doorn, T. Swierstra, B. J. Koops and H. Romijn (Eds.), *Responsible Innovation 1. Innovative Solutions for Global Issues.* Dordrecht: Springer Science and Business Media.

Wynne, B. (1992). Uncertainty and environmental learning. *Global Environmental Change*, 6(2), pp. 111–127.

Wynne, B. (1993). Public uptake of science: A case for institutional reflexivity. *Public Understanding of Science*, 2 (4), pp. 321–337.

Wynne, B. (2007). 'Taking European Knowledge Society Seriously. *Report of the Expert Group on Science and Governance to the Science, Economy and Society Directorate*, Directorate-General for Research. European Commission, Brussels.

9 RRI *versus* neo-liberal governance

Virgil Lenoir

Introduction

The risks and promises linked to science and technologies were first the subject of fiction, from Mary Shelley to Jules Verne and beyond. RRI is now in search of a scientific knowledge about it: "The hope is that, before these technologies are fully formed, we might be able to nudge their trajectories in various ways towards responsible, desirable futures" (Owen, Heintz and Bessant 2013; foreword). This implies a better grasping of the ways sciences develop in order to propose alternative ways of governing.

But the actual dominant ways of governing are dictated by neo-liberal logics of performance (Supiot 2015). They ask for benchmarking in order to evaluate performance, thus applying business management logics to state governance. I call this neo-liberal governance. This has been a mainstream tendency for the last thirty years (Arnaldi and Gorgoni 2016).

What I want to suggest here is that RRI could generate a general alternative to neo-liberal governance. It should be intuitively clear that the two models are incompatible from the fact that, for someone like Hayek (Hayek 1973–1979, chap. 2), for instance, the unpredictability of an agency process is in itself good. This is the case since all the agents, in a definite situation, can use all the available information, which is impossible for a single planner, with his or her predictive power, as clever would he be. So unpredictability is linked to efficiency. We can say that this concerns only economics, not the larger field of science and innovation. But precisely, what was first an economic theory has become a governance tool.

The opposition between governance praising unpredictability and one that tries to nuance its analysis in order to be responsible towards future generations may seem evident. But what I want here is to explore and formulate the conceptual dimension of that opposition. I will do it through the two concepts of contingency and *homo œconomicus*.

Something or some event is traditionally considered contingent if it could have occurred or not, or if it could have occurred differently[1] (Aristotle 1989). I use it here, as a first approximation in the sense of the unpredictable efficiency[2] of the logics of human action, as it is dependent on their relation to the possible at work in a given situation (Lenoir 2016). It can also be seen as a radical loosening of the link between cause and effect.[3] Small causes can have disproportionate effects and *vice versa*. This is particularly evident in research and innovation.

Contingency is certainly the mark of increasingly interdependent societies. Even if people always had to deal with it, its generalization is the main characteristic of our era. This is largely so because of the ever-more-rapid spreading of technologies, and their growing power to reshape our world. The important unpredictability and risks inherent to these processes make urgent the clarification of the responsibilities incumbent to the actors of research and innovation.

Important terminological and etymological distinctions have already been made concerning the different ways of expressing "responsibility" (see, for example, Owen *et al.* 2013, and Gianni 2016). There were also important contributions to the polysemy of the word (Vincent *et al.* 2012, Pellé and Reber 2016). I will not repeat them. I would like here to explore the implications of a robust concept of "contingency" for an RRI governance as opposed to a neo-liberal one. *What would be the implications of a robust concept of contingency on the management of efficiency?*

Economists often argue that efficiency is free from any reference to ethics. For them, efficiency is expressed by the Pareto optimum, and designates a situation where nobody's well-being could be improved without diminishing that of someone else. This equilibrium is attainable by purely economic processes.

Efficiency is often supported by a conception of actor's motivation as that of a *homo œconomicus*. This actor only has his personal, selfish interests in view. It is not despite this fact but thanks to it that the actions of all the actors coordinate to produce exactly what is needed and to make the maximum profit for most actors. In other words, the best way to be responsible in this sense (of the efficiency) is never to think about responsibility.

So, the model of an actor's motivation called *homo œconomicus* is best grounded by the idea that the actors do better by each pursuing his or her selfish interests than by (also or sometimes) adopting ethical motivations (Hayek 1973–1979, esp. vol. 1). In fact, this means that people not only do not adopt ethical motivations, but also that they are right not to do so. Both of these theses can be questioned.

What would be the implications of a robust concept of contingency regarding a model of responsible human agency's motivation? I will first examine this question under a hypothesis. I will try to show that what allowed Amartya Sen to powerfully oppose the *homo œconomicus* model is precisely an implicit concept of contingency. This concept works not as a foundation in the classical sense, but as a "process-efficiency" justification.

In a second step, I will put in evidence a complexity of the contingency's concept that Sen does not take into account (precisely because the concept remains, for him, implicit). I will ask to what extent this hidden aspect of contingency could weaken Sen's attempt to overcome the *homo œconomicus* model and his mastery of effort to introduce complexity and plausibility into a model of human motivation. I will suggest that the indeterminacy of the values, and the constant refusal by Sen to define ultimate moral principles, is linked to this aspect of the concept of contingency.

In a third step, I will make clear that all this concerns very closely the problematic field of RRI. I will ask why the five pillars formulated by the European Commission have the same indeterminacy as Sen's values. I will examine to what extent the contingency at work in the actor's situation allows or does not allow a more precise apprehension of those pillars, under a definite model of human motivation that could be very different from that of the *homo œconomicus.*

So contingency and the *homo œconomicus* model will appear as the conceptual core of what opposes RRI and neo-liberal governance. And the contingency concept will first be considered as implied in Sen's powerful calling into question of the *homo œconomicus* model.

Sen's implicit concept of contingency

The question of human agency's motivation is important for RRI. In research, an "interest" in knowledge naturally comes to the fore, along with the profit expected. But more relevant to the unpredictability of the effects of the discoveries, their reinterpretations, the renewal of their uses etc. is the complexity of "values", "moral principles", "interests" (selfish or not), "aims" and "objectives" interacting in human agency. A theory of motivation is important for prediction, but also for defining a robust concept of efficiency and, even more, it is required for a consistent thought of our freedom – all dimensions that are structurally at the core of RRI.

We have first to consider a very influential theory of human agency: the simplistic model of the *homo œconomicus.* Sen powerfully and influentially put into question this dogma, which (even today) is very widely shared among economists.

Rational Choice Theory (among others, Becker 1976) does not consider any reference to "ethics" as relevant to an analysis of human agency (Sen 2002). It (Rational Choice Theory) prefers to suppose a complex hidden mechanism that promotes selfish interests. This comes down to distinguishing the level of an apparent motivation (that can present itself as ethical), and that of the real (selfish) motivation. The appeal of the theory is not only that it offers a rational interpretation of human agency, but its claim that it knows better than the actors what their motives are. The problem is that, according to this theory, they only consider "rational" a selfish action. If an actor argues that he is driven by ethical considerations, not only is he considered naïve or a liar, but also as being irrational.

As Sen argues, if someone can rationally pursue his self-interests, it does not follow that pursuing self-interests is the only way to act rationally (also Sen 1991). It is even possible, on the contrary, that *Rational Choice Theory* (RCT) is actually at fault, offering an oversimplified motivation in place of the rich motivational variety and the rational complexity of "real" deliberation and "effective" choice. It is well known that empirical studies do not satisfactorily corroborate the predictions of RCT (Kahneman, Slovic and Tversky 1982). People do not systematically act in a way that maximizes their personal interests. Maybe it is not because of a "lack" of rationality, but because people in everyday life are much more rational than the "rational fools" (Sen 1991) of RCT.

Sen opened the theoretical perspective about motivation in several ways. I will mention only three of them here. I will not develop them fully because a growing literature exists on the subject (see de Munck and Zimmermann 2008).

The first is by distinguishing well-being from agency. Someone can pursue his well-being (let's assume it is equivalent to the satisfaction of his desires, which is only one interpretation among others). Alongside this, there is a dimension of "agency" that, we can argue, has a distinct appeal and is equally important for the actor. This person can attach particular importance to what she has accomplished. If she has devoted herself to a cause, she can attach more importance to the promotion of this cause than to her well-being. This is not to say that this is the case for everybody. But anyway, the distinction has to be formulated in order to better grasp the complexities of human motivation.

The second distinction is relative to freedom. It is not the same to consider what someone really chooses, and to consider it relative to the different choices that he was offered. The classic example is that of someone starving and someone fasting. Objectively, both persons do not eat. But the second "could" eat. He has the possibility to eat and voluntarily abstains from it. So, the freedom of both actors is certainly not the same (this is important for Sen's characterization of "capabilities"). And this freedom allows the realization of a more or less wide spectrum of possibilities. The motivation, in its link to objective options of choice, can be more or less efficient.

The third aspect is that of "rights". Utilitarianism, during its long domination of ethics, gave a purely instrumental view of rights. They were only considered inasmuch as they had "consequences" on the "utilities" (in one interpretation: "well-being") of the agents. Sen's contribution is to reconcile a consideration of the intrinsic importance of rights with consequentialism. Indeed, taking into account the real importance of rights that is not only instrumental is compatible with a consideration of the consequences (for example, in integrating the observation of the right as an important consequence). The point is to go beyond the simple alternative of considering "only" the consequences, with a purely instrumental view of rights, or on the contrary. Rights are an important part of motivation, but only when integrated into a complex view of what makes the actor's action (for these three steps, see Sen 1991).

I have tried to show, as briefly as possible, certain aspects of Sen's widening of the concept of human motivation. Alongside our selfish interests, each of us also takes into account, to various degrees, personal commitments, available choices and valorized rights when it comes to choosing. This is important if we want to predict the actor's choices: empirical studies show that people often do not follow the maximizing conduct that RCT would predict. It is also important for the definition of the concept of efficiency. If we consider it as the ability to reach an objective exterior to the agent, that doesn't correspond to his real objective, we would not be able to reach a plausible concept of efficiency. But it is also crucial for a measure of our freedom. A narrow conception of human motivation can't help but to ignore human freedom.

Interpreters generally consider that Sen introduces this widening by offering a new concept of rationality, much more flexible and less "algorithmic" (he doesn't necessarily want a complete ordering of choices, etc.). Is rational for him a choice that conforms to a reasoned scrutiny (Sen 2002: p. 49)? He knows it doesn't sound like a new concept. For some, it is just common sense. But, he argues, it allows us to overcome important trends in economic thought (for example, RCT). Nevertheless, his characterization of rationality contains an important indeterminacy.

This flexible concept allows us to take into account "rights", "values", "interests" and "objectives" of different sorts. But this seems less limiting for choice. This is so because every deliberation and every choice is seen in context. A concept of rationality can't be imposed from the outside to limit the actor's choice. This choice takes into account every element of the context. And it is why it is a free choice. A concept of (rational) choice cannot limit the freedom of choice of the agent. If this were the case, it would be a false concept, since rationality is precisely the ability to take into account everything important in a situation.

Nevertheless, Sen's concept of rationality is hardly a concept. If this is so, what guided him in his undertaking? Maybe it is not a concept of rationality, but an intuition about the importance of contingency. My thesis is that this intuition (even if it is not explicit in his works) can best justify his widening of the model of human motivation.

This can be best illustrated by Sen's more philosophical book *The Idea of Justice* (Sen 2010: p. 7). In this book, Sen distinguishes two methods of thinking about political justice: "transcendental institutionalism" and "realization-focused comparison". Noticing that the first is much more common among the theorists, he argues in favour of the second. The first method is in search of a definition of perfectly just institutions, whereas the second wants to reduce the existing injustices by proceeding comparatively in context.

I will try to explain in what sense this shift of perspective he proposes leans on and expresses a concept of contingency. First, it represents a considerable *broadening* of the perspective, which conduces to positively take plurality of theories and opinions into account, in order to realize a true pluralism. In this confrontation of different theories, coming from different horizons, various disciplines, expressing different (and sometimes incompatible) values, objectives and justifications, contingency manifests itself openly. But Sen uses it in a positive and optimistic way. The variety of reasons is a richness, not a default (citing John Grey, Sen 2010: p. 12, note). Good reasons can come from everywhere. So, pluralizing the perspectives can bring us to understand the others' ideas, which can in return make us revise ours, bringing us to a more precise and just awareness of their signification.

Second, Sen's shift in perspective promotes an *open availability* to the context of the choice and the action. This can be seen as an open relation to the creative possible at work in the situation, and accessible to every actor (Lenoir 2016). Contingency is the unpredictable but coherent manifestation of the creativity of the possible as an element of the situation. We can express it by saying that what is concretely given in a situation does not exhaust the situation. There is always an invisible dimension that works in the visible. And the situation never coincides completely with itself, because there are possibilities in it that bypass it. This means that there is no pre-determination of the concrete. It is not pre-definite somewhere before it comes to exist. But the creative dimension of the possible realizes it contingently.[4]

This broadening and this open availability to the creative power at work in the context fits with Sen's revision of the model of the *homo œconomicus*. Considering only the selfish interests as a motivation makes an incredibly narrow and impoverished model. It leads us to disregard all aspects of the situation that are not directly relevant to it.

Taking into account well-being and action, the whole spectrum of choice instead of only the final choice, the rights with the utilities, gives not only a wider, subtler account of human action (more apt to use the creative possible at work in the context). It is also a more plausible one. It can lead to improvement in the capacity of prediction of the theory, as well as reinforcing the concepts of freedom and efficiency.

But the concept of contingency remains implicit in Sen's works. Actually, it is for him more an intuition than a concept. Nevertheless, it has some definite features. Contingency is an actual capacity of opening possibilities. It brings into contact different perspectives, sometimes from remote horizons, and allows their mutual enrichment through dialogue. It broadens the spectrum of reasons pertinent to a choice and allows a more definite perception of what makes them valid. It can lead every actor to revise his choice, to test his reasons by discovering those of others. This is also a central concern for RRI, with its important participation pillar. In this view, contingency is this broadening of perspective. Contingency is an opening power.

I have tried to reconstitute Sen's implicit concept of contingency. I have argued that it is important in his attempt to broaden the model of human motivation. Now, I move to consider if the concept of contingency is not more ambiguous than that – if it does not hold another aspect that could weaken this attempt.

The duplicity of contingency

Contingency can also be a closure, a brutal closure of possibilities. As Sen notices, democratic institutions do not, by themselves, guarantee a free exchange of reasons and an open scrutiny. Even a "transcendental institutionalism" has to "suppose" that the actual behaviour of people complies with certain standards required for the correct functioning of society. Determinate institutions require determinate standards of conduct. This is also true for "realization-focused comparison". If the scope is not broad enough, people can always use the knowledge they have of the situation to "cultivate discontent and instigate violence" (Sen 2010, p. 354).

It is not because ethical motives are more widespread than the economists usually think that people do not *sometimes* (and some more than others) act in a selfish way. It is enough that some people (not many) occupying strategic positions act that way, manipulating the others, for the situation to deteriorate very quickly. This interaction is also contingent, manifesting a disproportion between small causes and big effects.

Democracies seem particularly vulnerable to those mass manipulations. This is especially the case in difficult periods, when crisis becomes a usual state and a habit, and when trust in the traditional representative parties is largely ruined. This creates space for manipulators, promoting a particularly narrow interest: that of a unique, national or religious identity, erasing all the others (Sen 2007).

But, obviously, this narrowing of the perspective takes place when the open discussion characteristic of democracy is already perverted. Free exercise of reason and free exchange of ideas are best guaranteed by a democratic system. If they have become pure hypocrisy, democracy has already ceased to be. This shows that democracy is not only a given set of institutions but also the compliance of the citizens with a kind of behaviour that allows the free functioning of these institutions. With this behaviour, there is open contingency; without, there is closed contingency. With it, a careful attention to the creativity of the possible at work in the situation allows an open invention of the future; without it, knowledge becomes a set of dead recipes tacked on the situation from the outside.

In fact, I evoked the political level first because Sen puts it to the fore. But this analysis is also valid for research and innovation. An open attention to the creative possibilities in the situation, to the lineaments of a new problem or new solutions that become possible because of a new configuration of the actual situation, new experiments, new data etc., is crucial for theoretical research. For technological innovation, this context, the expectations, the particular configuration of people's needs, are also crucial.

But closed contingency can also be true for research and innovation. This is the case, as was mentioned, when knowledge becomes purely a means to an end, whose meaning has been forgotten. It is so when it is not apprehended from the situation itself, but from the outside, as something external and general that is only brought in here to get a particular result, that itself comes quickly to lose its meaning. Maximizing … what? For what reason?

So, the duality of the concept of contingency (that of open and closed contingency) is at work, depending on whether the actors are aware of the creative possible in context and listen to it or not. It is a question of disposition. But this disposition is part of the possible at work in the situation. This possible is not something separated. It is shared by all the actors. And its creativity expresses itself through the actors' activities.

Once this has been said, one can ask, what about responsibility, given this double concept of contingency? To what extent is the broadening brought by Sen valid and effective? Sen's model of human motivation constitutes an important step towards a better apprehension of responsibility. This is certainly true as long as we consider the open side of contingency. Deliberation has to take into account not only selfish interests, but also values, rights, freely chosen aims and objectives, altruistic motives, commitments etc. Open discussion and exchange of reasons allow everybody to decide in a well-informed way, after having weighed his motivations, and having inscribed them in a wide perspective. This is what responsibility requires in a situation of open contingency. And, in this respect, the intuition of open contingency offers good support to Sen's wide model.

Closed contingency, as a real situational possibility, threatens it on the efficiency level. People's behaviour is no longer adapted to the demands of freedom. Discussion is not enough anymore, because of hypocrisy. But it can be argued that in these situations of closed contingency, the wide model is more necessary than ever. What appears in a crude way is that, even if we know what responsibility demands (a free and honest weighing of the widest range of motives), the situation can arise whereby most people will not act that way. So responsibility will not have its needed efficiency.

If we rely on contingency for an efficient expression of responsibility, we have to know that contingency can also ruin this efficiency. So it cannot be a "foundation", in the traditional sense. Does it mean that contingency is a "necessary" but not a "sufficient" condition for responsibility? In one way, I have to say that it is a sufficient condition. If the actor considers freely the possible at work in the situation, he will act responsibly. What about when closed contingency comes? What about when the reasons do not come anymore in an inner, integrated way (integrated into the situation's possible)?

I will try to show how Sen can be read as defusing this implicit objection to his implicit argument. He did so by refusing to define in an abstract way "universal" moral principles or values or rights. He simply doesn't believe that we can give such "universal" principles that would be valid in "all" and "every" context. The individual or collective decision can only be responsible if it is contextualized. Nobody can dictate a definite list of moral norms or of human rights that we would want every country to adopt. This would be a reintroduction of the idea of a "perfect" and once and for all definite "transcendental institutionalism". But what is important with such a list is precisely that it is subject to revision. So here, also, Sen's distinction between "transcendental institutionalism" and "realization-focused comparison" applies, and so does his choice for the second method.

This is true, I would suggest, because of the duality of the concept of contingency, which forbids it to be considered as a "foundation". It has this not only necessary but also sufficient justificatory role. But this has a cost: we cannot get a complete and definite (decontextualized) list of rights, values or principles.

The attempt of Martha Nussbaum to give such a list (Nussbaum 2000) was criticized by Sen. He did so even if she insisted on the necessity of getting such a list, even provisionally, to enforce the social actions in countries where human rights were severely violated. And it seems that in a "realization-focused comparison" perspective, to get such a temporary list could be useful to diminish relative injustices. But Sen did not approve of her attempt. Why such a reservation?

His permanent insistence on the importance of the contextualization shows that, even with the objection of the closed contingency, the widening of the range of motives to the ethical ones remains valid. This is true not on a "foundation", but on an "efficiency process" argument. This argument is not given by Sen, but it is congruent to his theoretical positions. Indeed, open contingency demands the widening of the motives to the ethical ones. But even if closed contingency comes into play, it will be only for a moment, and after that open contingency will come again. But to hasten this move to open contingency, ethical motives will be decisive. So if we consider the efficiency play of the two moments – open and closed contingency – as a process, ethical motives are justified as efficient on both sides.

So responsibility, in both cases, requires that ethical motives are taken into account, without being specified in a trans-situational abstractive way. This is particularly relevant for RRI. The spreading, rearrangement and reinvention of the uses, for concepts and technologies, take the undefined shape of contingent "efficiency processes" (Lenoir 2016; see also Lenoir (2018), where I consider four types of ethically structured processes.). These processes integrate a large spectrum of human motivation. Considering this spectrum to be as wide as possible, "from" the precise situation where the actors are concerned is a first step towards their efficient responsibility-taking. The participation, so important for RRI, is a requisite for this responsibility-taking if one follows this argument.

But, we can say, RRI already accepts that ethical motives are real ones. What it demands is that conflicts between values and conceptions of the good be decided in a rigorous and pluralistic manner. And in this respect, the impossibility of defining lists of relevant values, with, eventually, a precise ordering of priority, seems like a defect. And, actually, the five "pillars" offered by the European Commission as a characterization of the requirements of RRI suffer from such an indetermination. This is also the case for the often more abstract "conditions" proposed by the scholarly works on the subject (Pellé and Reber noticed that; 2016: p. 60). This means that the requirement of a "maximal" opening of the scope of the motives has to be ever reaffirmed. A concern centred too much on procedural features would quickly forget about this requirement. But defining a fixed list of values that would fit every context of evaluation would also lead to forgetting the importance of the context itself for the evaluation.

The option for this indeterminacy is justified in a double way. First, it imposes limits (even if they are not so precisely defined) to the neglecting of marks that bring closed contingency to efficiency. Second, it allows an openness to creative possibility in situations of open contingency. (This presupposes that people have not "only" selfish interests, but also some values or norms of some kind. And this seems a quite plausible point. But it doesn't presuppose that they adhere to "definite" values and norms, this one and not this one.)

Taking this for granted, the question becomes: Where do we put these limits, and how far do we have to tolerate the indeterminacy of moral principles?

An alternative concept of human agency?

Until now, I have argued for the duplicity of the concept of contingency. I have tried to show that (1) this concept is important in order to understand the "efficiency" of the processes at work in a given situation; (2) it can be used as a justification means for a broader model of human motivation – in this case, it justifies not as a foundation, but as a "process efficiency" conception; and (3) it can justify a certain indeterminacy of the moral principles that has to be completed in context.

Now, I want to add that a broader model of human motivation can be used by RRI as a predictive tool of the behaviour of the agents, allowing a better understanding of the risks. This could lead to completion of the content of the principles (here, the five pillars or the six keys of RRI) without demanding a complete, abstract and exhaustive determination of them.

First, I have to take a precise and non-caricatural definition of the *homo œconomicus* perspective:

> all human behaviour can be viewed as involving participants who maximize their utility from a stable set of preferences and accumulate an optimal amount of information and other inputs in a variety of markets.
>
> (Becker 1976, p. 14)

Acting this way, people are rational and are in a position to efficiently pursue their objectives, as long as they fit a plausible definition of "utility".

But people, most of the time, do not act that way. They simply do not choose to act in a way that only maximizes their final utilities. This was shown by empirical research (Kahneman, Slovic and Tversky 1982 among others). So, this theory is not a very good prediction tool.

Notice that, Jolls, Sunstein and Thaler, in a long article in 1998, suggest completing the model with data coming from Behavioural Economics. This would, as they think, introduce more complexity into the model, and bring its predictions closer to the objectively noted behaviours.

They want to proceed as follows. Becker's model is completed by three limitations of the actors: (1) "bounded rationality" (people's rationality is subject to bad evaluations); (2) "bounded willpower" (they do not always do what they want to do. Think of the smokers who want to stop); and (3) "bounded self-interest" ("people care, or act as if they care, about others, even strangers, in some circumstances") (Jolls, Sunstein and Thaler 1998, pp. 1477–1479).

An interpretation of this surprising concern about others is expressed as follows: "In many market and bargaining settings (…) people care about being treated fairly and want to treat others fairly if those others are themselves behaving fairly" (Jolls, Sunstein and Thaler 1998, p. 1479).

Is this so surprising? And doesn't it fit our daily experience after all? But why not go a step further? Is not this principle of "bounded self-interest" more simple and more general than that of purely selfish action? And what if this principle was not a limitation put on Becker's theory, but if the latter were a limitation, a useless complexification of the former?

Let's call the principle of "bounded self-interest" "motivation by reciprocity". It is a plausible and simple hypothesis that people want to act fairly to people they perceive as behaving fairly[5] to themselves and to others. This doesn't mean that "everybody" acts like that on "every" occasion. But maybe people act like that more often, on a purely statistical level, than they act in a purely selfish manner. The empirical surveys' results can be interpreted as fitting with the "motivation by reciprocity" principle at least as well as with the "selfish" principle.

But we should not be too enthusiastic. Indeed, the "motivation by reciprocity" model is far from being a moral one. People treat others well because they expect to be treated well in return, or because it is their pleasure to do so, choosing with whom to act fairly and with whom not to act that way. Morality asks that we treat others well because it is our duty to do so, and doesn't allow us to choose among the others those we want to be fair with.

So the "motivation by reciprocity" model has to be completed by a stronger, moral one. The first admits considerable violence towards people that are perceived as behaving in an inappropriate way (for cultural reasons, sexual orientation etc.) A moral counterpart to that model should emphasize the necessity of extending this fair treatment to every person in society, and beyond. This has to be established as the universality of the model. This is clearly not an ethical, substantial stance, but a moral,[6] principled one. At the same time, it is not an "abstract" principle put on the situation, but the generalization of the reciprocity link already at work in it.

We are now faced with a double model of human motivation. What would be its relation to the agents' responsibility? Couldn't it serve as a criterion of this responsibility? The big difference with the *homo œconomicus* model is that ethical and moral motives are integrated at the base. A purely selfish strategy is just a limitation, arbitrary but always possible, put on the motivational spectrum. The "motivation by reciprocity" model is apt to express ethical motives. Indeed, ethics has to do with freedom shared with people we are in affinity with. This is not possible for "every" single person. So the moral model adds a motivational duty to treat fairly everyone, even people we dislike.

In what we called ethics and morality, is it about responsibility? Ethically shared freedom implies mutual sympathy and mutual expectations. It shows responsibility as long as we are in this reciprocity (as opposed to a purely selfish behaviour). The moral model expresses responsibility as something disproportionate to human agents. Nobody can in every circumstance be fair to everybody. So it will never completely meet the actual behaviour of the agents.

What I want to suggest is that "taken together", both models can contribute to an understanding of people's effective responsibility. Since the moral model is more demanding than "motivation by reciprocity", we could proceed by subtracting the latter from the former. This could allow us to evaluate and foresee, in a non-mathematical way,[7] what the responsibility of people and its effectiveness would be in a given situation.

In a participation perspective, examining to what extent everyone complied with the "motivation by reciprocity" model, and, further, to the moral model can also show if, during the discussion, people really took up their responsibilities. Obviously, if nobody gave up anything, there was no real responsibility-taking.

"Motivation by reciprocity" can simultaneously be a tool to predict people's conduct (it will better fit their actual conduct that a purely selfish model) and a tool to evaluate participation in the debates. Indeed, if someone renounces his self-interest once confronted with a strong argument, this would show a strong and honest implication in the debate. But there, also, reciprocity is an important dimension.

This method keeps the two requirements originating from the contingency concept. The motivation spectrum is wide open: from selfish interests to values, rights, aims and objectives. And the task of choosing is that of the agents concerned, "in context". Nobody can come from the outside with a theory and impose it on the actors. What I called the moral model is just the generalization of the reciprocity link between the actors that is at the core of every social interrelation.

If there is no such reciprocity, every individual focuses on his immediate interests. And this, when the action results in the same outcomes, is one way false relation brings closed contingency to the fore. This ruins not only social relations, but the efficiency itself of the processes. It is so because it promotes unjust inequalities. Inequalities are unjust not when they are quantitatively important, but when the privileged ones are not responsible. When this is so, reciprocity is broken, and there is no efficiency.

RRI is an attempt, in the field of research and innovation, to re-establish the reciprocity between the actors, letting everyone express his perspective. If we handle this intelligently, it could lead to open contingency, in which responsibility and efficiency are both carried out.

Conclusion

I have argued that Sen's broadening of the spectrum of human motivation asks not for a foundation in the traditional sense, but for an "efficiency-process"-oriented justification. This means to put to the fore a robust concept of contingency. As I tried to show that this is a dual concept, between "open" and "closed" contingency, the justification holds for the opening of the spectrum of human motivation to ethics, but doesn't allow for a precise "abstract" specification of moral principles that would be valid in any circumstances. Their indeterminacy is the consequence of the way they were justified. Naturally, this doesn't prevent them from being very precisely specified in context.

The concept of contingency allows for the efficient broadening of the spectrum of relevant motives. But it does so against the background of "closed contingency", which means concrete violence. Avoiding this violence while keeping efficiency can be achieved not by expressing determined abstract moral principles, but two action-guiding criteria, related to each other.

These two criteria form a double way to be followed to foresee and evaluate the responsibility taken by actors in context. It is, in this sense, a subtraction between the "motivation by reciprocity" and the moral model, which is a generalization of this reciprocity. This model can not only help, in an RRI context, to evaluate the agents' responsibility taking, but it could also be developed and refined in a way that could allow it to replace the *homo œconomicus* model of the economists, as a better prediction tool. Not only does it represent a broadening of the motivation model to ethics, but it can help to apprehend responsibility, and to rethink efficiency together with a consistent concept of contingency.

Both concepts of contingency and "motivation by reciprocity" can be seen as expressions of the divergence between RRI and the neo-liberal approach, with its notions of the "Invisible Hand" and the *homo œconomicus*. This has a considerable impact on what these two fields can respectively propose as ways of governance. Where the second promotes benchmarking and open competition on what is seen as a "market", the former asks for free participation in the debate and responsibility. In this view, they are not only distinct but also irreconcilable. Can RRI become the spearhead of an alternative way of governance to today's triumphant neo-liberal one?

Notes

1 It is still the definition of contingency for Kant and Hegel.
2 By "efficiency", I mean the ability of the actors to reach their freely chosen objectives, which can but does not need to serve selfish interests. This opposes the simplistic picture offered by the model of the *homo œconomicus.*
3 I add this for clarification only. Causality is not the subject of this paper.
4 These points are much more developed in my previous book, *Ethical efficiency* (London: ISTE Wiley, 2016).
5 "Fairly" is voluntarily indeterminate here. It expresses that a behaviour fits reasonable reciprocality expectations.
6 "Ethics", here, expresses freedom shared in social relations, where each one spontaneously respects all the others in the group. "Morals" means the intervention of a definite rule or norm, which can be formulated, and has a dimension of generality that often exceeds the group.
7 This would have to be established in what Gianni calls, after Rawls, a "reflective equilibrium" (Gianni 2016), but it has to be contextualized. See also Reber (2016), with the concept of extra-large reflective equilibrium.

Bibliography

Aristotle, (1989). *Categories. On Interpretation. Prior Analytics.* London: Loeb Classical Library.

Arnaldi, S. and Gorgoni, G. (2016). Turning the tide or surfing the wave? Responsible Research and Innovation, fundamental rights and neoliberal virtues. *Life Sciences, Society and Policy*, 6, pp. 1–19. DOI : 10.1186/s40504-016-0038-2.

Becker, G. (1976). *The Economic Approach to Human Behaviour.* Chicago: The University of Chicago Press.

de Munck, J. and Zimmermann, B. (eds.) (2008). *La liberté au prisme des capacités*, Paris: Editions de l'EHESS.

Gianni, R. (2016). *Responsibility and Freedom. The Ethical Realm of RRI.* London and Hoboken: ISTE/Wiley.

Hayek, F. A. (1973–1979). *Law, Legislation and Liberty*, Vol. 1 1973, Vol. 2 1976, Vol. 3 1979. London: Routledge.

Jolls, C., Sunstein, C. R. and Thaler, R. (1998). A behavioural approach to law and economics. *Stanford Law Review*, 50(1), pp. 471–608.

Kahneman, D., Slovic, P. and Tversky, A. (1982). *Judgment Under Uncertainty: Heuristics and Biases*. Cambridge: Cambridge University Press.

Lenoir, V. C. (2016). *Ethical Efficiency. Responsibility and Contingency.* London and Hoboken: ISTE/Wiley.

Lenoir, V. C. (2018). *La liberté comme processus éthique*. London: ISTE

Nussbaum, M. (2000). *Women and Human Development. The Capabilities Approach.* Cambridge: Cambridge University Press.

Owen, R., Bessant, J. and Heintz, M. (eds.) (2013). *Responsible Innovation. Managing the Responsible Emergence of Science and Innovation in Society*. Hoboken: John Wiley & Sons.

Pellé, S. and Reber, B. (2016). *From Ethical Review to Responsible Innovation and Research*. London and Hoboken: ISTE/Wiley.

Reber, B. (2016). *Precautionary Principle, Pluralism, Deliberation. Sciences and Ethics*. London/New York: ISTE-International/Wiley.

Sen, A. (1991). *On Ethics and Economics*. Oxford: Blackwell Publishers.

Sen, A. (2002). *Rationality and Freedom*. Cambridge, MA: The Belknap Press of Harvard University Press.

Sen, A. (2007). *Identity and Violence. The Illusion of Destiny*. London: Penguin Books.

Sen, A. (2010). *The Idea of Justice*. London: Penguin Books.

Supiot, A. (2015). *La gouvernance par les nombres. Cours au Collège de France (2012-2014)*. Paris: Fayard.

Vincent, N., van de Poel, I. and Van den Hoven J. (eds.) (2012). *Moral Responsibility, Beyond Free Will & Determinism*. Dordrecht: Springer.

Part IV

The innovative management of Responsible Research and Innovation

10 Challenging the ideal of transparency as a process and as an output variable of Responsible Innovation

The case of "The Circle"

Vincent Blok, Rob Lubberink, Henk van den Belt, Simone Ritzer, Hendrik van der Kruk and Guido Danen

Introduction

In the literature on responsible (research and) innovation (henceforth abbreviated as RRI or RI), it is self-evidently assumed that transparency will help to enhance responsibility throughout the innovation process (von Schomberg, 2013; Owen et al., 2013); transparency enables multiple stakeholders to reflect and deliberate on emerging innovations in our society, assess their possible risks and, in the end, contribute to the determination of the goal of these innovations (Owen et al., 2013). This assumption is embedded in a broader perspective on transparency as one of the most celebrated ideals in our society and as a solution to the social and political problems society currently faces (Roberts, 2009).

Originally, objects were called transparent if light could shine through them, for instance in the case of a picture painted on glass or thin cloth. Likewise, organizations are considered to be transparent if their strategies and operations are open and publicly visible. This openness and visibility of organizations is found in their ability to provide information about their strategies and operations to their stakeholders, whether or not in order to hold the organization accountable. According to Christensen and Cheney (2015), transparency is nowadays "a common synonym of good governance in all sectors and an umbrella term for an important set of practices in most organizations, including financial disclosure statements, open meetings, reporting regimes, budgetary reviews, audits, dialogue forums, consistency policies, and so on" (Christensen and Cheney, 2015; cf. Florini, 2007). The ideal of transparency bears witness to the ambition for good governance through new regimes of openness, visibility and legibility (cf. Garsten and de Montoya, 2008), regarding, for instance, the societal acceptability and ethical acceptability of research and innovation outcomes. By being transparent about decisions, policies and actions, actors become increasingly accountable to their stakeholders (cf. Christensen and Cornelissen, 2015; Fox, 2007).

According to the European Commission, transparency is also a prerequisite for responsible research and innovation (Sutcliffe, 2011: p. 17). The applicability of the ideal of transparency in private sector innovation practices has been criticized, however. Transparency involves the reduction of information asymmetries among actors, while an innovative company survives precisely because of remaining and increasing information asymmetries (Blok and Lemmens, 2015). Nevertheless, the intuition that we need at least some degree of transparency in order to enhance stakeholder deliberation about the future impacts of innovations, increase responsiveness towards societal needs and secure societal goals of future innovations seems to be legitimate.

While in the current RRI literature transparency is often seen as a characteristic of the innovation *process* (Owen et al., 2013; Blok et al., 2015), it can also be seen as the *outcome* of responsible innovation. Thus the civil movement which is known in Europe under the name *Piratenpartei* calls for transparency and direct democracy, i.e. free access to public data and free access to publicly funded research and development, in order to prevent corruption and other irresponsible behaviour. From this perspective, the movement's efforts to institute an electronic petition system in order to secure and enhance direct democracy can be seen as responsible innovation that enhances transparency (cf. Eickhoff, 2011).[1] Although in a less radical way, the European Commission also sees transparency as a process and as an outcome variable of responsible innovation. In the MATTER report on RRI, the engagement of researchers and industries, gender equality, future-oriented science education, ethical considerations, open access to the results of publicly funded research and harmonious governance models are defined as aspects of RRI (Sutcliffe, 2011). In the case of engagement of researchers and industries, transparency can be seen as a necessary condition for a responsible innovation process. Sutcliffe mentions open access to the results of publicly financed research as an example of a responsible innovation. In this case, transparency is seen as an outcome of RI and as part of the process of RI.

In this paper, we explore the opportunities and limitations of the ideal of transparency in responsible (research and) innovation, by consulting the virtual case of "The Circle", a company which appears in Dave Eggers' recent novel *The Circle*.[2] The Circle is a high-tech company that provides services like Google and Facebook. The mission of The Circle is to end the anonymity of the internet – which only leads to excesses like pornography, cheating and violence – and to develop a human community in which mutual understanding, community and sharing are central themes. To this end, this innovative company develops technology and software that enhance transparency. The fundamental intuition of *The Circle* is that transparency prevents corruption, war and other bad habits, and promotes ethical behaviour. In this, the company echoes "the modernist conviction that more and better information reduces uncertainty, increases knowledge, and provide a bulwark against corruption, fraud and inefficiency" (Christensen and Cheney, 2015). Because *The Circle* furthers this ideal of transparency to the extreme – all information has to be public and there should be no privacy at all – we can reflect on the advantages and the limitations of the ideal of transparency as an *outcome* of responsible innovation based on this case. Because it concerns a privately owned company, the case also enables us to reflect on the advantages and the limitations of the ideal of transparency as characteristic of industrial-responsible innovation *processes* in this chapter.

In section one, we provide more detailed information about the company and its products. We will elaborate the purpose, products and processes of the company itself and the most important innovations that they developed. In section two, we analyse the innovations of The Circle as an *outcome* of responsible innovation processes: transparency as an outcome of responsible innovation. In section three, we apply the different dimensions of responsible innovation in order to analyse the innovation *processes* of The Circle: transparency as a characteristic of the process of responsible innovation. In section four, we draw conclusions regarding the ideal of transparency in RI.

The Circle: Its mission and its innovations

The Circle is a high-tech company with the main purpose of being responsive to societal needs. They want to eradicate unethical behaviour in society, enhance public health and make a positive impact on the environment. They do this by developing innovations themselves and by bringing in innovations developed by other actors in society. The word "they" is used because The Circle is both a community and a company at the same time. It was originally started by one engineer, and later on, two other "wise men" joined as leaders of The Circle, known together as the "three wise men". They are assisted by "the gang of forty" which functions as a board consisting of the forty most important employees of the company. The rest of the company consists of thousands of other employees. Everybody within the community basically shares the same vision, values and perspectives.

The original innovation that led to the start of the company is the so-called *TruYou*. This is an information technology that combines "users' social media profiles, their payment systems, their various passwords, their e-mail accounts, user names, preferences, every last tool and manifestation of their interests" and turns it into "one account, one identity, one password, one payment system, per person" (Eggers, 2013: p. 21). It requires people to use their real identity when signing up, which means that the identity of users is fully transparent to other users and can no longer be hidden by aliases. On the one hand, it is expected that users will no longer be involved in unethical behaviour when it is no longer possible to hide or conceal their identity. On the other hand, it is expected that an increasing number of users will provide full transparency about their identity, because this transparency is a necessary condition for using the innovations that are developed by The Circle. In the end, *TruYou* is expected to turn into a sort of social security number. This will then be used for a civil registration system where one can vote via his or her *TruYou* account. One cannot use any other services of the *TruYou* account until one has voted in order to reach 100% participation. The ultimate goal of The Circle is to reach full democracy and transparency by its innovations for transparency.

Another important innovation is *SeeChange*. This is a camera the size of a large thumb. This camera is affordable to everybody and is extremely durable and can record people's behaviour all over the world. The advantage of this camera is that one can access the recordings from everywhere and, in case of unethical behaviour – beating up peaceful protestors at the Tahrir Square in Istanbul, for instance – *Seechange* enables instant accountability for people conducting any kind of unethical behaviour. Because it is so small and hard to detect, one can never be sure that one is not being recorded. It is expected that this "not-knowing" will prevent abuses of power in the future (cf. Foucault, 1977).

A third example of an innovation is the *ChildTrack/TruYouth*. Children get a chip in their bodies so they can be tracked at all times. This should prevent children from getting kidnapped. If they do get kidnapped, the authorities can locate their whereabouts immediately and (hopefully) prevent bad things from happening.

Although we use The Circle as a virtual case, a quick search on the internet shows that there are real-life companies and innovations that are heading in the same direction as the virtual innovations of The Circle. In 2010, Facebook founder Marc Zuckerberg argued that the age of privacy is over. According to Zuckerberg, the social norms regarding sharing of information has evolved over time, and "we view it as our role in the system to constantly be innovating and be updating what our system is to reflect what the current social norms are" (Zuckerberg, 2010). miicard can serve as a real-life innovation which shares some of the characteristics of the TruYou. The general public should: "Think of miiCard as your virtual driver's license or digital passport that lets you prove your real identity online. [...] miiCard is a free service that puts you in control of your identity, taking the trust you already have with your online bank and the protection of strong authentication, to help you do everything from shopping, to proving your social accounts, trading on eBay and even buying a house – entirely online" (www.miiCard.com). There are also real-life innovations that are similar to the Seechange. For example, the vision by NGO "witness.org" is that video as a medium is key to registering and fighting against unethical behaviour. They have a special initiative, the "cameras everywhere leadership", which is about using the power of the public to record violations of human rights (http://www3.witness.org/cameras-everywhere). Also, the increase in privately owned drones with high-quality cameras is a step in the direction of a "cameras everywhere world" where people feel that they might be recorded and therefore be held accountable for their actions. Police departments also believe in the power of (video) recording. By wearing body cameras, they want to become more transparent as they (and others) can be recorded, controlled and therefore be held accountable for their actions. Although we will focus on the virtual innovations of The Circle in this chapter, the real-life examples of innovations do show that reflecting on the idea of responsible innovation and the concept of transparency is now more relevant than ever.

In all three cases of innovations by The Circle, transparency is enhanced in order to prevent unethical behaviour. The question now is: Can these innovations be considered as *responsible* innovations?

Transparency as an outcome of responsible innovation

Innovation can be considered as a process and as a product. In the literature on responsible innovation, there is no consensus yet regarding the conditions of responsible processes and products. Even though most theories on responsible innovation stress the importance of collective decision-making on the norms that innovation practices govern, there are different approaches to how these norms are defined (Pellé and Reber, 2013).

One stream of literature adopts a responsible innovation approach where the values and value systems are already (democratically) agreed upon beforehand. This is considered a substantive approach where agreement on the normative horizon is already achieved. An example of this substantive approach can be found in the definition of responsible innovation by von Schomberg (2013). With regard to the outcome of responsible innovation, he argues: "Responsible Research and Innovation is a transparent, interactive process by which societal actors and innovators become mutually responsive to each other with a view to the (ethical) acceptability, sustainability and societal desirability of the innovation process and its marketable products (in order to allow a proper embedding of scientific and technological advances in our society)". But according to von Schomberg, responsible innovation is not only achieved by embedding it in a transparent and interactive process, because we can make an appeal in this to *normative targets* which can be found in the European Treaty as the latter is democratically agreed upon in the EU context. Examples of these normative anchor points are sustainable development, high quality of life, competitive social market economy, social justice, equality and solidarity and, finally, the promotion of scientific and technological advancement. Innovating with a view to ethical acceptability, sustainability and societal desirability, as von Schomberg proposes, should thus cover such anchor points.

Innovations that substantiate these norms in new products and services can be considered "responsible" according to the substantive approach of responsible innovation. In the innovations for transparency of The Circle, transparency can be considered as such a pre-given norm. The necessity of transparency in order to prevent unethical behaviour is agreed upon beforehand within the company, and for this reason, the enhancement of transparency can be seen as the company's mission. Normally, transparency concerns the transparency of a window; a transparent window means that we can look through the glass without any hindrance. In the case of organizations, transparency can be defined as the attempt to make available "all legally releasable information – whether positive or negative in nature – in a manner that is accurate, timely, balanced, and unequivocal, for the purpose of enhancing the reasoning ability of publics and holding organizations accountable for their actions, policies and practices" (Rawlins, 2009: p. 75; cf. Christensen and Cheney, 2015). In the context of corporate innovation, transparency means, then, the *visibility* of their motivations, interests and actions (Menéndez-Viso, 2009).

In order to assess whether The Circle's innovations for transparency can be considered responsible, we have to answer the question of whether transparency as an outcome covers such pre-given norms. We will reflect on this question by considering three requirements of responsible innovations which are mentioned by von Schomberg; sustainability, societal desirability and ethical acceptability.

Sustainability

Sustainability is a so-called "big word", meaning that it has a positive connotation but in reality lacks definition and clarity. It gives some direction but its contents are flexible and open (Bos et al., 2014). When we look at sustainability as environmental friendliness or the balancing of people, planet and profit, we can say that it does play an important role for The Circle.

First of all, one can argue that the *SeeChange* cameras enhance sustainability. Their primary function, namely to identify and track down unethical behaviour, can easily be extended to environmental issues and social injustice, for instance in the case of child labour and sweatshops. But the innovation itself is also sustainable, since one of its main achievements is, for instance, its durability and the sustainability of its energy consumption. A second example of the sustainability of the innovations of The Circle comes from a smaller invention, which is called the *Homie*. This innovation is able to scan your home and assess what inventory is running low, and then restock it. The main advantage of this product is that it prevents the buying of too many unnecessary goods, and prevents pre-use disposal, and thus enhances sustainability within the household. A third example of an innovation addressing sustainability is a bracelet that tracks the health status of users. This device enables the prevention of diseases and injuries instead of their curing. The idea behind this is that prevention is better (cheaper) than curing. The bracelet provides full information so there are no knowledge gaps at the root of medical issues. This device thus enhances sustainability and public health. This is linked to the concept of "the quantified self", where people use technologies for measuring and improving their health and behaviour. Barrett, Humblet, Hiatt and Adler (2013) argue that this can even be expanded to communities and institutions, leading, in the end, to improved collective health driven by data. There are even social movements that live according to this principle. This shows that the virtuous case of The Circle is implemented in the real world in some cases.

We can conclude that the innovations for transparency meet the requirement of sustainability, because they focus on the improvement of public health while keeping their environmental impact as low as possible.

Societal desirability

The ultimate goal of The Circle is to reach 100% full transparency in the world, which is impossible without any societal desirability. In first instance, it is a free choice of people to accept and embrace the products and services of The Circle, who invest resources in keeping current customers happy and in raising awareness about the dangers of privacy. This very effort aims at a "transvaluation of values" as privacy, or "the right to be left alone", which is traditionally considered a cornerstone of liberal ethics and politics. Furthermore, the enormous increase in users who are willing to give up their privacy is, at least according to The Circle itself, an indication of the societal desirability of their innovations. This reflects the justification that social media like Facebook and Google routinely offer for their commercial practices (see the example of Facebook in the previous section). However, as José van Dijck critically remarks, the services delivered by social media may be nominally "free", but they are actually "'paid for' not in actual money but in users' attention as well as their profiling and behavioural data" (Van Dijck, 2013: p. 169). Or as another critic, Jaron Lanier, puts it, even more bluntly: "it has become commonplace to expect online services [...] to be given for free, or rather, in exchange for acquiescence to being spied on" (Lanier 2014: p. 6). In their eagerness to benefit from such online services, users hardly take the trouble to reflect on the conditions of the bargain and may find out later that they have given up much more of their privacy than they thought they had bargained for.

One can even argue that The Circle is responsive to the desires of society at large. Society wants a transparent government and the innovations for transparency offered by the Circle enable society to achieve this goal. For example, the *SeeChange* camera gets adopted by some politicians to enhance their transparency, and with this, the Circle contributes to increasing trust among society. Furthermore, The Circle's responsiveness to societal desirability becomes clear in the product presentation of *SeeChange* by the CEO: "I agree with the [international court of justice] in The Hague, with human rights activists all over the world. There needs to be accountability. Tyrants can no longer hide. There needs to be, and will be, documentation and accountability, and we need to bear witness." (Eggers, 2013: pp. 67–68). In this case, The Circle stresses the demands of society and makes clear that their innovations for transparency are responsive to societal needs.

This doesn't mean that everybody in society supports the actions, strategies and values that the Circle pursues. However, the Circle seems to follow a utilitarian approach where the greatest good for the greatest number of people should be attained. Small groups of people who resist transparency in their lives and do value their privacy more still exist, but have to adapt to the majority. In fact, The Circle argues that these people are basically old-fashioned, narrow minded and conservative. The early resistance against previous innovations – think of the invention of the car, the computer, the internet etc. – faded away over time and The Circle expects that the resistance against their innovations for transparency will disappear as well in the future. In the end, the ultimate goal of a 100% transparent world without unethical behaviour justifies the means of giving up privacy, according to The Circle.

This especially holds as the majority of the users favour the former over the latter. We can conclude that the innovations for transparency meet the requirement of societal desirability.

Ethical acceptability

The innovations for transparency should lead to moral behaviour by all actors within society. But is it also ethically acceptable to pursue this end of securing ethical behaviour by means of giving up privacy? In the world we live in, there is a continuous discussion about whether privacy should be given up in favour of transparency in order to secure ethical behaviour. For instance, Eric Schmidt, executive chairman of Google, argues: "If you have something that you don't want anyone to know, maybe you shouldn't be doing it in the first place". This discussion seems to become stronger with the introduction of big data and the terrorism debate. More important, however, is that the ethical acceptability of the innovations for transparency is dependent on the ethical perspective one takes.

According to Adam Smith, for instance, everyone acts out of his or her own interest and because we only have limited knowledge about the consequences of our actions, behaviour is ethically acceptable only when it serves the freely chosen interests of the decision-maker. Seen from this perspective, one could argue that the innovations for transparency of The Circle are ethically acceptable as long as they serve the interests of the users who have freely chosen to use these applications. A politician is, for instance, concerned about the trust of society. If he or she freely decides to use *SeeChange* in order to become fully transparent to society, this may increase his or her reputation as a politician and, in this respect, serves his or her interest. One can argue whether all users were really "free" to use *SeeChange* in the case of The Circle – all kinds of pressures on and manipulations of politicians are mentioned in the book – but this is not due to the innovation itself but to the offensive marketing strategy of the company (we will come back to this issue in section 3). From the perspective of Smith, we can conclude that the innovations for transparency are ethically acceptable as long as actors are really free to choose the product in order to serve their own interests. In general, this seems to be the case in The Circle. In the transparent world envisioned by The Circle, everyone would use the information for his or her own interest; a disabled person will be able to "experience" mountain biking via *SeeChange*, a student will use information and fora about the financial system to prepare for his exam, a researcher will use the health data of users to search for patterns and generate research output. One can argue, however, that this approach does not consider the indirect consequences: "As more people embrace this track-and-share mentality, those who refuse to participate in this great party will bear the brunt of the social costs" (Morozov, 2014: p. 242).

From a utilitarian perspective, the ethical acceptability of innovations for transparency is dependent on their contribution to the greater good. One can argue, for instance, that the ethical behaviour of people is dependent on personal characteristics (e.g. age, gender, culture, integrity or personal values) and situational factors (moral intensity, moral framing, authority, rewards) (Crane and Matten, 2010). In cases where these personal characteristics and situational factors of individual actors are transparent to society, we can expect a change in people's actual ethical behaviour (Bentley, O'Brien and Brock, 2014). This seems to be the assumption in The Circle as well; *if* everyone *could* be watched, "it would lead to a more moral way of life" (Eggers 2013: p. 292). If all information about a person is public, unacceptable behaviour will decrease while acceptable behaviour will increase. Because of this impact of the innovations for transparency on the greater good by more ethical behaviour in our society, one could argue that these innovations are ethically acceptable from a utilitarian perspective. The Circle's plea for full transparency as a means to prevent socially harmful behaviour reflects the same approach that informs the so-called Situational Crime Prevention (SCP) movement: the way to suppress crime is to create an environment which makes it virtually impossible to commit crimes in the first place, e.g. by installing cameras everywhere and also by maximally exploiting the opportunities offered by social media. However, critics argue that this would not only suppress crime but also the possibilities for people to grow into genuinely honest and moral citizens (Morozov, 2014: pp. 190–199).

A Kantian perspective provides another assessment of the ethical acceptability of the innovations of The Circle. According to Kant, people should act on principles that can be seen as universally valid, and in which humanity is treated as an end in itself instead of a means. From this perspective, people should act out of a sense of duty or principle and not only in their own interest or because of an external cause. This Kantian perspective qualifies, first of all, the importance of transparency of the actual behaviour of moral actors, because more weight is given to the moral principles one embraces. From a Kantian perspective, one can expect that full transparency of ones behaviour will not cause a change in ethical behaviour; this change is only caused by embracing universal principles. Moreover, one can argue that the innovations for transparency are ethically unacceptable from a Kantian perspective, because they treat humanity not as an end but as a means. Furthermore, one can question whether The Circle acts on principles that are universally valid. They would like their principles to become universally valid and eliminate people who oppose their principles. But at the start of the company, it is not universally held that "privacy is theft" by society.

The dependency of the ethical acceptability of the innovations for transparency on the ethical perspective one takes makes two things clear. First, that these innovations are in fact acceptable from some ethical perspectives. Second, that the applicability of the criterion of ethical acceptability is problematic to assess whether an innovation can be considered responsible or not (cf. Rene von Schomberg, 2013). The Circle assumes a utilitarian perspective, as we have seen, and in this respect, we can understand why, at least according to the company itself, their innovations for transparency are ethically acceptable.

Conclusions regarding transparency as an outcome of responsible innovation

If we look at transparency as an outcome of innovation, we can conclude that it can indeed be considered "responsible". It addresses, at least to a certain extent, sustainability; it is societally desirable and it is ethically acceptable according to the utilitarian perspective. But although The Circle makes a strong case for transparency as a hallmark of responsible innovation, most people will feel uncomfortable with this conclusion. And this intuition is legitimate: it provides a first indication of the insufficiency of the substantive approach of RI. The primary point we wanted to make clear in this section is that the application of the three criteria for more responsible innovations at the product level is at least insufficient to assess whether an innovation deserves to be qualified as fully "responsible". We therefore agree with Stilgoe, Owen and Macnaghten (2013) that the discussion about the normative ends of responsible innovation is important, but that the focus should be more on the means governing the innovation *process*. Let us therefore move on to another approach which is more process oriented.

Procedurally responsible innovation

In the previous section, we showed that the substantive approach of responsible innovation can lead to "good" outcomes, if we look at sustainability, societal desirability and ethical acceptability, but can still be considered "controversial". This subsequently raises the question of whether a procedural approach can lead to better results. Examples of authors that rely on deliberation, such as Habermas (1984) and Rawls (1971; 1993), embrace such a procedural approach (Pellé and Reber, 2014). In the procedural approach, the norms of responsible innovation are not predetermined. On the contrary, they ensue from the communicational capacities of the actors involved and from the process of deliberation itself.

Pellé and Reber (2014) mention the framework of Owen et al. (2013) as an example of such a procedural approach in responsible innovation, in which the capacity to change and shape the direction of the innovation is based on the responsiveness of actors to public demands and changes in the environment. This capacity to be responsive can be achieved by including societal actors in the innovation process and by fostering deliberation among them. This is also beneficial for anticipating future impacts and (negative) outcomes of the innovation process. Being responsive then results in a continuous reflexive decision-making process that enables an "informed incremental response" (Guston and Sarewitz 2002).

In this section, we will discuss whether the procedural approach of responsible innovation is present in the case of The Circle, by analysing whether the four dimensions of Owen et al. (2013) – anticipation, reflexivity, inclusion and deliberation and responsiveness – can be recognized in the case of The Circle. This helps us to analyse and assess whether their innovations can qualify as being responsible according to this approach.

Anticipation

Anticipation in responsible innovation means to consider the impacts, both intended and unintended, that an innovation can have. The scope of anticipation in RI theory thus goes beyond what could be (un)intended or (un)desirable impacts that are related to the function of an innovation, but also which effects it could have in economic, social and environmental domains (Owen et al., 2013). Proper anticipation requires innovators to take an approach that forces them to consider and reflect on an innovation and various scenarios that might play out in the future. It is not possible to predict the effects of an innovation in a future world, but it calls for a systematic way of thinking that leaves room to reconsider negative aspects of an innovation and, in the end, to abandon a project altogether (Owen et al., 2013).

Methodologies like foresight, constructive technology assessment and scenario thinking can be used, while simultaneously asking questions like: "What if" and "what else might happen?". However, these answers should not be used for prediction but more for exploration and discussion. As such, it is a useful input for reflexivity (Owen et al., 2013). But proper anticipation can be hard for companies. This can be due to the fact that organizational routines are often based on interpretations of the past, rather than on anticipations of the future (Velamuri and Dew, 2010). Difficulties can also ensue from a technology push or policy pull, neglecting ethical principles or lacking precautionary measures (Owen et al., 2013).

But to what extent is The Circle engaged in anticipating future impacts during their innovation process? The answer is that they are rather inconsistent regarding the assessment of future impacts of their own innovations and activities. An example of how they did not anticipate negative impacts is when an employee tested her own innovation, the *Pastperfect*. This is a program that has the ability to go through your family tree and cross-reference it with every document, photo or video that exists about your family to see what they did and who they were, as far back as the archives go. The employee is devastated when finding out that her ancestors were slave owners and that her parents refrained from helping a man drowning in front of their eyes. This information would become public in the next day. It seems ironic, in a sense, that she is the one to suffer from the consequences of not identifying the risks of the program at an earlier stage. It is safe to say that the board members of The Circle do not anticipate negative impacts. In fact, they are focused on meeting the right impact – total transparency – but do not think about negative or problematic events or circumstances that might affect the road leading to total transparency. Furthermore, one can question whether they engage in certain processes for doing the right thing or whether it is just for attaining customer satisfaction. The founding father of the first innovations by The Circle finally says that it was never his intention to achieve total transparency by the innovations developed in his firm. He just wanted to know whether his first invention was able to work (Eggers, 2013: p. 485). It is precisely this type of behaviour of engineers, who may be more interested in whether a new technology actually *works* than in its societal consequences in the future, that the call for anticipation and technology assessment is legitimized.

While scenario-thinking about future impacts is not included in the innovation process, the testing of customer satisfaction is widespread. Some evaluations and tests are done during the product presentation with employees or customers outside the campus of The Circle. However, it remains unclear whether this is done for customer satisfaction purposes alone or whether it is also done for reaching the right impacts. All in all, however, it is safe to say that there is a lack of attention to possible negative impacts at The Circle. If they do notice negative impacts, they are neglected or seen as "collateral damage". In other situations, they do anticipate well, but from a business perspective – assessment of customer satisfaction – and not from a responsible innovation perspective, i.e. anticipating possible negative social or ethical impacts together with stakeholders inside and outside the firm.

Reflexivity

Where anticipation is more focused on the object of innovation – i.e. the product and outcomes of the innovation – reflexivity is more about the subject who is innovating (i.e. the firm, the RandD department or employee). Reflexivity describes the need for organizations to not only consider their activities as integral to the organization, but to take a wider perspective on their role in society and consider their activities as part of society (Owen et al. 2013). Theory says that a company should hold a mirror to its own activities, commitments and assumptions, while acknowledging that certain goals are not universally held (Owen et al. 2013). Reflexivity also requires an awareness of the limits of one's knowledge. Organizations do not have access to all the information necessary and have to be aware that the knowledge within the firm is subjective. In order to innovate responsibly towards society, companies should reflect upon the values and motivations underlying their activities (Owen et al., 2012).

Gianni and Goujon (2014) go more into detail regarding the concept of reflexivity. They argue that the actor's cognitive framing (certain pre-conceptions and visions of the world) affects how they conceive situations and subsequently determine their decisions when facing ethical issues. They state, therefore, that "at a cognitive level, in order to conceive in a more appropriate way our relation to the context, we need to introduce the possibility for the agents to be reflexive and to revise not only their judgments, but also the way in which they size and understand the problem" (Gianni and Goujon, 2014: p. 72). This reflexivity consists of two parts, namely a part that is primarily about reflecting on one's own actions, strategies and decisions (first-order thinking) and a part that is about reflection on one's principles, values and value systems that determine the way we act (second-order thinking). In other words, the second-order reflexivity determines the first-order reflexivity.

Therefore, next to the fact that we look at The Circle and try to understand to what extent they reflect on their own strategies, actions and decisions, we also look whether they are aware of the way their values and principles frame and affect their own strategies, decisions and actions. "Actors [should] not only reflect on the adequacy of their norms and values, but also on the way in which they construct these norms and values. These norms and values can be focused on what is right – or false- (epistemic norms) or what is good, just or evil, unjust" (Gianni and Goujon, 2014: p. 73).

To what extent, then, is The Circle reflexive? The Circle engages (to some extent) in first-order reflexivity but does not engage in second-order reflexivity. An example is the case where an employee is being criticized for not sharing an experience. This is an example of first-order reflexivity, because they reflect on the ethical impact of employee behaviour: the deprivation of opportunities for others (a disabled person for instance) to experience (the experience of canoeing for instance). They reflect on the question of why they should share such information. When the company has to deal with negative impacts of its innovations (people fleeing from the transparent world they help to create, employees suffering from the innovations of the company etc.), however, they say that the end justifies the means *without any further reflexion on the topic*. Only by the end of the book, in the phase in which full transparency is almost reached, the founder of the firm reflects and says: "I didn't expect any of this to happen. And it is moving too fast [...] it is far beyond what I had in mind when I started this" (Eggers, 2013: p. 485). However, at that point, it is already too late and he has already lost control over his innovation.

With regard to second-order reflexivity, we can say that reflexivity is not part of the innovation process of The Circle. Gianni and Goujon (2014) say that actors should become aware of the fact that their knowledge is subjective and that their actions, decisions and views also result from the way they frame reality. It seems that The Circle only looks for technological innovations that need to fix ethical issues. This can be due to the fact that the frame of The Circle is narrowed by the fact that it is a technological company. Their world view is that technologies that enhance transparency will solve the problems of unethical behaviour in the world. In situations in which they are, in fact, reflexive, they primarily seem to justify their actions, decisions and world views, instead of taking a critical stance towards these issues. But we cannot claim that The Circle does not reflect on future impacts. Based on their utilitarian perspective on the innovations of The Circle, they do reflect and justify their decisions and actions. If we do not accept this position as "responsible", we should argue that being truly reflective does not only involve "reflection" but also a critical view towards oneself (cf. Blok, 2014). Incorporating different and even opposing views can help to develop such a critical stance. This is key in the dimension of inclusion and deliberation, which is explored in the next section.

Inclusion and deliberation

One of the most important aspects of responsible innovation is the inclusion of societal actors in the innovation process. Inclusion moves beyond involving just stakeholders and is about including the wider public as well. Blok (2014) mentions three reasons why inclusion of societal actors is essential for responsible innovation. First is because of the high complexity of the problems that innovations address and the uncertainties of the future impact of these innovations. Active involvement of stakeholders with conflicting interests and value frames is demanded in order to better understand these challenges and the risks and uncertainties involved (cf. Bellucci et al. (2002); Bulkeley and Mol (2003); Chilvers (2008)). Second, stakeholder engagement enables actors to learn from each other, which helps them to achieve shared objectives and decisions, and to set desired directions for future technology developments (cf. Andriof and Waddock (2002); Bulkeley and Mol (2003); Chilvers (2008); Gould (2012)). Third, because the responsibility and resources to deal with the grand challenges are allocated to different societal spheres – government, civil society and the private sector – the solution of these grand challenges requires the active involvement of multiple stakeholders (Blok 2014).

Deliberation is about opening up visions, purposes, questions and dilemmas through processes of dialogue, engagement and debate with multiple stakeholders (Owen et al. 2013). Companies can make more deliberative choices, which benefits responsible innovation. Where inclusion is about involving societal actors in the innovation process, deliberation is about the exchange of quality arguments and opinions and becoming conscious about the different frames that actors have. Pellé and Reber (2014) mention that there are two ways of exchanging information, opinions etc., namely consultation and co-construction. The consultation approach argues that "the legitimacy of technological development comes from the possibility for social actors to express their values and value systems. To avoid market failures and the backlash of innovation, consulting end-users and other stakeholders is an essential step" (Pellé and Reber, 2014: p. 38). It allows the public to co-manage the risks but still places the implementation of the responsible behaviour with experts. On the other hand, the co-construction approach calls for participation and deliberation to co-produce technology where innovators "are responsive towards social actors' value whereas the latter understand and take into account the imperatives and constraints of innovators and researchers" (Pellé and Reber, 2014: p. 39). Moreover, it allows for "incremental adjustment of science and innovation to address social norms and values, as science and innovation actually occur" (Owen et al., 2013: p. 41). Inclusion and deliberation are thus two different aspects and combining the two can be hard to manage. Furthermore, it is hard to manage deliberation when there are actors with opposing interests, and different power and epistemological backgrounds (Blok and Lemmens, 2015).

The Circle is highly engaged in inclusion activities and involves an incredible number of actors in their innovation processes. For example, they involve politicians in their innovation process by testing prototypes. Employees also test similar technologies. One can think of the health bracelet for keeping track of medical data, which results in the prevention of health issues instead of their cure. Not only employees, but also their friends and family members, are involved in testing the new technologies. However, innovations are also tested on societal actors who are unaware or not willing to participate. In all cases, however, The Circle determines under which conditions actors are involved. And people are mainly involved in tests in order to assess the market acceptance and/or product failures, rather than for the reasons found in the stakeholder engagement for responsible innovation literature.

Next to the question of who is included in the innovation process, it is also important to look at when they are included. Literature suggests that this has to be achieved already from the start of the innovation process (von Schomberg, 2013). However, this is certainly not the case in The Circle. Furthermore, most employees are not even aware of their company's own innovations, since they are notified on the day of launch most of the time. The Circle is therefore only inclusive at the final stages of the innovation process, mainly with the purpose of assessing market acceptance instead of the co-construction of innovations together with society. The difficulty with this is that the shape and direction of innovation processes are then hard, if not impossible, to adjust.

The Circle does a tremendous job in announcing its latest product launches by organizing Dream Fridays, which are broadcasted across the globe. The general public has the opportunity to respond in real time to the latest innovations by The Circle by sending messages and/or "smiles/frowns", which is similar to the "likes" of Facebook. However, the purpose of this seems more to receive feedback on innovation adoption than to open up The Circle's vision, purpose, questions or dilemmas. In this respect, the involvement of employees and other actors can be considered as market intelligence activities, rather than aiming for inclusion and deliberation. Therefore, it is safe to say that deliberation is absent during the innovation process of The Circle. Moreover, because of the sheer volume of data that is being created on a daily basis in the fictional world of The Circle, critical arguments can quickly become a voice in the wilderness. In this respect, the way that The Circle responds to its customers does not promote a balanced discussion. An example of this is related to the implementation of TruYou: "TruYou changed the internet, *in toto*, within a year. Though some sites were resistant at first, and free-internet advocates shouted about the right to be anonymous online, the TruYou wave was tidal and crushed all meaningful opposition" (Eggers, 2013: p. 22). There is a problematic distribution of power between the involved stakeholders where The Circle can individually decide how to deal with critics and stakeholders who want to deliberate. These power imbalances affect the deliberation and decision-making regarding responsible innovations (Blok and Lemmens, 2015). This can be one of the reasons why reflexivity is lacking and negative (un)expected impacts are neglected or seen as "collateral damage". The company lives in their own bubble of "doing good" while neglecting critical voices.

Responsiveness

Responsiveness in terms of RI refers to the idea that the corporation has the capacity to "change [the] shape or direction in response to stakeholder and public values and changing circumstances" (Stilgoe et al., 2013: p. 5). In that sense, responsiveness uses the aforementioned dimensions as a basis to act upon and sets "the direction and influence the subsequent trajectory and pace of innovation" (Owen et al., 2013: p. 38), while being aware of insufficient knowledge and control at the same time (Stilgoe et al., 2013). To be truly responsive, this process should be an iterative and open one that stimulates learning and adaptation (Owen et al. 2013). Responsiveness is "an encompassing yet substantially neglected dimension of responsibility" (Pellizzoni, 2004: p. 557, cited in Stilgoe et al., 2013). One should be able to adjust the courses of innovation while at the same time being aware that there can be insufficient knowledge and control.

The founder of The Circle, one of the current board members, says, in the end, that he had not intended the ideal of total transparency to be realized and that he had lost control over the process. This shows that the inventor of the innovation does not have the capacity anymore to be responsive at a certain moment. However, this is different from responsiveness of the company itself. The Circle is a rich company with dynamic capabilities. They have the capacity to be responsive from a resource-based view of the firm. However, when there is no deliberation, and thus no opening up of visions, purposes or dilemmas, it is hard to be responsive to other values and changing environments. Furthermore, they do not identify, and in some instances even neglect, negative outcomes. Therefore, it seems that The Circle does not see the need to be responsive to other, sometimes opposing, views and opinions. It also shows that a lack of engagement in other dimensions makes it impossible to be truly responsive.

Conclusion

In section 2, we studied the substantive approach to responsible innovation. There, we concluded that The Circle meets the requirements regarding the outcomes of responsible innovation, at least to a certain extent, while at the same time, one feels unease about certain activities they undertake. We subsequently looked into a procedural approach on responsible innovation in section 3 in order to determine whether The Circle innovates in a responsible way.

Although the outcomes of their innovation process seem to be sustainable, desirable and ethically acceptable, and in that sense can be considered "responsible", we conclude that The Circle does not meet the requirements for a proper responsible innovation process. Even though their innovation process is inclusive (in its later stages), The Circle does not reflect upon their cognitive frame which influences their decision-making regarding actions to be taken and strategies to follow (second-order reflexivity). This closely relates with the fact that they do not foster deliberation and they do not allow critical voices in their innovation process. Their reflexivity is not accompanied by a critical stance toward their own values, visions etc. This also means that they are not responsive toward societal actors who hold different views. In this respect, we can conclude that the innovation process of The Circle is highly in-transparent and therefore, highly ir-responsible.

There is a huge discrepancy between the outcomes of the innovations of The Circle (achieving full transparency) and the process of their innovations, which is not transparent at all. On the one hand, one can expect that increased transparency during the innovation process can help to embed responsibility in the innovation process itself. On the other hand, it is exactly the lack of transparency during the innovation process, and with this the lack of reflection, deliberation, inclusion etc., which makes the innovations of The Circle irresponsible. In case the outcomes of the innovation process of The Circle were legitimized by a transparent process of deliberation and inclusion, these innovations would really be "responsible". In this respect, the virtual case of The Circle clearly shows, first, that the substantive approach of responsible innovation is insufficient and should at least be extended with a procedural, transparency-increasing approach in order to render innovations that can really claim to be responsible.

At the same time, it will be clear by now why increasing transparency can be a perilous task for companies. Although the business model of The Circle is not elaborated upon in the book, we can understand why The Circle is not able to become fully transparent about their motives and strategies, as they invest heavily in the development of technologies and therefore need profits to cover these investments. Being transparent threatens to turn information asymmetries into information symmetries, and with this, the company's reason for existence (Blok and Lemmens, 2015). For a company, it is much easier to develop transparency-enhancing products that are sustainable, societally desirable and ethically acceptable than to develop a transparent process in which stakeholders are included. This is confirmed by research by Blok et al. (2015), who show that food companies are in fact engaged in responsible innovation for healthy food at product level, but are hesitant to engage stakeholders during the innovation process. The case of The Circle shows, second, that this difficulty may not seduce us to focus on output variables of responsible innovation alone without engaging stakeholders in a transparent and interactive innovation process (Blok et al., 2015). Although it is precisely this procedural, transparency-increasing approach that makes responsible innovation a perilous task for private companies, responsible innovation requires a combination of the substantive and procedural approach in order to claim to be responsible.

One particular way to deal with the difficulties of transparency in the private sector is to reflect on the concept of transparency itself. The presupposed concept of transparency in much of the literature is highly naïve, as scholars like Christensen and Cheney (2015) have already shown. They showed that the pursuit of transparency is often counteracted by new types of opacity and conditioned by our epistemic insufficiency. This means that the ideal of transparency or information symmetry can never be reached. On the one hand, structural information asymmetries may exactly *encourage* companies to engage stakeholders during the innovation *process*. On the other hand, structural information asymmetries will prevent these information asymmetries from turning into information symmetries and threaten the competitive advantage of innovative companies. However, the further elaboration of a proper concept of transparency and its role in responsible innovation in the private sector is beyond the scope of this chapter.

Notes

1 See www.sunlightfoundation.com for a US-based example of an organization that seeks to make governments and politics more accountable and transparent.

2 In this, we follow another strategy to eminent scholars like Christensen and Cheney (2015). While they criticize a naïve concept of transparency because it neglects the existence of ambiguity and opacity and argue for a better-informed concept of transparency that acknowledges these ambiguities, we 'accept' this naïve concept in this chapter in order to assess the opportunities and limitations of this ideal in the context of responsible innovation.

References

Andriof, J. and Waddock, S. (2002). Unfolding Stakeholder Engagement. In *Unfolding Stakeholder Thinking: Theory, Responsibility and Engagement.* Sheffield: Greenleaf Publishing Limited, pp. 17–42. doi: http://dx.doi.org/10.9774/GLEAF.978-1-909493-28-5_3.

Barrett, M. A., Humblet, O., Hiatt, R. A. and Adler, N. E. (2013). Big data and disease prevention: From quantified self to quantified communities. *Big Data*, 1(3), pp. 168–175. doi:10.1089/big.2013.0027.

Bellucci, S., Bütschi, D., Gloede, Bellucci, S., Bütschi, D., Gloede, F., Hennen, L., Joss, S., Klüver, L., Nentwich, M. Peissl, W., Torgersen H., van Eijndhoven, J. and van Est, R. (2002). Analytical Framework. In: S. Joss and Bellucci, S. (Eds.), *Participatory Technology Assessment. European Perspectives.* London: University of Westminster Press, pp. 24–48.

Bentley, R. A., O'Brien, M. J. and Brock, W. A. (2014). Mapping collective behavior in the big-data era. *The Behavioral and Brain Sciences*, 37(1), pp. 63–76. doi:10.1017/S0140525X13000289.

Blok, V. (2014). Look who's talking: Responsible innovation, the paradox of dialogue and the voice of the other in communication and negotiation processes. *Journal of Responsible Innovation*, 1(2), pp. 171–190. doi:10.1080/23299460.2014.924239.

Blok, V. and Lemmens, P. (2015). The emerging concept of responsible innovation: Three reasons why it is questionable and calls for a radical transformation of the concept of innovation. In: B.-J. Koops, J. van den Hoven, H. Romijn, T. Swierstra, and I. Oosterlaken (Eds.), *Responsible Innovation, Volume 2: Concepts, Approaches, and Applications* (2nd ed., vol. 2). Dordrecht: Springer, pp. 19–35.

Blok, V. Hoffmans, L. and Wubben, E. (2015). Stakeholder engagement for industrial responsible innovation: Critical issues and management practices in the Dutch food industry. *Journal of Chains and Network Sciences* (forthcoming).

Bos, C., Walhout, B., Peine, A. and van Lente, H. (2014). Steering with big words: Articulating ideographs in research programs. *Journal of Responsible Innovation*, 1(2), pp. 151–170.

Bulkeley, H. and Mol, A. (2003). Participation and environmental governance: Consensus, ambivalence and debate. *Environmental Values*, 12(2), pp. 143–154.

Chilvers, J. (2008). Environmental risk, uncertainty, and participation: Mapping an emergent epistemic community. *Environment and Planning*, 40(2), pp. 2990–3008

Christensen, L. T. and Cheney, G. (2015). Peering into transparency: Challenging ideals, proxies, and organisational Practices. *Communication Theory*, 25(1), pp. 70–90.

Christensen, L. T. and Cornelissen, J. P. (2015). Organizational transparency as myth and metaphor. *European Journal of Social Theory*, 18(2), pp. 132–149.

Crane, A. and Matten, D. (2010). *Business Ethics: Managing Corporate Citizenship and Sustainability in the Age of Globalization* (3rd ed.). Oxford: Oxford University Press.

Eggers, D. (2013). *The Circle*. New York: Vintage Books.

Eickhoff, D. (2011). The fallacy of transparency: Why radical openness is not enough to restore democracy. *SSRN Electronic Journal*. doi:10.2139/ssrn.2304213

Florini, A. (2007). The battle of transparency. In: A. Florini (Ed.), *The Right to Know: Transparency For an Open World.* New York: Colombia UP, pp. 1–18.

Foucault, M. (1977). *Discipline and Punish: The Birth of the Prison*. New York: Vintage.

Fox, J. (2007). The uncertain relationships between transparency and accountability. *Development in Practice*, 17(4/5), pp. 663–671.

Garsten, C. and de Montoya, M. L. (2008). *Transparency in a New Global Order*. Cheltenham: Edward Elgar.

Gianni, R. and Goujon, P. (2014). *Construction of an Analytical Grid* (p. 102). Retrieved from http://www.great-project.eu/deliverables_files/deliverables02. Last accessed 09-05-2018.

Gould, R. W. (2012). Open innovation and stakeholder engagement. *Journal of Technology Management and Innovation*, 7(3), pp. 1–11. doi: http://dx.doi.org/10.4067/S0718-27242012000300001.

Guston, D. H. and Sarewitz, D. (2002). Real-time technology assessment. *Technology in Society*, 24(1–2), pp. 93–109. doi:10.1016/S0160-791X(01)00047-1.

Habermas, J. (1984). *Theory of Communicative Action Volume One: Reason and the Rationalization of Society*. Boston: Beacon Press.

Lanier, J. (2014). *Who Owns the Future?* London: Penguin Books.

Menéndez-Viso, A. (2009). Black and white transparency: Contradictions of a moral metaphor. *Ethics and Information Technology*, 11(2), pp. 155–162. doi:10.1007/s10676-009-9194-x.

miiCard.org. (2015). *Online Identity Verification Service*. Available at: http://www.miiCard.org (accessed 16 May 2015).

Morozov, E. (2014). *To Save Everything, Click Here*. London: Penguin Books.

Owen, R., Stilgoe, J., Macnaghten, P., Gorman, M., Fisher E. and Guston, D. (2013). A Framework for Responsible Innovation. In: R. Owen, Bessant, J. and Heintz, M. (Eds.) (2013). *Responsible Innovation. Managing the Responsible Emergence of Science and Innovation in Society*. Hoboken (NJ): John Wiley and Sons Ltd, pp. 27–50.

Owen, R., Macnaghten, P. and Stilgoe, J. (2012). Responsible research and innovation: From science in society to science for society, with society. *Science and Public Policy*, 39(6), pp. 751–760. doi:10.1093/scipol/scs093.

Pellé, S. and Reber, B. (2013). *Theoretical Review* (No. 2.2), draft (p. 114). Available at: http://www.great-project.eu/deliverables_files/deliverables03. Last accessed 09-05-2018.

Pellé, S. and Reber, B. (2014). *Responsible Innovation Models Report* (p. 70). Available at: http://www.great-project.eu/research/Responsible_Innovation_Model_Report_version forsubmission.docx. Last accessed 09-05-2018.

Pellizzoni, L. (2004). Responsibility and environmental governance. *Environmental Politics*, 13(3), 541–565. doi:10.1080/0964401042000229034.

Rawlins, B. (2009). Give the emperor a mirror: Toward developing a stakeholder measurement of organizational transparency. *Journal of Public Relations Research*, 21(1), pp. 71–99.

Rawls, J. (1971). *A Theory of Justice*. Cambridge: Belknap Press of Harvard University Press.

Rawls, J. (1993). *Political Liberalism: The John Dewey Essays in Philosophy, 4*. New York: Columbia University Press.

Roberts, J. (2009). No one is perfect: The limits of transparency and an ethic for 'intelligent' accountability. *Accounting, Organizations and Society*, 34, pp. 957–970.

Stilgoe, J., Owen, R. and Macnaghten, P. (2013). Developing a framework for responsible innovation. *Research Policy*, 42(9), pp. 1568–1580. doi:10.1016/j.respol.2013.05.008.

Sutcliffe, H. (2011). *A report on Responsible Research and Innovation*. Available at: http://www.diss.unimi.it/extfiles/unimidire/243201/attachment/a-report-on-responsible-research-innovation.pdf. Last accessed 09-05-2018.

Van Dijck, J. (2013). *The Culture of Connectivity: A Critical History of Social Media*, New York: Oxford University Press.

Velamuri, S. R. and Dew, N. (2010). Evolutionary processes, moral luck, and the ethical responsibilities of the manager. *Journal of Business Ethics*, 91(1), pp. 113–126. doi:10.1007/s10551-009-0071-7.

Von Schomberg, R. (2013). A vision of responsible research and innovation. In: R. Owen, Bessant, J. and Heintz, M. (Eds.), *Responsible Innovation: Managing the Responsible Emergence of Science and Innovation in Society*. Hoboken: John Wiley and Sons Ltd, pp. 51–74.

Witness.org. (2015). *Cameras Everywhere Leadership Program*. Available at: http://www3.witness.org/cameras-everywhere [accessed 16 May 2015].

Zuckerberg, M. (2010). "I know that people don't want privacy. Interview with Marc Zuckerberg", *CNET*, January 2010. Available at: https://www.cnet.com/news/zuckerberg-i-know-that-people-dont-want-privacy/.

11 From responsible-innovation to innovation-*care*

Beyond constraints, a holistic approach of innovation

Xavier Pavie

Introduction: Innovation, responsibility and care

When François Rabelais wrote in the 16th century in *Pantagruel* his famous sentence "Science without consciousness is nothing but the death of the soul" (Rabelais 1854: p. 107), was he aware that five centuries later it would still be a topical question? Was it an early attempt to fight the modernity his century would enter with Descartes, his almost-contemporary? Whatever it was, if we look at the environment we live in today, we cannot deny that he had a vision. Electronics have invaded our everyday life with the objects through which we communicate, the 'digitalization of the world' is becoming a major stake and nanotechnologies are going to be everywhere, whether in food or in clothes. And it seems that it is only the beginning, considering the progress to come both in the exploitation of the human body and in its avatars, in terms of trivialized automatons.

In the meantime, these new technologies or these new ways to communicate have been related to the development of democratic movements in the countries where freedom of expression is limited. Besides, medical headways supported by technology are naturally praised by their beneficiaries. We could thus study the notion of innovation by using the famous term *deinon*. This term is difficult to translate because of its polysemy. It means both the ideas of the terrible and of the admirable which unite to say the power of opposite. Sophocles in *Antigone* illustrated this idea by the example of the man who has "resources, whose ingenuous skill is above all expectations, he moves sometimes towards evil, sometimes towards good" (Sophocles 1955: p. 86). But men, individuals, are those who innovate; they are the ones who can choose in which direction they want innovation to direct innovation: "sometimes towards evil, sometimes towards good", consciously or not. The responsibility to choose between 'to make or not to make' is finally borne by innovators. Nevertheless, the very word 'responsible' can take on several meanings, including an everyday acceptance. What does 'responsibility' mean today? For whom? For what? To which extent?

The unprecedented rise of technology and of its power occurs in a context of globalization which keeps on accelerating. Human beings henceforth have to assume their responsibility of the world and in the world. The innovator is particularly more concerned by the responsibility of the world to come. It is by its novelties, its launches of products and services that the face of the world is outlined. Thus it is appropriate to talk about responsible-innovation. It's necessary to question the role of responsibility in innovation one more time and to underline that it has a unique stake: taking care of humanity.

That is the reason why we suggest to focus in the first part on the fundamental question of responsibility by underlining, as Marc Neuberg suggest, that the responsibility of innovation remains in the consideration of situation within a value system shared by all the actors impacted by innovation (Neuberg 1997). We shall then describe what 'responsible-innovation' may be. It will also be the moment to point out criticisms concerning the wrong understanding or, more exactly, the shades of meaning of responsibility. As a result, we shall opt for a proposition which, it seems to us, casts a new light on the issue that every innovation has to deal with: the individual. That is why we shall use the notion of *care.* Having defined this term, we shall explore the meaning of 'innovation-*care*', its principles and its uses for society, for the company and for the innovator. In a conclusive moment, we shall be careful not to lose sight of the very essence of innovation according to Schumpeter: the economic performance (Schumpeter 1934; 1939).

The need for responsibility of the innovator

About the importance of responsibility

By its nature, innovation cannot be predicted. Even if a lot of surveys and market-studies are made before a new product or a new service is launched, there is no denying that it is only once the product is on the market that its outcome can be known. When Schumpeter described innovation, he particularly underlined this aspect: innovation occurs when the product is launched on the market and attracts enough customers to become significantly profitable (Schumpeter 1934; 1939).

This situation of uncertainty is the basis on which a lot of studies are made and thrive, aiming at reducing failures. Paradoxically enough, few people wonder about the consequences of this uncertainty, should it be successful or not (Nowotny 2015). Yet it is this very uncertain feature which gives birth to the stakes of responsible-innovation, whose essence is to question the consequences of an innovation.

In the recent financial crisis, the banking innovation was held responsible for the economic fall. And today, new topics on 'responsible-innovation' are often to be found in the media. This notion, which is both comforting and seemingly moral, aims at reassuring the customers about both the morals of their supplier and the security of the financial product they are offered. Yet if the popularizing and everyday acceptance of the expression appeared during the financial crisis, the 'responsible-innovation' theme appeared in Europe in 2004 through the French association Vivagora. Vivagora's purpose is to reflect on a new relation between society and innovation while keeping people and their quality of life at the core of its research.[1]

The understanding of the notion 'responsible-innovation' leaves room for a large number of interpretations. Its evolution is deeply rooted in the topic of the social responsibility of the firm whose stake is about the firm's basics, especially innovation, but not exclusively so. The stake of the social responsibility of the firm has, in fact, little to do with innovation. As it is mostly concerned with short- and middle-term issues, social responsibility cannot highlight the specificities of innovation, nor even mention its uncertain outcome. The social responsibility of firms mostly deals with the present time and the close future, but also, and mostly, with what it can forecast (Porter and Kramer 2011). And the very essence of innovation lies in its uncertainty: in the uncertainty of its results, of its outcomes on the market, of its uses etc.

Responsibility, a new dimension in the innovation world

We can only determine 'responsible-innovation' in parallel with the notion of progress, that is to say, the permanent desire of people to 'progress' towards a goal that is profitable for the individuals. It is only when we think in those terms that Descartes' sentence, which made the 16th century enter modernity and progress – in other words the race for innovation, can reach the full extent of its meaning: we, people, "have to render ourselves the lords and possessors of nature" (Descartes 2008: p. 168). This opinion, which was justified in the 16th century – all the more so because it was concerned with protecting people's health[2] (Faye 2005) – has rarely been questioned. The race for progress and innovation, which thrived on economic development, has kept increasing its speed[3] (Carlson 2002).

Even if this dimension became more tangible at the time, it dates back to the Ancient World. To quote two significant examples, one can think about the quest for immortality in the *Epopee of Gilgamesh* or the quest for the fountain of youth and for the elixir of immortality (Bostrom, 2005). Among the French philosophers of the 18th, we can quote Condorcet, who suggested to use the future outcomes of medical sciences to create an endless human life (Condorcet, 1988). Benjamin Franklin, whose phantasm was to be able to interrupt and start life again, showed similar interests (Franklin, 1956). It is also to be remembered that the great theorist of evolution, Charles Darwin, underlined that chances were that humankind, as we know it today, had not reached the end of its evolution, and was rather at its very beginning (Darwin, 2003).

Finally, Nietzsche, in the 19th century, was just the heir of these philosophers when he wrote about the "will for power" (Nietzsche 2003: p. 87) whose meaning was to "reach more essence". According to him, there is always a taste for power, which can be seen everywhere. However, it can take several forms or functions according to individuals or bodies.

The point of these philosophers is about 'progress', and whether it should be related to knowledge or to science (Kant, 1998). The notion of progress has been studied for a long time in close connection with medical headways or questions related to the conservation, creation and extension of human life. We shall not forget Paracelsus, who kept experimenting with the 'chemical' reproduction of life in the 15th century (Bensaude-Vincent, 2001). Even if religion has always limited some possibilities of progress, regarding the reproduction of life, for instance, the scientists had neither the knowledge nor the ability to realize such ambitious projects. But for the last ten or twenty years, the rhythm of medical progress has clearly become faster with the discovery of genetics and the DNA structures, and the first attempts to clone animals. The issue lies no longer in the ability of science to realize a project; it is now in the concerns of ethics and responsibilities regarding the choice between doing or not doing.[4]

Innovation, the daughter of progress, has kept developing while trying to improve or to ease all aspects of the lives of individuals, their conservation as well as their well-being. It has been helped in this particular area by the development and the progress of technology, which has enabled people to develop lots of products and services whose existence was pure fantasy less than a century ago. Today, for instance, 'transhumanism' has become a will whose public stake is the improvement of the human condition through techniques. These techniques, for instance, aim at ending old age and increasing our intellectual, psychological and bodily capacities.[5] The theorists of transhumanism, especially Raymond Kurzweil, highlight the fact that the rhythm of technological change is becoming faster, and that the next fifty years will witness both technological breakthroughs and a technological singularity which will deeply and definitely transform human nature (Kurzweil 1999). Even if those in favor of transhumanism show the possible risks stemming from the rise of new techniques and technologies, they are deeply convinced that the benefits are bigger than the risks, especially in terms of fighting poverty, sickness, disabilities, lack of food and dictatorships. The improvement of the quality of life of individuals being the ultimate goal, those theorists only see, in the concept of 'nature', something unclear and hampering progress (Bostrom and Sanders 2008).

These last dimensions cast a new light on the risks and threats to human values. There is, today, a new context which brings into line the modern period we live in and the quest for a sustainable and responsible development. Thanks to the progress of science and technology, we can understand the complexity and the exploitation of the world. These developments make way for a lot of actions which imply ethical, social and citizenship-related concerns. Yet the successes and uses originating from these developments result in new risks whose consequences cannot be foreseen, should they be successes or give birth to new behaviors. Responsibility should thus be given a new common acceptance, because it appears that "nowadays we are responsible, or at least responsible together, for common actions whose development and effects remain unknown; the circle of closeness which made me feel duty-bound only towards the close future and my neighbor is broken, just like the link of simultaneity which made me responsible for the present effects, or the effects directly inferring from the actions I made today" (Ost 1995: p. 267).

The way we think about being responsible and being careful evolves, because we act in a different manner to thirty years ago. Responsibility remains the property of individuals, but it spreads to all of society. It can now be devolved to a man, but not only to him. Moreover, whereas we used to think that responsibility and proximity were linked, that responsibility needed a strict boundary in space and time; it now evolves towards a time- and space-free notion with unlimited reciprocity. In other words, responsibility has to be defined more precisely because the constant journey between individual and common responsibility, which has become the norm, is as unclear as it is strongly rooted in the mindset: "Instead of personal actions easy to identify, we have to face numerous decisions which, all together, can have considerable effects. Responsibility is nowhere and everywhere. Actions have been made and decisions have been taken, whose consequences are sometimes tragic. But no one can identify who is responsible for it, unless we decide that the organizations or the network should bear it, which does not fit our intuition of responsibility. We keep thinking about it as a property of the individual", according to Jean-Louis Génard (2000, p. 105). In our opinion, it would also have made responsibility less clear.

The criteria of responsible-innovation

Three elements mentioned by Bensaude-Vincent[6] (2009) can help to determine what a responsible-innovation may be. We have to mention that if these can be studied together, they have to be clearly distinguished from one another in the meantime. The first one emphasizes the fact that, in the world today, every firm is – righteously – obsessed with listening to their customers, so that they will be able to meet their needs. Responsible-innovation questions this dimension by wondering if a new need should systematically be met. Should a firm systematically launch an innovation which allows it to meet a need just discovered? In other words, it's not because there is a need that an innovation must be launched. Should innovation strategies do everything they can to meet a new need? Should we launch an internet service which automatically does the student's homework because they do not want to do it?[7] Should we organize trips dedicated to special sexual desires because a part of the population has special sexual desires?[8]

The second aspect of responsible-innovation is a blatant fact: innovators cannot calculate or predict all the consequences of the products they launch. All the more so that, in the meantime, there is a race for innovation which entails quick decisions (sometimes even adopted in a hurry). As a result of the challenging business environment and of the increasing number of firms, all competitors can think about is launching their latest product on the market, whatever the consequences. The famous Ford Pinto is a telling example (Raymond 2003).

The third and last level of responsible-innovation is that innovation can result in new risks, whose consequences can impact everyday life and ways of life. This topic is of great importance and yet it is often sidelined. An innovation may have no bad consequences on the "eco-system" it is meant to reach but it can have an impact on an unforeseen target and result in some damage. In the case of launching a new more powerful, faster, and louder-sounding airplane, the consequences should not only be assessed on the members of the staff and on the customers. The damages stretch to all beings in contact with it, be they human or animal. It is the whole ecosystem around the airport which is harmed, as the *Grenelle de l'environnement* underlined, and decisions will have to be made.[9] It is the same when a car with air-conditioning is sold, because it consumes 15% more CO_2

emissions than a vehicle without this option (Gagnepain 2005). Carbon emissions will affect not only the driver, but also the man on his bicycle.

Responsible-innovation thus results in three axes, three questions that we repeat hereafter: Should a new need always be met? Do we really know the full extent of the consequences of the innovation once it is available on the market? Will this very same innovation have consequences on the ecosystem within which it will evolve?

From responsibility to care

Common misunderstandings about the meaning of 'responsibility'

The previous elements underline what responsible-innovation can be, that is to say, an innovation stemming from a client's need, a solution developed by the firm, an institution or an organization which enables it to grow with profit while being aware of the possible damages to society in the short, middle and long term.

Yet 'responsible-innovation' seems to face too many limits, resulting in an impossible understanding of the notion, and thus in an impossible implementation of it within the structures of innovative organizations.

The first point deals with responsibility as part of innovation. Who is responsible for the innovation in terms of implementation? Who 'has to account for its decisions', as the Latin etymology *respondere* suggests? Especially concerning suggestions about new products or services? In other words, who decides? This question is very important when it comes to analysis of the recent development of working groups firms have set up. The first consequence of these working groups is the dilution of responsibility (Baber 1983). We know that the dilution of responsibility in general, and of responsibility as part of innovation in particular, always results in a careless assessment of consequences. We obviously feel less concerned by the impact of innovation when it's not well defined who in the management chain makes decisions (Baber 1983). Responsibility can only be approached when one chairs an entire item – even a small one – and not only a part of it.

Secondly, responsible-innovation is often shown as hampering innovation. Just as much as 'innovation' is characterized by development, growth, headway and progress, 'responsible' is a synonym of brakes, slow motion and patience. Because one may have 'to account for' what he did, the rhythm of the innovation automatically has to be slower. The fear of bearing responsibility for one's acts is an incentive to a wait-and-see policy, should it be because of a lack of courage or because of a will to avoid problems.

The third point is the common acceptance of the term 'responsible'. For what and for whom would an innovation be responsible? We could imagine a responsible-innovation dedicated to the sole preservation of the stakes of the shareholders. If so, the actions implemented would not matter. What is the object of responsibility? Is it the preservation of the generations to come? Or the current generations? Is responsibility about groups, communities or individuals? These questions have to be raised, all the more so as the word 'responsibility' dates back to the 18th century and also covers the notion of solidarity. The evolution of this term is closely linked to the restructuration of the schemes of civil responsibility, including the prevention of risks. It is in that period that the notions of responsibility and fault broke apart, just like insurance, indemnification etc. In fact, it became a tool allowing people to assess risks more than a regulative principle of the behaviors. And yet, it had a paradoxical consequence: the "relieving responsibility of each act" (Ewald 1996: p. 86). From this moment on, "Responsibility without fault tends to lead to the weakening of responsibility. Above it, before the making of a decision, and because it results in a dilution of responsibility without allowing to question the role of the people being inquired, it turns action into an anesthesia, which is completely opposite to that of responsibility. Beneath, because it does not analyze the faults which may have existed, responsibility without fault kills the feeling of responsibility, because the person who indemnifies can openly say that 'this is not my fault'", as Laurence Engel reminds us (Engel 1997: p. 80).

In between those two steps, the substance of the responsibility of the subject has been lost, both for himself and for the others. It is thus the judiciary evolution of responsibility which rocks its very essence (Gorgoni 2006). Responsibility has a consistent meaning as long as it is an application chosen by individuals for individuals. It weakens as soon as it falls under the yoke of executive organs (Ewald 1996). François Ewald explains that "what makes us responsible is the fact that we make decisions when we are responsible for others. This dimension cannot be seized by law because law thinks responsibility in terms of norms and of the breaking of those norms. Yet we are not completely feeling responsible when we are submitted to norms. The experiment of responsibility begins with making a decision in which norms had no part" (Ewald 1996: p. 11). We can note that this dimension was the one adopted by Petersen when he underlined the space we implement in responsibility between the 'do not harm' and the 'do good' (Pedersen 2010). The question of submission to norms thus differs from doing good. Doing good is going positively beyond norms.

The last point of this criticism of the term 'responsibility' is the fact that the very notion is no longer accurate. Since the financial crisis, everything has become magically 'responsible'. From consumer credit to the latest cellphones, everything is coated with responsibility. We experienced the 'green washing' trend; it seems that the 'responsibility washing' will be its heir.

There is a need for responsible innovation but the word is no longer keeping pace with its meaning – it is too unclear and trivialized. Not only does it have a passive and defensive coloration, but it does not enable the particularities of its object to be pointed out precisely enough, and thus remains of little use.

Herbert Hart suggests that we adopt the notion of 'role-responsibility' (Hart 1968). It is an interesting idea because it characterizes the situation of one who is in charge of taking care of someone else's interests. The 'role-responsibility' refers to a meaning of the responsibility that brings into play a nexus of transverse responsibilities at the intersection of ethics and law. Nevertheless, even if the concept shows interesting aspects regarding our problematic, it seems to us that it cannot fit. Indeed, just like the notion of 'responsibility', 'role-responsibility' and what it covers in terms of 'being in charge of taking care of someone else's interests' can only deal with the preservation of the shareholder's stakes, whatever the means.

Paul Ricœur shows that the term *respondere* is often misunderstood and suggests that we replace it by *imputare*, the imputation. According to him, the notion of responsibility should be stretched towards imputation so as to increase the value of the relation with each other. Ricœur's speech almost questions responsible-innovation. He says that "the new meaning responsibility has been given in our technological period needs an orientation openly directed towards a far future, which goes beyond the time of consequences we can predict" (Ricoeur 2000). Yet imputation seems too close to juridical questions because imputation seeks the 'fault' and characterizes it for the subject, which is useful but in no way sufficient. If we were to scare innovators with imputation, the direct risk would be the slowing-down or the giving-up of every innovation. Moreover, imputation seems to focus on the past whereas we are trying to think about an innovation which is yet to come.

It is thus necessary to find a new concept, a new dimension, a new understanding which would provide us with an answer to this lack of substance. This concept should, in the meantime, enable us to understand more completely what is at stake in the relation of the individual, with himself as with someone else. In other words, the point is to think about innovation just as a means whose result would be better for the individuals, because it would take care of them. It would highlight a point which responsible-innovation does not tackle enough. Taking care of the individuals naturally leads society towards a better end. This is the reason why we suggest to use the British and American notion of *care*. This one, coupled with the notion of innovation, should enable us to reach a new paradigm, including a new conception of the innovator's role, and help us to set up a more accurate approach of what responsible-innovation should be. This paradigm could be placed under the aegis of Plato, who said in *The Republic* that the City should be established not only for "a single class of privileged citizens, to whom the possession of happiness would be granted, but so that happiness would belong to the higher number of people we can reach, to the whole State" (Plato 1950: p. 980). Thus, reformulating the Athenian, innovate-*care* is to innovate for the City while seeking not only the exceptional happiness of a single group, but happiness for as many individuals as possible, that is to say, all the City.

Emergence of the care beyond social sciences

What does care consist of?

Care can be understood as solicitude, taking care of someone or kindness (Laugier and Paperman 2008). It is the universal expression of human concern about the world we live in (Gilligan, 2008). This concept is used by sociologists, psychologists, politicians, jurists, philosophers, geographers, anthropologists, engineers and social workers. And yet, it seems important today to question its dimension within the managerial circle, especially concerning innovation (Tronto 2009).

If the concept of *care* is closely linked to the relationships between individuals, Joan Tronto, one of the most influential specialists of *care*, underlines the need for questioning the concept by institutions, cities and States (Laugier and Paperman 2008). It is a consistent project, because, for the advocates of the ethics of *care*, morals infer from everyday life experiences, and from moral problems faced by real people in their routine (Laugier and Paperman 2008). This is the reason why we think that firms should be added to this list.

In the beginning, Joan Tronto and Berenice Fischer defined *care* as "a typically human activity which includes everything we do so as to maintain, preserve or fix our 'world', aiming at living in it in the best conditions. This world includes our bodies, our individualities and our environment, because we try to mix it in a complex pattern which is the underlying basis of life" (Fisher and Tronto 1990: p. 37). Innovation associated with *care* does not completely match this definition, because every technological, scientific and economic innovation does not aim at 'fixing' the world or our bodies – even if it might have been the aim of progress. Yet, according to this definition, innovation-*care* can be partly defined as enabling to avoid what *care* tries to implement. In other words, innovation should not run the risk of destroying the world, the environment or individuals.

This definition reveals also that *care* is focused on the present time and innovation-*care* on the future. While *care* aims at taking care of the one who currently needs it, innovation-*care* aims at meeting the future needs of individuals without forgetting to care for them. We should note that this research is strongly correlated with ethics, and with responsible-innovation. In order to make it clearer, we underline that we consider ourselves as heirs of Bernard Williams, whose thesis is that the basis of ethics is to be found in Socrates' question "How should we live?"(Williams 2015). This question is a need, a demand for ethics with which philosophers try to deal when thoroughly reflecting upon ethics. This reflection is even more Socratic: by which knowledge can we reach the 'good way of life'? Innovation-*care* is based on these two pillars: first 'taking care of oneself' – *epimeleia heautou* – and secondly, ethics, which is here linked with Socrates but can also refer to Kant, as we will see later.

These details are important for our study, because from its beginning, and under the influence of Carol Gilligan, *care* was understood as an ethics, a specifically female one, for it appears first within the families – we take care of the ones who are around us and that we love without conditions –and is passed from mothers to daughters through generations. Several analyses have shown that no one is born *caring*, it is something we become (Laugier and Paperman 2008). 'Passing on' is not genetics, but it is achieved through education, and thus the gender barriers disappear. If *care* transcends genders like it transcends cultures and borders, it seems that, in the meantime, it could transcend social classes and become rooted in the economy and business management.

Innovation-care or care-innovation?

Before going further in our analysis of the notion, we need to define more accurately the two possible articulations of innovation with *care*. These possibilities can be summed up in two words: innovation-*care* and *care*-innovation. In order to grasp the meaning of these notions, we have to explain that *care* consists of four phases, according to Joan Tronto and Berenice Fisher: *caring-about* someone or something; *care-for* someone; *care-giving* to someone; and *care-receiving* (Tronto, 2009).

First, innovation associated with *care* is to be found in no less than three of the categories mentioned. An innovation can indeed aim at 'giving care to someone', such as medical innovations, for instance; it is thus *caring giving*. It is also the possibility to 'care for someone', and institutions offering services such as cleaning-ladies, help for homework and nursery-school attendants are related to this point. In these first two articulations, services or products, whose *care* is to some extent at the core of the economic offer, can be developed. And then, innovation can also be associated with *caring-about*. The point is not here to develop a new product or service. *Caring-about* deals with innovating (whatever the sector, the market, the product or the service) while caring about the individuals in society. And therefore it implies *caring-about* others. *Caring-about* must be taken as a general solution, but it is rather an answer to the consequence of innovation on the individuals. In other words, when a new banking service is launched, is it sure to care about its customers? Is there no risk that it would harm them or take them as hostages?

We must thus distinguish innovation-*care* from the notion *care*-innovation. The latter focuses more particularly on innovations whose purpose is to meet the need for care (school attendants, baby-sitters, cleaning-ladies, and so on). Innovation-*care* is thinking about individuals when assessing the consequences of innovation, and as such, it is real innovation (should it be technological, scientific or economic.) Among these different areas, the question of *care for* the others will arise and root.

Characterization of the purpose of innovation-care

The purpose of innovation-*care* is first to bring innovation back into society so it is as close to the people as it can be, because, as we said earlier, innovation is trapped within managerial circles and freed only to listen to consumers and detect commercial prospects. Innovation-*care* will, on the contrary, consider the society within which the product is to be launched, so as to enable the innovation to focus on people. We can wonder whether innovation within this framework is a return to Descartes' thought, for his will to see men "as lords and possessors of nature" (Descartes 2008) was, as we said, strongly correlated with progress for the preservation of the individual and of health.

Fields of expression of care

Care must run through a collective consciousness for Joan Tronto, because all of us benefit from it. It means that it is the attention we pay to the caring for somebody else which enables the existence of a collective *care*. Yet it raises the question of ability: What do we know about the techniques of caring for someone? What do we know about what is done for us? The movements and the will which the others give and have for us weave the preservation, coherence and even the aesthetics of our lives (Fisher and Tronto 1990). How could the manager know about caring for someone? These questions are just as accurate when it comes to innovation: What do we want for our lives? How should we answer it? What are the intentions, and is it coherent?

Innovation-*care* raises these questions once more about every form an innovation can adopt, in order to formulate them according to personal inner needs. It questions the decision to launch an innovation onto the market when its finality is opposed to, or clearly contrasting with, universal principles which have been agreed on. If the economic aspects of innovation are clearly studied by the corporate strategic services, the point here is to reflect beyond the market share this or that innovation will provide. In the end, the vulnerability of a firm does not have so much influence on its balance sheet but rather on the individuals – should they be employees, customers or citizens – who work for or benefit from it. The point is thus to innovate for the others in the same manner that we would innovate for ourselves, as Kant would have said.

Joan Tronto highlights that in *care*, there is a dyad which articulates two kinds of individuals, the *care-giver*, on the one hand, who gives the care, and the one who benefits from it on the other hand. We can see that the balance of power shifts in favor of the first one (Tronto 1994). However, it is slightly different; this superiority of the giver is to be found in the notion of innovation-*care*. Just like the innovator, the firm which innovates has power over its customers – who benefit from it and whom he/she knows, because he/she studied their needs and habits. This power, which the innovator may be tempted to abuse, is a main aspect of innovation-*care* which is written hereafter: To what extent can I exploit the weakness of someone who needs me? Let us take an extreme – but nonetheless real – example: To what extent does a weapon dealer, who innovates by creating a more effective weapon, really take into account his customer? As we know, this topic does not only deal with the extreme case of weapons, but also with products from the food and new technologies industries. To quote one but significant example, the question of the possible consequences of high-voltage electric lines remains unsolved[10] (Raoul, 2010).

The individual's spheres

This innovative environment raises the problematic of the private life *versus* the professional-one, especially for the innovator. For several years, Western firms – and governments – have been promoting the necessity of a strict boundary between one's career and citizen life, the famous *work/life balance.* The point is to enable individuals to have a personal life protected from their work. However, this policy results in a potential unawareness or voluntary denial of the consequences of each of them on the other. The fact that we want the manager to be a citizen who does not think about his work implies that we also want him to stick to his work when he is at his office; we want him to give up his citizenship and everything it implies when he enters the firm's building. The most important consequence this dichotomy implies – among others – is that the manager's main focus should be the company rather than the city. Indeed, to what extent does a manager wonder, "I have before my eyes an innovation which could be successful and thus good for the firm, its success could even enable me to get a promotion. Should I give up because it has negative impacts?" We can notice the disparity between power, concern and *care*, and this can result in several possible conflicts for the manager. How will the manager answer this question? Using his values? His morals? But values and morals are very difficult, if not impossible, to establish on a worldwide basis (Schwartz 2005). We know that moral values differ from Asia to Africa, for instance. Moreover, a man's moral sensitivity will not be the same as a woman's (Laugier and Paperman 2008). The most significant innovations in the world today transcend borders and continents. The dichotomy of manager/citizen should be explored once more. Is the separation between manager and citizen to be backed, or should we, on the contrary, articulate these two roles in order to strike a happy medium?

Responsibility within the innovation area has to be defined in another manner by listening to all its members, that is to say, a responsibility which reflects on the individuals the innovation can reach – be they customers, citizens, potential customer etc. Not only must the innovator understand that he is also a citizen, but that his/her professional sphere aims at taking care of his/her private life. This is what Empedocles tried to teach us, reformulated by Jean-François Balaudé: "There cannot be a human community fair and living in harmony if its members do not think and behave like members of the superior community of living beings" (Balaudé 2010: p. 117). In other words, innovators must always remain citizens, citizens working for the city and the community in which they fit.

The interaction between the private and professional spheres is the interdependence between manager and citizen, between innovators and innovation-benefiters as a whole. In the end, private and public spheres merge.

Competitiveness, interdependence and short-term plans

Innovation-*care* underlines the fact that we cannot pretend that we are self-sufficient, and the innovator has to accept this reality. Nonetheless, even if the state of interdependence existing between the innovator and its direct or indirect benefiters can be understood, it is often sidelined because of exogenous and endogenous corporate factors.

Exogenous conditions

Exogenous conditions hamper our understanding of the state of interdependence, and thus of innovation-*care*. They are closely linked to the economic pressure in which firms work, and especially to a globalized, strong competitiveness which results in the stressing of the innovation process. Firms must keep up with a competitive environment and a strong and perfect productivity, or they will be killed by this very same competitiveness. It seems that a kind of economic Darwinism is working, which entails a fight for economic survival and results in the elimination of the weakest.

To understand the way this works, we might want to take look at a study, conducted between September 2009 and January 2010. It interviewed 1,541 CEOs, presidents and directors of public and private organizations and firms of different sizes in 60 different countries and 33 sectors.[11]

What attracted our attention in this study were the firms pointed out as 'over-productive', especially in terms of innovation. The difference between the 'over-productive' organizations and the others was measured by their economic results in the short and long term. The indicator used was the rate of annual growth of their operating margin over a four-year term, from 2003 to 2008 for the long-term measure, and the same rate for the years 2008–2009 for the short term. This method emphasizes the over-productive organizations, the ones that managed to improve their operating margin both in the long and the short term.

We can also take notice of the fact that these 'over-productive' firms have better overcome the crisis than the others, because they built themselves in the strongest way in this economic environment, and they have kept improving.

Two specificities of these 'over-productive' firms can be identified. First, these organizations accept to bear responsibility for taking decisions in uncertainty. Indeed, 16% more of them implement reiterated processes of strategic planning, in place of a formal annual planning process. Second, they are able to make up their minds faster than the others. More exactly, 54% of them are in favor of quick decisions. Yet these are precisely the two factors which damage the responsibility of innovation and enable the negative consequences of an innovation to not be taken into account: making up one's mind in a state of uncertainty leads to risks. Being able to make up one's mind quickly is as risky as having no control over the factors and the consequences. We will not conclude immediately that being 'over-productive' means *de facto* damaging the responsibility of innovation. We would need to go into the details and analyze the innovations and process of these 'over-producers' to say such a thing. Moreover, we would need to analyze a panel of firms whose innovations can be qualified as 'responsible', and compare their production to the average in their production sector of the market and to those of the 'over-producers'.

Endogenous conditions

Endogenous factors are closely linked to the exogenous ones. They deal with two major issues. First is the fact that the duration CEOs spend in their position keeps decreasing. In the last ten years, the average lifetime of a CEO decreased by 25% (Favaro et al. 2010). When they are asked about it, CEOs answer that they have barely enough time to imagine a strategy when they come into office. Their concern and obsession must be the publication of the results to come. But this publication cannot be made separately from the announcement of a strategy, of future innovations and projects, even if they are at the very beginning of their development. They criticize what they call the syndrome of 'announcement effect' that they have to accept to reassure the market and/or the shareholders and/or their co-workers. From this moment on, no doubt is admitted, no question can be raised, even if it is the very essence of innovation to be in a state of uncertainty. In order to keep their work, these CEOs have to maintain the 'announcement effect' and guarantee the success of the innovation. This results in an explosion of the announcement effect among their competitors. The point is no longer to launch the innovation of the year but to reach fame through the announcement effect of the year, which can be measured easily by the evolution of the stock exchange's value. Because this system is difficult to stretch in the long range, the CEOs are always granted a shorter lifetime in their job. The pressure of the market and of shareholders for short-term profitability is responsible for the shorter lifetime of CEOs, who complain about their constant lack of time for implementing a concrete strategy or a range of successful innovations.

Another factor which does not stem from the firm and whose responsibility is often borne by the CEO should be mentioned. CEOs have a particularly close link with innovations, and are often considered as their 'fathers'. In a study carried out among 1,130 directors, from all areas and continents, the directors claimed that the responsibility of innovation belonged to them. Fifty percent of them said, "I am the innovator" or that innovation belonged "to all the employees"[12] which implied, in the last case, that the directors remained the owners of innovations through the hierarchy process. This underlines several difficulties concerning a possible innovation-*care*, especially an ecological question. If an innovation fails, is the director responsible for this? If he is, what made him responsible for it and to what extent? Is there an obsession to innovate as soon as pride and ambition are stressed? (Raymond 2003)

About the understanding of interdependence as related to exogenous and endogenous conditions

Innovation-*care* deals with both the exogenous and endogenous conditions of the firm through the conscience of interdependence. There is interdependence in today's globalization of products and services; there is interdependence between individuals, should they be directors or employees; there is interdependence in the inner-self of an individual between the manager and the citizen. Interdependence is everywhere, whether we like it or not. And the goal of *care* is to accept this interdependence while taking care of oneself and of others. Being aware of interdependence is understanding that violence always turns against oneself, just as we benefit from the *care* given to someone else (Gilligan 2008). This is why the *care* theories always underline the importance of showing that all of us depend on the services of others to meet our basic needs (Laugier and Paperman 2008). In the *care* perspective, oneself and others are not represented as distinct items: the relationship is the central object from which the moral subject perceives needs and meets this perception. Each of these perspectives deals with seizing the relations between you and the others (Laugier and Paperman 2008).

From medicine to driving on a road, from education to information, from management to collaboration within a project group, there is always some sort of interdependence. In order to understand this concept, one has to leave one's own sphere, and this is precisely what – most of the time – firms and directors find the most difficult, especially within the innovation framework. The offer of innovation-*care* is, on the one hand, to show that innovation is no lonely stake, and on the other hand, that failure does not mean weakness but is due to human characteristics. To quote one significant example, a study about airplane accidents showed that pilot instructors proved that if the crew members only know about the situation through the pilot, they are unable to correct a mistake. If pilots and crew learn to recognize their mistakes and accept their weaknesses, they solve problems much more effectively (Tronto 2009).

Innovation-*care* and self-control

Innovation-*care* is focused on the awareness of our relationship with others, but its most important concern is the awareness of the interdependence between individuals, firms, countries etc. Innovation-*care* is the awareness of possible exchanges at the boundary between private and public spheres. The innovator is able to understand the notion of *care* only when he is aware of living with a process where he receives *care* and benefits from innovations. In other words, he must personally aim at being 'caring'.

Once these mixed processes are understood, innovation can no longer pretend to bring happiness to people, which is something that innovation can naturally do but which may have a consequence on *care*. Joan Tronto distinguishes between 'good' and 'bad' *care* by referring to the significant example of the colonizers who did not think that they were taking advantage of the people they wished to rule (Tronto 2009). The same criticism may be raised about innovation.

It seems that the 'over-productive' firms we talked about start listening to people, and are more particularly concerned with listening to their customers in order to focus their research on them. Putting the customer at the core of one's strategy is even becoming an obsession. For 95% of these firms, that is to say, 14% more than the others, "tying closer bonds with the customer" is the priority.[13] Yet, there is more to innovation-*care*. If the innovator thinks that something is 'good' for him or herself of for the customer, it may not be for the rest of the society. Innovation-*care* will thus endeavor to listen to the opinions of others. But the opinions of others do not necessarily match the opinions of potential customers. It seems important to take into account the opinions of all the people who could suffer from the consequences of a future innovation.

This question is particularly accurate because innovation, from the customer's perspective, is – most of the time – valuable when it comes to incremental innovations. Yet the most topical issues concerning the possible consequences of an innovation deal with breakthrough innovations. Incremental innovations are, by nature, more predictable, because there is at least a small part of them on the market. A breakthrough innovation requires more attention because its consequences are completely unknown. A new difficulty emerges because the very notions of 'breakthrough' and 'incremental' have no worldwide acceptance.[14]

In order to define innovation-*care*, we need to adopt a holistic approach. This means acting not only for the sake of oneself, of the firm or of one's nation. It means acting for the sake of these elements but also for the sake of all of society. A cigarette producer must think about non-smokers; a producer of domestic cleaners about the treatment of water after its products have been in contact with it and about the children playing with this water; a car-seller about the pedestrians and the cyclists with whom cars share the road.

In the end, the evolution of the paradigm innovation-*care* is just resurgence of the thinking act of the application of Kantian principles, more particularly of the universal maxims. The first is important because it deals with our subject: "Act that your principle of action might safely be made a law for the whole world" (Kant, 2006, p. 97). This highlights the interdependence scheme, the obligation to look for the global consequences and the fact that others, in the meantime, can have the same concerns as oneself, instead of a personal and individual view. In other words, this principle could be the maxim of innovation-*care*: always acting while caring, that is to say, bringing into line our actions with a universal view of what we are just about to do.

The second maxim is "Act in such a way that you treat humanity, whether in your own person or in the person of any other, always at the same time as an end and never merely as a means to an end" (Kant, 2006, p. 108). Here, innovation-*care* is particularly emphasized as there is humanity to preserve, and this is a goal in itself. This Kantian maxim, just as the last one, tries to put individuals as a necessary prerequisite for any action. There is no doubt that Kant did not think about innovation when he wrote those maxims, yet he remained an observer of the French philosophers of the 18th century, and thus of the numerous issues linked with progress and sciences, topics which Rousseau criticized as well (Rousseau 1992).

From the innovator to the innovator-caring?

The maxims of Kant and, more generally, the innovation-*care* require a completely new human behavior, concerning others and oneself. When Hans Jonas introduced the 'responsibility principle', he wondered if humanity had a right to exist (Jonas 1984). If the answer to this question is yes, then it is essential that human beings evolve towards a new behavior, a behavior of caring for the world, a new stance that individuals must largely accept. Faced with the rise of technology and its power, with worldwide globalization, human beings have to bear their responsibilities for the world and in the world.

This depends on the innovator, and it raises the question of the innovator profile. The latter should adopt a *caring* behavior, which should stem from his/her inner self. Yet, the usual studies about innovation, should it be in business, economics or sociology, are much more interested in the innovation as a process, and thus more in what innovators do rather than who they are (Guichard and Servel 2006). Even if this issue is tackled, the question of the responsibility of the innovator remains sidelined. Schumpeter saw the innovator as an athlete with a strong taste for conquest, a '*wild* spirit' who yearned for success (Schumpeter 1934; Perroux 1965). Recent literature on entrepreneurship questions the personal characteristics of the innovator-entrepreneur, but neither Robert (Robert 1991) nor Sahlman (Sahlman 1997) deal with the question of their responsibility. Whatever the innovator types we can quote, following Alter's typology, the 'central', 'specialized', 'link' or 'followers', none has to worry about this characteristic (Alter 2002). The only aspect stemming from the different research carried out on the innovator's profile is that innovators are often considered as iconoclasts, eccentrics, exceptions to the norm, marginal or even deviants "because their behaviors are in opposition with the established social norms" (Alter 2003: p. 18). This last element must be emphasized and it can be brought in parallel with Michel Foucault who often used the word 'innovation' to point out behaviors, and especially sexual ones, which were exceptions to the norms (Foucault 2001; 2009).

Some books tackle the issue of the innovator's profile more often, but they do not mention the responsibility they are to bear. For instance, one of Tom Kelley's last books, *The Ten Faces of Innovations*, makes no mention of the responsibility of the innovator. The author classifies innovative behaviors into three categories – the 'learners', the 'promoters' and the 'builders' (Kelley 2005) – whose specificities are explained; none of them ever possess, or should possess, responsible qualities.

Stigmatization of innovation, of innovators and self-control

Turning one's behavior into a responsible one does not mean more constraint. There is no point in stigmatizing innovations, or in agreeing with Rousseau who saw progress as the symbol of men's degradation, or in trying to establish that the state of nature would be more profitable (Rousseau 1989).

We must mention two necessary qualities the innovator should have. First, as we said earlier, is the ability to question the capacity of a responsible-innovation, and thus to come to grips with the three aspects Bernadette Bensaude-Vincent underlined. Second is the ability to slow down innovation in an attempt to bring it into line with the economic, social and societal sphere in which it will be implemented. This last concern naturally evolves towards self-control, which echoes the Stoicism techniques. Self-control was closely linked with the notion of freedom (Schuhl and Bréhier 1962) for the Stoicians. Being able to control oneself is being free from one's passions, from exterior events and so on. Being able to control oneself for the innovator-*caring* means to be free from the market, from the economic pressure, from the situations which would see the launch of an innovation without having assessed its possible consequences. One must not be completely unaware of the context in which the innovation was born, but one must not be dependent on it either. If the service or the product launched is really innovative, these questions are no longer accurate.

Being able to control oneself for the innovator-*caring* also means knowing what makes us act and launch this innovation. Why is this innovation good? Is it good by nature, or for me, or for others? That is the control of the innovation process in its deeper consequences. Being able to control oneself also means giving up, just as the Stoic masters showed their ability to give up on their passions. Even if they were attractive and gave pleasure, they endeavored to control their passions so as not to yield to them (Schuhl and Bréhier 1962). Innovator-*caring* must reach some wisdom which no other person can understand: they notice the needs of others but they must act only according to what they know, because others rely on them (Schuhl and Bréhier 1962). They must be able to foresee the actions which could result in pain, because they among others are responsible for everybody's well-being. The entire ethics of *care* which relies on the principles of non-violence and of not harming anybody will thus prevail in the innovation area (Schuhl and Bréhier 1962).

Thus, even if an innovation can significantly increase the turnover, reach the objectives and generate a consistent premium, one should be able to give up on it if it damages the 'care' of the individuals and of society. The innovator-*caring* is a conscience, not only for them but for their firms, their organizations and their society. They act, not only in their own interest, but in the common interest. If the responsible-innovation could assess the consequences on the community, innovation-*care* pictures itself as caring for the community. Innovation-*care* has a positive and benevolent role to play in the community and in the city, and the innovator-*caring* is the first student of the ethical Kantian principle "What should I do?" (Kant 1998). Responsible-innovation would stick to a predetermined role concerning its consequences while innovation-*care* takes care of others as a prerequisite.

Conclusion

How to combine care and performance

Kindness and care for others are key notions concerning innovation-*care* and contribute to the evolution of the very notion of *care*. As we have said, the meaning of care for its creators is 'to care for the others'. For Janet Finch and Dulcie Groves, care is even a "combination of affectionate feelings and responsibilities" (Cancias and Stacey 2000: p. 36). From the mother to the cleaning-lady and the nurse, there are jobs and professional features linked to care. The first approach to care was very feminist. We shall mention that it would be useful to question innovation-*care* through a female prism, for we know that, on the one hand, women are very sensitive and adapt themselves much more easily to innovations (Garbarinoa and Strahilevitzb 2004; Mazman et al. 2009), and that on the other hand, women's lives, compared to men's lives, are rooted more in social interactions and personal relationships (Gilligan 2008).

Yet managers and innovators should be added to this list, maybe even before the 'usual female deliverers' of care, because they are the people in charge of the individuals' care through the innovations they might launch.

We would like to underline the fact that the word *care* in the expression 'innovation-*care*' is nevertheless linked to a hierarchy at whose top is innovation. Even if we have just underlined that a caring-innovator should know when to give up on innovations, there is no denying that his first attribute is to innovate while aiming at economic performance. Care is not responsibility, it is not the social responsibility of firm nor the sustainable development issues. Last but not least, care is not a frame or a brake to innovation. It is a process which can be articulated to it and with it, but is not the final goal. For it is innovation as a well-known factor of performance, growth, sustainability and improvement of the individuals' lives which has to recover a primacy. A final primacy, without ambiguous meaning, for innovation being first by nature, care comes first for organizations, leaders and innovators. In fact, the well-being, the care mentioned at the start of this movement, has never meant sacrifices (Gilligan 2008).

This means that performance is at the core of innovation-care, and that there is no possible amphibology in this new generation, and this is very important. Any other interpretation would be a misunderstanding of the meaning of care in general, and of innovation-care in particular. If it is easy to understand as far as innovation-care is concerned, in the case of care it doesn't mean providing a basic service of an inferior quality, pretending that what is important is the 'care for the others'.

Care develops itself through occasions. Care in itself does not mean anything, or is not just a new form of sympathy. On the contrary, care developed on the American continent keeps pace with the pragmatic movement and deals with concrete events, with reality. Innovation-care without its focus on innovation would remain a given-without-gift. The integration of tools able to deal with innovation-care exists nowadays, or will exist soon, should it be the *Chasm* from Moore (Moore 1999) or the *Matrix Virtue* of Martin, (Martin, 2002) for instance. Its concrete aspect can also be found within the assessment methods of the strategies of existing firms, such as the *Dow Jones Index*,[15] for example. It can also rely on a quantitative axis integrating indicators of its components which would enable one to assess and to be assessed according to one's ability to innovate-care.

The Antic philosophy considered that commitment was the necessary condition to implement a philosophic way of life. This commitment was to be found in the mind as well as in actions; it is the very famous articulation of *theoria/praxis*. It is also the Greek *elenchus* – the commitment – which means "think well to be able to act well" (Balaudé, 2010: p. 188).

Innovation-care is just at the very beginning of its existence and its stance remains to be drawn more accurately so that it can be integrated into economic models. Just as the Ancient is for philosophy, innovation-care is to be thought of as a commitment. This commitment has two faces: it can be intellectual models, theories and speeches, but also actions. Like other sciences, running a business and management must integrate these two schemes in innovation-care, for its own development as well as for that of the individuals and of the city.

Notes

1 http://www.vivagora.org.
2 Emmanuel Faye shows that to get all the possible 'commodities' on earth is not the prevailing aim; it is in fact the 'preservation of health' with the intent to make mankind

'wiser'. It implies to have knowledge of the 'reasons' for our sicknesses and of 'all remedies provided by nature'. Cf. E. Faye, *Heidegger, l'introduction du nazisme dans la philosophie: autour des séminaires inédits de 1933–1935*, Albin Michel, 'Idées', 2005.

3 The appearance of the first criticisms at the beginning of the 1960s can be noted, for one Rachel Carlson in *Silent Spring,* Mariner Book Edition, 2002.

4 Among a very large range of examples, the recent birth of the first 'life-saving baby' can be noted. The parents of a little girl suffering from a genetic disease decided to have another child that could save her. The parents of this 'life-saving baby' benefited from a double pre-implantation diagnostic. First, the embryos that carried the sickness were ruled out; then, among the remaining ones, the one that best matched the gene pool of the sibling was selected, and finally it was implanted in the mother's womb. If such a technical achievement should be celebrated, one can wonder about the development of such a technique which opens the way for eugenics.

5 www.transhumanism.org.

6 Bernadette Bensaude-Vincent, au Colloque innovation responsable du 29 avril 2009, Collège de France.

7 *Libération* du 7 mars 2009, 'Faismesdevoirs.com ferme déjà ses pages'.

8 For instance, several internet websites: pleasuretours.com; alternativephuket.com; globalfantasies.com; temptation.originalresorts.com; affordable-adult-vacations.com; wildwomenvacations.com; pornweek.com.

9 http://www.legrenelle-environnement.fr/Convention-avec-les-acteurs-du.html. For that matter, the measures intended to reduce noise pollution for the sake of local residents' well-being increase the planes' consumption of kerosene at the same time.

10 Cf. le rapport du sénateur Daniel Raoul sur 'Les effets sur la santé et l'environnement des champs électromagnétiques produits par les lignes à haute et très haute tension', handed out to the Parliamentary Office for the Evaluation of Scientific Choices and Technologies, May 2010.

11 IBM, 2010, *Institute for Business Value, Capitalizing on Complexity* (IBM Corporation).

12 IBM, 2008, *Global CEO Study* (IBM Corporation).

13 IBM, 2010, *Institute for Business Value, Capitalizing on Complexity* (IBM Corporation).

14 Conference held in CEIBS (China Europe International Business School) in Shanghai, 30 June 2010. During that conference, Norma Harisson came back to the subject of incremental innovation versus disruptive innovation and highlighted the fact that what is incremental for the American market can be disruptive for the Chinese market. This explains why, all in all, innovation in China is incremental, based on occidental innovations, principally on the business model.

15 http://www.sustainability-index.com/.

References

Alter, N. (2002). Les innovateurs du quotidien. L'innovation dans les entreprises. *Futuribles*, 271, pp. 5–23.

Alter, N. (2003). *L'Innovation ordinaire.* Paris: Presse Universitaire de France.

Baber, W. (1983). *Organizing the Future: Matrix Models for the Post-industrial Policy.* Alabama: The University of Alabama Press.

Balaudé, J-F. (2010). *Le Savoir vivre philosophique.* Paris: Grasset.

Bensaude-Vincent, B. (2001). *Histoire de la chimie.* Paris: La Découverte.

Bensaude-Vincent, B. (2009). Introduction au Colloque innovation responsable du 29 avril, Collège de France, Paris.

Bostrom, N. (2005). A history of transhumanist thought. *Journal of Evolution and Technology*, 14(1), pp. 1–25.

Bostrom, N. and Sanders, A. (2008). The Wisdom of Nature: An Evolutionary Heuristic for Human Enhancement. In: J. Savulescu and N. Bostrom (eds.), *Human Enhancement.* Oxford: Oxford University Press, pp. 375–416.

Cancias, F. and Stacey, O. (2000). *Caring and Gender.* Walnut Creek (CA): Altamira.

Carlson R. (2002). *Silent Spring.* Boston, MA: Mariner Books.

Condorcet, M. J. A. N. C. (1988) *Esquisse d'un tableau historique des progrès de l'esprit humain.* Paris: Flammarion.

Darwin, C. (2003). *The Origin of the Species.* New York: Barnes & Noble Classics.

Descartes, R. (2008). *A Discourse on the Method of Correctly Conducting One's Reason and Seeking Truth in the Sciences.* Oxford: Oxford University Press.

Engel, L. (1997). Réguler les comportements. In: T. Ferenczi (ed.), *De quoi sommes-nous responsables?* Paris: Éditions Le Monde, pp. 11–36.

Ewald, F. (1996). *Histoire de l'État-Providence.* Paris: Grasset.

Favaro, K, Karlsson, P-O. and Neilson, G. L. (2010). CEO Succession 2000-2009: A Decade of Convergence and Compression. *Booz&Co, Strategy Business,* (n 59). Available at: http://www.favaro.net/publications/CEOSuccession.pdf.

Fisher, B. and Tronto, J. (1990). Toward a feminist theory of caring. In: E.K. Able and Nelson, M. (eds.), *Circles of Care: Work and Identity in Women's Life.* Albany: State University of New York Press.

Faye, E. (2005). *Heidegger, l'introduction du nazisme dans la philosophie: autour des séminaires inédits de 1933–1935.* Paris: Albin Michel, 'Idées'.

Foucault, M. (2009). *Le Courage de la vérité, Le gouvernement de soi et des autres II: Cours au Collège de France. 1984.* Paris: Gallimard-Seuil.

Foucault, M. (2001). Le triomphe social du plaisir sexuel: une conversation avec Michel Foucault. In: *Dits et Ecrits II, 1976-1988.* Paris: Gallimard, p.1127–1133.16. Franklin, B. (1956). *Mr. Franklin: A Selection From His Personal Letters.* New Haven: Yale University Press.

Garbarinoa, E. and Strahilevitzb, M. (2004). Gender differences in the perceived risk of buying online and the effects of receiving a site recommendation. *Journal of Business Research,* 57(7), pp. 768–775.

Gagnepain, L. (2005). La climatisation automobile, Impacts consommation et pollution. In: *Repères* (published by l'Agence de l'environnement et de la maîtrise de l'énergie – département Technologies des transports). Available at: http://www.ademe.fr/climatisation-automobile-impacts-consommation-pollution.

Génard, J.-L. (2000). Le temps de la responsabilité, in G. Philippe, O. François and M. Van de Kerchove (eds.), *L'Accélération du temps juridique.* Bruxelles, Publications des Facultés universitaires, Saint-Louis, pp. 105–125.

Gilligan, C. (2008). *Une voie différente. Pour une éthique du care.* Paris: Flammarion.

Gorgoni, G. (2006). La responsabilité comme projet. In: C. Eberhard (ed.), *Traduire nos responsabilités planétaires. Recomposer nos paysages juridiques.* Bruxelles: Bruylant, pp. 131–146.

Guichard, R. and Servel, L. (2006). Qui sont les innovateurs? Une lecture socio-économique des acteurs de l'innovation. *Sociétal,* 52(3), pp. 26–31.

Hart, H. L. A. (1968). *Punishment and Responsibility. Essays in the Philosophy of Law.* Oxford: Oxford University Press.

Jonas, H. (1984). *The Imperative of Responsibility: In Search of Ethics for the Technological Age.* Chicago: University of Chicago Press.

Kant, I. (1998). *Critique of Pure Reason.* Cambridge: Cambridge University Press.

Kant, I. (2006). Fondation de la métaphysique des mœurs, in Métaphysique des mœurs, trad. Alain Renaut. Paris: Groupe Flammarion, pp. 97–108.

Kelley, T. (2005). *The Ten Faces of Innovation: IDEO's Strategies for Defeating the Devil's Advocate and Driving Creativity Throughout Your Organization*. New York: Doubleday.

Kurzweil, R. (1999). *The Age of Spiritual Machines*. Berkeley (CA): Viking Penguin.

Laugier, S. and Paperman, P. (2008). La voix différente et les éthiques du care. In: C. Gilligan (ed.), *Une voie différente. Pour une éthique du care*. Paris: Flammarion, pp. 8–35.

Mazman, S., Usluel, Y. K. and Çevik, V. (2009). Social influence in the adoption process and usage of innovation: Gender differences. *World Academy of Science, Engineering and Technology*, 3(1), pp. 31–34.

Martin, R. (2002). Virtue matrix: Calculating the return on corporate responsibility. *Harvard Business Review*, 80(3), pp. 68–75.

Moore, G. A. (1999). *Crossing the Chasm, Marketing and Selling High-Tech Products to Mainstream Customers*. New York: Harper Collins Publishers.

Neuberg, M. (1997). *La Responsabilité: questions philosophiques*. Paris: Presses universitaires de France.

Nietzsche, F. (2003). *Fragments posthumes sur l'éternel retour*. Paris: Allia.

Nowotny, H. (2015). *The Cunning of Uncertainty*. Oxford: Polity.

Ost, F. (1995). *La Nature hors la loi, l'écologie à l'épreuve du droit*. Paris: La Découverte.

Pedersen, E. R. (2010). Modelling CSR: How managers understand the responsibilities on Business toward society. *Journal of Business Ethics*, 91(2), pp. 155–166.

Perroux, F. (1965). *La Pensée économique de Joseph Schumpeter*. Geneva: Librairie Droz.

Plato, (1950). *République*. In: Plato, *Œuvres complètes I*. Paris: Gallimard.

Porter, M. and Kramer, M. (2011). Shared value. How to reinvent capitalism – and unleash a wave of innovation and growth. *Harvard Business Review*, 89(1–2), pp. 62–77.

Rabelais, F. (1854). Pantagruel. In: *Œuvres*. Paris: J. Bry Ainé.

Raoul, D. (2010). Les effets sur la santé et l'environnement des champs électromagnétiques produits par les lignes à haute et très haute tension. Handed out to the Parliamentary Office for the Evaluation of Scientific Choices and Technologies, May 2010.

Raymond, J. (2003). La Ford Pinto: le contre-exemple américain. *Le Polyscope* (Le journal de l'École polytechnique de Montréal), vol. 36.

Ricœur, P. (2000). *The Just*. Chicago: Chicago University Press.

Robert, E. B. (1991). *Entrepreneurship in High Technology: Lessons from MIT and Beyond*. New York: Oxford University Press.

Rousseau, J. J. (1989). *Discours sur l'origine et les fondements de l'inégalité parmi les hommes*. Paris: Flammarion.

Rousseau, J. J. (1992). *Discours sur les sciences et les arts*. Paris: Garnier-Flammarion.

Sahlman, W. A. (1997). How to write a great business plan. *Harvard Business Review*, 75(4), pp. 98–108.

Schumpeter, J. A. (1934). *The Theory of Economic Development: An Inquiry into Profits, Capital, Credit, Interest and the Business Cycle*. New Brunswick: Transaction Publishers.

Schumpeter, J. A. (1939). *Business Cycles: A Theoretical, Historical, and Statistical Analysis of the Capitalist Process*. New York: McGraw-Hill.

Schuhl, P.-M. and Bréhier, E. (1962). Introduction. In: *Les Stoïciens*. Paris: Gallimard.

Schwartz, M. (2005). Universal moral values for corporate codes of ethics. *Journal of Business Ethics*, 59(1), pp. 27–44.

Sophocles, (1955). *Antigone*. Paris: Les Belles Lettres.
Tronto, J. (1994). *Moral Boundaries: A Political Argument for an Ethic of Care*. London: Routledge.
Tronto, J. (2009). *Care* démocratique et démocraties du care. In: P. Molinier, S. Laugier and P. Paperman (eds.), *Qu'est-ce que le care?* Paris: Petite Bibliothèque Payot, pp. 36–54.
Williams, B. (2015). *Ethics and the Limits of Philosophy*. London: Routledge.

12 Responsibility in research and innovation

The potential of care ethics

Sophie Pellé

Introduction

Attempts to think of, understand, and regulate the governance of emerging technology and science have recently crystallised into the idea of Responsible Research and Innovation (RRI). Drawing on several well-known traditions in sociology and the philosophy of science (Owen et al., 2012; Pellé and Reber, 2016), including Technology Assessment (Grunwald, 2014), Participative Technology Assessment, Ethical Legal and Social Impact or Assessment (ELSI, ELSA approaches), or Value Sensitive Design (Kelty, 2009; van den Hoven, 2013), various frameworks of interpretation have been proposed to define and conceptualise RRI. Some of them rest on "keys" (such as those promoted by the European Commission for the current framework programme Horizon 2020, for instance); others highlight the "conditions" of RRI, as in Stilgoe et al. (2013), Owen et al. (2012, 2013b), Guston (2014), Grunwald (2011, 2014), Robinson et al. (2013), Nordmann (2014), Pavie and Egal (2014), Lee and Petts (2013), Sykes and Macnaghten (2013). Although these frameworks differ on several points (Pellé and Bernard, 2015, 2016; Pellé, 2016a), they defend similar requirements for RRI (e.g. the idea of including relevant stakeholders, citizens, or the public at large in the governance process of science and technology).[1]

Among the various conditions or requirements that have been advanced to define RRI, it has been claimed (Owen et al., 2012, 2013b; Stilgoe et al., 2013; von Schomberg, 2013; Grunwald 2011, 2012; Guston, 2014) that responsible Research and Innovation (R&I) processes demand *transparency* (an effort to render outcomes of R&I visible to the public, including possible benefits and harms); *anticipation* (understanding and normatively assessing the possible outcomes of science and technology and the visions of the world associated with it); *responsiveness* (i.e. the individual or systemic capacity to react to a specific situation and to respond to it adequately); *reflexivity* (i.e. the individual and organisational capacity to reflect about one's own frame); and *inclusion* (participation and/or deliberation of the different relevant stakeholders to ensure a collective and pluralistic identification of norms).

Some of these approaches have proposed the idea that the responsibility of the various research and innovation actors (scientists, research institutes, entrepreneurs, companies, funding institutions, policy-makers, end-users, citizens, etc.)

could be conceived with the help of care ethics (Owen et al., 2013b; Adam and Groves, 2011; Grinbaum and Groves, 2013; Groves, 2009, 2014; Pavie, 2014; Pellé, 2016a, b, 2017; Pellé and Reber, 2015, 2016).

This chapter aims at investigating the attempt to conceptualize responsibility in innovation and research through the notion of care. As shown elsewhere (Pellé and Reber, 2015, 2016), responsibility is a polysemic concept with no less than ten different meanings,[2] one of which is care. Beyond backward-looking understandings of responsibility or meanings based on the role social actors play or the obligations they have, proponents of responsibility in R&I conceived as care argue that such an interpretation provides a normative content to the conditions of RRI mentioned above, and sketch a theoretical and practical framework for the assessment and management of R&I activities. This chapter explores some of the benefits of considering responsibility in R&I as related to the idea of care, as well as some of the limits and issues raised when care ethics is taken out from its traditional arena and applied to the specific challenges posed by the development of science, technology and innovation.

Section 1 presents a definition of care borrowed from Joan Tronto's work (1993, 2013) and investigates its correspondence with the RRI conditions found in the literature. Section 2 analyses three different reasons to adopt an interpretation of responsibility in R&I based on the notion of care, related to a) the way in which context is taken into account, b) the possibility of building a collective notion of good, and c) compatibility with moral pluralism. Section 3 focuses on what has to be reinterpreted when applying care ethics to R&I practices, including the specific problem of how to define a need (who is in need and what is the need) in the assessment of science and technology. Finally, section 4 investigates the central notion of connectedness in care ethics and emphasises how it can be useful to elaborate a framework for the governance of RRI.

Some aspects of care ethics

The idea of caring for or caring about is anchored in different philosophical trends which include, among others, the phenomenological tradition (Heidegger and Levinas), Hans Jonas' concern for future generations, Aristotle's virtue ethics and his emulators, and the work of feminist authors that emerged during the 1980s against an alleged hegemony of universalist and principled theories in psychology, political theory and political philosophy (e.g. Carol Gilligan (1982), Sara Ruddick (1980), Nel Nodding and Paul Shore (1984)). Among these various perspectives, I will concentrate on the feminist approach of care ethics,[3] and, more precisely, on the one offered by Joan Tronto.

In her conception (first developed together with Berenice Fisher in 1990), caring is defined as "a species activity that includes everything that we do to maintain, continue, and repair our 'world' so that we can live in it as well as possible" (Tronto, 2013: p. 19). The broadness of this definition has been criticized (e.g. Held, 2006; Engster, 2007; Groves, 2014) because it could contain activities such as "plumbing" or "house building," which are not straightforwardly defined as care practices (*ibid.*).[4] Yet, this definition is suited to our purpose, precisely because it comprises many different types of activities (including the development of science, technology, and innovation). It is characterised by the *intentions* behind the actions that seek to "maintain, continue, and repair our 'world'" in order to "live in it as well as possible" rather than the *conditions* for responsibility or *objective outcomes* to achieve.[5] Although each term of the definition could be subjected to a deeper analysis, I will point out only two elements briefly.[6]

First, the idea of maintaining and repairing the world echoes a concern that is behind both ideas of precaution and sustainable development, which can be synthesized, among other formulations, as follows: we should conduct human activities without jeopardizing the right of future generations to live and enjoy what will be their world. The idea of continuation and repair offers a first interesting step for R&I because it provides a far-ranging normative horizon that can steer the development of science and technology to preserve and take care of the riches of our world (understood in a broad sense). This, however, cannot be the sole aspect of responsibility in R&I. Innovation – as already claimed by Joseph Schumpeter in 1934 – has the potential to disrupt and destroy previous social organisations and equilibria in ways that are not univocally dangers or damages (as in the case of the internet, for instance). Disruption and destruction do not always imply repair. This brings us to the second related point: Tronto's conception does not clearly define what constitutes 'appropriate repair' or what a world in which we would live 'as well as possible' would look like. One way of addressing this issue advocates for a collective assessment process to define what 'good' means. Yet, this raises many questions concerning how deliberation and representation are to be conceived and put into practice in a democratic governance process of science and technology (see section 2).

This is why another aspect of Tronto's approach – the various *moral moments* she identifies as characterising caring practices – might offer a more practical basis to conceive RRI, compared with the definition mentioned above. Surprisingly,[7] these moral moments echo most of the conditions of responsibility identified in the recent literature on RRI.

Tronto identifies four steps in the process of care: caring about, caring for, care giving and care receiving. These steps correspond to four elements of an ethics of care: attentiveness, responsibility, competence and responsiveness, which should not be understood as individual virtues, but as 'moral moments' of caring practices, since Tronto's ethics of care is relational and does not seek to define what a virtuous individual should be.

Related to the requirement of caring about, a relation of care implies *attentiveness* on the part of the care-giver who becomes aware of others' needs. Deficiencies of attention and ignorance – i.e. when we fail to identify (deliberately or not) needs that should be taken care of – are moral evils, moral failures. An ethics of care seeks instead to promote "a capacity genuinely to look for the perspective of the one in need" (Tronto, 2013: p. 34). To adequately care for others (or for the environment), we first need to identify their needs. Yet, as we shall see in section 3, this question is more complex than it seems since a part of what is recognized as a "need" is socially constructed and might be subject to different (sometimes conflicting) interpretations. Finally, if *care-based relationships* demand that we take care of others' needs, this does not mean that we should forget our own needs. As argued by Gilligan's (1982) seminal work, beneficial care implies good self-care. Among the practical reasons that are advanced, there is the idea that taking care of ourselves helps us to be aware of the kind of needs that are expressed by others; it fosters our availability to be attentive to the demands of others. In addition, care-givers neglecting to care for themselves might be unable to take care of others in the long run, leading to situations of exploitation and abuse (Held, 2006; Engster, 2007).

The second ethical element of care is *responsibility* (related to the second step of caring for). In contrast to a backward-looking conception of responsibility as a set of obligations and formal rules to follow, Tronto adopts an anthropological perspective according to which our responsibility to others is something flexible, rooted in political motivation, cultural practices and individual psychology (Tronto, 1993: p. 132). Both the things that we do or that we don't do make us responsible for *taking care* of a need. In other words, once needs have been identified (attentiveness), someone or some group must take the responsibility of meeting those needs. In section 4, I shall add some elements to this idea.

Third, when defending an ethics of care, the *competence* of the care-giver to provide good and successful care should count as a moral issue.[8] The willingness or the virtue of the care-giver to provide good care alone never ensures that the need of the care receiver will appropriately be met. According to Tronto, it is only by looking at outcomes of caring practices, in a consequentialist perspective, that it becomes possible to assess 'good' care. Adding a consequentialist dimension, which focuses on the competence of the care-giver, leads Tronto to reaffirm the crucial role of professional ethics. Codes of conduct and guidelines for good practices, which are collectively defined within a specific profession, become a constitutive part of the worker's competence and abilities.

The fourth[9] "moral moment that arises out of caring" (op. cit. p. 134) is *responsiveness*, which designates the response of the care receiver to what is being provided to him/her. This 'moment' supposes that the care-giver not only adopts his/her own perspective but also adapts to that of others. Her own way to identify good caring practices has to be confronted and mitigated with the perspective of the care receiver. This would prevent possible abuses and omnipotent positions in which care-givers could impose their own perceptions of what good is, regardless of the assessment of the one in need.

As we can see, Tronto's four dimensions of care ethics refer to most of the "conditions" of RRI highlighted in the introduction. Because it focuses on needs, care ethics contains a form of *anticipation* – it is a future-oriented approach for Groves (2009) – but in a much less rationalistic way than traditional technology assessment activities (Koehn, 2011; Grinbaum and Groves, 2013). *Responsiveness* is not understood in the same way as Owen et al. (2012, 2013b) suggest it. However, the individual disposition to which Tronto refers, when complemented with attentiveness, favours the capacity to adapt, to change situations, and to elaborate answers that would mitigate conflicting interests. The condition of *responsibility*, as highlighted above, appears directly as an ethical component of the definition of what good *care* is. While this could lead to semantic issues, given that Tronto's conception is focused on the responsibility of taking needs into account – a perspective that would be too reductive for RRI (see sections 3 and 4) – it acknowledges the moral engagement of the care-giver (individual or institution).

Finally, the conditions of *reflexivity* and *inclusion* seem to be only implicitly addressed in Tronto's care ethics (when she considers the relationship between care-givers and care receivers). Yet, reflexivity is an explicit and important element in other care-based approaches, such as in MacIntyre (1999: p. 95). Moreover, the next section shows that it is both possible and beneficial to combine care ethics with inclusion, understood as a collective process of determining the good.

Care ethics and governance of RRI

The preceding discussion showed that Tronto's care ethics shares similar concerns with the recent literature on RRI and that both perspectives can be compatible. Yet, this alone does not explain why it is fruitful to interpret responsibility in R&I through the idea of care. I would like to emphasize three reasons to favour this interpretation.

Context-dependant moral theory

First, it is widely agreed among its proponents that care ethics is a context-dependant moral theory in which what is defined as "good" caring practices comes neither from a paternalistic (or maternalistic) attitude towards those in need, nor is it subject to moral relativism.

Let me tackle the problem of paternalism first.[10] In traditional care relationships, because care-givers usually have more competence and capabilities related to their practice than those they are taking care of, there can be a risk of bypassing the interest, values and even preferences of the care receiver. In R&I, scientists, engineers and innovators are placed in an asymmetrical position compared with end-users and citizens due to their specific skills, knowledge and competence. However, this does not necessarily imply that, while taking care of social needs or needs raised by the development of science and technology, they will reinforce a paternalistic top-down mode of governance that was typical of the post-World War II management of science in Western countries. As expressed by Joan Tronto (1993, pp. 153–154):

> Because care is a practice, there is no guarantee that the moral problems that we have pointed to will be solved. There is no universal principle that we can invoke that will automatically guarantee that, as people and society engage in care, that care will be free of parochialism, paternalism and privilege. But the absence of such a solution only points to the fact that, as a practice, care also has a context and a location. Only when care is located in a society in which

> open and equal discussion can occur, when there is a consensus about some notions of need and or justice, can these problems be mitigated.

It is possible to recognize here a traditional claim of feminist care ethicists (Gilligan, 1982; Nodding and Shore, 1984; Ruddick, 1980; Tronto, 1993, 2013) against "universalist" neo-Kantian theories of justice – Rawls being one prominent example – in which principles for the allocation of resources are determined according to procedures and abstract reasoning, regardless of the specific context in which the recipients of the allocation evolve. In contrast, many care ethicists draw on an Aristotelian framework (Nussbaum, 1988, 1992; MacIntyre, 1999) in which the resolution of ethical dilemmas involve a practical wisdom (*Phronesis*), which helps us take decisions, mitigate conflicting interests and find the appropriate solution by adapting rules to the unique circumstances of each situation. In this view, the way in which norms of good care are discovered is historically, culturally, and socially bounded and good care depends more on the quality of human relations than on the application of fair abstract rules.[11]

In R&I activities, such sensitivity to the context can be both an individual virtue and an institutional capacity, as when social organisations such as companies or research institutes decide to reduce their emissions of greenhouse gases in order to respond to climate change and international competition. However, it might be easier to produce norms that emanate from the context in local and medium-scale projects than in large international networks of actors (individuals or institutions) ruled by different legal and moral sets of norms. In the latter case, the possibility of producing norms of care in R&I would be closely related to the ability to generate norms in a pluralist environment.

Collective understanding of good

The whole issue is then to define what a morally 'appropriate' answer is in a given situation and how such an answer is elaborated among social actors expressing different value systems and normative theories. Interestingly, Joan Tronto adds a political layer to her conception of care based on the four "moral moments": what is considered as "good practices" does not only rest on an individual basis; it has to be settled through collective processes that allow for fair discussion.[12] In R&I, this would mean that innovators and scientists could not be left alone in identifying what are and will be the needs and vulnerabilities of citizens and other stakeholders and what appropriate solutions can be. Here, we can connect the framework of care ethics to a core idea of RRI inherited from various forms of technology assessment practices: to identify what is considered as an issue in R&I, as well as the kinds of solutions that can be proposed in a normatively adequate way, different affected parties must somehow be involved.

Political and institutional infrastructures and designs have to be thought of to ensure a collective understanding of what "good" caring practices are. All authors recently working on RRI have outlined the central role of a constructivist perspective of RRI where inclusion, inclusive deliberation or participation plays a major role (Stilgoe et al., 2013; Owen et al., 2012, 2013b; von Schomberg, 2013; Lee and Petts, 2013; Sykes and Macnaghten, 2013).

However, it is not always clear what is subject to collective deliberation (the assessment of R&I, of their outcomes, the construction of what the problem is, the types of scenarios that can be envisioned and the related course of actions, which can be anticipated), and how this process of deliberation will be constructed (among the variety of available social "devices" such as consensus conferences, mini-public, workshops, focus groups, forum, citizens' juries, surveys etc.). As I have claimed elsewhere (Pellé and Reber, 2016), going back to several aspects of the theory of deliberative democracy can be of some help to assess the different types of devices according to their context and to define the conditions of a quality deliberation. In this work, we gave many examples to illustrate how such a reflection can be organised in R&I to elaborate appropriate devices that ensure deliberation around issues, assessment, outcomes and pathways of development of technology and science.

Moral pluralism

Finally, care ethics is of particular interest for the governance of R&I because it offers a sound basis on which to make moral pluralism flourish. Following Tronto's conception of care, it is possible to connect two distinct moral theories, namely *virtue ethics* and *consequentialism*, in the building of a moral framework based on caring. Two of the dimensions of care ethics identified by Tronto, attentiveness and responsibility, correspond to moral qualities or dispositions (in the sense of virtues),[13] which the person providing care has to experience and use. And the whole concept of *good care* involves a dynamic process through which the care-giver exerts his/her capacities (virtue) of empathy, responsiveness (in the sense of being responsive to the care receiver's demands), practical wisdom and, eventually, things such as human warmth.

In the case of R&I practices, this means that we could depict actors of innovation and research as exerting specific virtues: honesty, patience and rigor in the case of scientists, for instance; creativity and reactivity for innovators; and perseverance, honesty, and clearness in the case of non-governmental organisations (NGOs) etc. This list is only an (non-exhaustive) example of a set of virtues that corresponds to different stakeholders. Its content and attribution could be discussed, opposed, modified etc. The point here is to highlight that when bonds between R&I actors are interpreted in terms of caring, social players discuss, deliberate and act according to some *dispositions* oriented towards a common normative horizon, without necessarily implying any form of consensus on particular values or means to achieve a generic end such as that of "maintaining and repairing our world".[14]

Together with individual virtues, which make caring practices adequate in the face of a certain situation, Tronto also insists on the *competence* of care-givers, introducing, as it has already been mentioned, a consequentialist component that helps ensure that certain outcomes will come about or not. The efficiency of caring practices does not solely stem from good dispositions and intentions. It also takes outcomes into account. The appropriateness and goodness of caring has to be assessed from different perspectives, including that of the one receiving care, eventually leading to professional ethics and the elaboration of codes of conduct. For R&I actors, this would mean that good intentions (e.g. social innovation, R&I conducted to answer a demand or a need) have to be complemented with adequate actions and decisions that ensure the specific need is met in an appropriate way. The skills of scientists, innovators and engineers are not only technical. Actors of innovation also have to show an ethical ability to understand, follow and contribute to creating codes of conducts, for instance.

In this sense, Tronto's conception of care ethics makes moral pluralism possible insofar as it calls up different moral theories to assess moral judgments. Moreover, adding a consequentialist dimension to the assessment process also helps to answer the frequent criticism (outlined in paragraph 2.1.) of care ethics being relativist.

Indeed, the sensitivity to the context of care ethics, which rests on an individual and collective capacity to adapt one's own moral assessment (and corresponding acts and decision) to the specific features of the context, does not lead to the impossibility of grounding moral judgements (a form of relativism), because it rests on a normative horizon that is well defined. An example of this is the attempt to maintain and sustain our world so that we can live in it as well as possible, in the case of Tronto. With this consequentialist dimension, R&I processes can be both assessed from the point of view of the dispositions of the various actors involved and also by looking at the occurrence of outcomes that are recognised as being morally desirable, or as evils.

In conclusion, care ethics provides a theoretical framework which favours a dynamic, reactive and collectively shaped process of R&I that echoes many of the requirements of RRI proponents. It helps in giving a more precise normative content to the concept of responsibility in R&I, organized around the idea of taking care of the various human, environmental and institutional dimensions of our world in a way that allows for moral pluralism. Yet, to be applied to RRI, Tronto's particular perspective should be adapted and revised.

Attentiveness and the problem of the "need"

Indeed, her definition of caring has been conceived in the specific cases of caring practices in the family, hospitals and child care when dependant, deprived, handicapped or diseased persons need daily physical care, help in their movement, emotional attention or cuddling. In the case of R&I, there are also some vulnerabilities at stake, but many of the situations that have to be dealt with do not involve vulnerable people of the kind feminist care ethicists have been keen to reintroduce in the reflection on social justice. The concept of a person being "in need" has to be reinterpreted to fit in the specific context of RRI.

Needs in R&I practices

In the course of the development of science and technology, Tronto's conditions of attentiveness and responsiveness can be interpreted as follows: innovators and researchers would have to be aware of the needs they contribute to creating whenever technology destroys the environment or affects the health of particular individuals or groups, and would have to seek to respond adequately. Citizens, end-users, and stakeholders such as local communities or suppliers can be seen as vulnerable persons in the sense that they lack the power to influence processes as well as detailed knowledge about science and technology, including information on the ways in which they could be positively or negatively affected. However, as objects of care, they are different from children, the elderly, the diseased, the disabled, the handicapped or the unemployed. The dynamics of science and engineering sometimes has a close correspondence with the traditional situations analysed by care ethics, for instance, when research staff have to take care of animals or humans involved in their experiments. But there are many other cases (e.g. the analysis of friction forces in the components of a turbine) for which the "vulnerability" of others will not appear in a straightforward fashion.

Then, we might ask, how accurate is it to identify the issues raised by R&I activities with the need to deal with specific vulnerabilities (whether of individuals or of the environment)? This focus on *needs* created by the development of science and technology is not uncommon: authors belonging to other philosophical trends also adopt a perspective in which addressing weaknesses is important. For instance, Callon, Lascoumes and Barthe (2009) argue that the central problem a democratic polity has to solve is how minorities (expressing different types of vulnerabilities) are able to represent themselves in the public realm (in which publicly funded innovation is included). Moreover, the recent Grand Challenges identified by the European Union and tackled within its Horizon 2020 research program (including health and wellbeing, food security, transport, energy, climate action, society and security) can be interpreted as a way of addressing specific needs and vulnerabilities through the production of new techniques.

Finally, it is often acknowledged among care ethicists that vulnerability and dependence are constitutive of the human condition. In line with the work of Virginia Held or Joan Tronto (among others), which firmly rejects the ideal of autonomy promoted by liberal justice theories, MacIntyre (1999) insists on the dependence (and the correlated vulnerability) that characterizes our animal condition. We are bound to each other in order to meet our needs. This is particularly true in the case of the deprived, the diseased or the handicapped, or in the case of children. But it is also true for everyone who belongs to one or several communities and networks related to others by "their and our roles" (op. cit.: p. 122). In a broad sense, daily needs (housing, catering and public hygiene), but also the whole set of institutional, professional and business relationships that involve dependence and connectedness. Section 4 shows how this view is transposed in R&I activities where connectedness and dependence play a crucial role.

Another connected difficulty in defining responsibility through care is the strong focus of many care-ethicists on parent/child or mother/child dyads (Ruddick, 1980; Held, 1993). In the case of RRI, Grinbaum and Groves (2013), for instance, invoke a parent/child metaphor to analyse the relationship between creators and their outputs. Using the analogy of parents and children, they focus on the vulnerability of others (and future generations) and claim that scientists and innovators have the responsibility to 'teach' or 'encode virtues' into their artefacts in the same manner that parents try to do so with their children. Groves (2014: p. 117), although acknowledging that this might be "risky", further uses the mother/child dyad to focus "on the concept of secure space as a 'medium' of attachment, through which security identity, agency and also the capacity to put oneself in the position of the other are fostered" (*ibid.*).

At least in the latter case, the particular practices of care that a mother/parent is able to deliver to her/his child does not serve as an interpretation of all caring practices but as a specific case by which to understand the emergence of agency for individuals that can be described as both dependant and autonomous. Joan Tronto (1993) and Marilyn Friedman (1993), among others, have strongly opposed the tendency of reducing or understanding all care relationships through the archetype of the mother/child metaphor. Objects of care can vary and include non-human beings such as animals and plants, the environment (Tronto, 1993) and specific places, but also communities, institutions, practices or cultural objects (Groves, 2014).

In the context of R&I, even if specific care relationships can be of some help for the analysis, the relationship of innovators and scientists with their stakeholders (local communities, policy-makers, funders, citizens, end-users) and the public at large is more complex than the dyad care-giver or care receiver, and roles can be exchanged. Of course, the development of science and technology creates vulnerabilities and needs. It also provides answers to specific issues and sometimes to the needs initially identified. However, research and innovation actors face a complex environment that might be better represented as a *network* of relationships than as a face-to-face dual bond. Caring practices will involve different actors of innovation and research, and not only scientists, engineers and policy-makers. Stakeholders, NGOs, in their way of addressing what they consider as an issue and in the quality of the dialogue that they establish with partners whose interests might conflict with theirs, can show various levels of care.

The needs race

In parallel with the perspective that points to the needs created by science and technology and to the related vulnerabilities that have to be taken care of, there is another interpretation of being attentive to others' needs which is mostly relevant in a business context: firms and commercial organisations are often said to seek to satisfy the needs of their consumers. In cases of social innovation (where a company attempts to address a "need" that is widely recognized as such, such as illness, old age, malnutrition or illiteracy, for instance), but also in other cases in which communication plays a major role, the business discourse is focused on the ability of firms to satisfy consumers' needs. However, this could be a misleading route towards a conception of responsibility as care in R&I. As highlighted by Xavie Pavie (2014), consumers' needs do not all have the same moral importance. We can think, for instance, about the difference that exists between supplying starving children with a nutritional supplement adapted to their specific living conditions (e.g. lack of drinking water), which requires innovation, and providing a new smartphone to already well-equipped executives, bewitched by the novelty.

Here, we would need to define what a need is in the context of research and innovation. It is perhaps morally inappropriate to try to satisfy all needs. Without entering the endless discussion of a definite list of needs that should be met[15] (because such a list, grounded in possibly conflicting value systems, would be difficult to establish), it is possible to focus on the significance of the needs. In the case of smartphones (ironically presented by Pavie (2014)), what makes the "need" to change devices every six months problematic has to do with the harmful effects of electronic waste on the environment and our limited ability to recycle components. Here, "attentiveness" and responsiveness will require that actors of R&I (researchers, companies, policy-makers and NGOs, among others) arbitrate between different needs (that of individuals as consumers and that of individuals as human species living in an endangered environment). To ensure that such a collective process of arbitrating between different interpretations of a *need* takes place and to react with concrete actions involving the production of new technologies and science, care ethics needs to be combined with a theory of collective assessment and decision making.

To sum up, an understanding of RRI based on the idea of care requires us to identify some specificities of R&I practices and to adapt accordingly so as to integrate the network of actors involved in mutual relationships (while not necessarily reciprocal, as claimed by Groves (2009)), along with the different degrees of dependence and connectedness. Therefore, without excluding the cases in which scientific and technological development creates vulnerabilities and needs that have to be taken care of, the central notion of understanding care-based relationships in R&I might not be the idea of *need*, but the ideas of *connectedness* and *dependence*.

Connectedness, dependence and the individual reasons for caring

Another criticism that is usually directed against cultivating *care* in R&I practices raises the issue of the *contingency of individual virtues*.[16] As in any social ecosystem, there would be a good proportion of actors convinced (whatever the reason – instrumental, deontological or by virtuous disposition[17]) of the necessity to acknowledge, delineate and face their own responsibility in a responsive and reflexive manner. But there could also be a large proportion of actors who might tend to reduce their own sphere of responsibility and the ethical constraints they impose on their activities. Whether by ignorance, motivated by malevolent intentions, or because they do not perceive their own activities as problematic, the idea of taking care of other stakeholders and the environment might be at odds with the priorities of certain R&I actors. The history of techno-scientific and industrial scandals is full of examples where not only institutional design was inadequate (not reflexive and responsive enough), but also in which actors sought to escape some of their responsibilities: the political and industrial denial until the 1980s of the risks of the use of asbestos (which were known since antiquity[18]); the lack of counterweights to the quest for efficiency and profit in agriculture, which favoured the development of bovine spongiform encephalopathy; the scandal of the Love Canal in the Niagara Falls;[19] or Monsanto's strategies to conceal the toxic effects of its activities (PCB, agent Orange, GMOs etc.), to name only a few.

As a way of escaping the moral problem of the contingency of virtue, most of the proponents of an ethics of care oppose the liberal political ideal of perfectly autonomous and independent human beings (such as rational choice theory's assumption of methodological individualism) and focus on the connectedness that defines the human condition (Gilligan, 1982; MacIntyre, 1999; Tronto, 1993, 2013; Held, 2006; Engster, 2007). Without denying that social actors have spheres of autonomy and independence, they seek to outline the importance of relationships, bonds and dependence to others that have been neglected by traditional neoliberal-inspired philosophies. In her seminal analysis of the emotional and psychological development of individuals, Gilligan (1982) highlighted the crucial role of attachment to others: decision making comes from our attempt to maintain and cultivate relationships with those we care about rather than from a principled will to follow an abstract rule, as fair as the rule might be. In this view, the paradigm of good care is exemplified[20] by the mother/child relationship in which the child acquires agency, a perception of her identity and autonomy through a secure attachment bond.[21] In the process of their development, young adults who received enough and appropriate care acquired a capacity to care for what is of value to them, i.e. close individuals (family, friends, lovers) but also "objects" of their environment, including geographical places, communities, cultural objects, institutions (Groves, 2014).

In the end, human beings are bound to what exists in the world, what has a meaning for them – other human beings, monuments, values or ideals – by attachment. As claimed by Groves (2014: p. 127) "objects of attachment sustain and preserve the secure space of emotional and cognitive future possibilities that provide the matrix for our sense of identity and agency".

Our propensity to hold "objects of attachment" and to care for elements of the world that are meaningful for us creates an ontologically forward-looking link between responsibility, our actions and the objects of our attachment.

> Attachment implies that there is a non-reciprocal responsibility owed to particular kinds of others by virtue of the constitutive role they play for the subject and its world, a role which is expressed in concrete, empirical historical actualities and the determinable virtual futures that inhabit them".
>
> (op. cit.: p. 129)

In the context of R&I, the nature of the relationships between social actors might not be the same as the one explored by care ethicists (i.e. fundamentally asymmetrical and related to the vulnerability of the one in need). But attachment and interdependence are also prominent. Concerning *attachment*, researchers and innovators care for what they develop and contribute to creation, whether it be models, algorithms, technologies or paradigms. As citizens, they might also want to defend political or moral values that are of meaning to them and which infuse their work. Other actors such as NGOs or civil society have objects of attachment (geographical places; characteristics of the world, such as biodiversity; or political ideals, like democracy) they might want to preserve and allow to flourish.

When it comes to *connectedness*, Xavier Pavie (2014, 2017) emphasises the interrelations existing in economic ecosystems between different departments of the same corporation or various members of a supply chain. A goods or service production unit depends on many other economic social actors within and outside a firm to supply it with input, intermediate goods, supplies, advertising, marketing, information etc. R&I activities also imply connectedness and dependence. Innovation in new technologies, tools and machines broadens research and enables discovery across fields, as happened with the atomic force microscope and the development of nanotechnology (both as a research field and as an industrial issue), for example. The network of funding institutions will also play a major role in deciding which type of research should be fostered or banned, as is the case with the Grand Challenges of the European Union or the scientific policy of the US National Science Foundation. These different groups of social actors (researchers, research institutions, entrepreneurs, funding institutions) are related to each other and aim at "preserving attachment objects' singular potential for meaning within the context of a secure space and a common fate", to take Christopher Groves' definition of care (Groves, 2014: p. 129).

Then, as soon as the interdependence between actors of innovation and research is acknowledged, caring practices can be found to be at work. Scientists, innovators, decision makers and investors can be seen as connected to each other but also to the citizens, consumers, NGOs, Civil Society Organisations, local communities and other stakeholders who will be impacted by their activities. Innovation and research activities, since they imply a network of interrelated actors, raise the responsibility for the actors to take care not only of the outputs of their activities, but also of other beings, objects or institutions affected by the process. These various social actors are linked together around the development of technology, which becomes an object of attachment together with the places where they live, the institution they belong to etc.

Here, one might ask the question of how to mitigate between conflicting strategies in order to make these objects of attachment flourish or how to choose between various objects of attachment which imply conflicting solutions. Such a question requires that we move from the individual level to the political one and justifies what has been said in section 2: the process by which objects of attachment that have to be taken care of (over others) are identified and the way in which good caring practices are defined is the result of a collective assessment. It is historically and culturally shaped. And the rules, characteristics and practices of such a collective process have to be discussed, experienced and revised, so as to adapt as closely as possible to the specific requirements of the context.

Of course, as mentioned above, virtuous processes of care that allow for objects of attachment (which are constitutive of human life) to flourish do not always take place; relationships between R&I actors can be tarnished by manipulation, abuses, political strategy or the pre-eminence of economic interests. The development of caring relationships has to be taken as a) something that already exists and on which we can count (since it is constitutive of our integration in the world) and b) something which should be fostered by institutional design, education (including education to moral thinking) and political will. In this sense, it is not an unachievable ideal, which could appear as naïve and utopian. It is both an already-existing feature of the ethical attitude we adopt to objects and a normative horizon that can guide RRI governance. At a political level, grounding RRI in care ethics would mean that one of the normative tasks of a responsible R&I governance will be to promote the flourishing of care relationships between R&I actors by different means: appropriate conceptual frameworks which put a theoretical emphasis on interdependence and relationships instead of abstract and only backward-looking responsibility (such as liability or blame) (Pellé and Reber, 2015, 2016), training and education to make the need for caring practices in R&I widely acknowledged and an institutional design that allows caring relationships to be established between funders, scientists, companies, incubators, local communities and citizens. In addition to cultivating individual virtues, RRI governance should be designed so as to steer cultural organizations through soft and hard law (Sander-Staudt and Hamington, 2011) towards an enhancement of care relations between social actors of R&I.

Conclusion

The chapter aimed at showing that the ethics of care is a powerful and fruitful framework through which to understand and fashion human practices. First, it presented how conditions of RRI are in fact closely connected with various dimensions of care ethics and how a conception of responsibility can benefit from an interpretation focused on care-based relationships between R&I actors. Through the idea of care, responsibility is approached as a context-dependant notion whose specific norms and injunctions emerge through attentiveness and sensitivity to the requirements of a given situation. In this view, the condition of inclusion can be interpreted as a collective process to determine the objects of care and the norms of good care, which ensures various forms of moral pluralism (plurality of values and value systems defended by social actors and plurality of normative theories used to justify moral assessment). Yet, some dimensions of this ethical framework have to be reinterpreted in the specific context of R&I (compared with that of traditional care ethics), in particular the concept of need. Rather than defining responsibility only in terms of vulnerabilities that should be reduced or repaired, I have tried to show how the ethics of care based on attachment and connectedness provides a dynamic and flexible way of approaching responsibility. This perspective allows for various forms of creativity and moral innovation to emerge in order to provide answers to the challenges of technology, science and innovation.

Finally, I have argued that understanding responsibility as care in R&I does not imply that individual virtues should be considered in isolation. This approach offers a normative framework in which to conceive of the role of institutions and of various aspects of RRI governance.

Notes

1 For an extensive discussion on these conditions and the European pillars, see Blok and Lemmens (2015), Gianni (2016), Pellé and Reber (2015, 2016) and Pellé (2016a), among others.
2 We claimed that responsibility can be understood as cause, task (or role), authority, capacity, blameworthiness, obligation, liability, responsiveness, accountability and virtue (which includes care).
3 See Groves (2014) for an ambitious attempt to connect aspects of the phenomenological tradition with feminist care ethics.
4 Although Tronto would include such activities, when they are carried out with the aim of taking care of the places where people live.
5 See Pellé (2016a) for a presentation of the three normative strategies – procedural, outcome-oriented or based on virtue ethics – behind most RRI approaches.
6 See Pellé (2017) for further analysis.
7 Tronto's approach to care is elaborated a decade before the idea of RRI emerged. In addition, if this approach is mentioned by Xavier Pavie in this book, the correspondence between the moral elements of caring practices and the conditions of RRI has not been fully stressed yet.
8 "To be competent to care, given one's caring responsibility is not simply a technical issue but a moral one" (Tronto, 2013, p. 35).
9 In her 2013 book, Tronto adds a fifth element which is "plurality, communication, trust and respect: solidarity, caring with" (Tronto, 2013, p. 35).
10 See paragraph 2.3. for an answer to the second kind of criticism according to which care ethics would be a relativist philosophical framework.
11 In *Political Liberalism*, Rawls acknowledges a form of sensitivity to the context by highlighting the "burdens of judgement", i.e. the possibility of reasonable disagreements in factual judgements and in religious, philosophical and moral convictions among people, regardless of how reasonable and rational people are.
12 Here, I depart from Nussbaum's account of a common set of human capabilities or Tronto's belief in the possibility of a consensus about needs. It might be the case that it happens for basic needs, but the hypothesis of consensus is not needed to describe a deliberative process allowing for conflicting interests to be confronted and mitigated.
13 If responsibility must be understood as ontologically bound to human condition and action (as I try to defend it here), it cannot solely be conceived as a "moral quality". Nevertheless, as we have shown elsewhere (Pellé and Reber, 2015, 2016), being a "responsible" person – one of the ten meanings of responsibility we identified – is a moral quality (*Idem*).
14 Consensus is only one form of agreement among others such as compromise or deliberative disagreement; see Reber (2012).
15 As done by Martha Nussbaum (1988, 1992, 1993) in her list of human capabilities, for instance.
16 See Lenoir (2019), Chapter 9 in this book.
17 Other normative theories such as intuitionism, contractualism or teleology could also be mentioned.
18 Roman philosopher and naturalist Pliny the Elder (first century A.D.), in his *Natural History*, already reported that slaves who mined asbestos suffered from a sickness of the lungs and died at an early age.

19 The Love Canal, named after utopian entrepreneur William T. Love, was constructed in the late 19th century in the neighbourhood of Niagara Falls City to connect the Niagara River to Lake Ontario. After Love's project failed, the portion of the canal that had been already dug was used by Hooker Electrochemical Company as a toxic waste burial site. In the 1950s, the city of Niagara Falls experiencing a major economic boom, needed land and purchased the property to build schools and houses over the canal, creating a major environmental and health disaster.

20 But not limited to, as shown by the debate between feminist philosophers.

21 Which also supposes a growing autonomy of the young adult. As recalled by Groves (2014: p. 99) connectedness is not opposed to autonomy since, following Jonas (1982), the more autonomous we are, the more the world around us is of concern to us.

References

Adam, B. and Groves, C. (2011) Futures Tended: Care and Future-Oriented Responsibility, *Bulletin of Science Technology & Society*, vol. 31, no. 1, pp. 17–27.

Blok, V. and Lemmens, P. (2015) The Emerging Concept of Responsible Innovation. Three Reasons why it is Questionable and Calls for a Radical Transformation of the Concept of Innovation, in Van den Hoven, J. Koops, E.J., Romijn, H.A., Swierstra, T.E. and Oosterlaken, I. (Eds.), *Responsible Innovation: Issues in Conceptualization, Governance and Implementation*, vol. 2. Dordrecht: Springer, pp. 19–35.

Callon M., Lascoumes P. and Barthes Y. (2009) *Acting in an Uncertain World. An Essay on Technical Democracy*. Cambridge: MIT Press.

Engster, D. (2007) *The Heart of Justice: Care Ethics and Political Theory*. Oxford: Oxford University Press.

Friedman M. (1993) *What Are Friends For? Feminist Perspectives on Personal Relationships and Moral Theory*. Ithaca: Cornell University Press.

Gianni, R. (2016) *Responsibility and Freedom: The Ethical Realm of RRI*. Paris: Wiley-ISTE.

Gilligan, C. (1982) *In a Different Voice – Psychological Theory & Women's Development*. Cambridge, MA: Harvard University Press.

Grinbaum, A. and Groves C. (2013) What is the 'Responsible' in Responsible Innovation? Understanding the Ethical Issues. In Owen, R., Bessant, J. and Heintz, M. (Eds.) (2013a), pp. 119–142.

Groves, C. (2009) Future Ethics: Risk, Care and Non-Reciprocal Responsibility, *Journal of Global Ethics*, vol. 5, no.1, pp. 17–31.

Groves, C. (2014) *Care, Uncertainty and Intergenerational Ethics*. London: Palgrave Macmillan.

Grunwald, A. (2011) Responsible Innovation: Bringing Together Technology Assessment, Applied Ethics, and STS Research, *Enterprise and Work Innovation Studies*, vol. 7, pp. 9–31.

Grunwald, A. (2012) *Responsible Nanobiotechnology: Philosophy and Ethics*. Singapore: Panstanford Publishing.

Grunwald, A. (2014) Technology Assessment for Responsible Innovation, in van den Hoven, J., Doorn, N., Swierstra, T., Koops, B.J. and Romijn, H. (Eds.), *Responsible Innovation 1: Innovative Solutions for Global Issues*. Dordrecht: Springer, pp. 15–32.

Guston, D.H. (2014) Understanding Anticipatory Governance, *Social Studies of Science*, vol. 44, no. 2, pp. 219–243.

Hamington, M. and Sander-Staudt, M. (2011) Introduction: Care ethics and Business Ethics, in Hamington, M. and Sander-Staudt, M. (Eds.), *Applying Care Ethics to Business, Issues in Business Ethics*, vol. 34. New York: Springer, pp. vii–xxii.

Held, V. (1993) *Feminist Morality: Transforming Culture, Society, and Politics*. Chicago: Chicago University Press.

Held, V. (2006) *The Ethics of Care: Personal, Political, and Global*. Oxford: Oxford University Press.

Jonas, Hans (1982) *The Phenomenon of Life*. Chicago: University of Chicago Press.

Kelty, Chistopher M. (2009) Beyond Implications and Applications: The Story of *'Safety by Design'*, *NanoEthics* vol. 3, no. 2, pp. 79–96.

Koehn, Daryl (2011) Care Ethics and Unintended Consequences, in Maurice Hamington and Maureen Sander-Staud (Eds.), *Applying Care Ethics to Business*. Dordrecht: Springer, pp. 141–153.

Lee, R.G. and Petts, J. (2013) Adaptive Governance for Responsible Innovation, in Owen, R., Bessant, J. and Heintz, M. (Eds.) (2013a), pp. 143–164.

MacIntyre, A. (1999) *Dependant Rational Animals: Why Human Beings Need the Virtues* (The Paul Carus Lectures). London: Duckworth.

Nodding, N. and Shore, P. (1984) *Awakening the Inner Eye: Intuition in Education*. New York: NY Teachers College Press.

Nordmann, A., (2014) Responsible Innovation, the Art and Craft of Anticipation, *Journal of Responsible Innovation*, vol. 1, no. 1, pp. 87–98.

Nussbaum, M.C. (1988) Nature, Function, and Capability: Aristotle on Political Distribution, *Oxford Studies in Ancient Philosophy*, vol. 1 (suppl.), pp. 145–184.

Nussbaum, M.C. (1992) Human Functioning and Social Justice: In Defence of Aristotelian Essentialism, *Political Theory*, vol. 20, no. 2, pp. 202–246.

Nussbaum, M. C. (1993) Non Relative Virtues: An Aristotelian Approach, in Nussbaum, M. and Sen, A. (Eds.), *The Quality of Life*. Oxford: Clarendon Press, pp. 242–269.

Owen, R., Macnaghten, P. and Stilgoe, J. (2012) Responsible Research and Innovation: From Science in Society to Science for Society, with Society, *Science and Public Policy*, vol. 39, no. 6, pp. 751–760.

Owen, R., Bessant, J. and Heintz M. (Eds.) (2013a) *Responsible Innovation: Managing the Responsible Emergence of Science and Innovation in Society*. Hoboken (NJ): John Wiley & Sons.

Owen, R., Macnaghten P., Stilgoe J., Gorman M., Fisher E. and Guston D. (2013b) A Framework For Responsible Innovation, in Owen, R., Bessant, J. and Heintz, M. (Eds.) (2013a), pp. 27–50.

Pavie, X. (2017) From Responsible-Innovation to Innovation-Care. Beyond Constraints, a Holistic Approach of Innovation', in Gianni, R., Reber, B. and Pearson J. (Eds.), *RRI. Concept and Practices*. London: Routledge (forthcoming).

Pavie, X. (2014) The Importance of Responsible-Innovation and the Necessity of 'Innovation-Care', *Philosophy of Management*, vol. 13, no. 1, pp. 21–42.

Pavie, X., Scholten, V. and Carthy, D. (2014) *Responsible Innovation: From Concept to Practice*. Singapore: World Scientific Publishing.

Pavie, X., and Egal, J. (2014) Innovation and Responsibility: A Managerial Approach to the Integration of Responsibility in a Disruptive Innovation Model, in van den Hoven, J. Doorn, N., Swierstra, T., Koops, B.J., and Romijn, H. (Eds.) (2014), Responsible Innovation 1: Innovative Solutions for Global Issues. Dordrecht: Springer, pp. 53–66.

Pellé, S. (2016a) Process, Outcomes, Virtues: The Normative Strategies of Responsible Research and Innovation and the Challenge of Moral Pluralism, *Journal of Responsible Innovation*, http://dx.doi.org/10.1080/23299460.2016.1258945.

Pellé, S. (2016b) 'Responsibility as Care for Research and Innovation', in Schertz, C., Michalek, T., Hennen, L., Hebakova, L., Hahn, J. and Seitz, S. B, (Eds.), *Proceedings of the PACITA Conference*, 25–27 February 2015. *The Next Horizon of Technology Assessment*,

Pellé, S. (2017) *Business, Innovation and Responsibility*. New York and London: Wiley-ISTE.

Pellé, S. and Reber, B. (2015) Responsible Innovation in the Light of Moral Reponsibility, *Journal on Chain and Network Science*, vol. 15, no. 2, pp. 107–117.

Pellé, S. and Reber, B. (2016) *Ethics of Research and Responsible Innovation*. Paris: Wiley-ISTE.

Reber, B. (2012) Argumenter et délibérer entre éthique et politique, in Reber B. (Ed.), Vertus et limites de la démocratie délibérative, *Archives de Philosophie*, Tome 74, pp. 289–303.

Robinson, D.K.R., Huang, L., Guo, Y. and Porter, A.L. (2013) Forecasting Innovation Pathways (FIP) for New and Emerging Science and Technologies, *Technological Forecasting and Social Change*, vol. 80, no. 2, pp. 267–285.

Ruddick, S. (1980) Maternal Thinking, *Feminist Studies*, vol. 6, no. 2, pp. 342–367.

Schumpeter, J. (1934) *The Theory of Economic Development: An Inquiry into Profits, Capital, Credit, Interest and the Business Cycle*. New Brunswick: Transaction Publishers.

Stilgoe, J., Owen R. and Macnaghten, P. (2013) Developing a Framework for Responsible Innovation, *Research Policy*, vol. 42, no. 9, pp. 1568–1580.

Sykes K. and Macnaghten P. (2013) Responsible Innovation – Opening Up Dialogue and Debate, in Owen, R., Bessant, J. and Heintz, M. (Eds.) (2013a), pp. 85–108.

Tronto, J. (1993) *Moral Boundaries: A Political Argument for an Ethics of Care*. New York: Routledge.

Tronto, J. (2013) *Caring Democracy, Market, Equality and Justice*. New York: NY University Press.

Tronto J. and Fisher B. (1990) Toward a Feminist Theory of Caring, in Abel, E. and Nelson, M. (Eds.), *Circles of Care*. Albany: SUNY Press, pp. 36–54.

van den Hoven, J. (2013) Value Sensitive Design and Responsible Innovation, in Owen, R., Bessant, J. and Heintz, M. (Eds) (2013a), pp. 75–84.

von Schomberg, René (2013) A Vision of Responsible Innovation, in Owen, R., Bessant, J. and Heintz, M. (Eds.) (2013a), pp. 51–74.

13 Design-thinking approach to ethical (responsible) technological innovation

Ganesh Nathan

Introduction

There is growing interest in and importance of responsible research and innovation (RRI) among academic scholars and policy-makers, especially in relation to emerging technologies such as nanotechnology. It is also to be noted that, although the design-thinking approach has been around since the 1960s, there is renewed interest in this approach to innovation with an increasing number of related publications over the last couple of decades. Furthermore, it is currently introduced in a number of schools and community projects. However, there is a gap in bridging the design-thinking approach to RRI, and this chapter attempts to address this need.

This chapter aims to show that a design-thinking approach is potentially conducive to ethical (responsible) technological innovation, especially within emerging and converging technologies, due to its emphasis on human-centred design and other core attributes such as empathy – although it poses many challenges to implement.

This chapter first introduces morally contentious technological innovations and their implications. Then, I will show why these implications pose challenges and constraints for ethical (responsible) innovation, especially within emerging and converging technologies. In doing so, I attempt to underscore the importance of responsibility as one of many ethical aspects of innovations; hence, the title of this chapter refers to 'ethical (responsible) technological innovation'. Following this section, I briefly discuss the shortcomings of linear innovation process models and I introduce an improved circular responsible innovation process model, especially for non-linear wicked problems, which are difficult to solve due to their complexity and changing requirements and conflicting or contradicting values among the stakeholders concerned (Buchanan 1992; Blok and Lemmens 2015). However, many emerging technologies may introduce ethical issues embedded at machine level, for example autonomous vehicles, drones and next-generation robotics that require an understanding of machine-level ethical concerns and considerations. These concerns have been increasingly addressed by the emerging new field of 'machine ethics'. However, it is important to integrate ethical decision-making at both the organizational-level innovation process and at machine level. From this perspective, this chapter introduces the design-thinking approach to innovation and attempts to show its potential applicability to ethical (responsible) technological innovations, along with challenges for the implementation of the approach.

Morally contentious technological innovations and implications

In practice, technological innovations change the way we do things, and this can challenge our normative values. 'Technologies can be not only contentious – overthrowing existing ways of doing things – but also morally contentious – forcing deep reflection on personal values and societal norms' (Cole and Banerjee 2013; quoted in Nathan 2014a). Technological innovations inevitably introduce changes to our ways of doing things: for example, social media and mobile phones have changed the way we communicate. However, most importantly, these changes can also be morally contentious: social media has introduced ethical concerns about cyber bullying, infringement of privacy and fake news distribution that raises serious concern for ethical journalism within the so-called 'post-truth era' (see ethicaljournalismnetwork.org). Moreover, technological innovations can have undesirable consequences for society and the environment. Just to give some examples: DDT was a pesticide which caused harm to other species such as birds; the pharmaceutical thalidomide, prescribed as morning sickness treatment for pregnant women, caused deformities in their children; chlorofluorocarbons (CFCs), used as refrigerants and propellants, were blamed for causing ozone layer depletion and are currently thought to be among the various greenhouse gases causing global warming (see Bessant, 2013; Nathan 2014a).

These examples illustrate the significance of organizational-level decision-making during innovation processes that can have impacts on the linkages at macro level when introducing these products to the market within a socio-cultural-political-ecological context; therefore, these linkages can be morally contentious, leading to harmful effects on society and the environment (Hanekamp 2010; Nathan 2014a). Furthermore, it is plausible to argue that many innovation decision-making processes have been blind to ethical impacts and concerns – 'innovation ethical blindness' (Nathan 2014a); due to their focus on return on investment in the economic dimension, organizational decision-makers do not give equal attention to the potential impacts on social and ecological dimensions in the early stages of innovation. For example, the Dutch government had to cancel the EPRS (Electronic Patient Record System) due to unresolved privacy issues after the investment of 300 million Euros over a 15-year period. The initiative to introduce smart electricity meters in every household within the Netherlands was also rejected by the upper house of the Dutch parliament due to privacy concerns after some years of R&D efforts (Van den Hoven 2013; also Nathan 2015). Therefore, it is important to consider how technologies shape our social reality and the associated ethical concerns and impacts.

Reijers and Coeckelbergh (2016) assert that technological structures 'constitute and create' new social realities in line with Searle's social ontology (Searle 2010); moreover, they turn to theories in the philosophy of technology and in social studies of science and technology (STS) to show that social relationships are shaped by technologies (cf. Van Den Eede 2011). This reality of social relationships raises many ethical concerns and dilemmas (Nathan 2014a). For example, as already mentioned, social media raises ethical issues of cyber bullying, infringement on privacy and recently emerging fake news (during the recent US presidential election campaign).[1] Furthermore, the distribution and installation of surveillance cameras in public places introduces the ethical dilemma of public safety versus privacy concerns. Although a technological innovation can support new constructive possibilities, it can also be exploited for destructive purposes by actors within the technological field. For example, 3D printers can be used for reconstructive surgery and to make prototypes for architectural designs; however, 3D printers can also be used to print handguns. These exploitations are not confined to the field of technology; they intersect with other fields such as regulation and media – for example, social media are exploited by fake news distribution and cyber bullying. Therefore, it is also important to consider moral contestation through exploitation that can have impacts on other intersecting fields such as media and regulation (Cole and Banerjee 2013; Nathan 2014a).

With emerging technologies, technological innovations are rapidly increasing; however, these can introduce new ethical concerns and, sometimes, dilemmas. Emerging technologies are becoming available in many forms; for example, in 2015, the top 10 emerging technologies listed by the World Economic Forum (WEF, 2015) were fuel-cell vehicles, next-generation robotics, recyclable thermoset plastics, precise genetic-engineering techniques (e.g. CRISPR), additive manufacturing (from printable organs to intelligent clothes), 3D printing to 4D printing (a new generation of products that can alter themselves with environmental changes), emergent artificial intelligence, distributed manufacturing (the final product is manufactured close to the end customer), 'sense and avoid' drones (sense and respond to the local environment), neuromorphic technology (computer chips that mimic the human brain) and the digital genome (health care – genetic code on a USB stick). Each of these emerging technologies can lead to ethical concerns and tension along with impacts on intersecting fields that may be hard to predict at the early stages of development and, furthermore, may even be difficult to resolve at the latter stages of innovation. These emerging technologies can branch into new forms, adding more complexity and ethical tensions; complexity can increase the unpredictability of ethical concerns because it may introduce new ethical issues. These issues are increasingly constituted by 'human-technology relations' (see Verbeek 2005; also Zwier et al. 2016) that may not be easily understood with our present 'being-in-the-world' experience. As an example, 'Pokemon Go' – a game on mobile devices with augmented reality – has recently become a new, somewhat disruptive, social phenomenon (Isbister 2016) that shapes social relations among the people playing it.

Now let's look at ICT, one of the emerging technologies, in order to illustrate the point on adding complexity; ICT branches into many new forms such as affective computing, ambient intelligence, artificial intelligence, bioelectronics, cloud computing, future internet, human-machine symbiosis, neuroelectronics, quantum computing, robotics and virtual/augmented reality (Sutcliffe, 2011;

Nathan 2014a, 2015).[2] These emerging technologies create novel forms of human-technology relations that introduce ethical tensions; for example, should we suppress our ethical norms of human interaction in virtual reality environments? Moreover, these emerging technologies can converge into new, complex technological fields; innovations within these fields can pose serious ethical concerns and constraints. For example, ICT in its various forms and nanotechnology converge into new forms of technologies such as nanomedicine and nanopharmacy that can enable us to anticipate illnesses and to take pre-emptive measures (Bennett-Woods 2008). However, this sort of technological innovation certainly raises some fundamental ethical concerns in relation to our understanding of an illness and human capability, thereby putting into question our concept of 'what it means to be human' (Bawa and Johnson 2009) and human identity (Nathan 2015); human beings by nature have limitations due to the human body of flesh – aging, frailty and death, and overcoming its finitude through technological innovations, may lead to the idea of creating 'superhumans', although it is a far-fetched idea (Dalton-Brown, 2015). These issues are not easy to resolve with our current understanding and experience of being-in-the-world social relations; as pointed out earlier, technologies shape our social relations and it will be hard to predict future ethical concerns of human-technology relations that may arise with new emerging and converging technologies. Furthermore, these concerns challenge and may transform our taken-for-granted social relations and roles – for example, doctor–patient and parent–child.

Responsible innovation may not address some of the future ethical impacts and implications based on our current values and legal compliances (Nathan 2015; cf. Von Schomberg 2013); values can change over time and people may value different things for the same reasons and may value the same thing for different reasons (Nathan, 2010). Therefore, it is important to understand how to value and what kinds of attitudes and actions are called for (Nathan 2010; cf. Scanlon, 2000: p. 99). These attitudes and actions underscore many ethical concerns that need to be addressed within responsible innovation, and therefore the title emphasizes ethical aspects with the phrasing 'ethical (responsible) technological innovation' (see also Nathan 2015). The above examples lead us to ask: What are the challenges and constraints in addressing these ethical concerns, especially innovations within emerging and converging technologies?

Some of the potential problems with early innovations within emerging and converging technologies may be considered as 'wicked problems' (Curedale 2013: p. 59), for example, 'Doctor in a Cell' (Casci 2004; see also Nathan 2015), a molecular computer that could be used as pre-emptive gene therapy – diagnosing, detecting and destroying defective DNA; another example is targeted gene editing using the CRISPR technological tool. Gene editing can potentially lead to changes in our ecosystems through the intervention in processes of natural selection (see Talbot 2016). These examples raise the ethical concern of curing genetic disorders versus human enhancement based on certain preferences of traits. These also show that information regarding these innovations and potential applications at early stages may be ill-formulated or ill-structured due to complexity along with contradicting or conflicting values among stakeholders such as decision-makers and customers or end users; moreover, requirements may be dynamic, and ramifications can therefore be confusing (Buchanan 1992; Blok and Lemmens 2015). Furthermore, it is also complicated when we consider Collingridge's dilemma; as already briefly mentioned, some of the ethical concerns and dilemmas may not be obvious or predictable at the early stages of the innovation process and, by the time they become clearer, it may be too late to remedy them due to technological lock-in (Collingridge 1980; Nathan 2015). Another challenge that one may face is 'moral overload'; even if one identifies those ethical dilemmas, it may be difficult to resolve conflicting moral obligations or values or to implement them at the same time (van den Hoven 2013; Nathan 2015). The normative framework of RRI of the EC (European Commission 2012) consists of six main keys: ethics, gender equality, governance, open access, public engagement, and science education.[3] This chapter focuses on ethics, even though other aspects are important. So, the next question is: What sort of innovation process models may be suitable to address the above-mentioned ethical challenges and constraints? The next section attempts to answer this question.

Circular responsible innovation process model

There is a variety of innovation process models. These include traditional stage-gate and funnel-phased approaches, as well as newer open innovation models; however, these are all linear innovation process models (see Nathan 2015). These models simplify complex innovation processes in order to emphasize critical innovation elements and stages. A simplified innovation process model consists of the following critical stages: searching for innovation opportunities, selecting the most suitable or viable ones and then implementing them for capturing the benefits in the market (Tidd and Bessant 2009; Bessant 2013). However, linear progressive stage models may not be suitable for wicked problems that require iterations with progressive and regressive stages, as there can be ethical concerns that may not be identified in the previous stages and the stages need to be regressed to be addressed fully. Furthermore, these models do not explicitly integrate ethical decision-making at each stage to identify potential ethical concerns and dilemmas among various stakeholders, as the main focus is about commercial success based on return on investment at each stage-gate of the process. It is plausible to integrate some of the concerns towards the environment, for example in the decision-making process, to be legally compliant. However, there is no deliberation about ethical concerns among the various stakeholders who might be affected by the innovation. Decisions at each stage-gate are made by senior managers based on economic viability without much regard for ethical impacts and concerns. Most importantly, as it is a linear open-ended model, there is no explicit feedback loop that could capture any unpredictable ethical concerns as early as possible following the launch of products and services. The absence of such feedback loops means there is no mechanism for re-evaluating the issues and or for going back through the innovation process stages to rectify them and re-launch or terminate the products or services (Nathan 2015).

However, this simplified model could be modified as a circular responsible innovation process model including the evaluation stage and embedding ethical decision-making that incorporates internal and external stakeholders at the organizational level[4] for deliberation to seek solutions that take into consideration ethical concerns from various stakeholders' perspectives. A stakeholder map identifying all stakeholders and their interests, along with ethical concerns and dilemmas as well as their rights and responsibilities, may enable us to embed ethical decision-making within the innovation process at the organizational level; this framework could also integrate multiple perspectives and a systems-thinking approach (Nathan 2015). At organizational level, we could integrate stakeholder mapping and an ethical decision-making process within a circular responsible innovation process to address ethical dilemmas and concerns at each stage of the innovation process, even though it can be difficult to identify all relevant stakeholders and to anticipate ethical concerns and issues at each stage. However, it becomes more complex when we take into consideration ethics at machine level such as robots, autonomous drones and transport vehicles. Therefore, it has become increasingly important to integrate machine-level ethics in decision-making processes for ethical (responsible) innovation. The next section looks into the challenges of what is called machine ethics or robot ethics.

Welcome to the machine: Machine ethics and challenges

The phrase 'Welcome to the machine' was inspired by Pink Floyd's song lyrics. Machines such as Roomba vacuum cleaners are already used as service robots in domestic environments (Guizzo 2010). Other robots are used for mowing lawns, ironing clothes and washing floors (Lin 2014). Humanoid robots (resembling the human body with controllable arms and legs) such as NAO have been evolving since 2006 at SoftBank Robotics (previously known as Aldebaran), and 7,000 models of the fifth version of them have already been sold throughout the world. New forms of emerging and converging technologies enable us to develop intelligent autonomous machines such as drones, next-generation robots and autonomous transport vehicles. Robots as co-workers; human–robotic interaction for health care, surgery and rehabilitation; robots as co-inhabitants for housekeeping, child care and elderly care ('robot caregivers') (Borenstein and Pearson 2012; also Sharkey and Sharkey 2012); robots for military ('killer robots') (Lokhorst and van den Hoven 2012) and for security ('robots that spy') (Calo 2014); robots for personal companionship ('robot lover') (Whitby 2012); and last but not least, robots for sex ('robot prostitutes') (Levy 2012) are being developed and used (Wallach and Allen 2010; Lin et al. 2014). Although robots certainly enable us to benefit in different contexts, they also raise many ethical concerns and dilemmas apart from the issues of safety and errors. For example, in health care, a robot may be monitoring Alzheimer patients and administering medication according to prescriptions; in this case, human dignity may be jeopardized – if a patient refuses to take the medication, should we allow the robot to forcibly administer it? And if so, what sort of moral cognition, communication and actions are required so that the intervention may not be considered as an arbitrary, even violent, intervention? In child care, robots may take care of children by reading bed-time stories while their parents are free to take their own time away from home; in this scenario, children may develop emotional bonds with robots ('unidirectional emotional bonds') (see Scheutz, 2014) instead of reciprocal bonding with their parents. The bonds are unidirectional because robots will not be able to develop authentic reciprocal emotional bonds. In warfare, military robots may be directed to kill enemies. These robots will need to react to difficult situations such as making a decision whether to take care of a wounded soldier from its own side or to keep moving and fighting the enemy; the point of contention is about the making of moral choices by humans versus robots and the respective normative consequences (see Lokhorst and van den Hoven 2012). An autonomous vehicle needs to respond not only to children crossing the street unexpectedly (and not just on designated crossings), but also to a cat or a dog crossing in certain situational contexts. Furthermore, the vehicle should also be able to detect temporary detours and be able to read those signs in different contextual situations and be able to redirect itself. A companion robot may be problematic on the issues of privacy; for example, it may be possible to hack the companion robot, or the robot may be accessible by security authorities.

The above-mentioned robots and scenarios bring about several ethical problems such as empathy and sociability, emotional bonding, ethical decision-making in unforeseen situations, privacy and accessibility, social meaning of different roles, loss of autonomy and liberty, and perceived agency and anthropomorphism of robots (Zlotowski et al. 2015) that raises the issue of whether to grant some basic human rights to anthropomorphic robots. These sorts of ethical problems have fostered growing interest in the emerging field of machine ethics over the last decade (Anderson and Anderson, 2006). This discipline includes 'moral machines' which are also referred to as artificial moral agents (AMAs) (Allen and Wallach 2012) because the idea behind them is that they can be taught right from wrong. It is important to address these ethical problems as we innovate intelligent autonomous machines. Simply following rules may not be appropriate (and may even be irresponsible) in certain situational contexts; for example, military robots may be programmed to kill enemies first and foremost without any regard either for wounded soldiers of its faction or to civilian victims. 'Ethicality' goes beyond compliance with rules and regulations and sometimes even goes against them; for example, taking refugees from a war-torn country into another country as illegal immigrants is ethical (saving innocent lives) even though it is illegal (breaking the border regulations). Moreover, responsible practices may fall short in an ethical dimension. For example, tobacco harms people ('smoking kills'); however, tobacco companies could pursue responsible practices on supply chain management – organically grown tobacco without using pesticides, efficient irrigation systems, fair wages and working conditions for the workers of tobacco plantations and low carbon emission transportation etc. Building ethical robots is a challenge; embedding rule-based ethical decision-making in predictable situations may not be effective in unpredictable situations, and enabling machine-learning to make ethical decisions – for example, decisions based on right from wrong and justice as fairness – in new situations may create a problem of trust (Deng 2015). Lokhorst and van den Hoven (2012: p.154) claim that

> it should never be assumed that human beings, in their role of designer, maker, manager, or user of robots and other artifacts or technological systems, can transfer moral responsibility to their products in case of untoward outcomes, or can claim diminished responsibility for the consequences brought about by their products.

There are many design strategies that could be adopted in addressing this variety of design issues. One of them may be to integrate ethical decision-making using ethical theories such as teleology – utilitarianism, and deontology – ethics of duty: Kantian Maxims, and theory of rights and justice; however, it is also plausible to develop a strategy to 'focus on whether a technological intervention is likely to advance or hinder human flourishing' (Borenstein and Pearson 2012: p. 251).

Taking into consideration the above ethical problems and challenges faced by machine-level ethics as well as organizational-level ethics, the next section attempts to explore the potential applicability of the design-thinking approach to the ethical (responsible) innovation process.

A potential application of design thinking approach

Design thinking has been around since the 1960s. However, design movement evolution can be traced back to the 1980s with cognitive reflections (user-centred design approach) to service design (human-centred design approach) in 2000; from 2010 onwards, the movement has evolved to design taking into consideration the above ethical problems and challenges at both levels – machine and organizational (Curedale 2013). Design thinking may be understood in many different ways with some core attributes. The design-thinking approach to innovation consists of three core elements: technology, business and (most importantly) humans. It is not a consumer or customer-centred approach; rather, it is human-centred in a broader sense, and, from this perspective, it is not just about focusing on existing or target customers. Therefore, it can also take into consideration potential new customers and is not restrictive but broadens the scope. However, I would add that these three elements – technology, business and human-centric – need to be contextualized within the social and ecological environment as the interactions of these elements within this context may raise societal and environmental ethical concerns. IDEO, today a global design company, has popularized design thinking for innovation with a simplified model consisting of six critical elements: understand, observe, point of view, ideate, prototype and test with iterative feedback processes.

The core attributes of a design-thinking approach during the innovation process are ambiguity, collaborative, constructive, curiosity, empathy, holistic, iterative, non-judgemental and open mindset (Curedale 2013). As I already mentioned, one of the problems with early innovations within emerging and converging technologies is the unpredictability of ethical problems and issues; however, traditional innovation processes often do not acknowledge or anticipate such issues and thus fail to integrate them into the process; on the other hand, the design-thinking approach encourages innovators to be comfortable with such ambiguity and to not be judgemental at early stages. Therefore, it allows these ambiguities to be dealt with using an open mindset through the iterative process (which is non-sequential and may include feedback loops and cycles which are compatible with the circular responsible innovation process model), making prototypes to be tested and re-tested. Therefore, it enables innovation process actors to understand and anticipate potential ethical concerns from multiple perspectives of various stakeholders. Moreover, the decisions can be made with empathy through the collaboration of (potential) users from a human-centric perspective.

It appears that some of these core attributes may be conducive, most importantly, to at least developing an awareness of ethical concerns (and not being blind to them) and, to some extent, may enable stakeholders to address the ethical problematic context that was discussed in the previous sections. These core attributes are integrated with certain design-thinking principles such as being action-oriented, comfortable with change, and human-centric; integrating foresight; a dynamic constructive process; promoting empathy; reducing risks; and creating meaning (Mootee 2013). These may appear to be simplistic, although each principle may be elaborated to accommodate ambiguity due to complexity; for example, integrating foresight and promoting empathy may encourage preparedness for alternative realities and challenges. Furthermore, design thinking, in essence, addresses human needs in many dimensions such as physical sustenance, security, leisure/relaxation, affection, understanding, autonomy, meaning, mattering (which includes care, compassion, empathy, mutual recognition etc.), sense of self (which includes dignity, integrity etc.) and transcendence (Curedale 2013: pp. 25–26). Certainly, the design-thinking approach captures many important elements, such as empathy and dignity, that need careful consideration at both the organizational- and machine-level of ethics. However, the challenge is how to integrate organizational-level ethics and machine-level ethics to address ethical concerns and problems at the early stages of the innovation process. The next section briefly attempts to show some potential directions for implementing a design-thinking approach to the ethical (responsible) innovation process.

Some directions for implementation and challenges

The design-thinking approach could be integrated with multiple perspectives and the system-thinking approach to embed ethical decision-making (see Nathan 2015). The system-thinking approach encourages us to consider systems as some sort of moral agents – even though this may not be fully transparent. The moral agency of systems arises because the 'structure, interrelationships, and goals of a particular system produce outcomes that have normative consequences' (Werhane 2002: p. 35). Integrating the systems-thinking approach is conducive to 'moral imagination', which seeks a potential variety of possibilities and assesses the moral consequences of decisions in order to counter organizational factors that may 'corrupt ethical judgement' (Werhane 1998; 2002: p.33). Furthermore, systems thinking emphasizes the need to understand all the interrelationships and linkages among sub-systems and the normative consequences of decisions at different levels. In this regard, interrelationships between organizational-level and machine-level ethical aspects need to be carefully considered for any normative consequences. It can be challenging, as we already discussed above, to anticipate future scenarios and contexts to consider all the potential normative consequences. However, as Grunwald (2011: p. 9) states: 'The postulate of responsible innovation adds explicit ethical reflection to Technology Assessment (TA) and science, technology and society (STS) studies and includes all of them in integrative approaches to shaping technology and innovation'. In this regard, ethical decision-making needs to be integrated within the design-thinking approach, taking into consideration various aspects of all relevant stakeholders' perspectives. Some of the aspects that are relevant to both the organizational and machine level are legal, ethical, socio-cultural and ecological from different stakeholder (including management and employees) perspectives. This kind of matrix structure – organizational and machine level with multiple perspectives – may enable us to map out all potential ethical concerns and anticipate those normative consequences. This could be embedded into responsible (ethical) innovation governance in four dimensions – anticipatory, reflective, deliberative and responsive (Owen et al. 2013; Nathan 2015). Once we identify these ethical issues and potential normative consequences through anticipatory and reflective processes, it may be plausible to engage with relevant stakeholders to seek solutions through deliberation, based on modern civic republicanism (see Nathan 2014b), that no stakeholder can reasonably reject in order to be responsive.

However, this approach is problematic, given that we live in an ethically plural society and that stakeholders may have unequal and asymmetrical power and influences on decisions. Therefore, for this kind of deliberation for justice, it is important to ensure that the minimal and common conditions of freedom as non-domination and recognition in three dimensions of acknowledgement, authorization and endorsement prevail (see Nathan 2014b; also Nathan 2010; cf. Pettit 1997). Acknowledgement ensures that all stakeholders are accepted in their specificities; authorization enables their differing viewpoints to be fully heard; and, finally, it is important to ensure that the endorsement of solutions does not violate any of the above conditions (Nathan, 2010; cf. Honohan, 2002). The challenge then arises as to how we should implement freedom as non-domination at the machine level. As I already mentioned, should we give any (or limited) basic human rights to robots due to anthropomorphism? What should be our rights and responsibilities when interacting with robots? Ethical and rights concerns are connected because normative consequences invariably include the issues of rights, responsibilities/duties and justice. It is also important to consider that we humans have two-sided (double-sided) morality (Nathan 2010); that is, we have internal morality, based on using our own conscience to determine what is right and wrong, and external morality, based on societal moral norms of what is right and wrong. These two forms of morality may come into conflict. Ethicality, on the other hand, is based on what is good in the longer term for a society that promotes human flourishing. Therefore, the inclusion of all relevant stakeholders and freedom as non-domination become significant requirements for deliberation. However, at machine level, the question of how we should integrate AMAs (Artificial Moral Agents) for human flourishing remains a challenge; making AMAs autonomous and giving them reflective, evaluative and creative attributes may jeopardize our autonomy as moral agents and, therefore, our human dignity. From this perspective, ethical innovation goes further than responsible innovation in dealing with ethical concerns that may not be clear at the early stages of innovation process, and in responding to those issues.

The Watson computer system at IBM has been shown in experiments to be able to both win the *Jeopardy*! game and to diagnose medical problems. It may be argued on the basis of these experiments that Watson can be considered reflective and evaluative. However, one may also argue, based on Searle's Chinese room argument (Searle 1980), that Watson is not capable of understanding. Some refute this argument based on systems, the virtual mind and other perspectives (see Searle 1990). Understanding is subjective and, therefore, it may be argued that understanding requires conscious experience; this line of argument can lead to a philosophical query on whether there are different kinds of minds (see Nathan 1997). Is it possible to create artificial consciousness? Is there any artificial conscious experience?[5]

Conclusion

This chapter has briefly shown morally contentious technological innovations and their implications, especially with regard to emerging and converging technologies, in order to emphasize the importance of integrating ethical decision-making in the innovation process at organizational level. Although the circular responsible innovation process model is an improvement over linear innovation process models at organizational level, it showed the challenges emerging from machine-level ethics, especially in relation to AMAs. From this perspective, it attempted to show the potential applicability of the design-thinking approach to ethical (responsible) technological innovations to address some of the ethical problems at machine level as well as organizational level. Despite the applicability of the design-thinking approach to integrating both the organizational and machine levels, taking into consideration various aspects from different stakeholder perspectives, it showed that there are challenges in anticipating and addressing normative consequences from different perspectives at both levels, and in being responsive to these consequences. This chapter has raised many questions about the problems we may face but without necessarily giving specific solutions; nevertheless, it is important to understand the problems before we embark on the solutions (in accordance with a quote from Albert Einstein).[6] Addressing these challenges requires further research from a range of multi-disciplinary approaches in this exciting field.

Acknowledgement

This chapter is based on my keynote presentation given with the same title at Symorg 2016 in Zlatibor, Serbia. The author is indebted to Bernard Reber for his critical feedback on this chapter.

Notes

1 See more information on www.thetrustproject.org.
2 Later in this chapter, I will address ethical concerns of the next-generation robotics within the topic of machine ethics.
3 https://ec.europa.eu/research/swafs/pdf/pub_public_engagement/responsible-research-and-innovation-leaflet_en.pdf.
4 See Nathan (2015) for more details.
5 These challenges revolve around the philosophy of mind and theory of consciousness, existentialism and phenomenology. As the scope of this chapter does not include these philosophical problems, I shall not delve into them further.
6 'If I had an hour to solve a problem I'd spend 55 minutes thinking about the problem and 5 minutes thinking about solutions'. Albert Einstein; http://www.goodreads.com/quotes/60780-if-i-had-an-hour-to-solve-a-problem-i-d; retrieved on 15 December 2016.

References

Allen, C. and Wallach, W. (2012). Moral Machines: Contradiction in Terms or Abdication of Human Responsibility? In Lin, P., Abney, K. and Bekey, G. A. (Eds.), *Robot Ethics: The Ethical and Social Implications of Robotics*. Cambridge (MA): MIT Press, pp. 55–68.

Anderson, M. and Anderson, S. L. (2006). *Machine Ethics*. IEEE Intelligent Systems 21(4), pp. 10–11.

Bawa R, and Johnson, S. (2009). *Emerging Issues in Nanomedicine and Ethics. Nanotechnology and Society*. Dordrecht: Springer, pp. 207–223.

Bennett-Woods, D. (2008). *Nanotechnology: Ethics and Society*. Boca Raton (FL): CRC Press.

Bessant, J. (2013). Innovation in the Twenty-First Century. In Owen, R., Bessant J., Heintz M. (Eds.), *Responsible Innovation. Managing the Responsible Emergence of Science and Innovation in Society*. Hoboken (NJ): John Wiley & Sons, pp. 1–25.

Blok, V. and Lemmens, P. (2015). The Emerging Concept of Responsible Innovation. Three Reasons Why It Is Questionable and Calls for a Radical Transformation of the Concept of Innovation. In Van den Hoven, J., Koops, E. J., H. A. Romijn, Swierstra, T. E. and Oosterlaken, I. (Eds.), *Responsible Innovation 2: Concept, Approaches and Applications*. Dordrecht: Springer pp. 19–36.

Borenstein, J. and Pearson, Y. (2012). Robot Caregivers: Ethical Issues across the Human Lifespan. In Lin, P., Abney, K. and Bekey, G. A. (Eds.), *Robot Ethics: The Ethical and Social Implications of Robotics*. Cambridge (MA): MIT Press, pp. 251–265.

Buchanan, R. (1992). Wicked Problems in Design Thinking. *Design Issues*, 8(2), pp. 5–21.

Calo, M. R. (2014). Robots and Privacy, In Lin, P., Abney, K. and Bekey, G. A. (Eds.), *Robot Ethics: The Ethical and Social Implications of Robotics*. Cambridge (MA): MIT Press, pp. 187–202.

Casci, T. (2004). Doctor in a Cell. *Nature Reviews Genetics*, 5(6), p. 406. DOI:10.1038/nrg1369.

Cole, M. B. and Banerjee, M. P. (2013). Morally Contentious Technology-Field Intersections: The Case of Biotechnology in the United States. *Journal of Business Ethics*, 115(3), pp. 555–574.

Collingridge, D. (1980). *The Social Control Of Technology*. London: Francis Pinter Ltd.

Curedale, R. (2013). *Design Thinking: Process and Methods Manual.* Topanga, CA: Design Community College Inc.

Dalton-Brown, S. (2015). *Nanotechnology and Ethical Governance in the European Union and China: Towards a Global Approach for Science and Technology*. New York: Springer.

Deng, B. (2015). Machine Ethics: The Robot's Dilemma. *Nature*, 523(7558), pp. 24–26. Available at: http://www.nature.com/news/machine-ethics-the-robot-s-dilemma-1.17881.

Grunwald, A. (2011). Responsible Innovation: Bringing together Technology Assessment, Applied Ethics, and STS Research. *Enterprise and Work Innovation Studies*, 7, IET, pp. 9–31.

Guizzo, E. (2010). IEEE Spectrum: World Robot Population Reaches 8.6 Million, April, 14. Available at: http://spectrum.ieee.org/automaton/robotics/industrial-robots/041410-world-robot-population.

Hanekamp, G. (Ed.) (2010). *Business Ethics of Innovation. An Introduction, Business Ethics of Innovation*. Berlin: Springer-Verlag.

Honohan, I. (2002). *Civic Republicanism*. London: Routledge.

Isbister, K. (2016). Why Pokémon GO Became an Instant Phenomenon. *The Huffington Post*, updated 19 July 2016; accessed 1 December 2016.

Levy, D. (2012). The Ethics of Robot Prostitutes. In Lin, P., Abney, K. and Bekey, G.A. (Eds.), *Robot Ethics: The Ethical and Social Implications of Robotics*. Cambridge (MA): MIT Press, pp. 223–231.

Lin, P., Abney, K. and Bekey, G. A. (2014). *Robot Ethics: The Ethical and Social Implications of Robotics (Intelligent and Autonomous Agents series)*, Paperback edition, MA: The MIT Press.

Lokhorst, G.-J. and Van den Hoven, J. (2012). Responsibility for Military Robots. In Lin, P., Abney, K. and Bekey, G. A. (Eds.), *Robot Ethics: The Ethical and Social Implications of Robotics*. Cambridge (MA): MIT Press, pp. 145–156.

Mootee, I. (2013). *Design Thinking for Strategic Innovation*. Hoboken (NJ): Wiley.

Nathan, G. (1997). *Shades of Minds: Towards an Understanding of Complexities of Kinds of Minds*. Available at SSRN: https://ssrn.com/abstract=2552220 or http://dx.doi.org/10.2139/ssrn.2552220.

Nathan, G. (2010). *Social Freedom in a Multicultural State: Towards a Theory of Intercultural Justice*. London: Palgrave Macmillan.

Nathan, G. (2014a). Technological Innovation and Ethics. In Bastos, J.-C. and Stuekelberger, C. (Eds.), *Innovation Ethics: African and Global Perspectives*. Globethics.net series 'Global', pp. 37–44.

Nathan, G. (2014b). Multi-Stakeholder Deliberation For (Global) Justice: An Approach From Modern Civic Republicanism. In Schepers, S. and Kakabadse, A. (Eds.), *Rethinking the Future of Europe: A Challenge of Governance*. Basingstoke (UK): Palgrave Macmillan, pp. 10–27.

Nathan, G. (2015). Innovation Process and Ethics in Technology: An Approach to Ethical (Responsible) Innovation Governance. Special Issue: *Responsible Innovation in the Private Sector, Journal on Chain and Network Sciences*, Wageningen Academic Publishers, 15(2), 119–134.

Owen, R., Stilgoe, J., Macnaghten, P., Gorman, M., Fisher, E. and Guston, D. (2013). A Framework For Responsible Innovation. In Owen, R., Bessant, J. and Heintz, M. (Eds.), *Responsible Innovation. Managing the Responsible Emergence of Science and Innovation in Society.* Hoboken (NJ): John Wiley & Sons, pp. 27–50.

Pettit, P. (1997). *Republicanism*, 2nd edition. Oxford: Oxford University Press.

Reijers, W. and Coeckelbergh, M. (2016). The Blockchain as a Narrative Technology: Investigating the Social Ontology and Normative Configurations of Cryptocurrencies. *Philosophy of Technology*. DOI 10.1007/s13347-016-0239-x.

Scanlon, T. M. 2000. *What We Owe to Each Other*. Cambridge, MA and London: The Belknap Press of Harvard University Press.

Scheutz, M. (2014). The Inherent Dangers of Unidirectional Emotional Bonds between Humans and Social Robots. In Lin, P., Abney, K. and Bekey, G. A. (Eds.), *Robot Ethics: The Ethical and Social Implications of Robotics*. Cambridge (MA): MIT Press, pp. 205–222.

Searle, J. (1980). Minds, Brains, and Programs. *The Behavioural and Brain Sciences*, 3(3), pp. 417–424.

Searle, J. (1990). Is the Brain a Digital Computer? *Proceedings and Addresses of the American Philosophical Association*, 64(3), pp. 21–37.

Searle, J. R. (2010). *Making the Social World: The Structure of Human Civilization*. Oxford: Oxford University Press.

Sharkey, N. and Sharkey, A. (2012). The Rights and Wrongs of Robot Care. In Lin, P., Abney, K. and Bekey, G. A. (Eds.), *Robot Ethics: The Ethical and Social Implications of Robotics*. Cambridge (MA): MIT Press, pp. 267–282.

Sutcliffe, H. (2011). *A Report on Responsible Research & Innovation*, MATTER. Available at: https://ec.europa.eu/research/science-society/document_library/pdf_06/rri-report-hilary-sutcliffe_en.pdf.

Talbot, D. (2016). Precise Gene Editing in Plants/10 Breakthrough Technologies 2016. Massachusetts Institute of Technology. Retrieved 7 December 2016.

Tidd, J. and Bessant, J. (2009). *Managing Innovation*. Chichester, UK: John Wiley & Sons.

Van Den Eede, Y. (2011). In Between Us: On the Transparency and Opacity of Technological Mediation. *Foundations of Science*, 16(2–3), pp. 139–159. DOI:10.1007/s10699-010-9190-y.

Van den Hoven, J. (2013). Value Sensitive Design and Responsible Innovation. In Owen, R., Bessant, J. and Heintz, M. (Eds.), *Responsible Innovation. Managing the Responsible Emergence of Science and Innovation in Society.* Hoboken (NJ): John Wiley & Sons, pp. 75–83.

Verbeek, P. P. (2005). *What Things Do: Philosophical Reflections on Technology, Agency, and Design*. Pennsylvania: Penn State University Press.

Von Schomberg, R. (2013). A Vision of Responsible Research and Innovation. In: Owen, R., Bessant, J. and Heintz, M. (Eds.), *Responsible Innovation. Managing the Responsible Emergence of Science and Innovation in Society.* Hoboken (NJ): John Wiley & Sons, pp. 51–74.

Wallach, W. and Allen, C. (2009). *Moral Machines, Teaching Robots Right from Wrong*. Oxford: Oxford University Press.

Werhane, P. H. (1998). New Approaches to Business Ethics. In Freeman, R.E. (Ed.), *The Ruffin Series Of The Society For Business Ethics*. New York: Oxford University Press, pp. 75–98.

Werhane, P. H. (2002). Moral Imagination and Systems Thinking. *Journal of Business Ethics*, 38(1), pp. 33–42.

Whitby, B. (2012). Do You Want a Robot Lover? The Ethics of Caring Technologies. In: Lin, P., Abney, K. and Bekey, G. A. (Eds.), *Robot Ethics: The Ethical and Social Implications of Robotics*. Cambridge (MA): MIT Press, pp. 233–248.

Złotowski, J., Proudfoot, D., Yogeeswaran, K. and Bartneck, C. (2015). Anthropomorphism: Opportunities and Challenges in Human–Robot Interaction. *International Journal of Social Robotics*, 7(3), pp.347–360. DOI 10.1007/s12369-014-0267-6.

Zwier, J, Block, V. and Lemmens, P. (2016). Phenomenology and the Empirical Turn: A Phenomenological Analysis of Postphenomenology. *Philosophy of Technology*, 29(4), pp. 313–333. DOI 10.1007/s13347-016-0221-7.

Conclusion

Moral responsibility can be explained by an analogy with a conversation. The relation between a responsible agent and those holding him or her responsible is like the relation between a speaker and his or her audience (McKenna, 2012). This conclusion aims at opening up a discussion between all the chapters of this book, integrating them into a general perspective. Nonetheless, this problematic is still a singular perspective, taking responsibility for its own position. Many other conversations may be possible.

If we analyse the several European funded projects dedicated to Responsible Innovation and Research (RRI), which have been promoting this new conception and enrolling numerous and different kinds of actors (academics, teachers, business people, NGO activists, civil servants etc.), we may be surprised by two aspects. First, most of these projects seem to start from scratch, apparently overlooking the important research in the closely related fields of Participatory Technological Assessment (PTA; Pellé and Reber 2016; Reber 2016, 2017a; Callon et al. 2009; Gianni and Goujon[1]), ethics of emerging technologies, deliberative democracy (Parkinson and Mansbridge, 2012) or reflexive governance (Maesschalck, 2017). Indeed, all these fields of research have developed experiments, surveys, indicators and theories.[2] Second, when trying to define a general understanding of RRI, most of the projects limit their scope to the ones provided by René Von Schomberg and Owen et al. (2013). If these texts are quoted in this collection, too, we have not seen a coherent and continuous use of these two first proposals in practice. It should be added that Richard Owen – author of the foreword to this book – has moved forward from his first attempt at a definition. It is as if these definitions should be mentioned without any follow up. One of the articles in the present volume (Blok et al.) addresses interesting critiques of a common principle embedded in both definitions: the ideal of transparency. It is self-evidently assumed that transparency enhances responsibility throughout the innovation process. The chapter concludes that the ideal of transparency contains a double bind.

These two problems are probably linked with the fact that most of the projects try to describe forerunners or explicit RRI practices, while others aim at implementing what they understood as RRI based only on a brief analysis. The latter sometimes affirm that giving a definition of RRI or specifying its understanding would be arbitrary. But describing or implementing a still-unclear or unknown conception is problematic and perhaps more contestable.

Another hypothesis behind these two problems is genealogic. RRI has perhaps been an umbrella term introduced during a European Commission meeting to cover existing research programmes, via the six RRI keys. This hypothesis is factually plausible, confirmed by interviews and by the structure of the different EC RRI calls, which provide some supporting evidence to it. However, it is not self-evident that these pillars all fit together, with each having its own specificity and logic (Lenoir, 2015). Different relationships among them are possible as well as their links to different understandings of responsibility (Reber). Each key covers different research debates and communities (Pellé and Reber, 2016), with their own history. Moreover, RRI is not only the sum of its keys and its components. This is one of the main reasons why responsibility should be conceived as a conceptual and practical resource.

This hypothesis can be matched with a broader perspective. The European Commission's RRI research calls are part of the former *Science and Society* programme. Incidentally, this is not typical of European research. The concern is an international one. The relationship between science and society has moved towards closer cooperation, expressed in the new name for the programme: *Science for and with Society*. Moreover, science and society are not on the same level. They are not only two worlds, the former integrated in the latter: science is made of practices and theory. Besides that, different sciences have society as their research objects. But here too, the change from the pairing of *Science and Society* to RRI or RI is not obvious. Innovation and responsibility are indeed a part of the former pairing, but the relationship is complex. Science can contribute to innovation, but it is only part of an incomplete process. Science's goals may be turned towards knowledge acquisition only. Innovations meet societal needs (Pavie), answering to them in different and always-changing ways. It is true that new needs are not always met, that the full extent of the consequences of innovations when they are available on the market are not known – be they impact on the ecosystem as a whole, or on parts of the societies. As the two sides of one coin, responsibility may be considered as the reverse of the innovation action, process or product. Responsibilities are attached to innovations at all levels – from simple actions to complex emerging technologies. Because each action is embedded in a normative and physical environment, and in intersubjective interactions, simultaneous or along generations, it has to cope with responsibilities. A link can be made between RRI and *Science and Society* in this way. Science is responsive to societal needs or challenges. The reverse is true, too. A society has to take care of the development of science for its own development. Here, too, in the relationships between innovation and responsibility, we encounter the title of this book: its constructive part (innovation) and its reflexive, critical or (r)-evaluative one (responsibility).

The last hypothesis, compatible with the two last mentioned above, is that RRI may be identified with models of governance and the Charter of Fundamental Rights of the European Union. A general regulatory approach of the EU is generally referred to as "New Governance", which aims at pursuing some objectives such as power sharing, multi-level integration, coordination of decision-making and actions, strengthening of diversity, decentralization, participation and/or deliberation processes, flexibility of norms and regulation (soft regulation), experimentalist governance (Pearson) or second-order reflexivity (Gianni and Goujon; Maesschalck 2016). These institutional tools are suitable for dealing with situations in which knowledge is uncertain and consent is contested, so that traditional approaches addressing responsibility ex post facto by the means of liability or compensation are unsatisfactory (Arnaldi et al.).

Besides, we also find differences between academic RRI research and science policy actors' expectations (Klaassen et al.). Furthermore, RRI is understood differently and implemented according to the territory: national, European or international. Different policies conflate key terms such as deliberation, engagement, inclusion and participation. Further clarity is needed as well as changes in governance as a means to legitimize research and innovation too (Pearson). Finally, RRI goes beyond addressing ethical concerns connected to research and innovation activities such as publicly controversial technologies like genetically modified organisms (GMOs). Rather, it also aims at including societal actors in the whole research and innovation process to align research with the needs and expectations of society (Guske and Jacob).

To tackle these problems and avoid some of these limitations, this book has shared a twofold perspective: both constructive and critical. Indeed, with emerging notions, both are needed iteratively in a reflexive circle. From very different disciplines (descriptive and normative), origins and familiarity with different types of knowledge of responsibility and innovation, the authors have given more precise outlines to RRI and made interesting critiques of impoverished, naïve or cynical RRI presentations. Moreover, they have opened original ways of letting RRI be incarnated. Finally, they have put these new debates in the context of larger, well-documented fields of research and philosophy. Indeed, responsibility is probably the most perfect regulator of human actions (Gianni).

This book has embraced the normative turn in science and society research (Gianni and Goujon; Reber 2017a). It has tried not to shy from the need to take the risk of discussing the very core of moral and political responsibility. It has realized this from an analytical perspective (Reber; Pellé; Pavie), taking seriously the different moral meanings and perspectives (deontologism, consequentialism, virtue ethics) on responsibility, but matched with the long history of this concept. This return to history is not a luxury. History encompasses different contexts that have permitted the emergence of the responsibility concept and perpetually modified it. This dynamic and informed genealogy shed light on the underlying and sometimes conflicting objectives of responsibility with its function throughout history. For instance, the shift that responsibility had to support is that from an individual who finds the interpretation for his actions in sources other than himself, to an individual called to respond to the requests through reason and able to distinguish between his intentions and external rules (Gianni; Gianni and Goujon). The passage from Antiquity to Modernity has radically shifted the understanding of agency and the modalities of responsibility: knowledge, will, power and duty.

This journey to the past is true for innovation too. Sophocles' famous term *deinon* in *Antigone*, meaning both the ideas of the terrible and of the admirable, exemplifies the ingenuous skill to move sometimes towards evil, sometimes towards good (Pavie).

The twofold pairing of innovation and responsibility did not originate when the term RRI was coined, and we can look to other sources besides the RRI projects to understand it. We may find it in the debate between hope (Ernst Bloch) and responsibility (Hans Jonas) principles (Gianni, Grunwald, Pellé), or in the famous pragmatist Dewey's *The Public and its Problems* (1954; Reber, 2017a, 2017b; Gianni and Goujon). The articulation between individual and collective responsibilities is an old problem (Gianni) and the possibility of a collective life in a permanently innovative society (Nathan) too.

Responsibility as the first step

According to a general and common narrative, innovation is an imperative of our societies: a condition of growth, employment and, often, of a better life. Responsibility is seen as a second step after innovation, either as part of the socio-legal systems that innovation must respect, or a way to correct some side-effects of innovations. We may add that innovation and responsibility evolve in the space between the imperatives "do not harm" and "do good" (Pavie).

But if we think more carefully, this common-sense view, putting innovation before responsibility, perhaps misses an important point. Responsibility belongs at the beginning of innovation. For instance, innovations answer (are responsive) to existing or potential needs. In this way, some authors have expressed this point of the precedence of responsibility over innovation in different ways.

They have shown such relations in three types of research: excellence-oriented research, innovation-oriented research and applied policy-relevant research. If it becomes accepted that scientists in the context of policy-making shape the world they study by the way they frame problems and by the assumptions underlying their research, all researchers have to demonstrate the likely societal impacts of their research projects when applying for funding too (Guske and Jacob) – not to mention the fact that this demand regarding societal impacts is increasing. But the ways to develop scenarios or provide narratives to represent and analyse these societal impacts are diverse and sometimes opposite. Often, there is plenty of room for conflicts and uncertainties.

These scientific-technological impacts do not result just in unanimously welcomed progress, but also raise new questions concerning equity, the balance of risks and benefits, the impacts on human rights, the possible shifts of the relation between humans and nature or between humans and technology. Because of uncertainties and controversies, the epistemological dimensions of innovations at stake do not enable us to apply consequentialist patterns of orientation. Therefore, responsibility considerations, according to a hermeneutic analysis, should focus on what is happening in actual reality and on its ethically relevant aspects.

If we take into account, for instance, synthetic biology, the subject of responsibility should be seen more in the processes of current research rather than in speculative future products (Grunwald).

Such understanding echoes the thoughts of Amartya Sen. Sen has defended the need to recognize ethics, both as prior to, or/and embedded within, economical theories as underlying assumptions. The scope of RRI is crucial to have a strong focus on the creative possibilities in the situation, on the lineaments of renewed solutions that become possible because of a new configuration of the actual situation (Lenoir). The rearrangement and reinvention of the uses, for concepts and technologies, take the undefined shape of contingent "efficiency processes" (Lenoir). Moreover, these processes bring us to understand others' ideas, leading to a more precise and just awareness of their signification.

From a legal perspective, Kelsen has shown, too, that the *individual is free because one imputed a sanction to his behaviour* (Gianni).

Innovative constructive proposals

All the chapters here have analysed responsibility in contexts (especially Gianni and Goujon; Nathan; Klaassen et al.) and in taking contingency (Lenoir) seriously. They have shown how RRI governance (Pearson) can be structured around the idea of connectedness (Gianni) and interdependence, drawing on care, for instance, on ethics as a context-dependent theory allowing moral pluralism (Pellé). Indeed, shortcomings often appear because of a formal, rationalistic framework, following an abstract justificatory path instead of contextualizing actions, without considering the actual performativity of norms.

All the contributions to this book have offered some warnings. For instance, it has been shown that simply following rules may not be appropriate and may even be irresponsible in certain situational contexts. Ethics goes beyond compliance with rules and regulations (Nathan; Pellé and Reber, 2016). The understanding of responsible governance cannot be reduced to liability, accountability or compliance. It cannot simply be another justification register for regulatory devices, but must engage responsibly with a view to the transformation of forms of life brought about by changing norms (Gianni and Goujon). A careful attention to the creativity of the possible at work in the situation allows an open invention of the future. Without it, knowledge becomes a set of dead recipes used in the situation from the outside (Lenoir). This means that the requirement of a "maximal" opening of the scope and the motives has to be reaffirmed. A concern focused too much on procedural features would quickly forget about creativity and openness. Defining a fixed list of values that would fit every context of evaluation would lead us to overlook the importance of the context of their evaluation.

Both innovation and responsibility are probably closer than people may realize, feeding each other and addressing mutual requirements. Indeed, in innovation, some of the core attributes of design thinking approached in non-linear innovation are collaboration; constructiveness; curiosity; empathy; a holistic, iterative and open mind-set; human-centricity, integrating foresight and dynamic constructive process or trying to reduce risks (Nathan). These attributes are compatible with responsibility. Responsibility has to be innovative too: both constructive and critical.

Notes

1 Where I do not give the publication date next to a cited author's name, I am referring to a chapter from this book.
2 A series (20 books published or forthcoming) is dedicated to RRI: http://iste.co.uk/index.php?f=a&ACTION=View&id=1078. There is also a journal series: http://www.tandfonline.com/toc/tjri20/current.

References

Callon M., Lascoumes P. and Barthes Y., *Acting in an Uncertain World. An Essay on Technical Democracy* (trans. Burchell G.). Cambridge: MIT Press, 2009.

Dewey, J., *The Public and Its Problems*. Athens, OH: Swallow Press, 1954.

Lenoir, V., *Ethical Efficiency: Responsibility and Contingency*. London: ISTE and New York: Wiley, 2015.

Maesschalck M., *Reflexive Governance for Research and Innovative Knowledge*. London: ISTE and New York: Wiley, 2017.

McKenna, M., *Conversation and Responsibility*. Oxford: Oxford University Press, 2012.

Owen, R., Bessant, J. and Heintz, M. (Eds.) (2013). *Responsible Innovation. Managing the Responsible Emergence of Science and Innovation in Society*. Hoboken (NJ): John Wiley & Sons.

Parkinson J. and Mansbridge J. (eds), *Deliberative Systems: Deliberative Democracy at the Large Scale*. Cambridge (UK): Cambridge University Press, 2012.

Pellé, S. and Reber, B., *From Ethical Review to Responsible Research and Innovation*. London: ISTE and New York: Wiley, 2016.

Reber, B. *Precautionary Principle, Pluralism and Deliberation: Science and Ethics*. London: ISTE and New York: Wiley, 2016; in French: *La délibération des meilleurs des mondes. Entre précaution et pluralisme*, 2017a.

Reber, B., RRI as the Inheritor of Deliberative Democracy and the Precautionary Principle, *Journal of Responsible Innovation*, 2017b. ISSN: 2329-9460 (print) 2329-9037 (online). Journal homepage: http://www.tandfonline.com/loi/tjri20.

Von Schomberg, R. (2013). A Vision of Responsible Research and Innovation. In: R. Owen, Bessant, J. and Heintz, M. (Eds.), *Responsible Innovation. Managing the Responsible Emergence of Science and Innovation in Society*. Hoboken (NJ): John Wiley & Sons, pp. 51–74.

Index

Note: page references in bold indicate tables; italics indicate figures; 'n' indicates chapter notes.

For Product Safety Concerns and Information please contact our EU representative GPSR@taylorandfrancis.com
Taylor & Francis Verlag GmbH, Kaufingerstraße 24, 80331 München, Germany

www.ingramcontent.com/pod-product-compliance
Ingram Content Group UK Ltd.
Pitfield, Milton Keynes, MK11 3LW, UK
UKHW021017180425
457613UK00020B/968

* 9 7 8 0 3 6 7 5 8 8 2 1 2 *